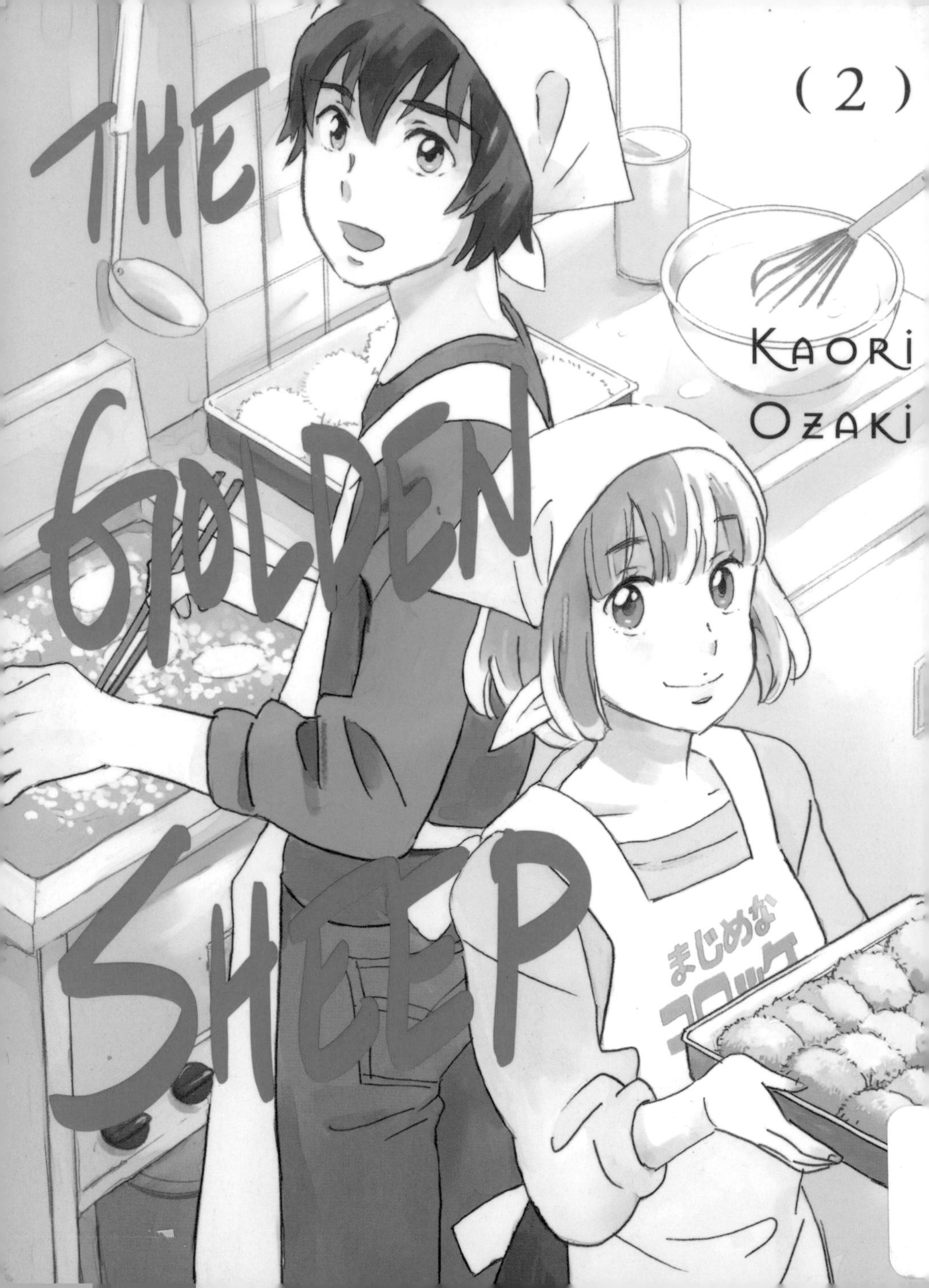
THE GOLDEN SHEEP
(2)
KAORI OZAKI
まじめな

contents

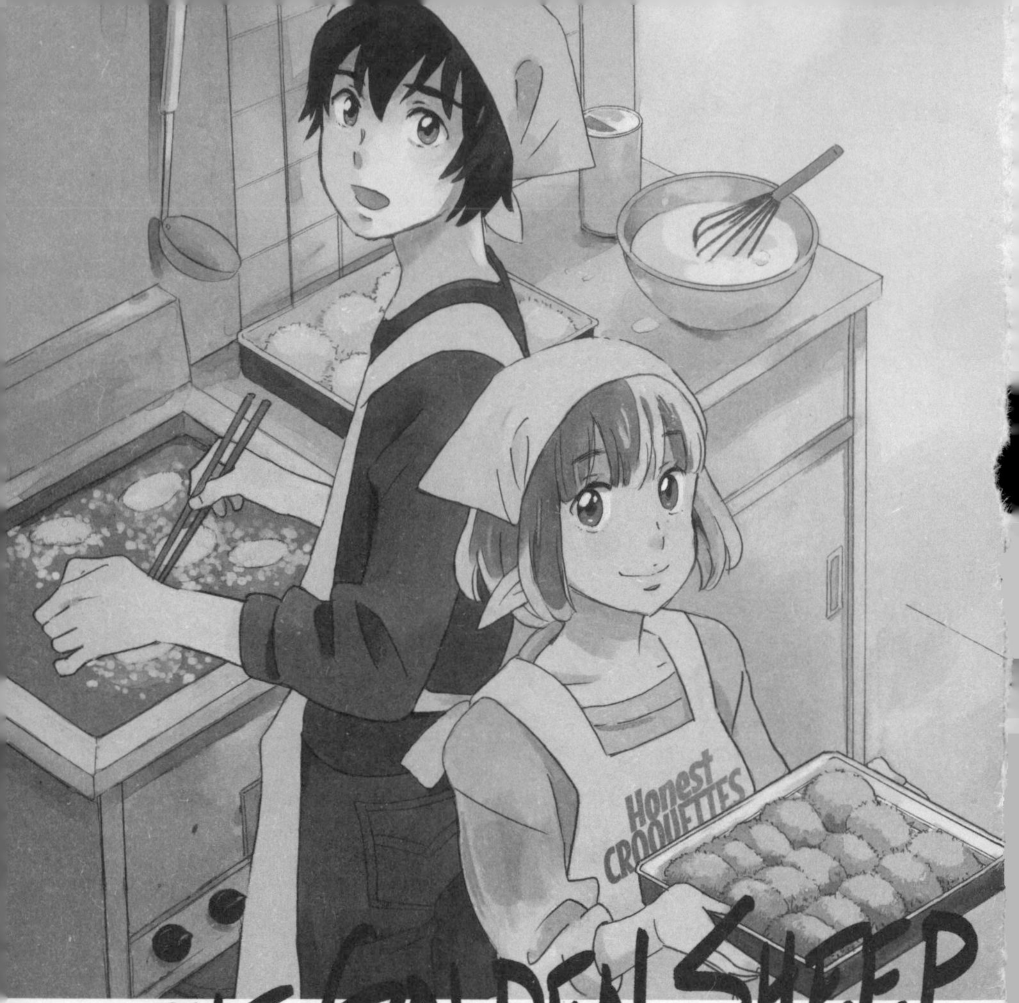
Honest
CROQUETTES

THE GOLDEN SHEEP

(2)

KAORI OZAKI

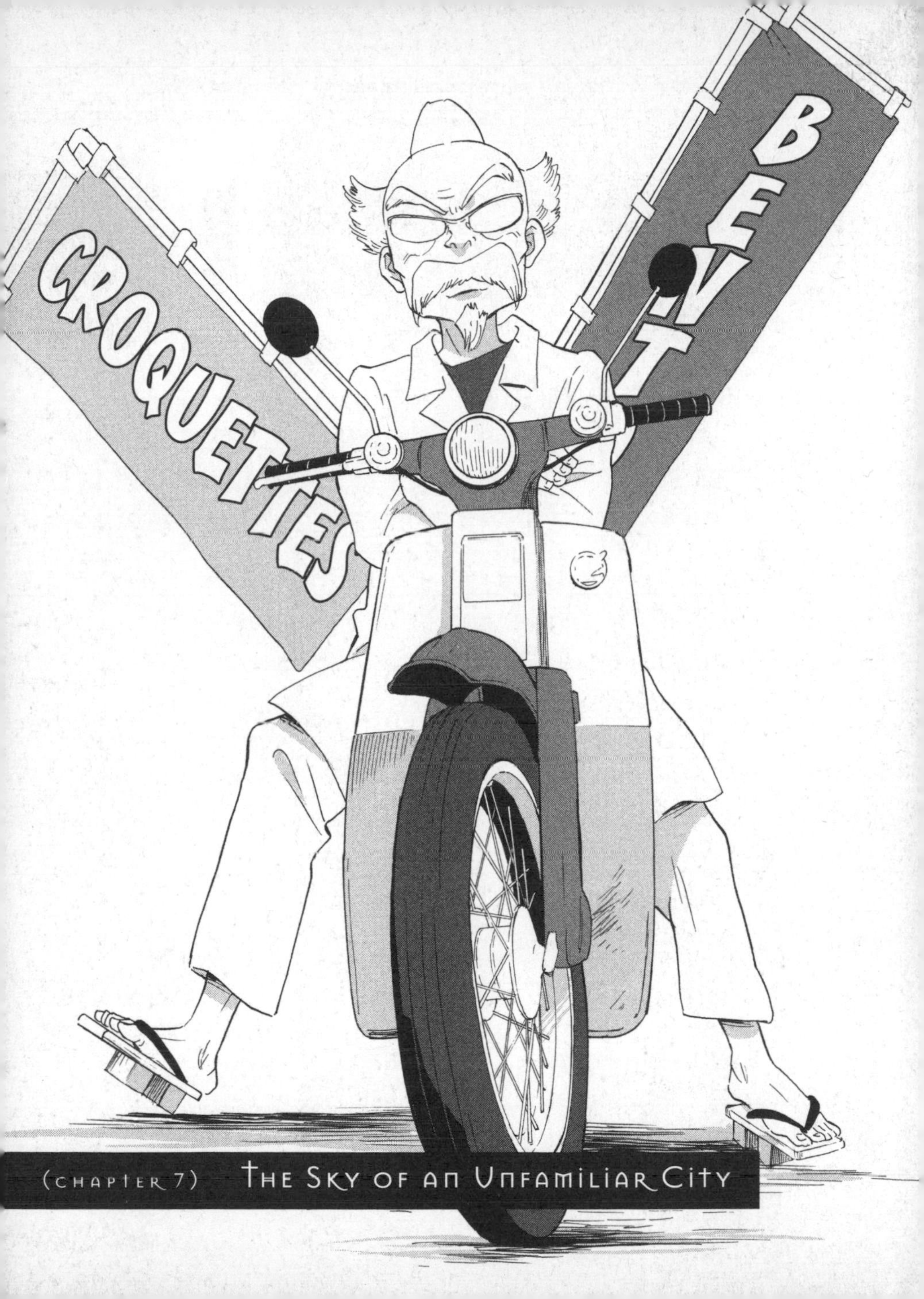
CROQUETTES

(CHAPTER 7) THE SKY OF AN UNFAMILIAR CITY

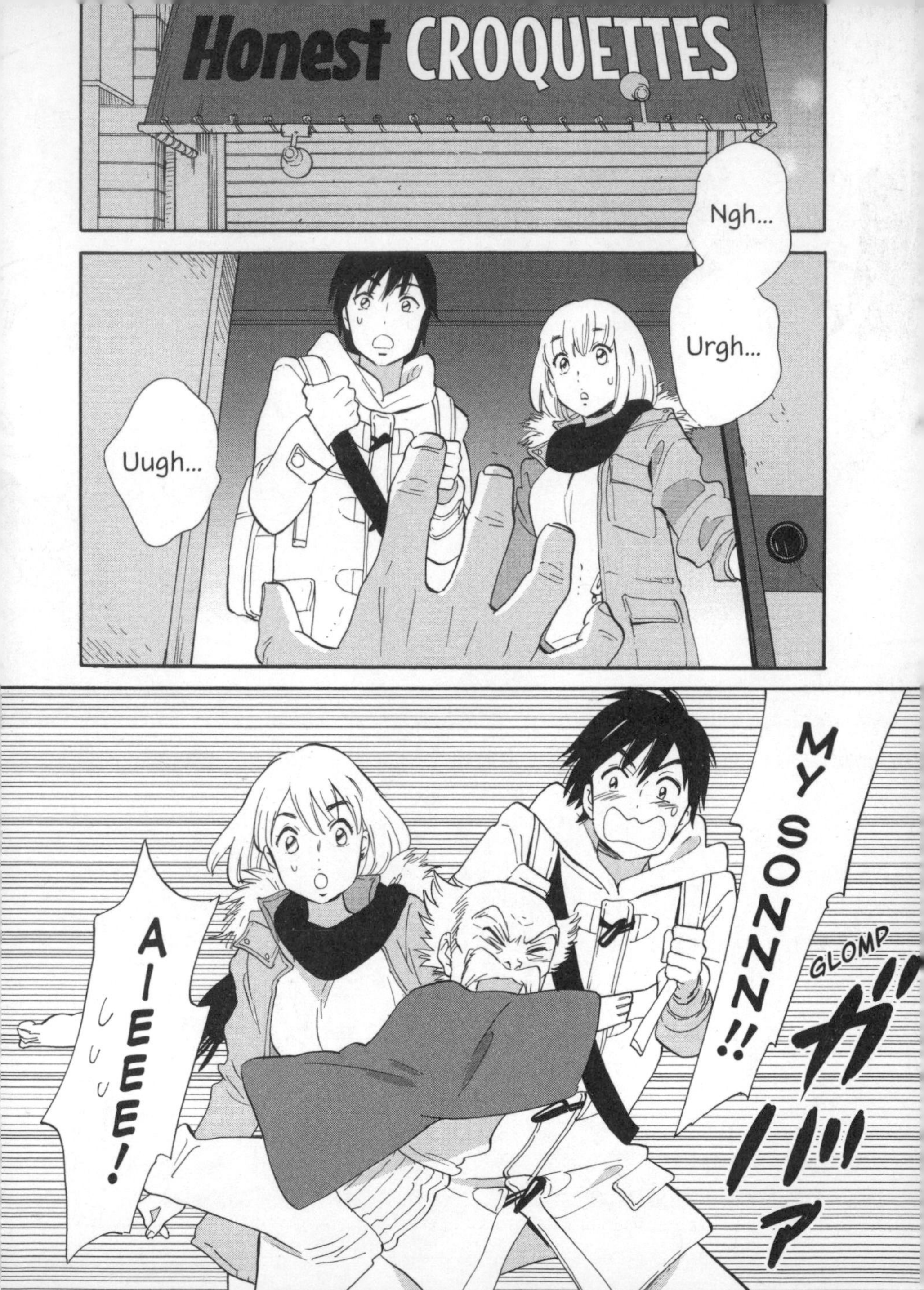
Honest CROQUETTES
Ngh...
Urgh...
Uugh...
MY SONNN!!
GLOMP
ガバァ
AIEEEE!

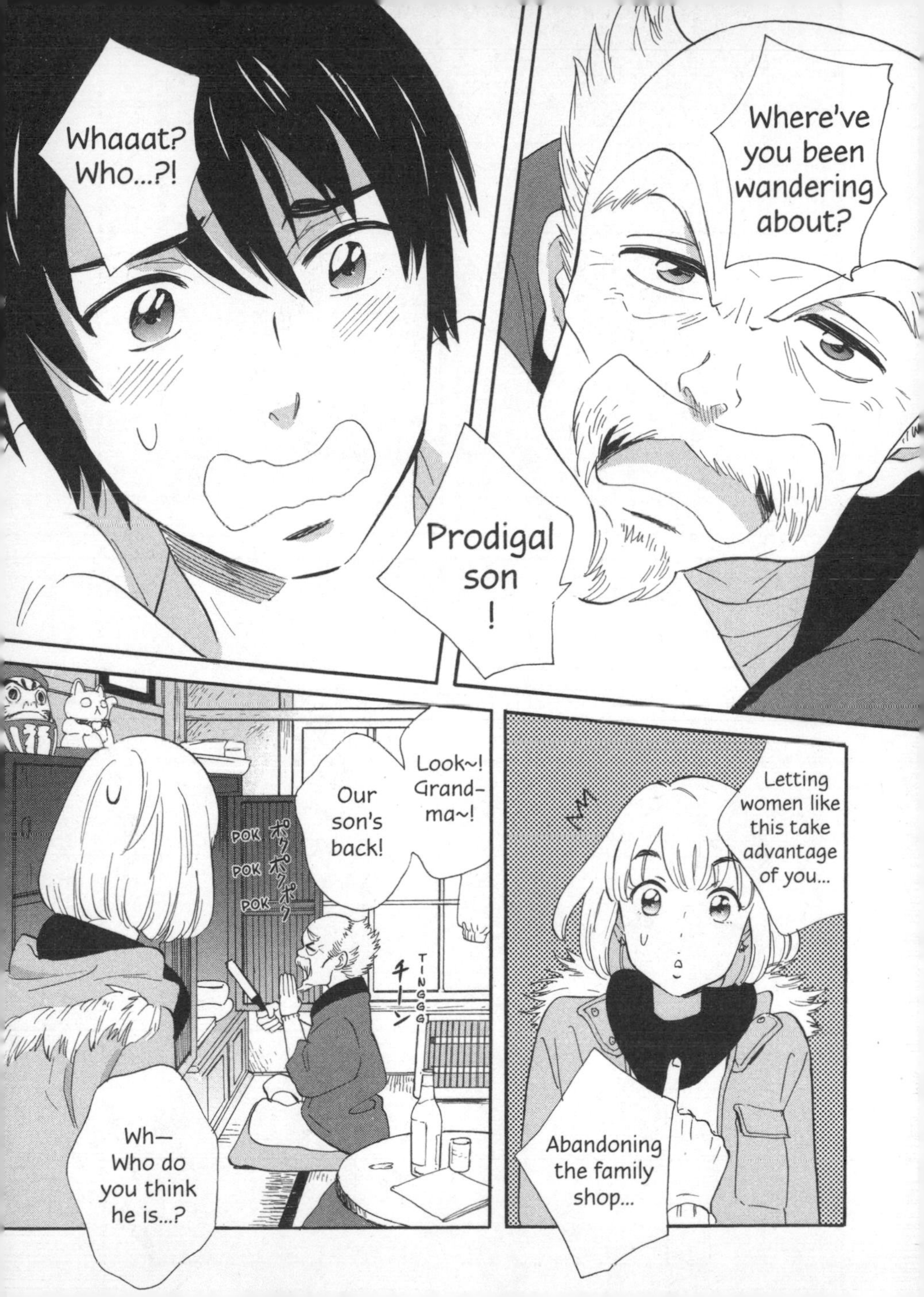
Where've you been wandering about?
Prodigal son!
Whaaat? Who...?!
Letting women like this take advantage of you...
Abandoning the family shop...
Look~! Grand-ma~!
Our son's back!
ポクポクポク
POK POK POK
チーン
TINGGG
Wh— Who do you think he is...?

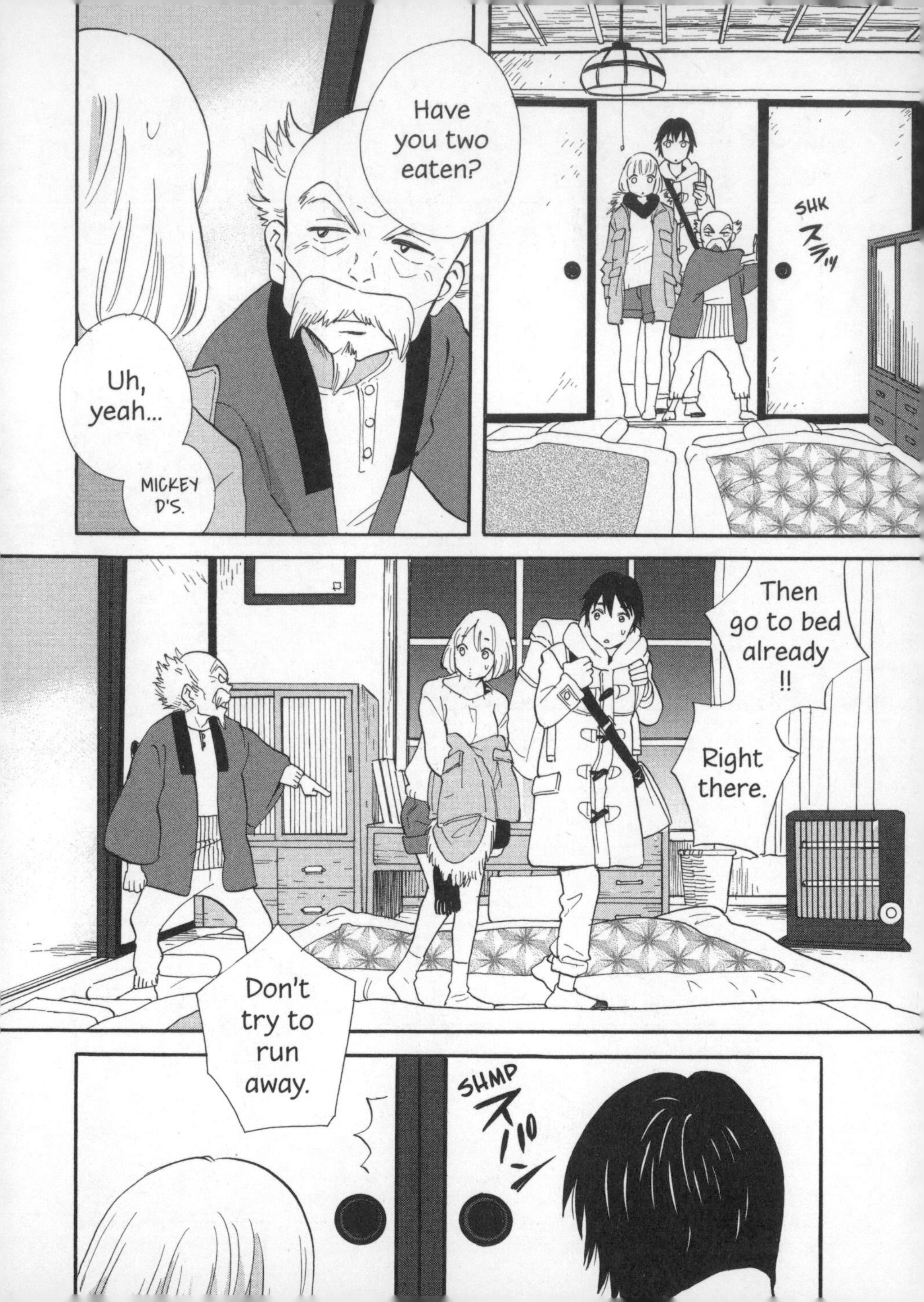
SHK
Have you two eaten?
Uh, yeah...
MICKEY D'S.
Then go to bed already !!
Right there.
Don't try to run away.
SHMP

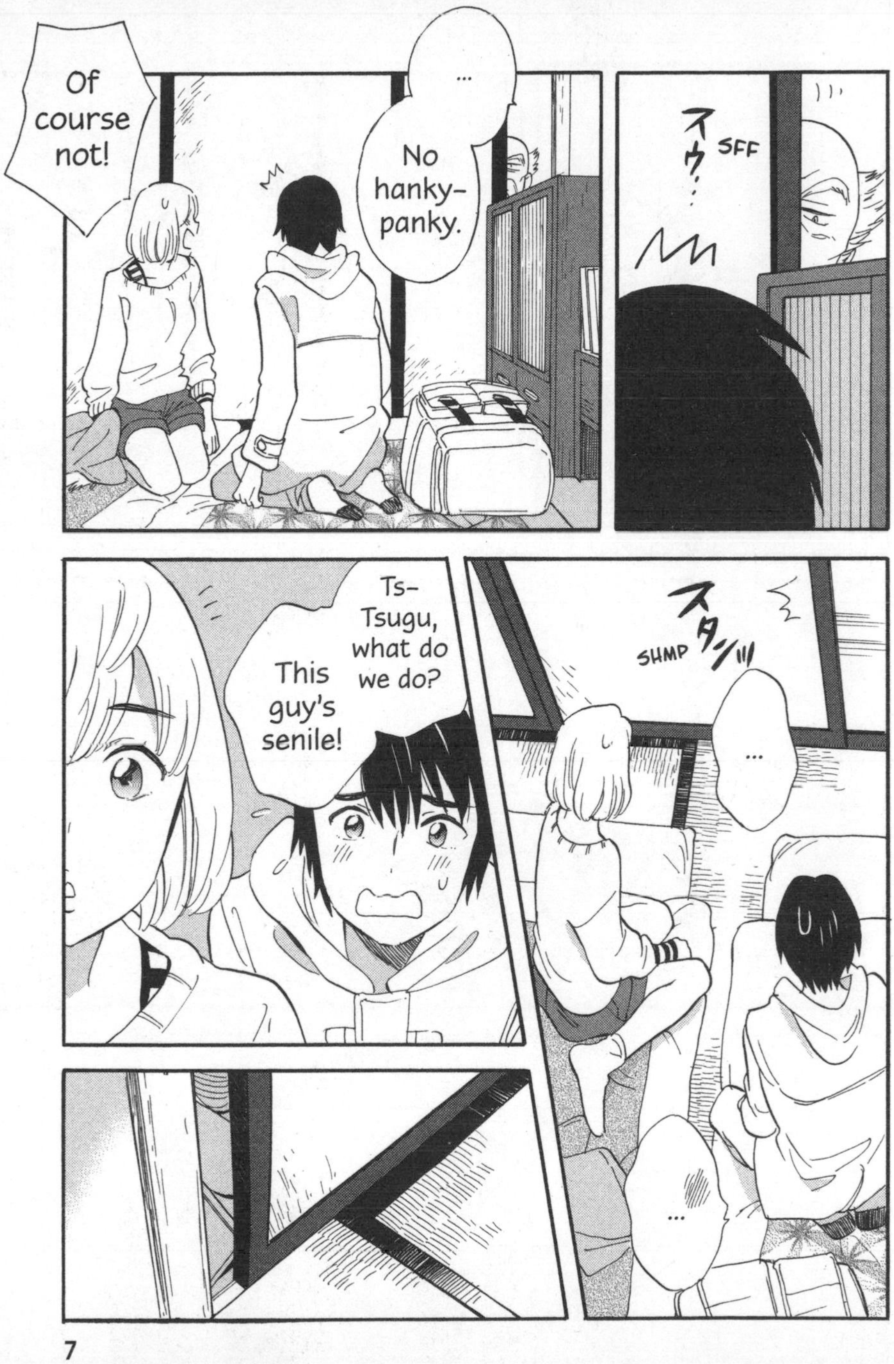
スウ
SFF
...
No hanky-panky.
Of course not!
スタン
SHMP
...
...
Ts-Tsugu, what do we do?
This guy's senile!

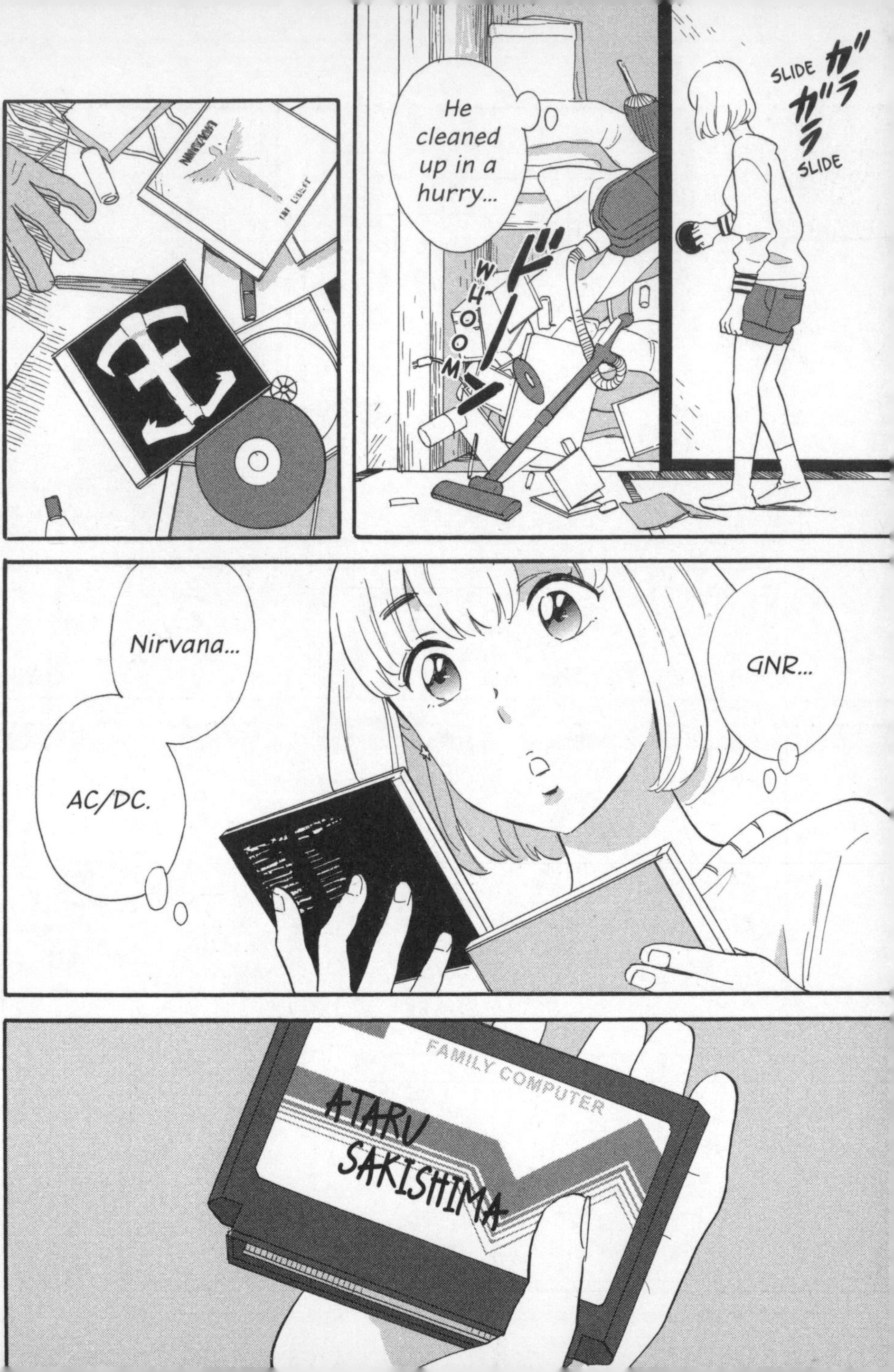
SLIDE
ガラガラ
SLIDE
He cleaned up in a hurry...
WHOOM
ドーン
GNR...
Nirvana...
AC/DC.
FAMILY COMPUTER
ATARU SAKISHIMA

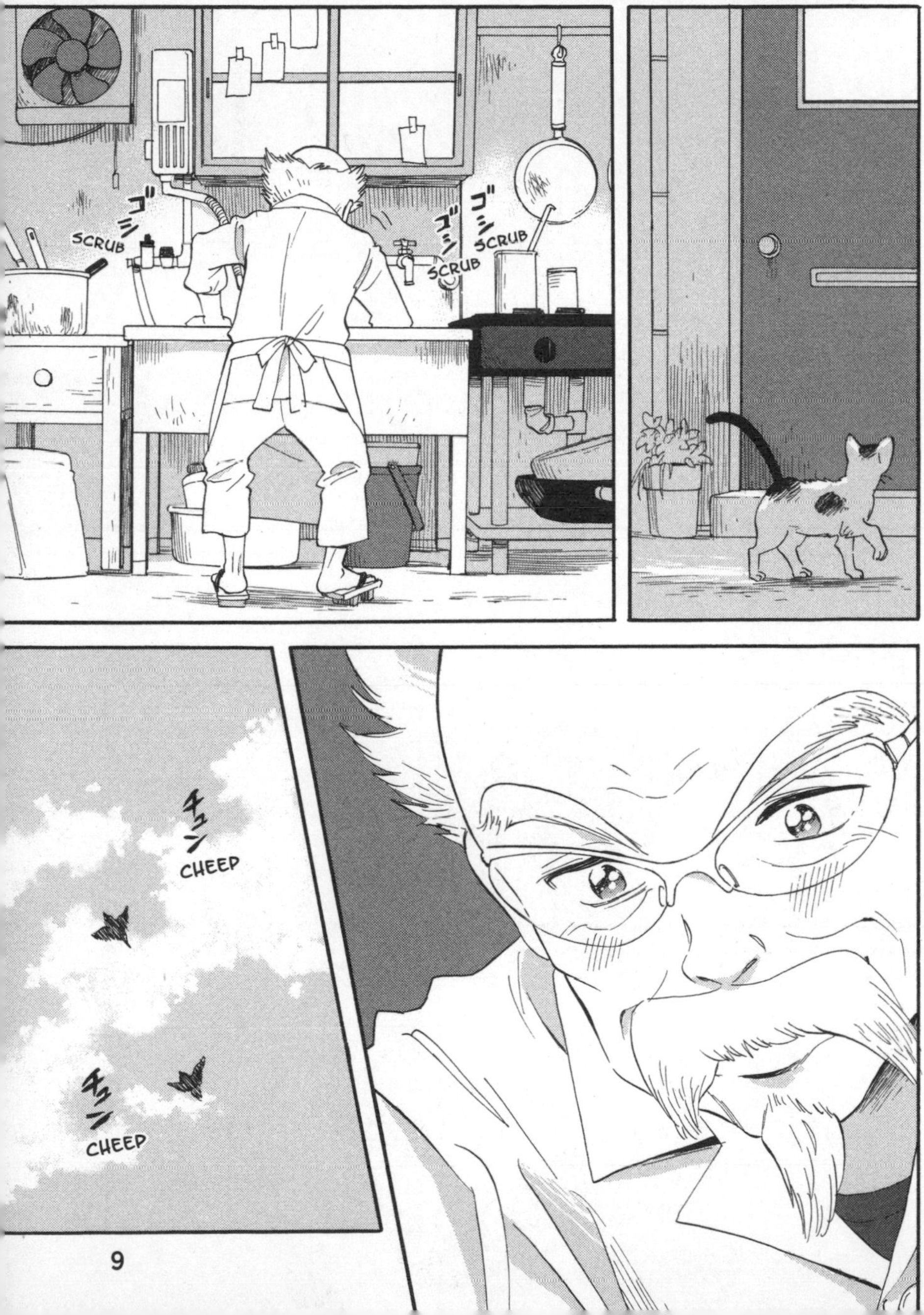
ゴシ
SCRUB
ゴシ
SCRUB
ゴシ
SCRUB
チュン
CHEEP
チュン
CHEEP

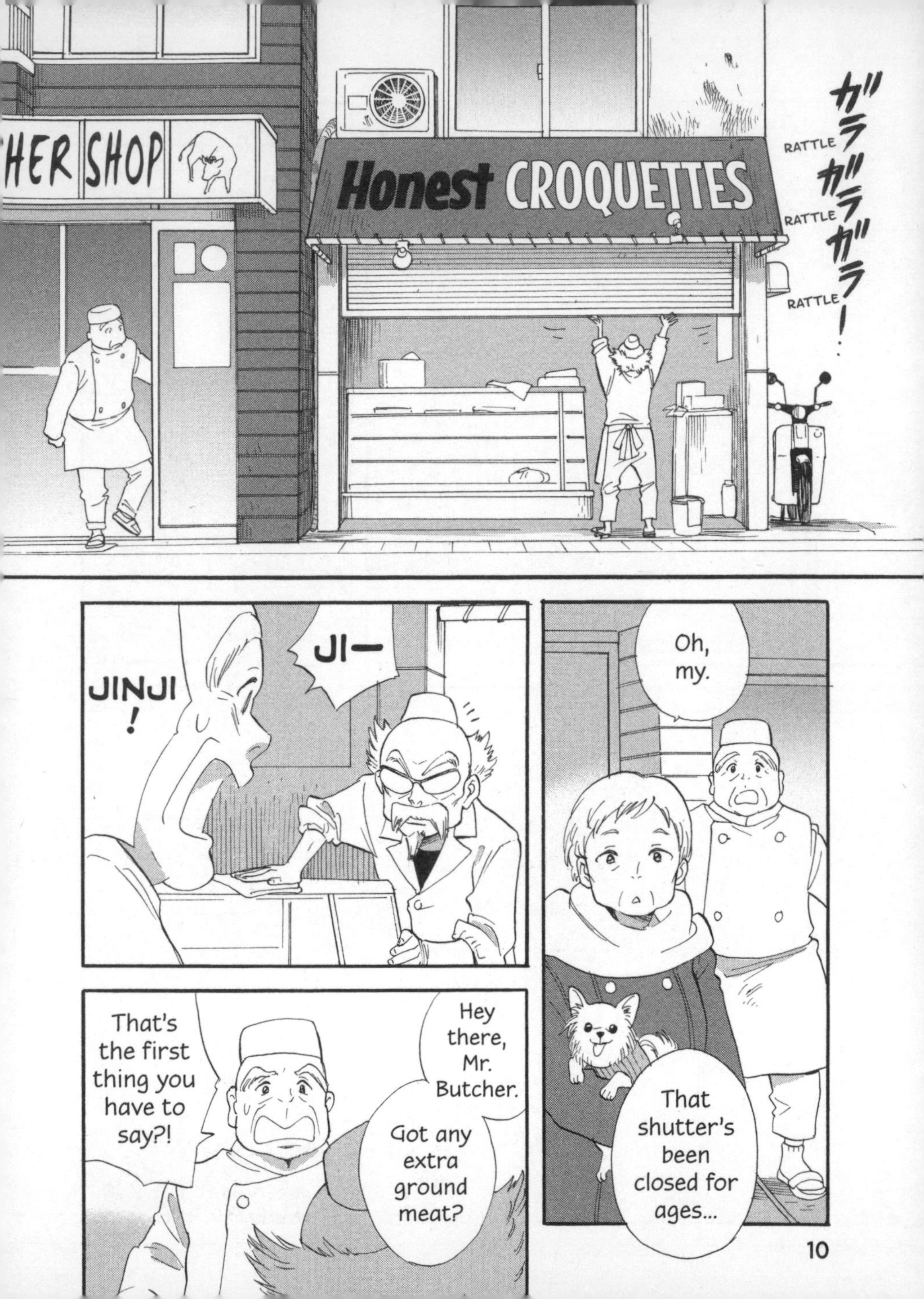
HER SHOP
Honest CROQUETTES
ガラガラガラ!
RATTLE
RATTLE
RATTLE
Oh, my.
That shutter's been closed for ages...
JI—
JINJI!
Hey there, Mr. Butcher.
Got any extra ground meat?
That's the first thing you have to say?!

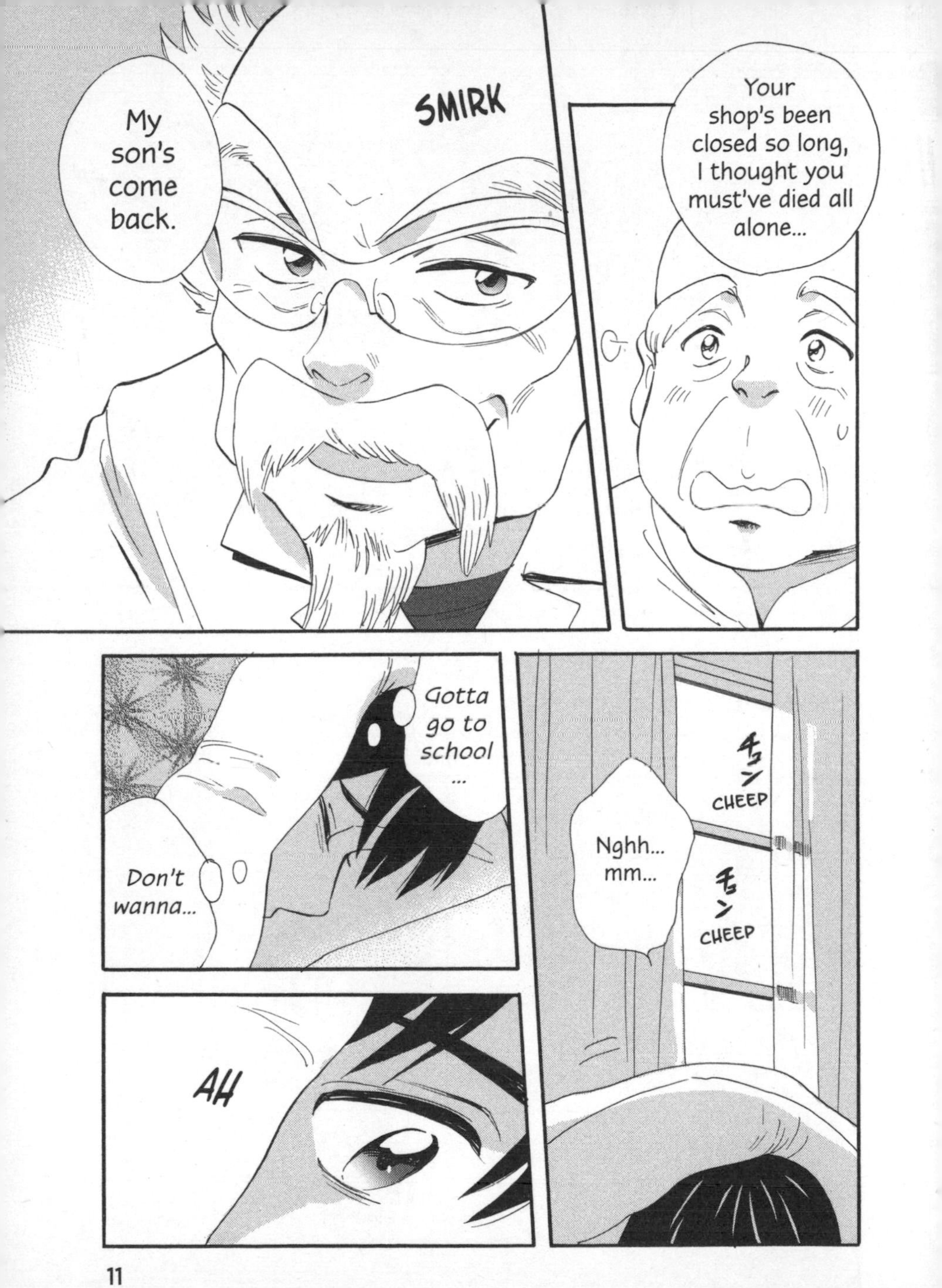

Your shop's been closed so long, I thought you must've died all alone...
SMIRK
My son's come back.
チュン
CHEEP
Nghh... mm...
チュン
CHEEP
Gotta go to school ...
Don't wanna...
AH

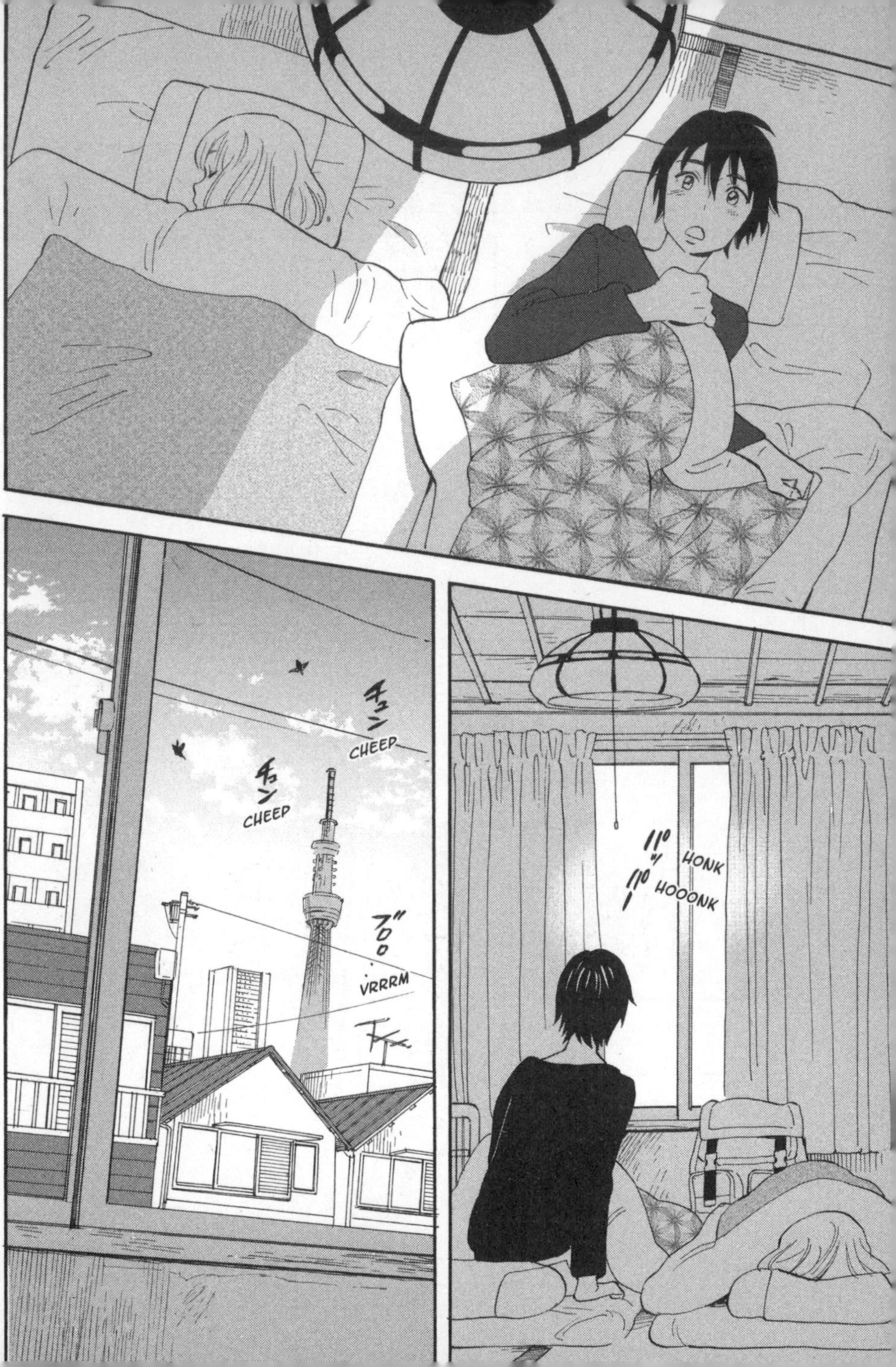
HONK
HOOONK
CHEEP
CHEEP
VRRRM

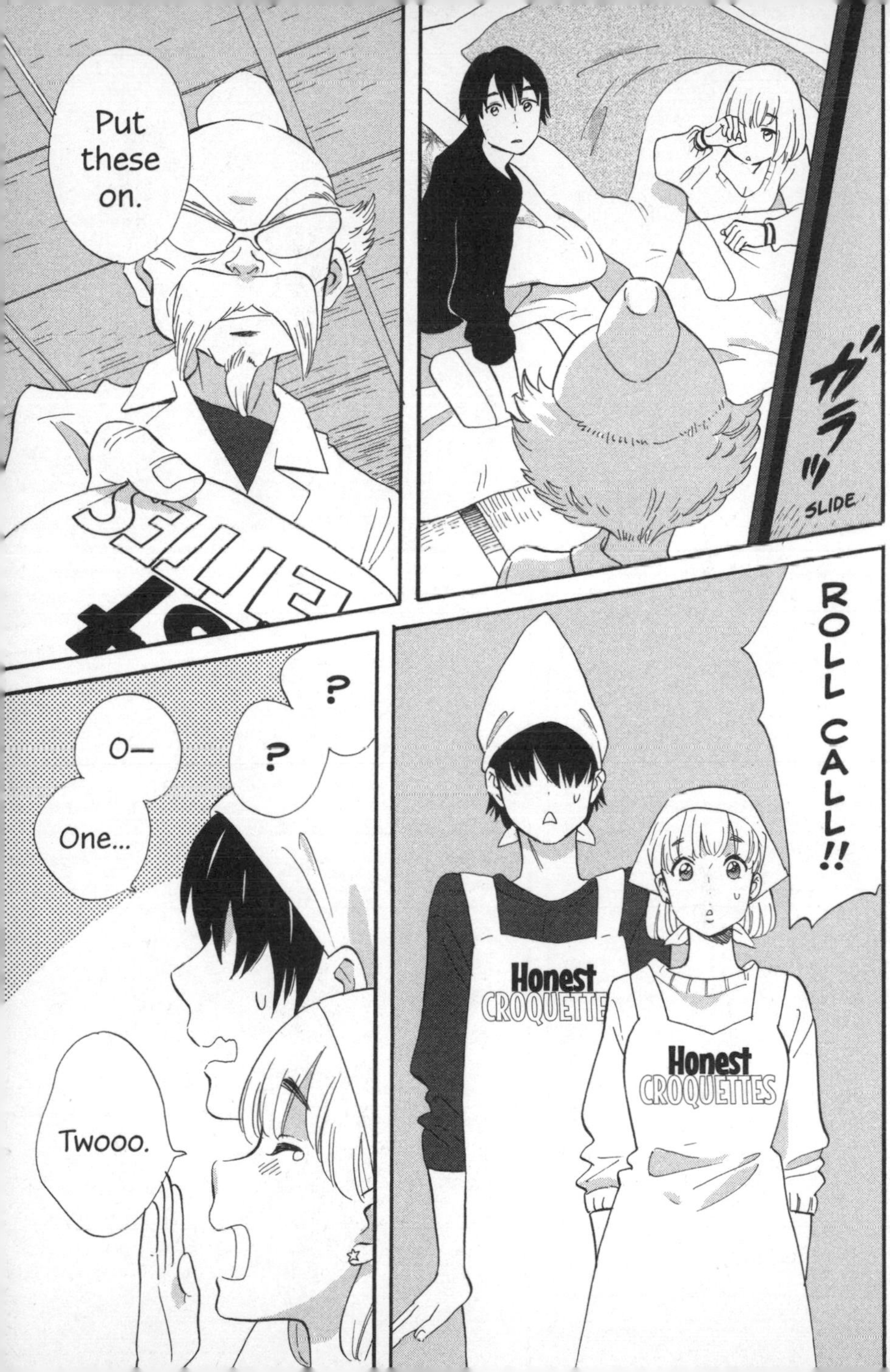
ガラッ
SLIDE
Put these on.
ROLL CALL!!
Honest CROQUETTE
Honest CROQUETTES
?
?
O— One...
Twooo.

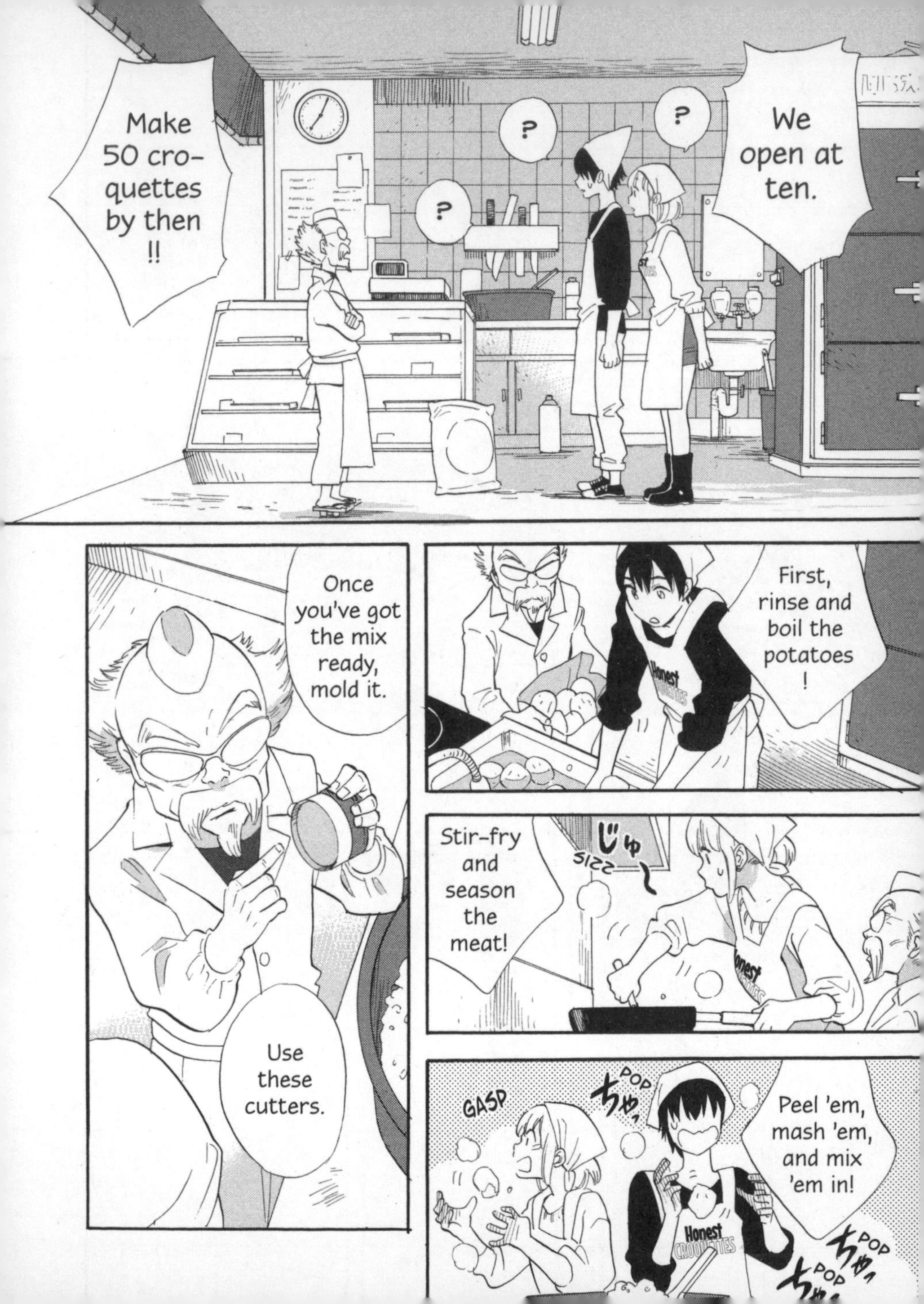
We open at ten.
?
?
?
Make 50 cro-quettes by then !!
First, rinse and boil the potatoes !
Stir-fry and season the meat!
じゅ~
SIZZ
Peel 'em, mash 'em, and mix 'em in!
ちゃ
POP
GASP
ちゃ
POP
ちゃ
POP
Honest CROQUETTES
Once you've got the mix ready, mold it.
Use these cutters.

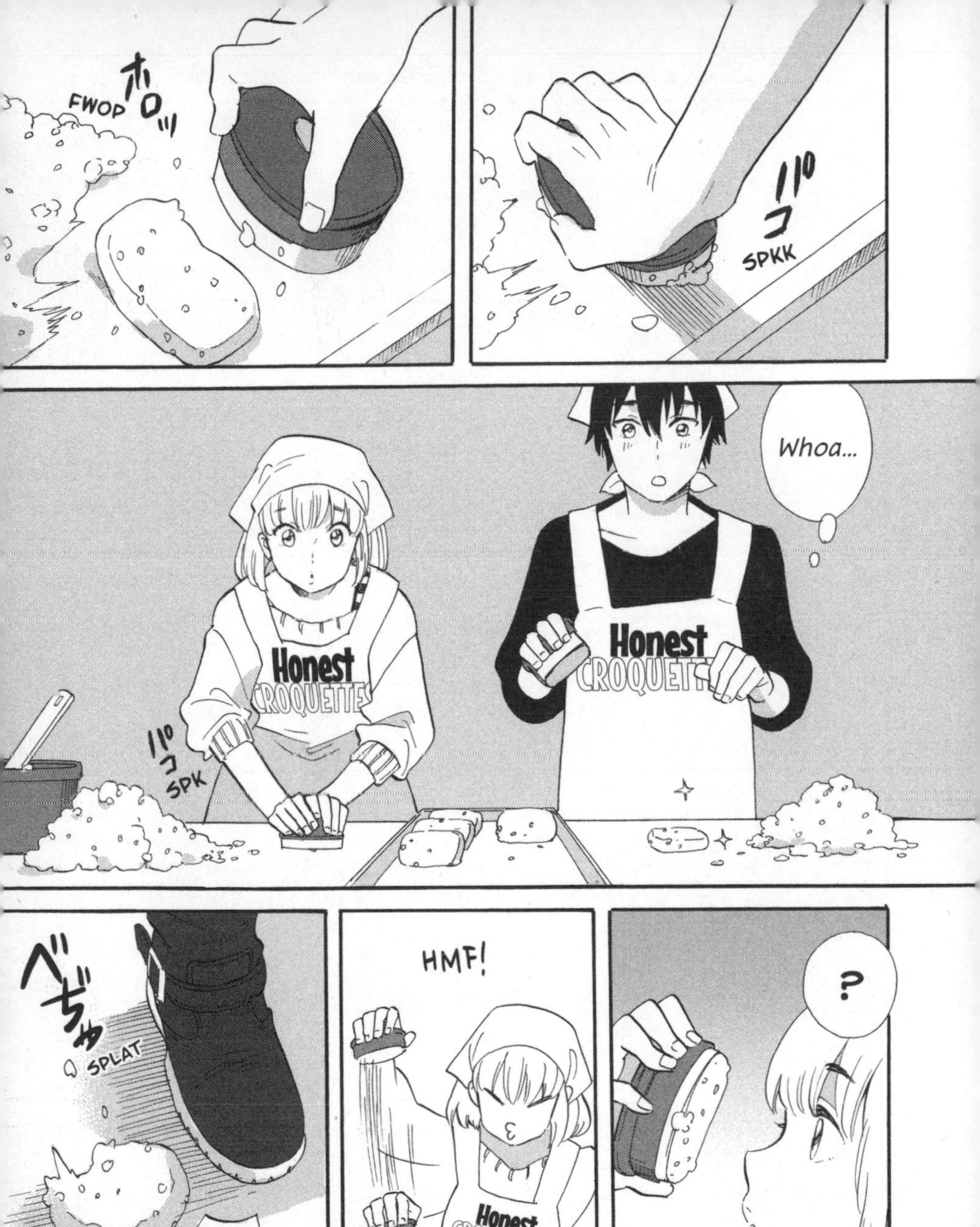
パコ
SPKK
ホロッ
FWOP
Whoa...
パコ
SPK
?
HMF!
べちゃ
SPLAT
!!

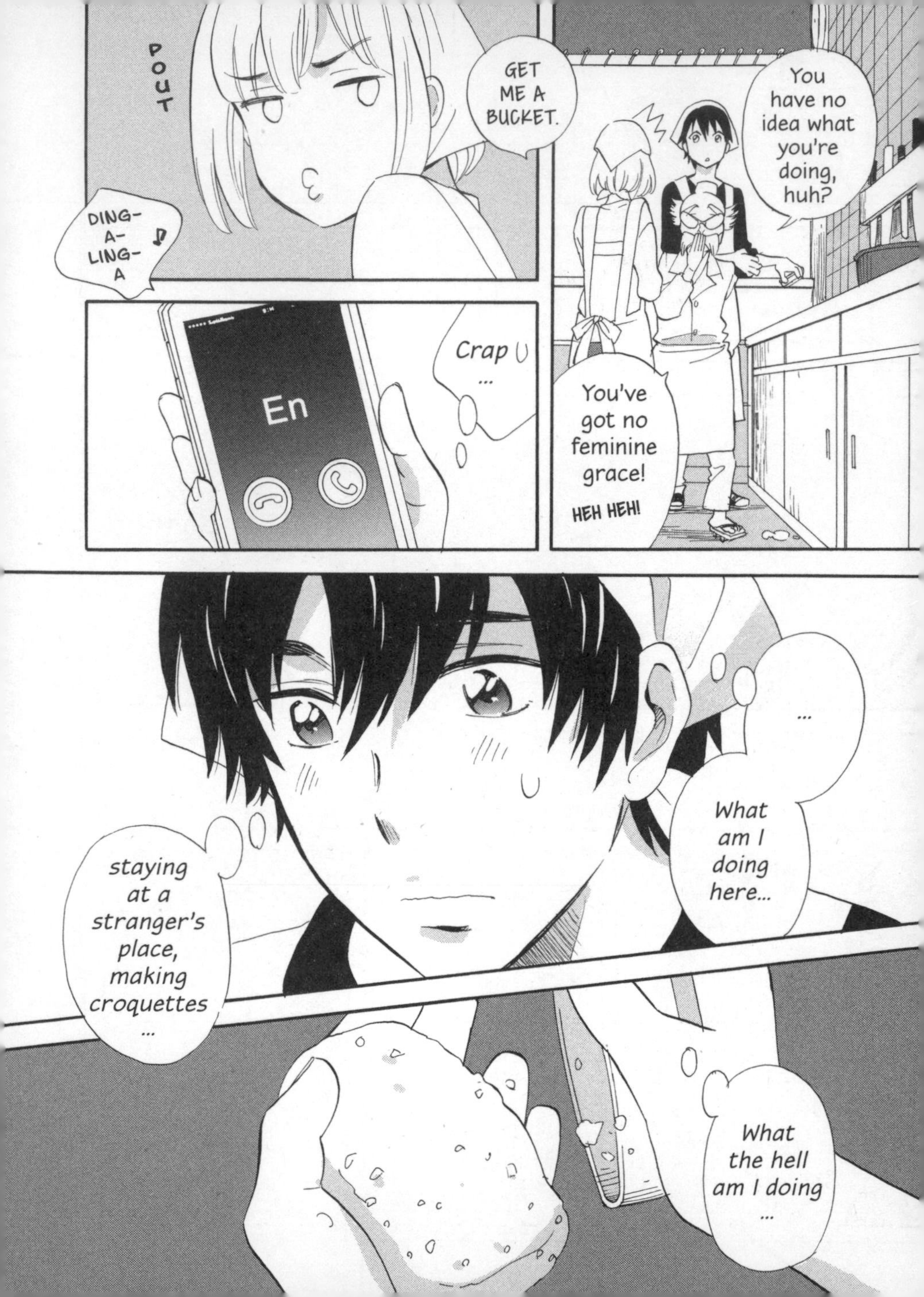
You have no idea what you're doing, huh?
You've got no feminine grace!
HEH HEH!
GET ME A BUCKET.
POUT
DING-A-LING-A ♪
Crap ...
En
...
What am I doing here...
staying at a stranger's place, making croquettes ...
What the hell am I doing ...

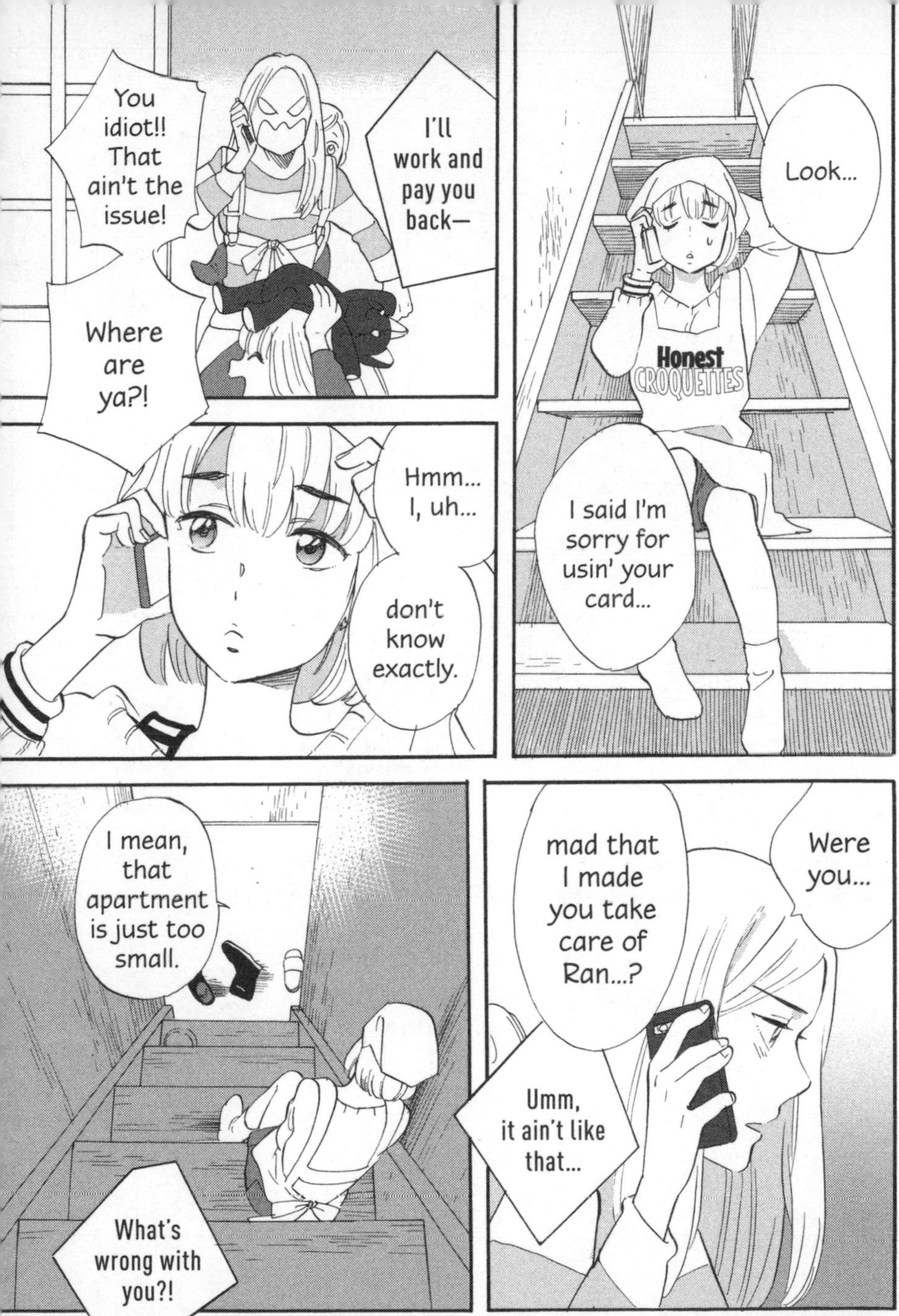
Look...
Honest
CROQUETTES
I said I'm sorry for usin' your card...
I'll work and pay you back—
You idiot!! That ain't the issue!
Where are ya?!
Hmm... I, uh...
don't know exactly.
Were you...
mad that I made you take care of Ran...?
Umm, it ain't like that...
I mean, that apartment is just too small.
What's wrong with you?!

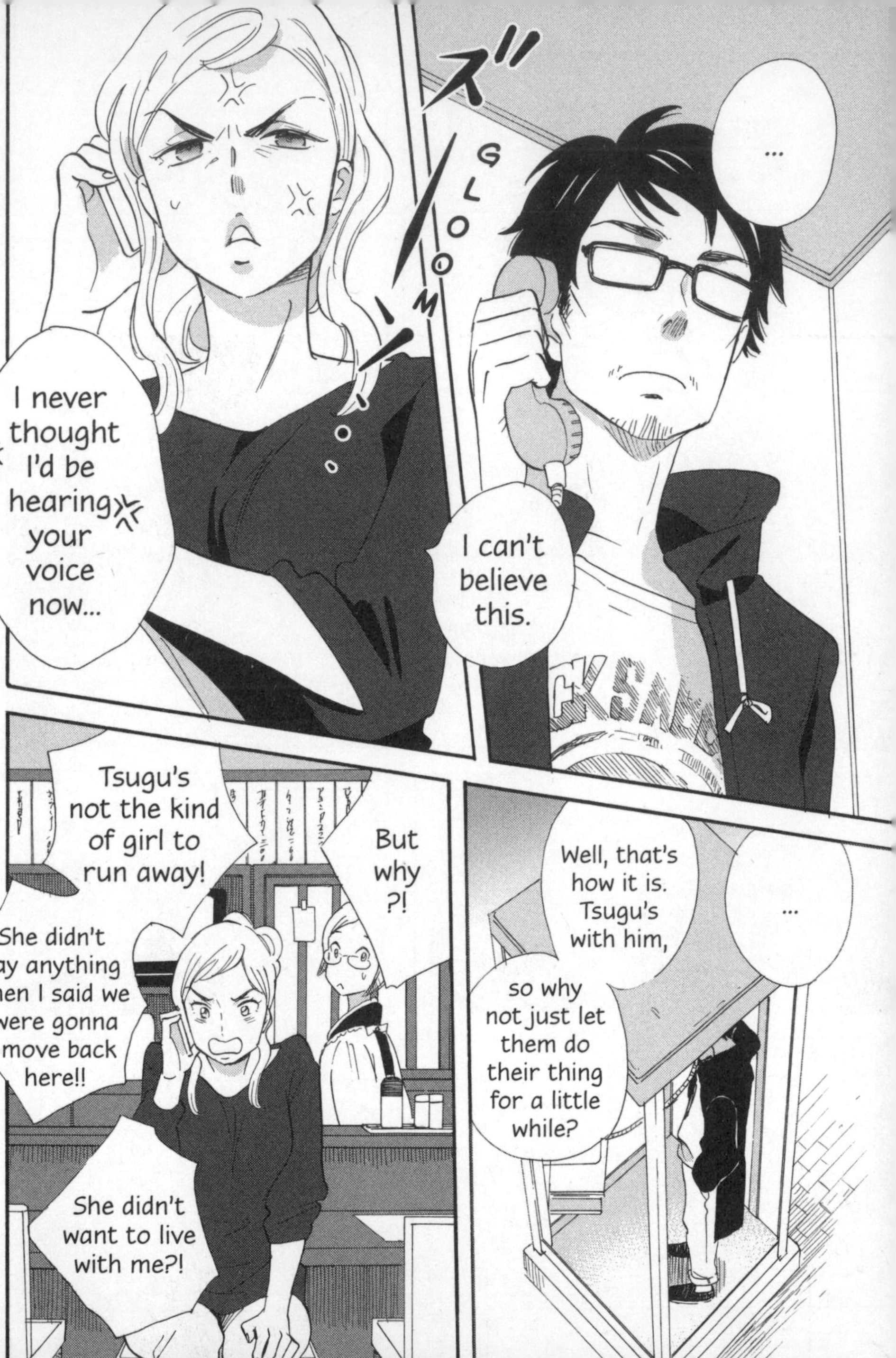
...
I can't believe this.
ズ
GLOOM
I never thought I'd be hearing your voice now...
...
Well, that's how it is. Tsugu's with him,
so why not just let them do their thing for a little while?
But why?!
Tsugu's not the kind of girl to run away!
She didn't say anything when I said we were gonna move back here!!
She didn't want to live with me?!

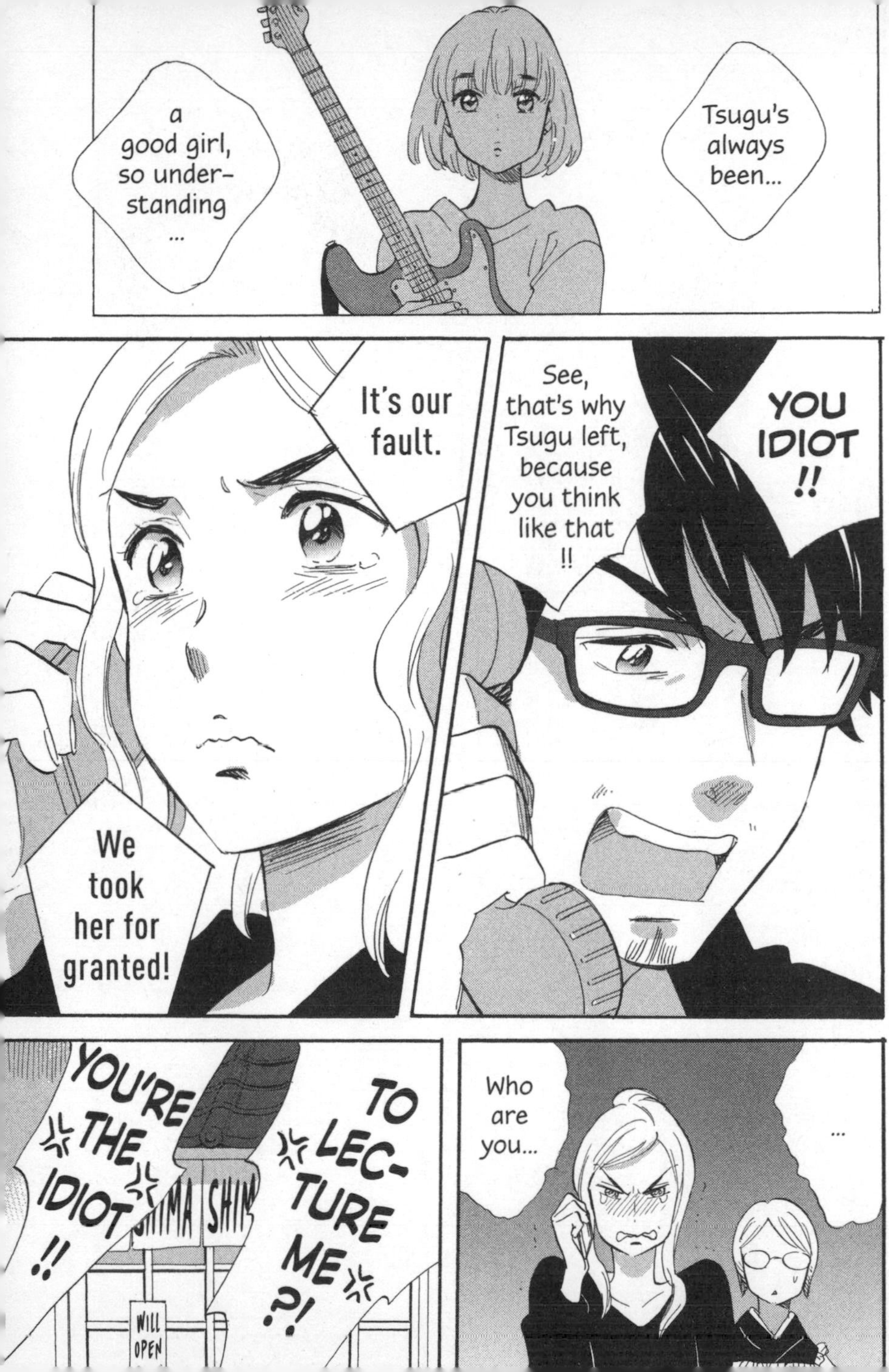
Tsugu's always been...
a good girl, so under-standing ...
YOU IDIOT !!
See, that's why Tsugu left, because you think like that !!
It's our fault.
We took her for granted!
...
Who are you...
TO LEC-TURE ME ?!
YOU'RE THE IDIOT !!
WILL OPEN

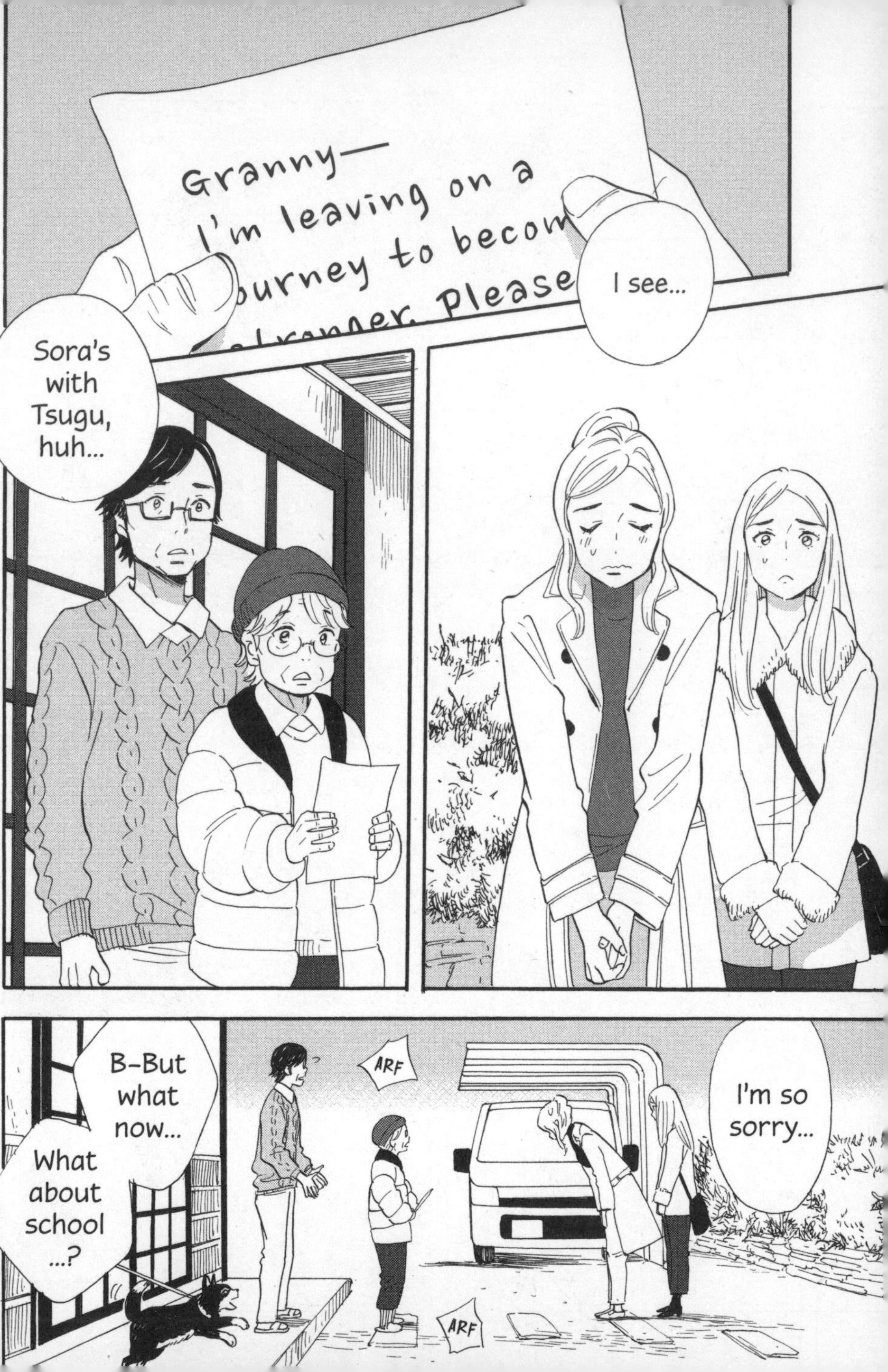
Granny—
I'm leaving on a
ourney to becom
Please
I see...
Sora's with Tsugu, huh...
I'm so sorry...
ARF
B-But what now...
What about school ...?
ARF

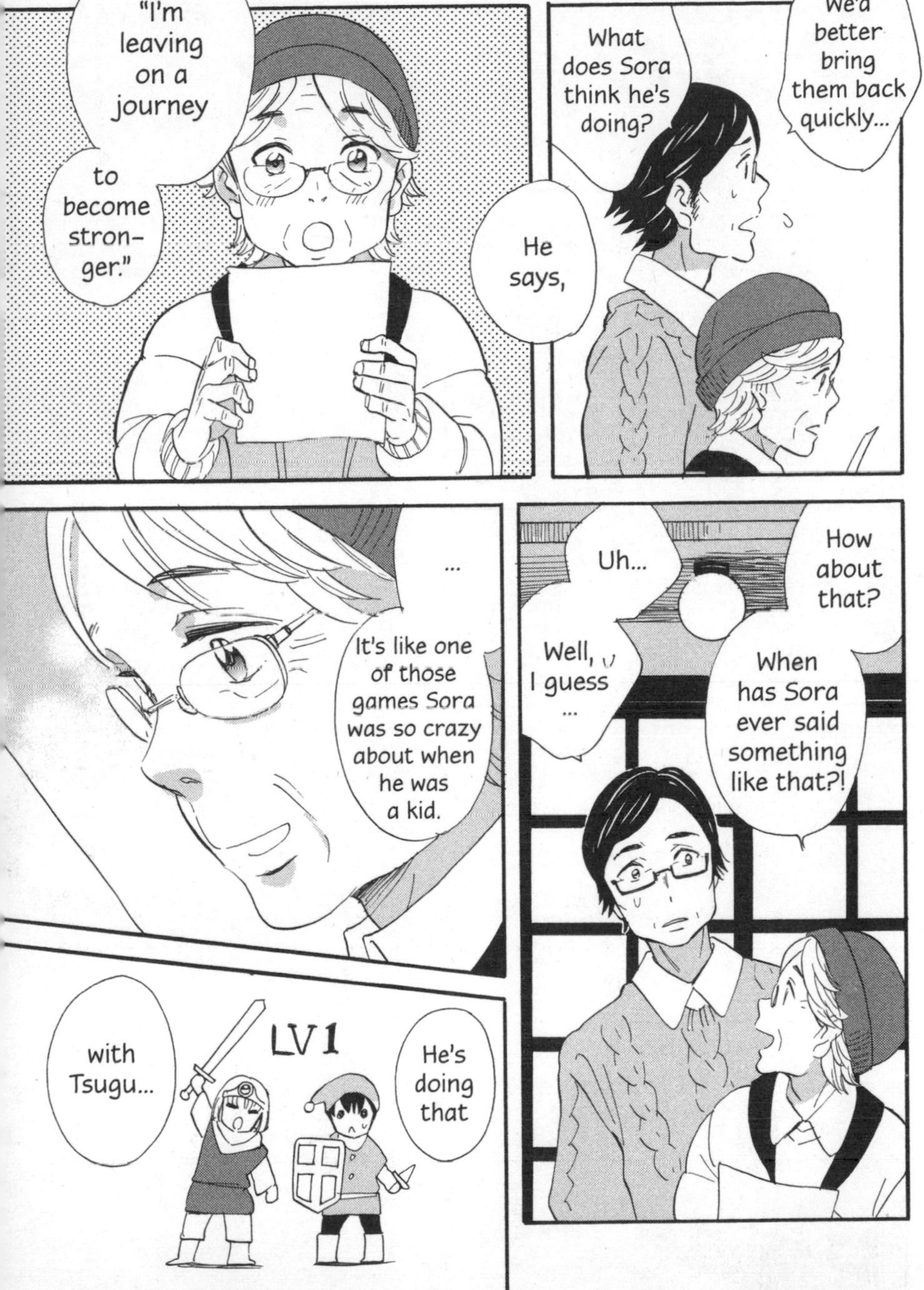
We'd better bring them back quickly...
What does Sora think he's doing?
He says,
"I'm leaving on a journey
to become stronger."
How about that?
Uh...
When has Sora ever said something like that?!
Well, I guess ...
...
It's like one of those games Sora was so crazy about when he was a kid.
He's doing that
LV1
with Tsugu...

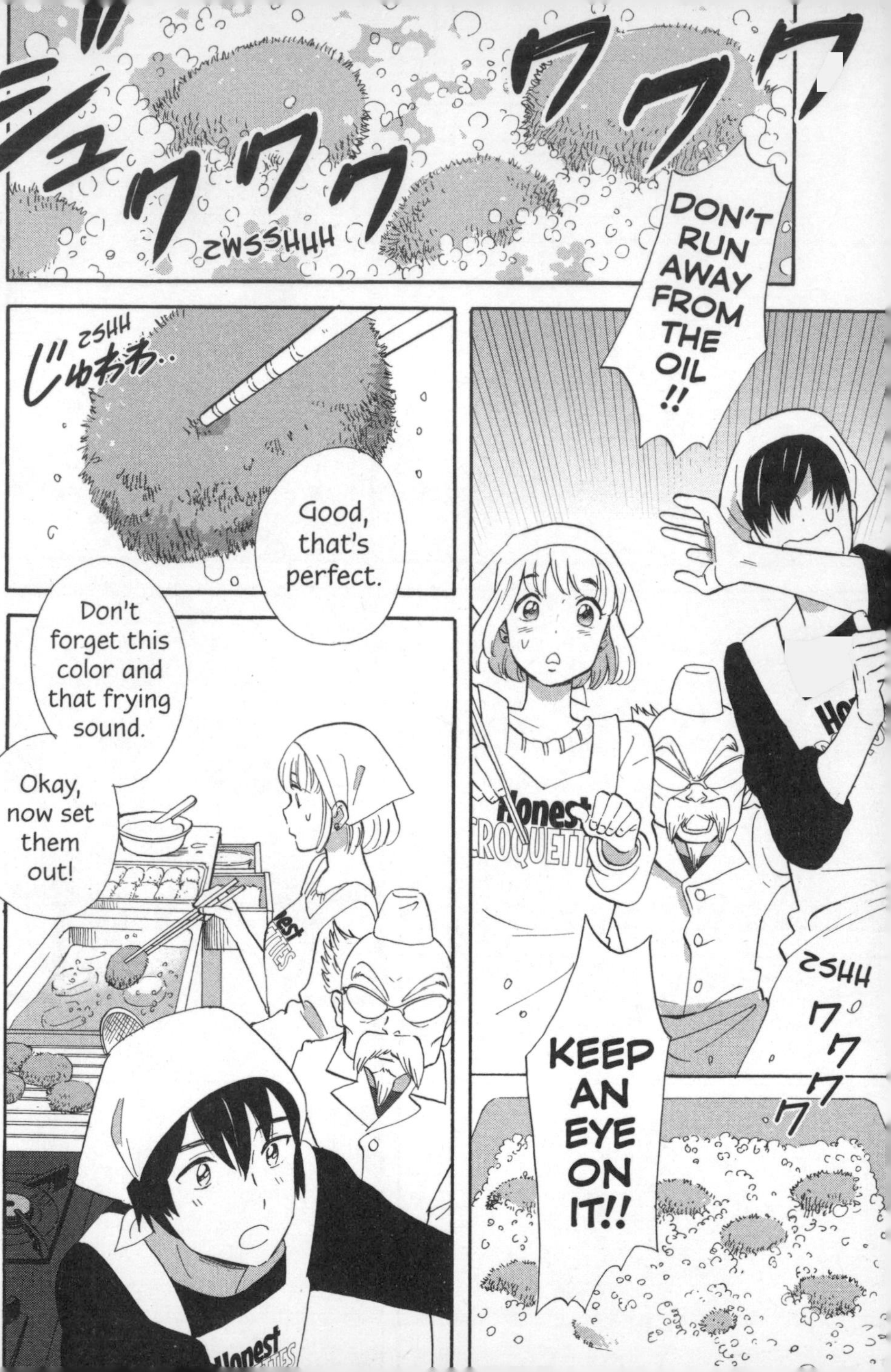
ジュワワワワワワ
ZWSSHHH
DON'T RUN AWAY FROM THE OIL!!
じゅわわ..
ZSHH
Good, that's perfect.
Don't forget this color and that frying sound.
Okay, now set them out!
KEEP AN EYE ON IT!!
ワワワワ
ZSHH

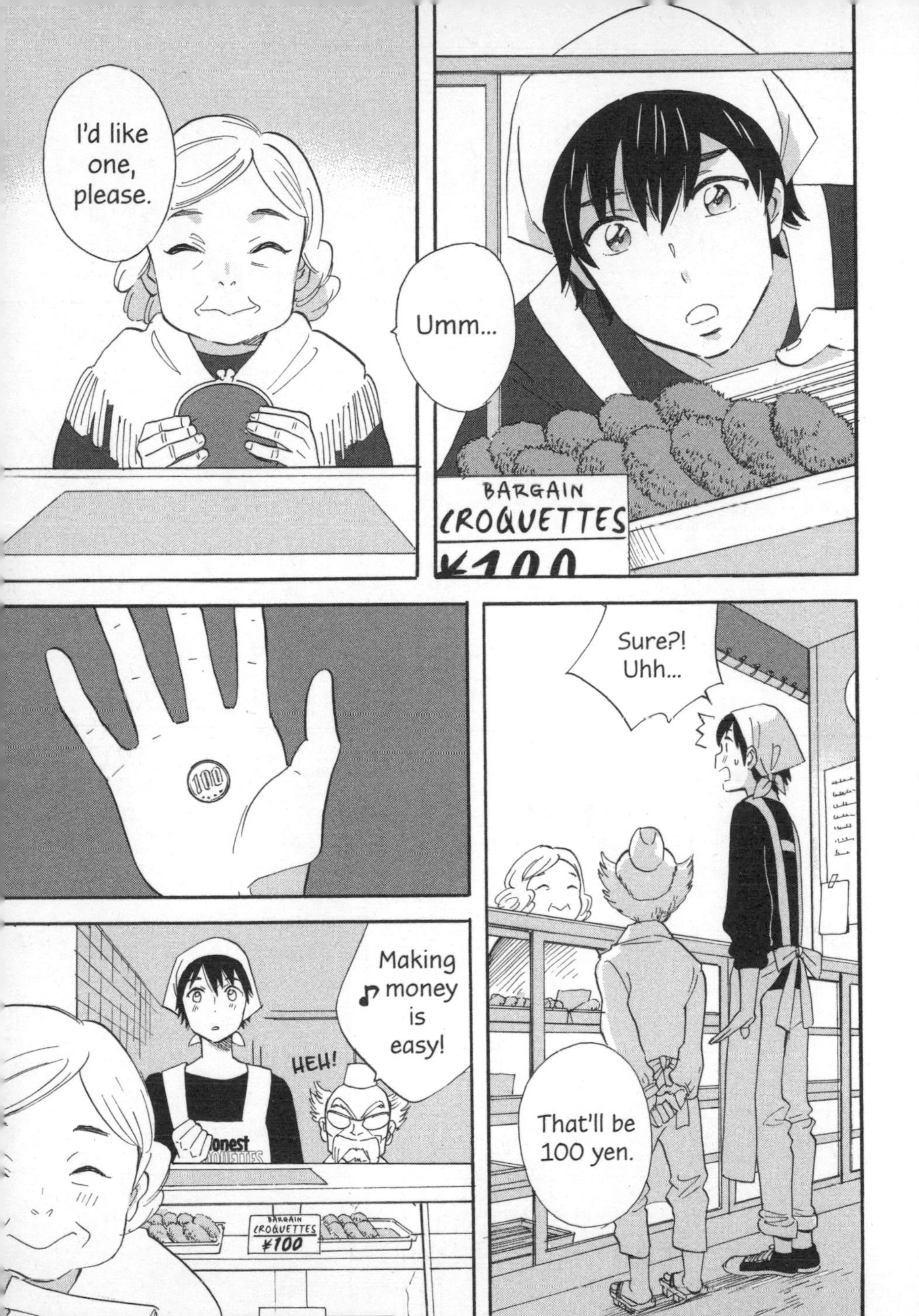
Umm...
BARGAIN
CROQUETTES
I'd like one, please.
Sure?! Uhh...
That'll be 100 yen.
100
Making money is easy!
HEH!
BARGAIN
CROQUETTES
¥100

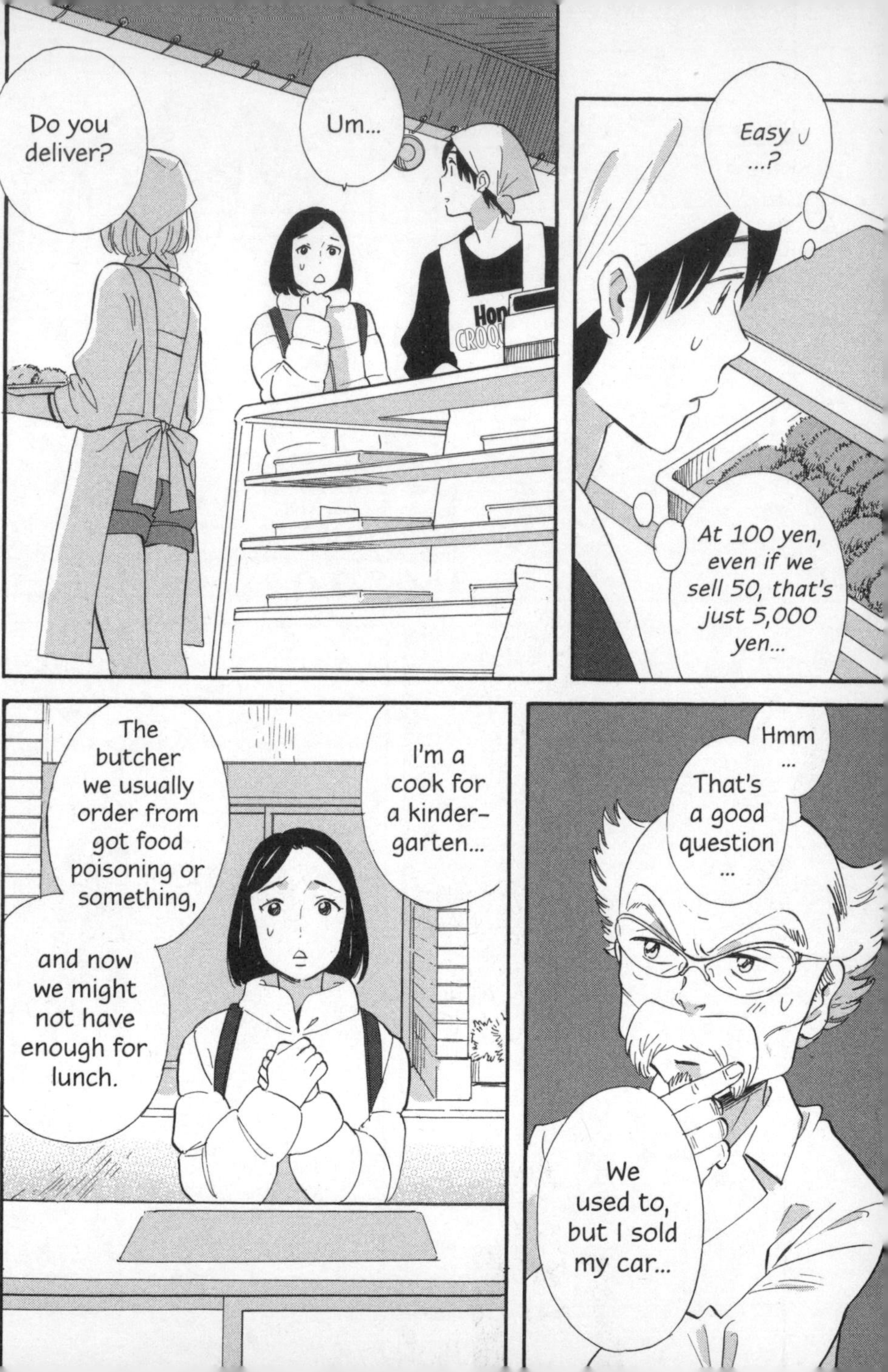
Easy ...?
At 100 yen, even if we sell 50, that's just 5,000 yen...
Um...
Do you deliver?
Hmm ...
That's a good question ...
We used to, but I sold my car...
I'm a cook for a kinder-garten...
The butcher we usually order from got food poisoning or something,
and now we might not have enough for lunch.

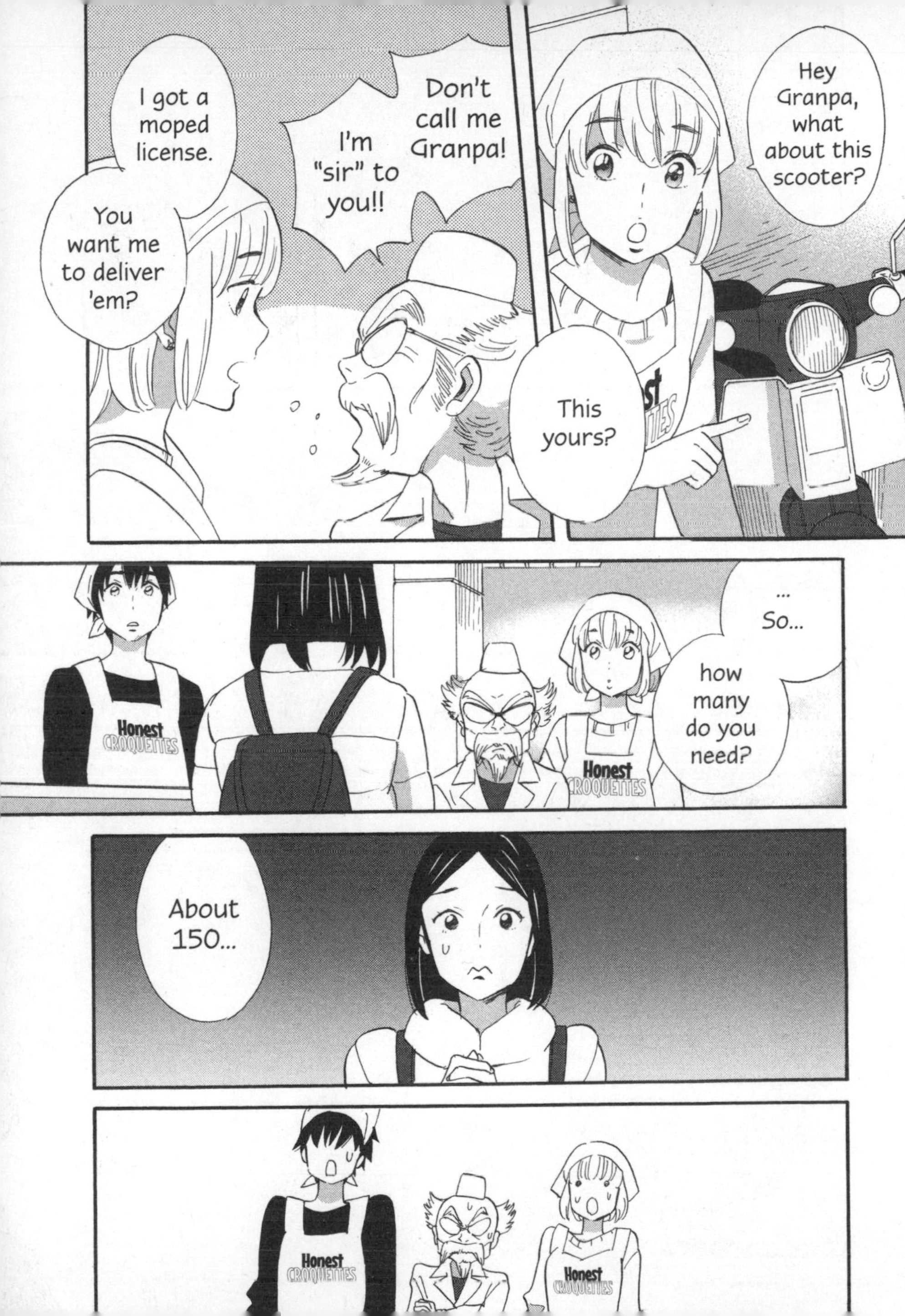
Hey Granpa, what about this scooter?
This yours?
Don't call me Granpa!
I'm "sir" to you!!
I got a moped license.
You want me to deliver 'em?
... So... how many do you need?
About 150...

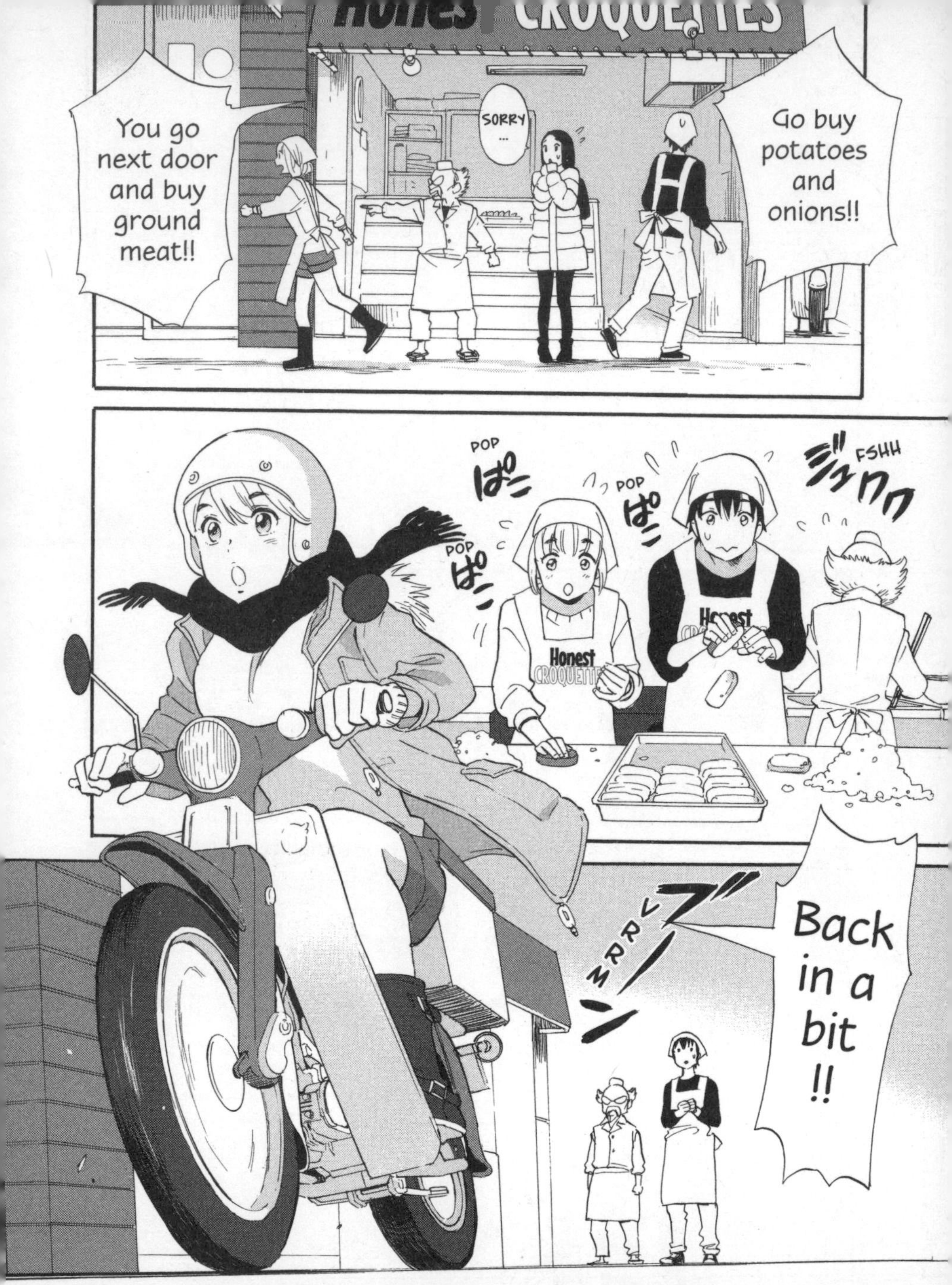
CROQUETTES
Go buy potatoes and onions!!
SORRY ...
You go next door and buy ground meat!!
FSHH
POP
POP
POP
Honest CROQUETTES
Honest CROQUETTES
Back in a bit !!
MRRRV

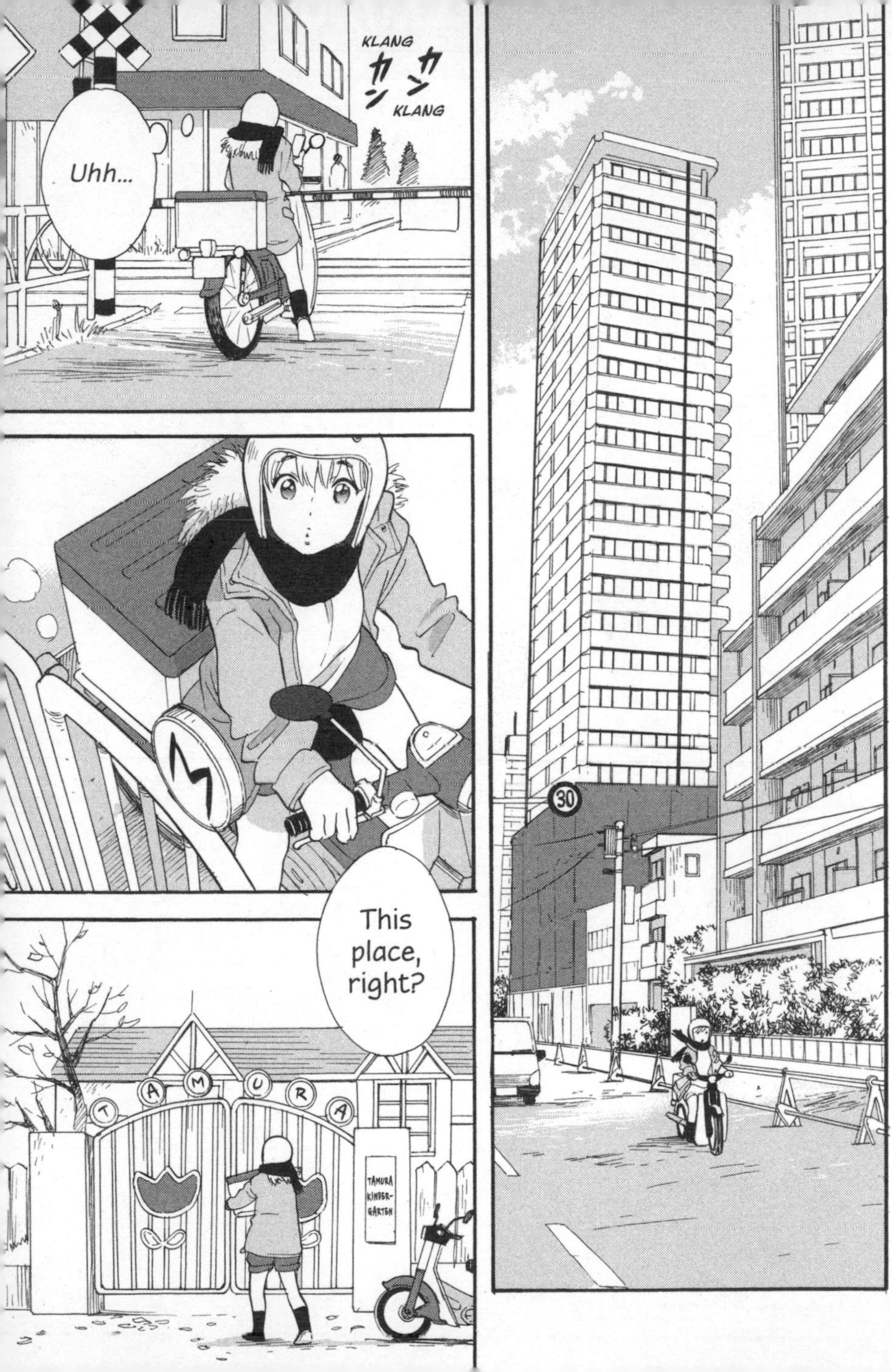
30
KLANG
カンカン
KLANG
Uhh...
This place, right?
TAMURA
TAMURA KINDER-GARTEN

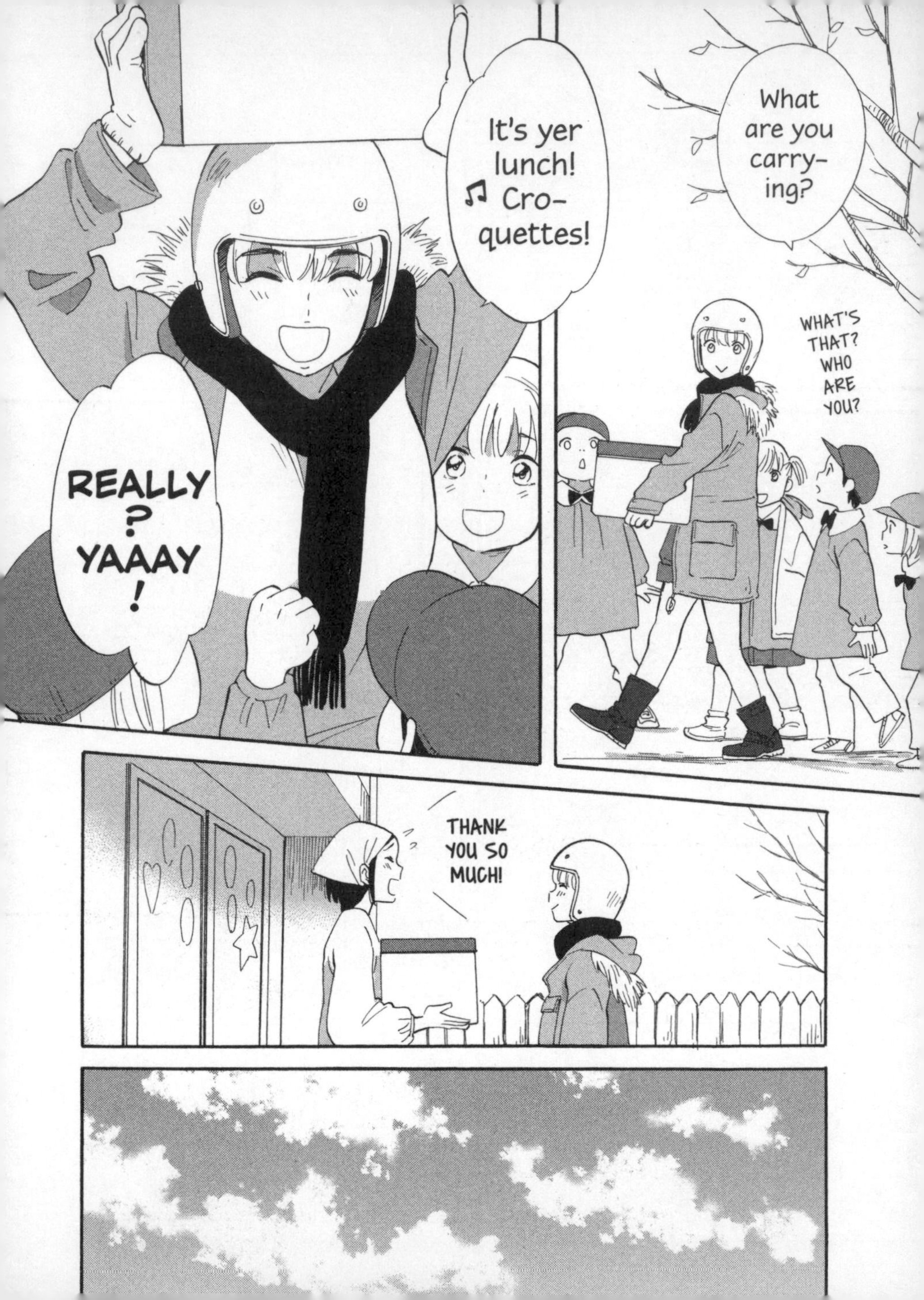
What are you carrying?
WHAT'S THAT? WHO ARE YOU?
It's yer lunch! ♫ Croquettes!
REALLY? YAAAY!
THANK YOU SO MUCH!

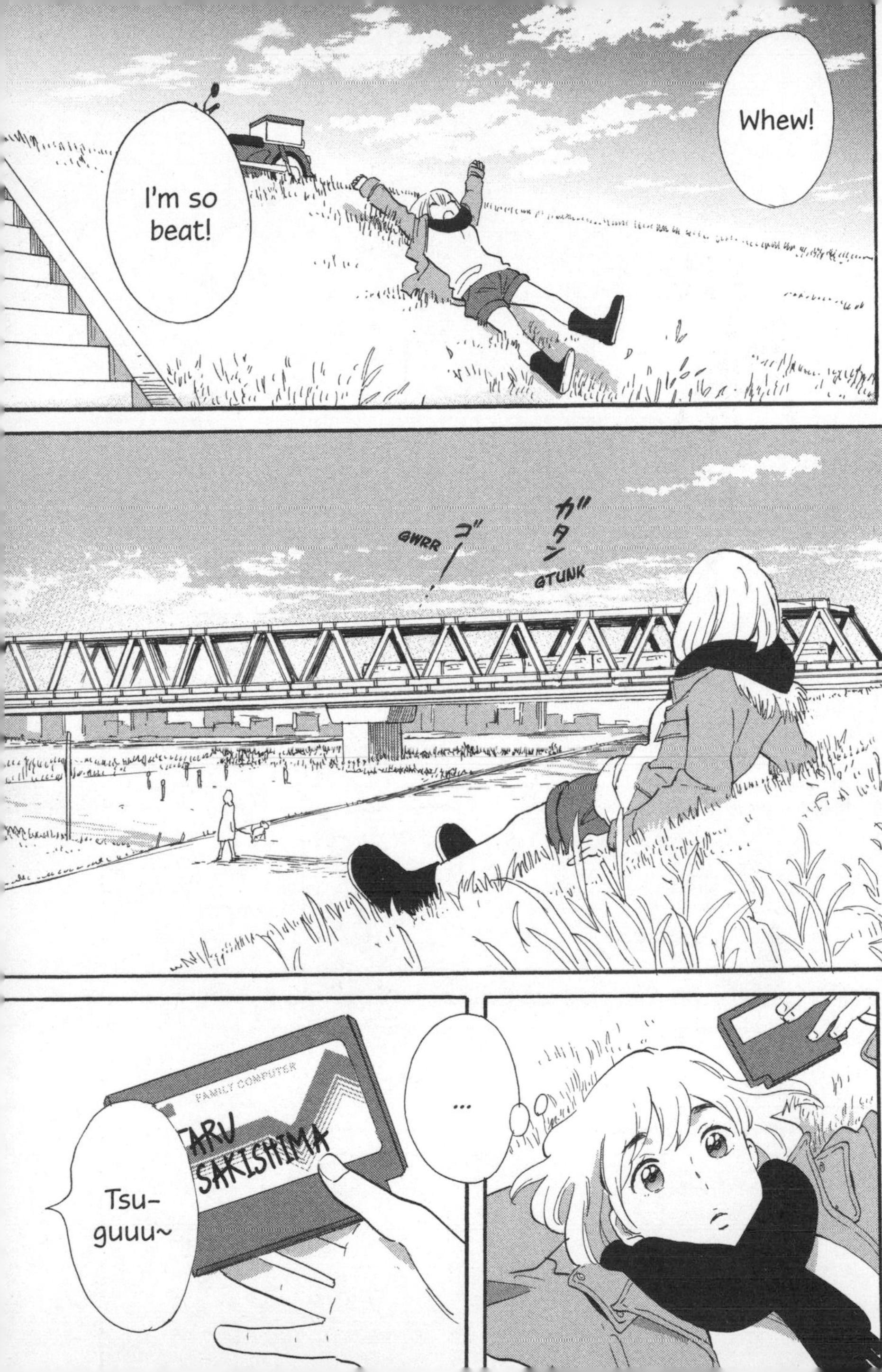
Whew!
I'm so beat!
ガタン
GTUNK
ゴー
GWRR
...
FAMILY COMPUTER
TARU SAKISHIMA
Tsu-guuu~

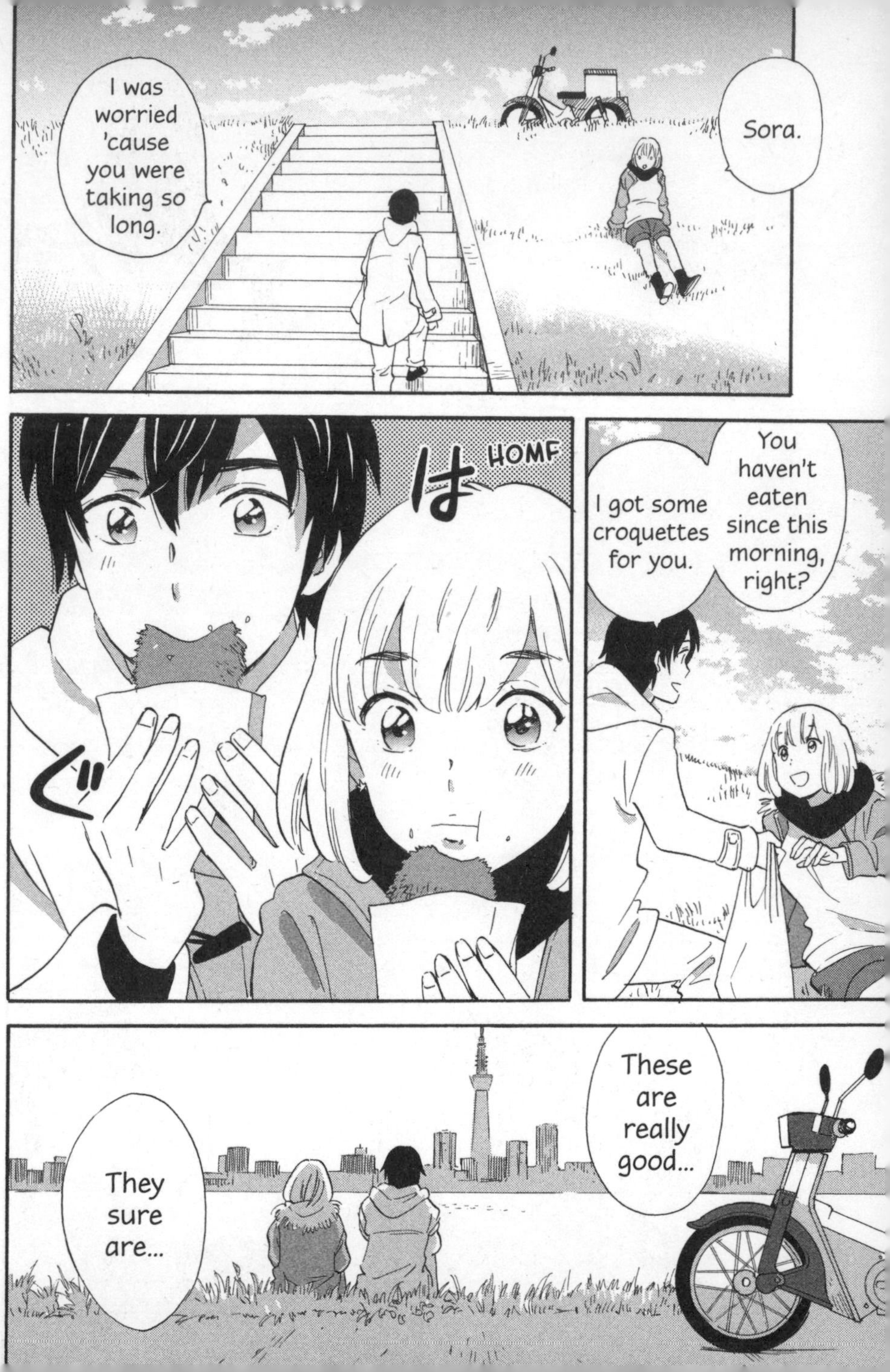
Sora.
I was worried 'cause you were taking so long.
You haven't eaten since this morning, right?
I got some croquettes for you.
は
HOMF
These are really good...
They sure are...

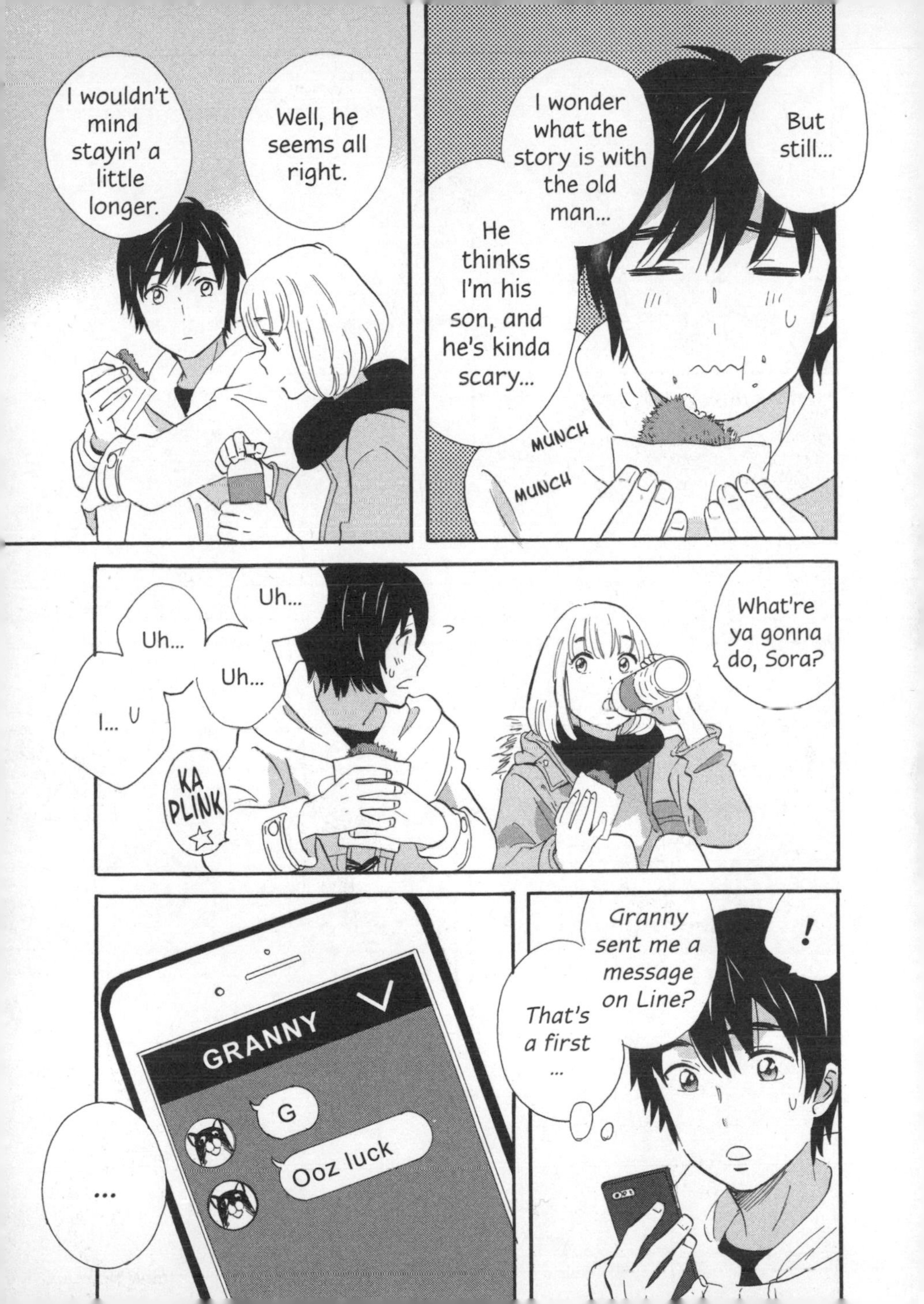
But still...
I wonder what the story is with the old man...
He thinks I'm his son, and he's kinda scary...
MUNCH
MUNCH
Well, he seems all right.
I wouldn't mind stayin' a little longer.
What're ya gonna do, Sora?
Uh...
Uh...
Uh...
I...
KA PLINK ☆
!
Granny sent me a message on Line?
That's a first ...
GRANNY
G
Ooz luck
...

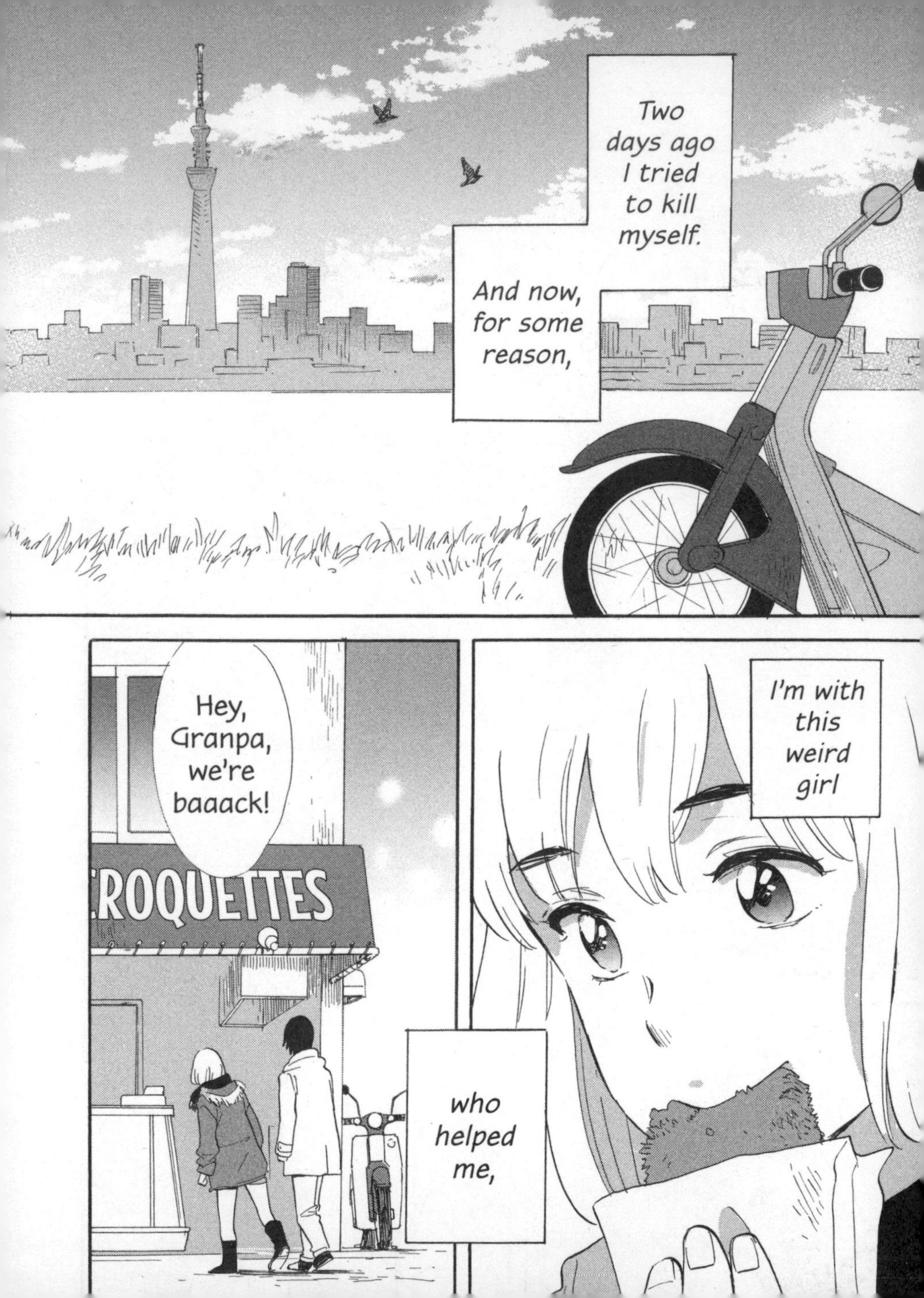
Two days ago I tried to kill myself.
And now, for some reason,
I'm with this weird girl
who helped me,
Hey, Granpa, we're baaack!
CROQUETTES

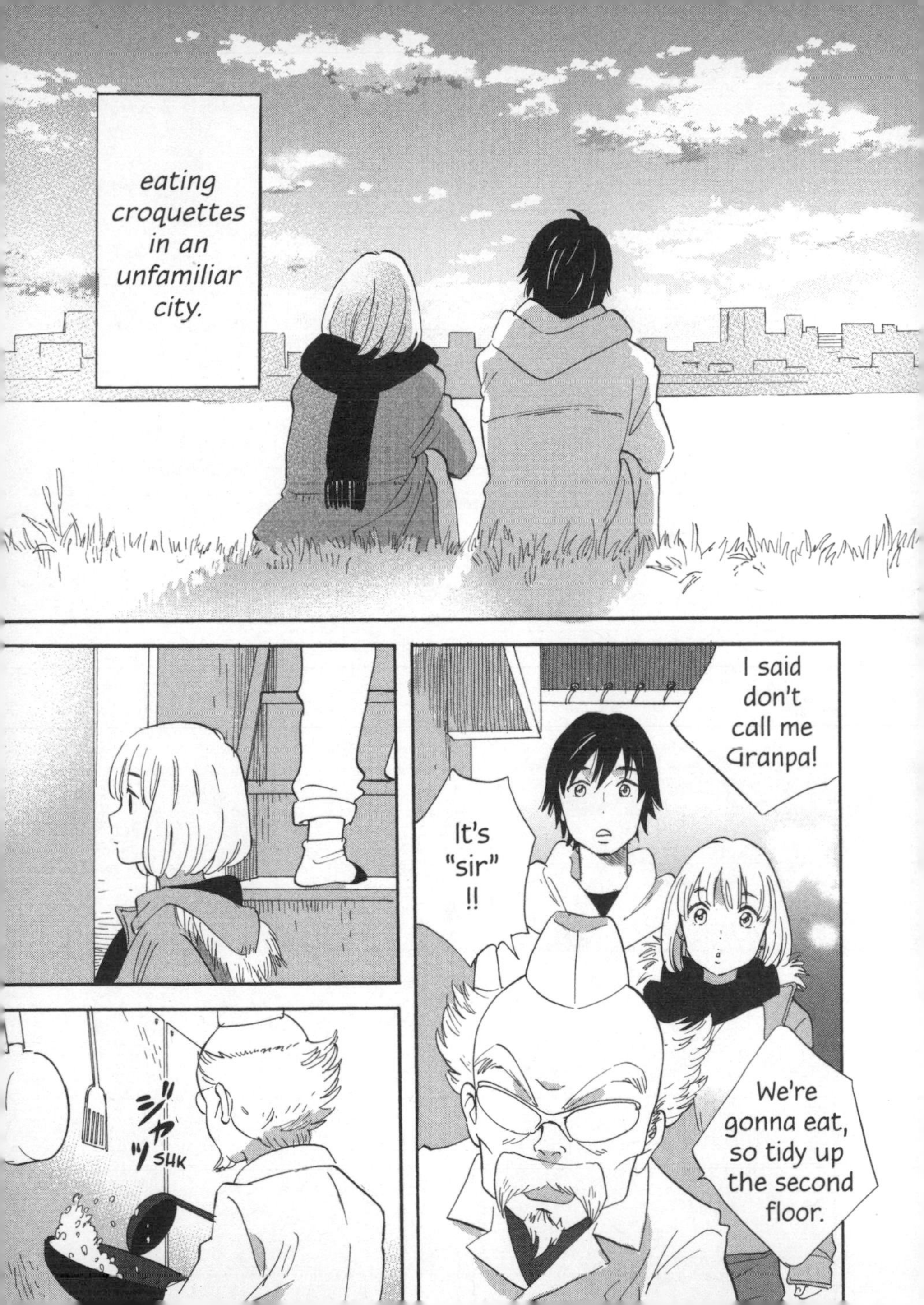
eating croquettes in an unfamiliar city.
I said don't call me Granpa!
It's "sir" !!
We're gonna eat, so tidy up the second floor.
ジャッ
SHK

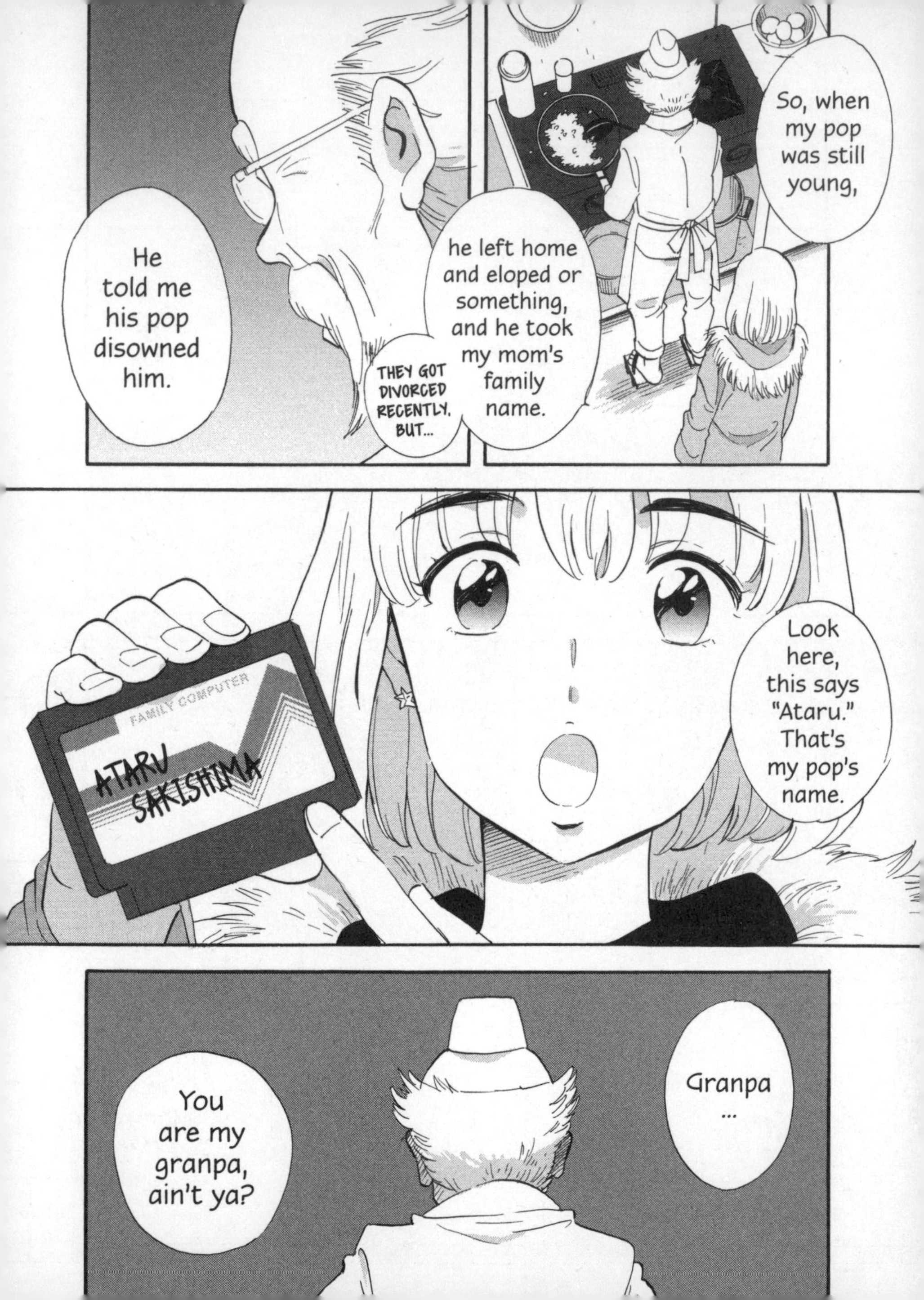
So, when my pop was still young,
he left home and eloped or something, and he took my mom's family name.
THEY GOT DIVORCED RECENTLY, BUT...
He told me his pop disowned him.
FAMILY COMPUTER
ATARU SAKISHIMA
Look here, this says "Ataru." That's my pop's name.
Granpa ...
You are my granpa, ain't ya?

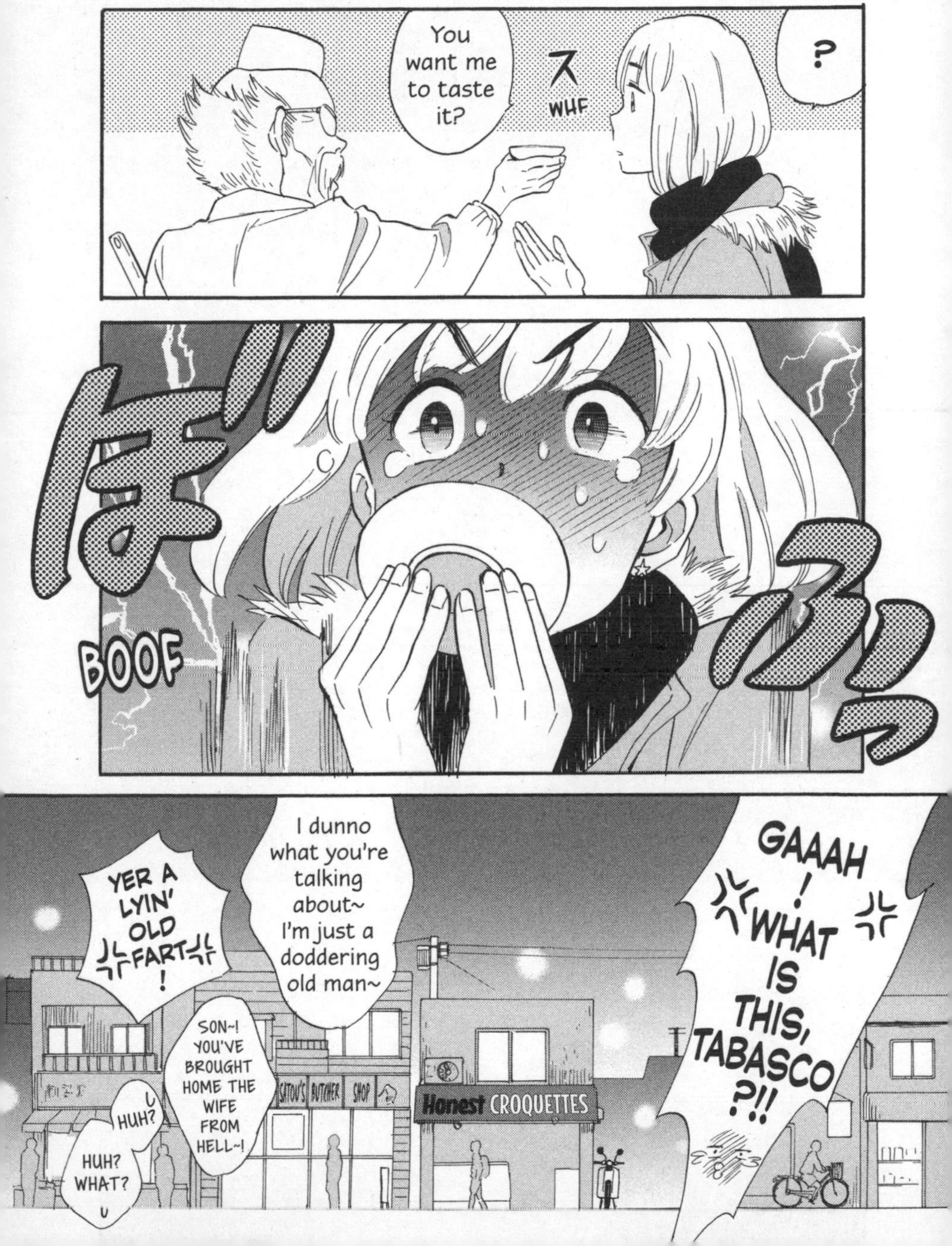
?
You want me to taste it?
WHF
BOOF
GAAAH! WHAT IS THIS, TABASCO?!!
I dunno what you're talking about~ I'm just a doddering old man~
YER A LYIN' OLD FART!
SON~! YOU'VE BROUGHT HOME THE WIFE FROM HELL~!
SATOU'S BUTCHER SHOP
Honest CROQUETTES
HUH?
HUH? WHAT?

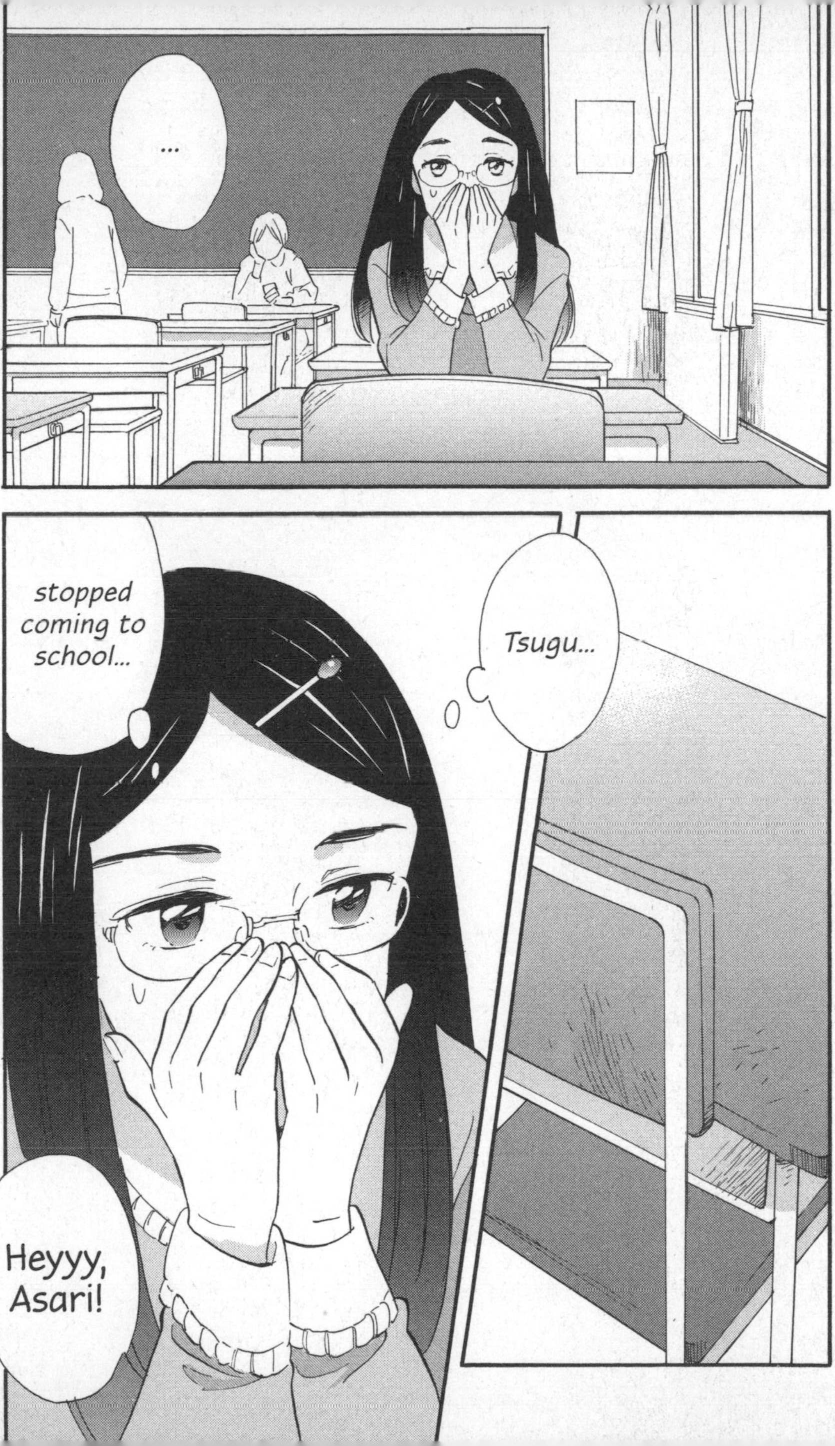
...
Tsugu...
stopped coming to school...
Heyyy, Asari!

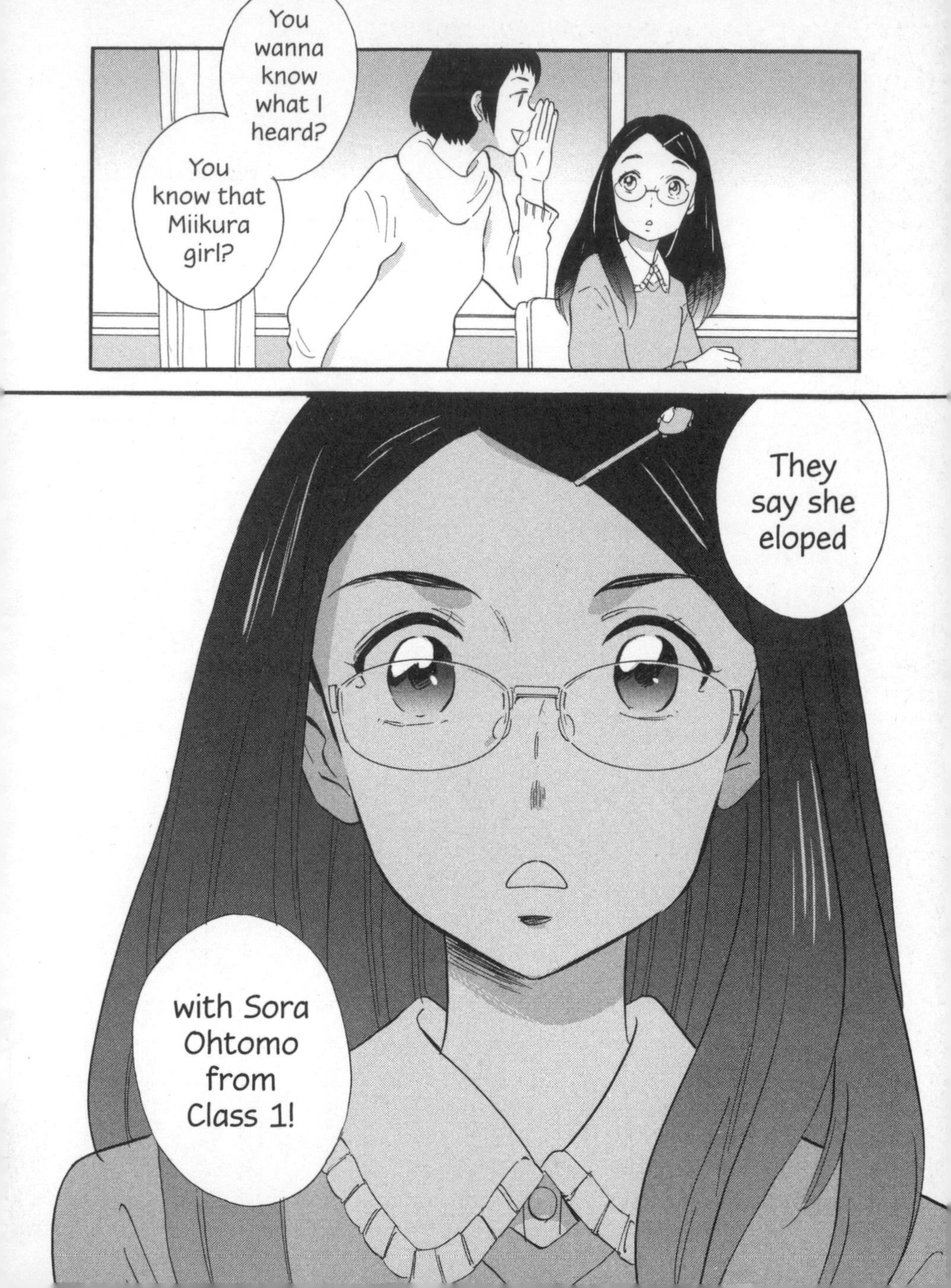
You wanna know what I heard?
You know that Miikura girl?
They say she eloped
with Sora Ohtomo from Class 1!

(CHAPTER 8) Is This a Date?!

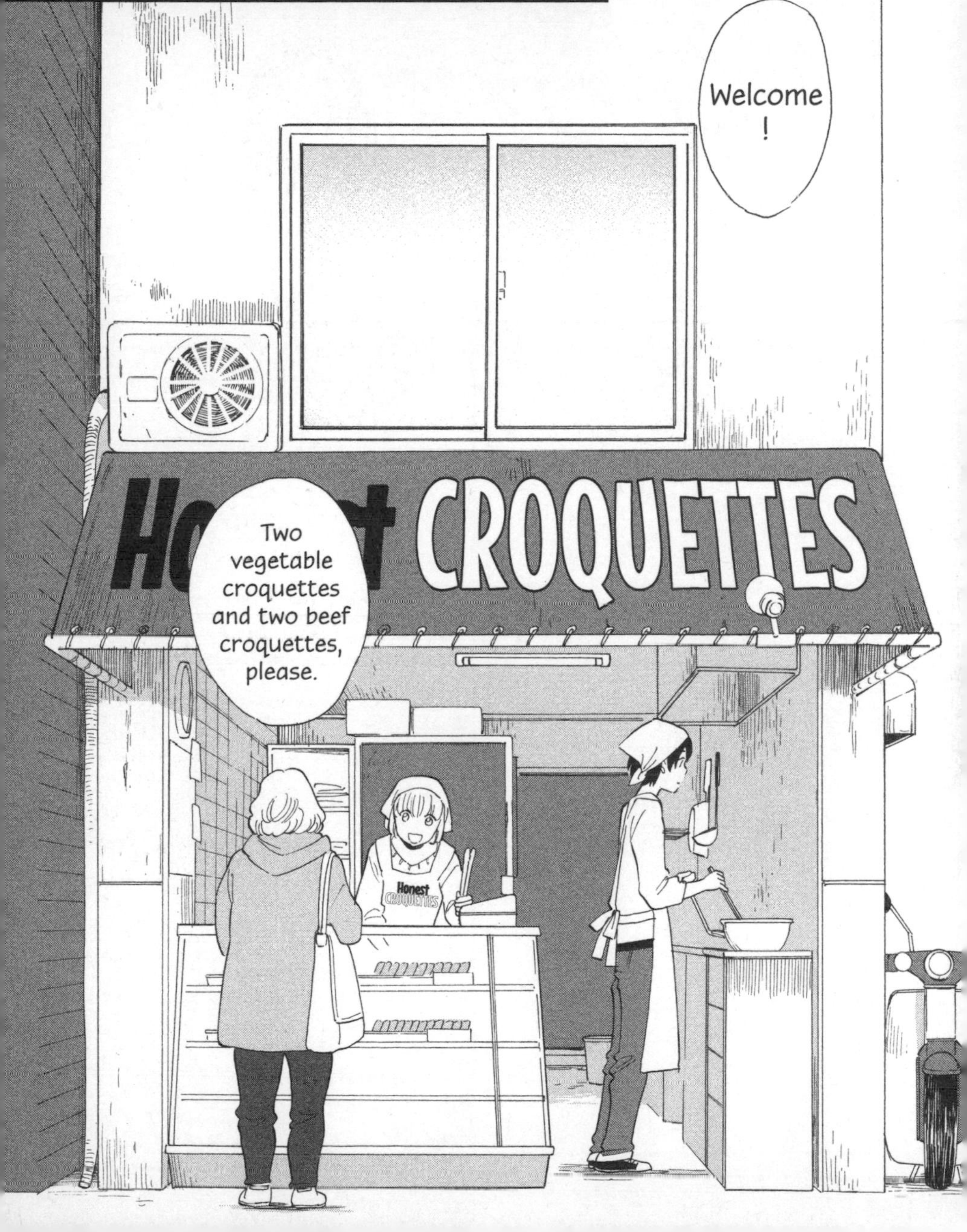
Welcome!
Two vegetable croquettes and two beef croquettes, please.
CROQUETTES
Honest CROQUETTES

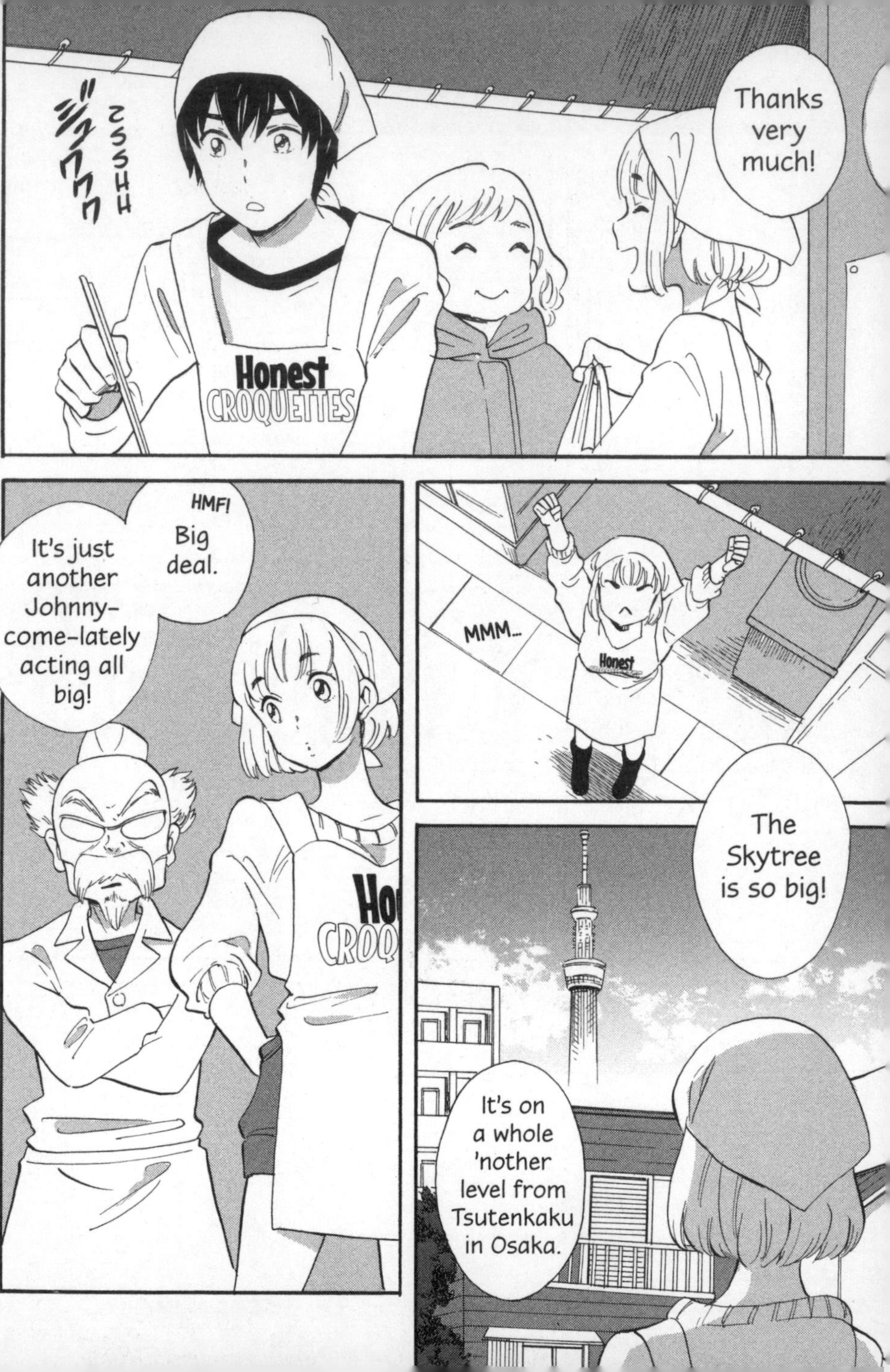
Thanks very much!
ジュワワワ
ZSSHH
Honest CROQUETTES
MMM...
Honest
The Skytree is so big!
It's on a whole 'nother level from Tsutenkaku in Osaka.
HMF!
Big deal.
It's just another Johnny-come-lately acting all big!
Honest CROQUETTES

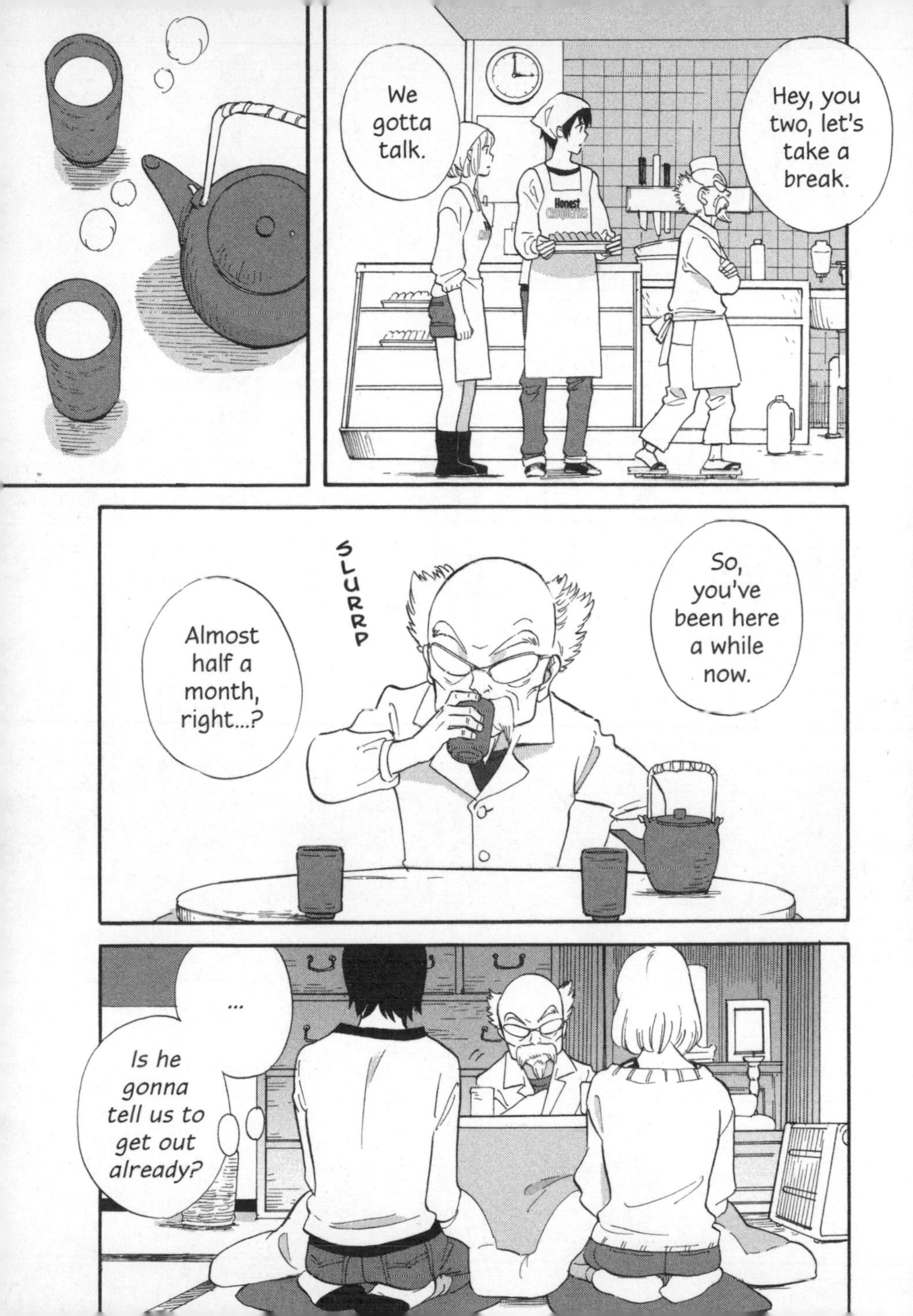
Hey, you two, let's take a break.
We gotta talk.
Honest CROQUETTES
So, you've been here a while now.
SLURRP
Almost half a month, right...?
...
Is he gonna tell us to get out already?

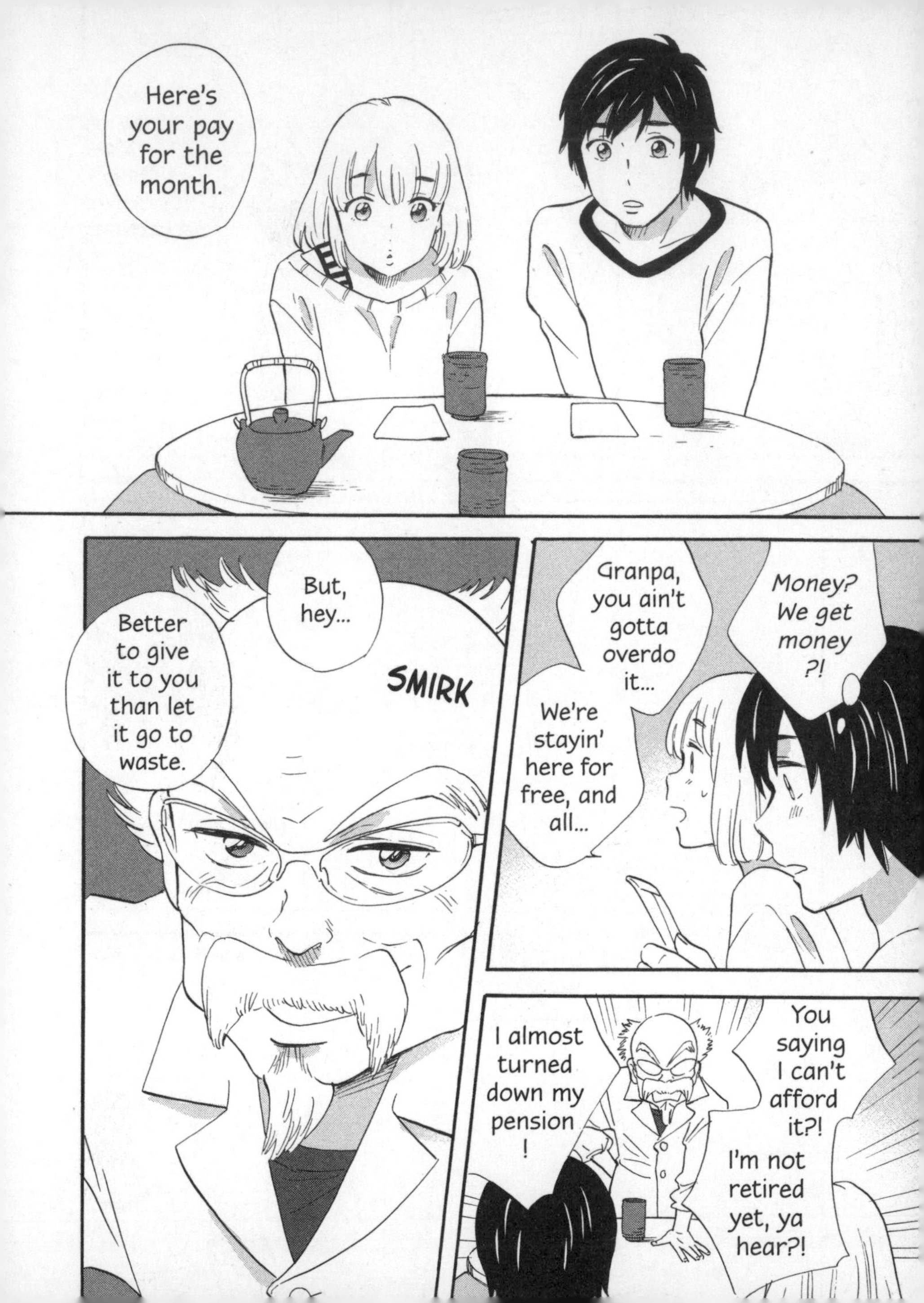

Here's your pay for the month.
Money? We get money?!
Granpa, you ain't gotta overdo it...
We're stayin' here for free, and all...
You saying I can't afford it?!
I'm not retired yet, ya hear?!
I almost turned down my pension!
But, hey...
SMIRK
Better to give it to you than let it go to waste.

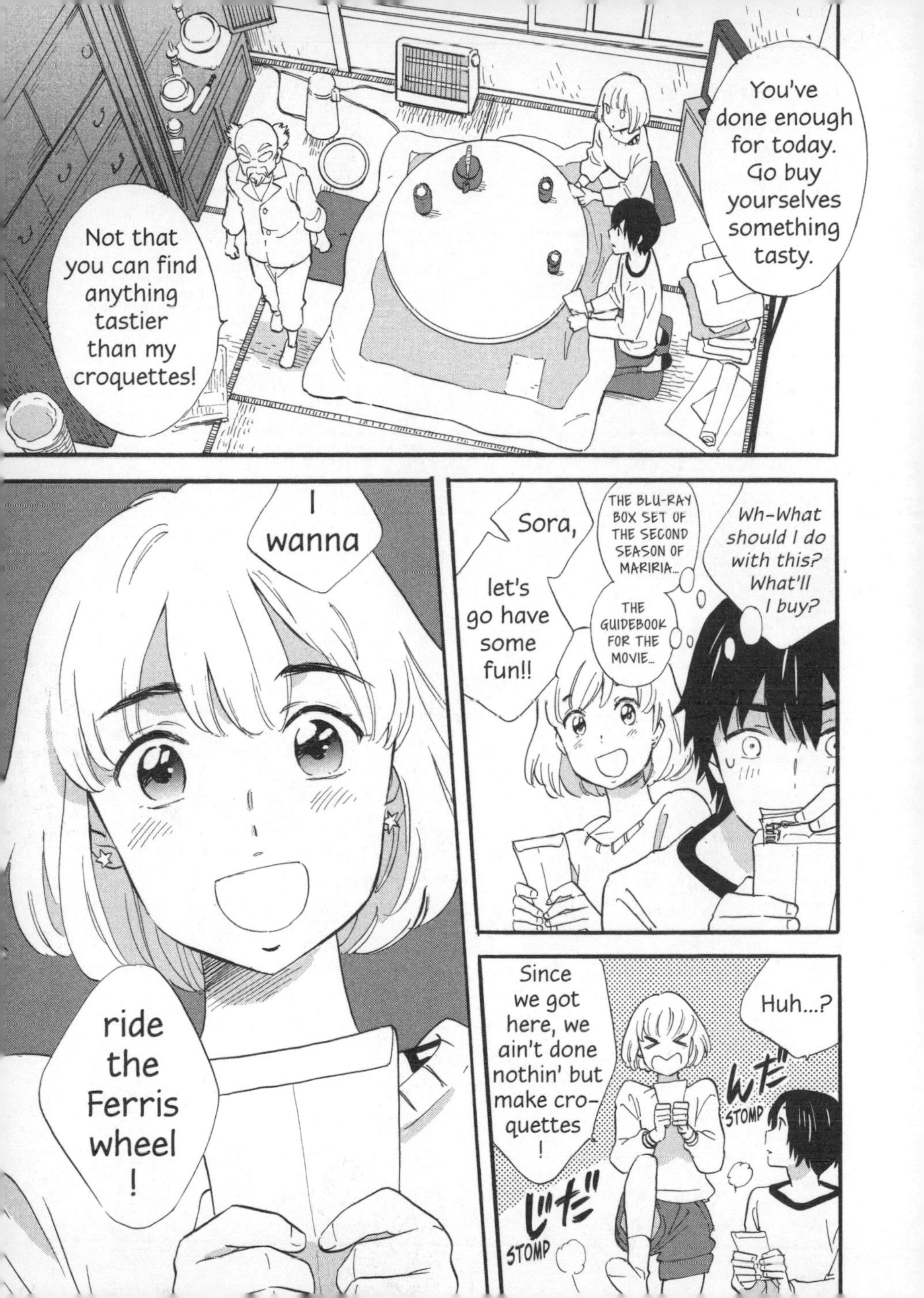
You've done enough for today. Go buy yourselves something tasty.
Not that you can find anything tastier than my croquettes!
Wh-What should I do with this? What'll I buy?
THE BLU-RAY BOX SET OF THE SECOND SEASON OF MARIRIA...
THE GUIDEBOOK FOR THE MOVIE...
Sora, let's go have some fun!!
Huh...?
Since we got here, we ain't done nothin' but make cro-quettes!
STOMP
STOMP
I wanna ride the Ferris wheel!

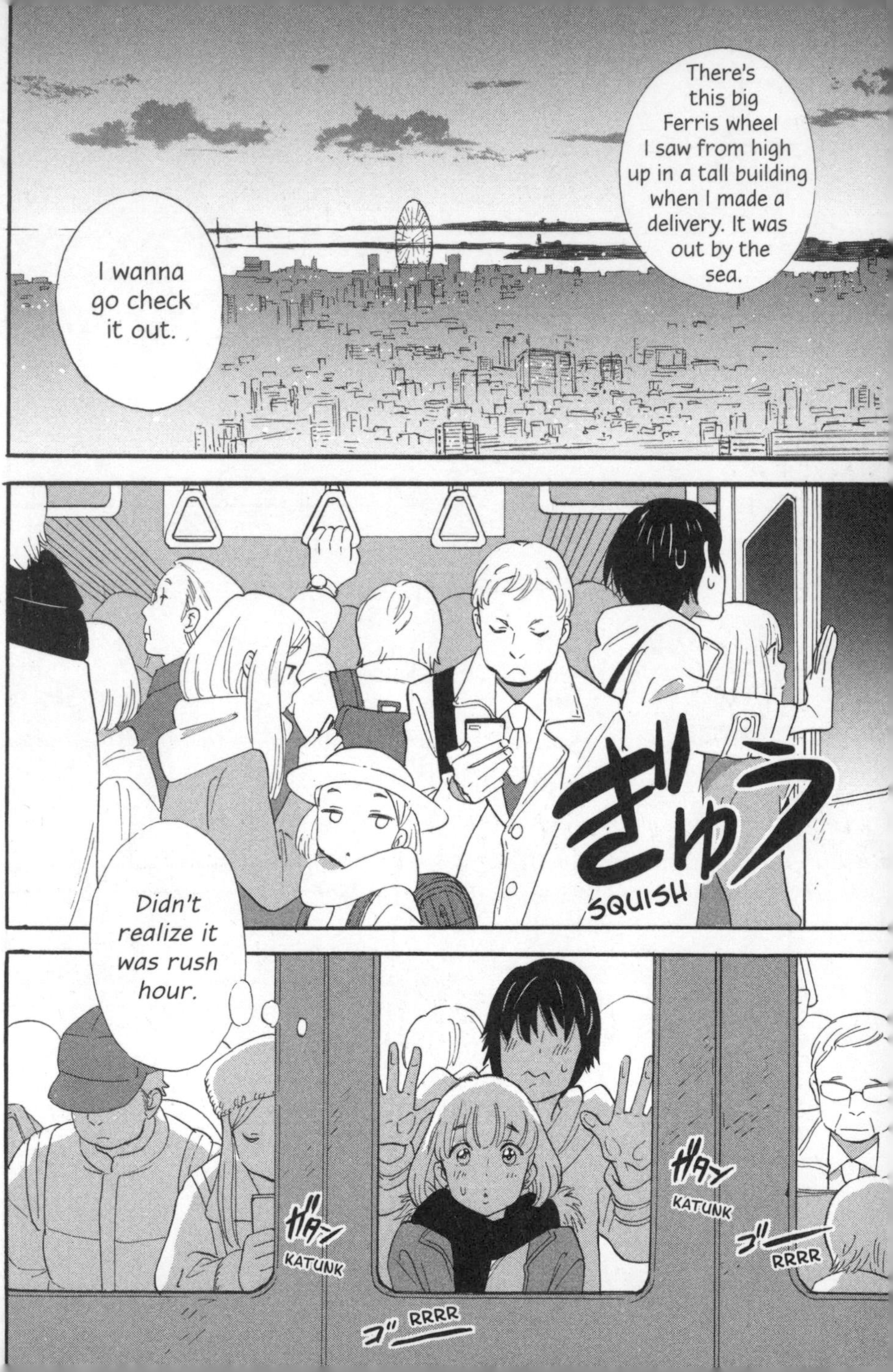
There's this big Ferris wheel I saw from high up in a tall building when I made a delivery. It was out by the sea.
I wanna go check it out.
ぎゅう
SQUISH
Didn't realize it was rush hour.
ガタン
KATUNK
ゴー
RRRR
ガタン
KATUNK
ゴー
RRRR

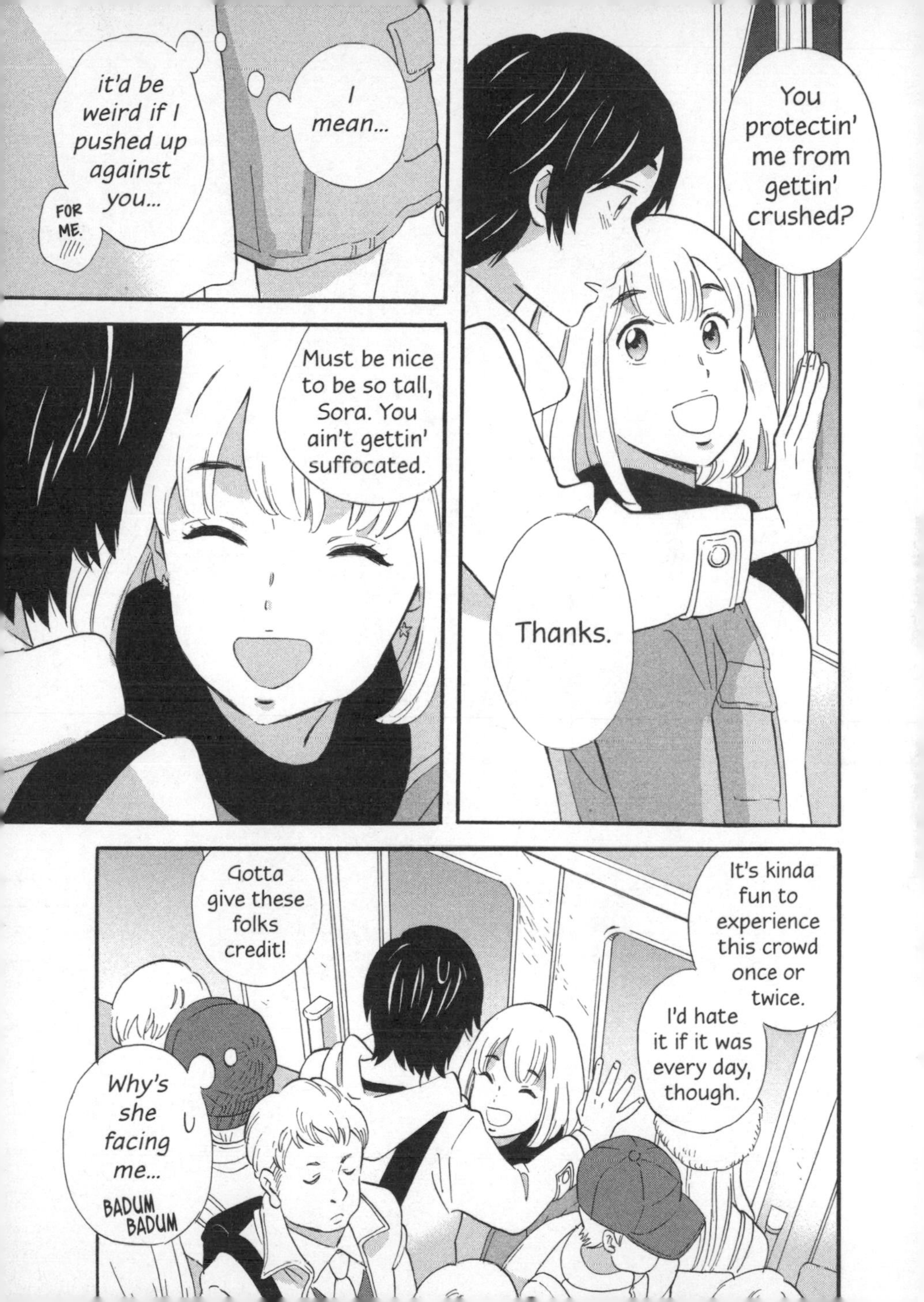
You protectin' me from gettin' crushed?
Thanks.
I mean...
it'd be weird if I pushed up against you...
FOR ME.
Must be nice to be so tall, Sora. You ain't gettin' suffocated.
It's kinda fun to experience this crowd once or twice.
Gotta give these folks credit!
I'd hate it if it was every day, though.
Why's she facing me...
BADUM BADUM

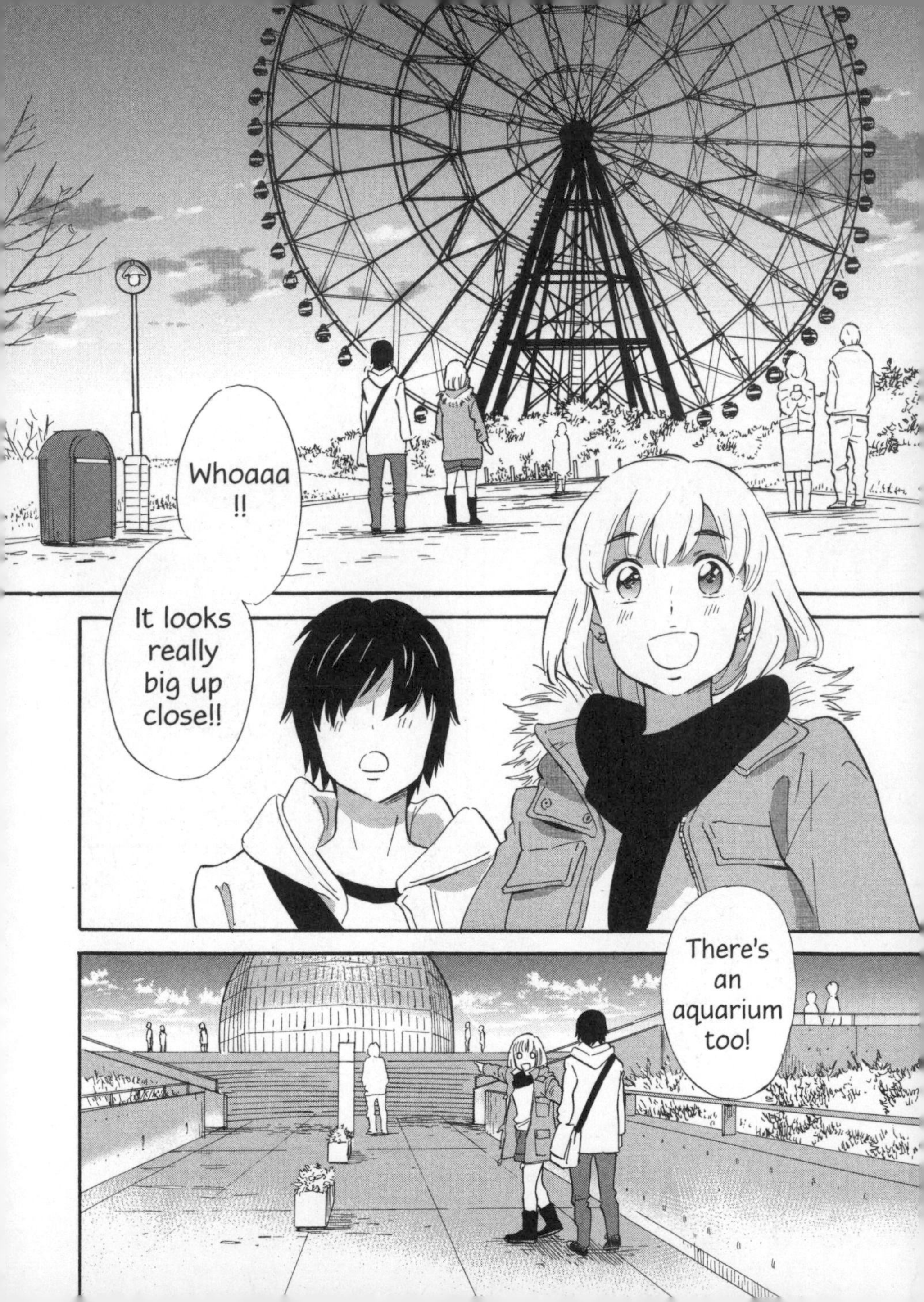
Whoaaa !!
It looks really big up close!!
There's an aquarium too!

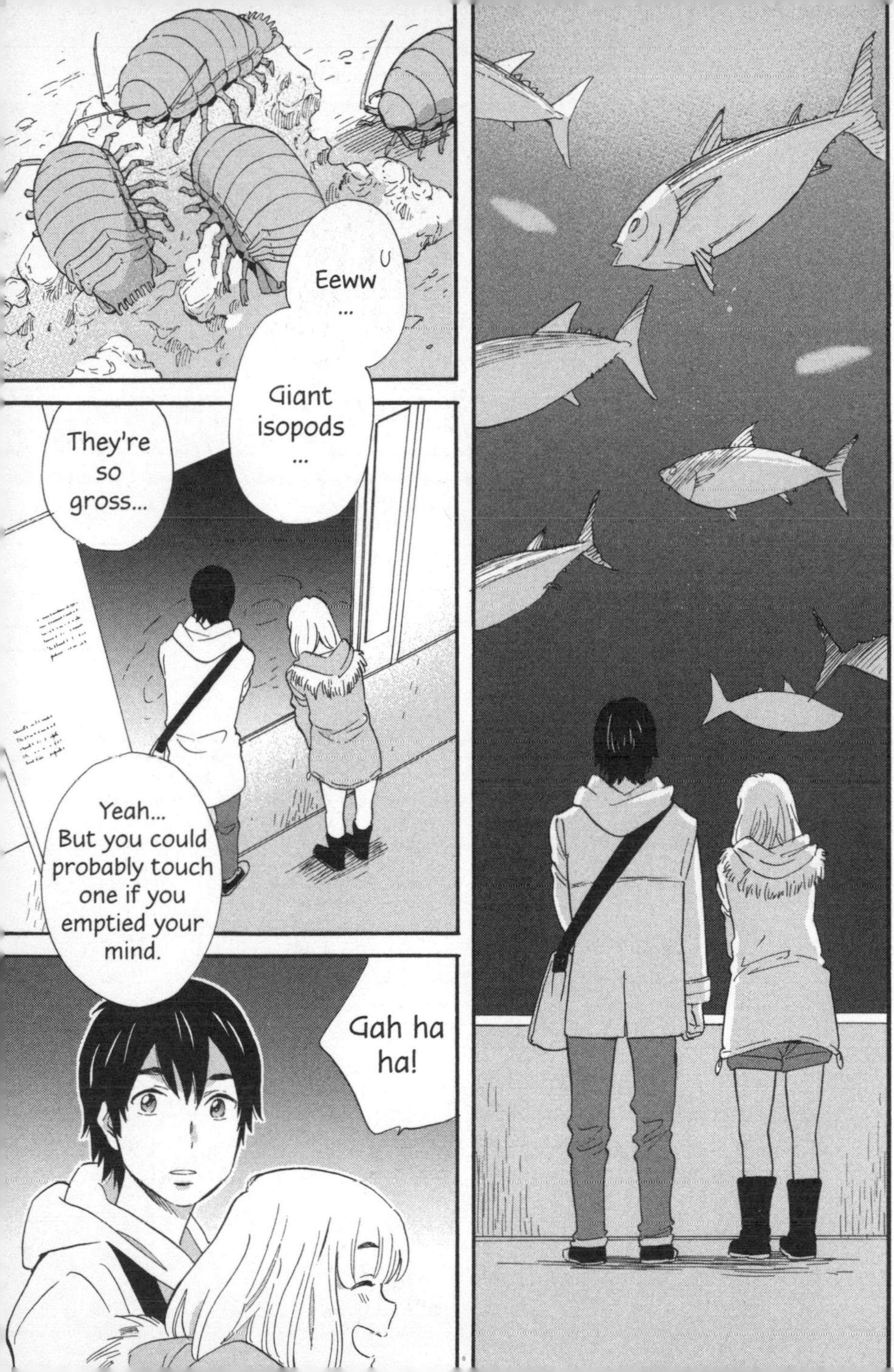
Eeww ...
Giant isopods ...
They're so gross...
Yeah... But you could probably touch one if you emptied your mind.
Gah ha ha!

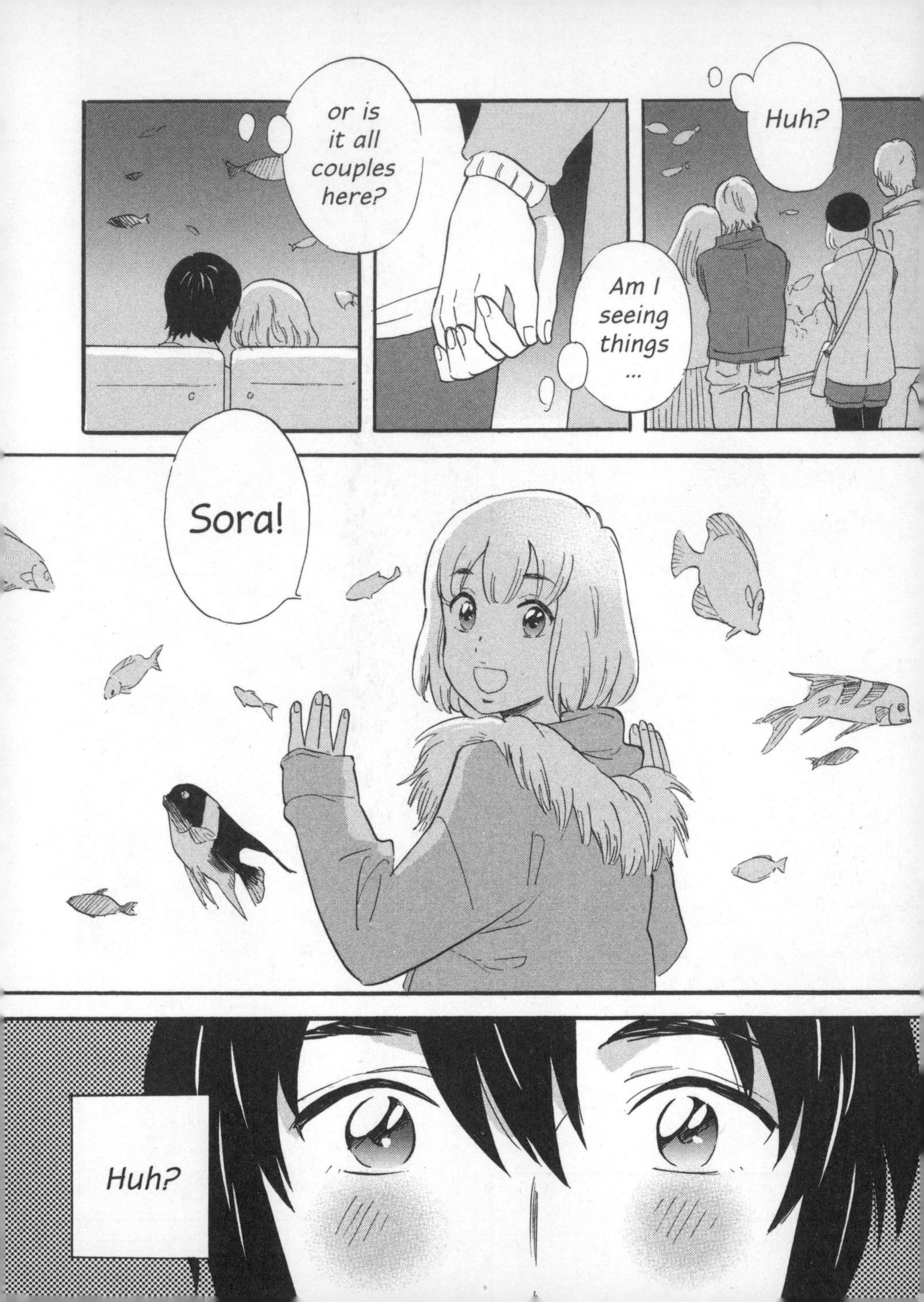
Huh?
Am I seeing things ...
or is it all couples here?
Sora!
Huh?

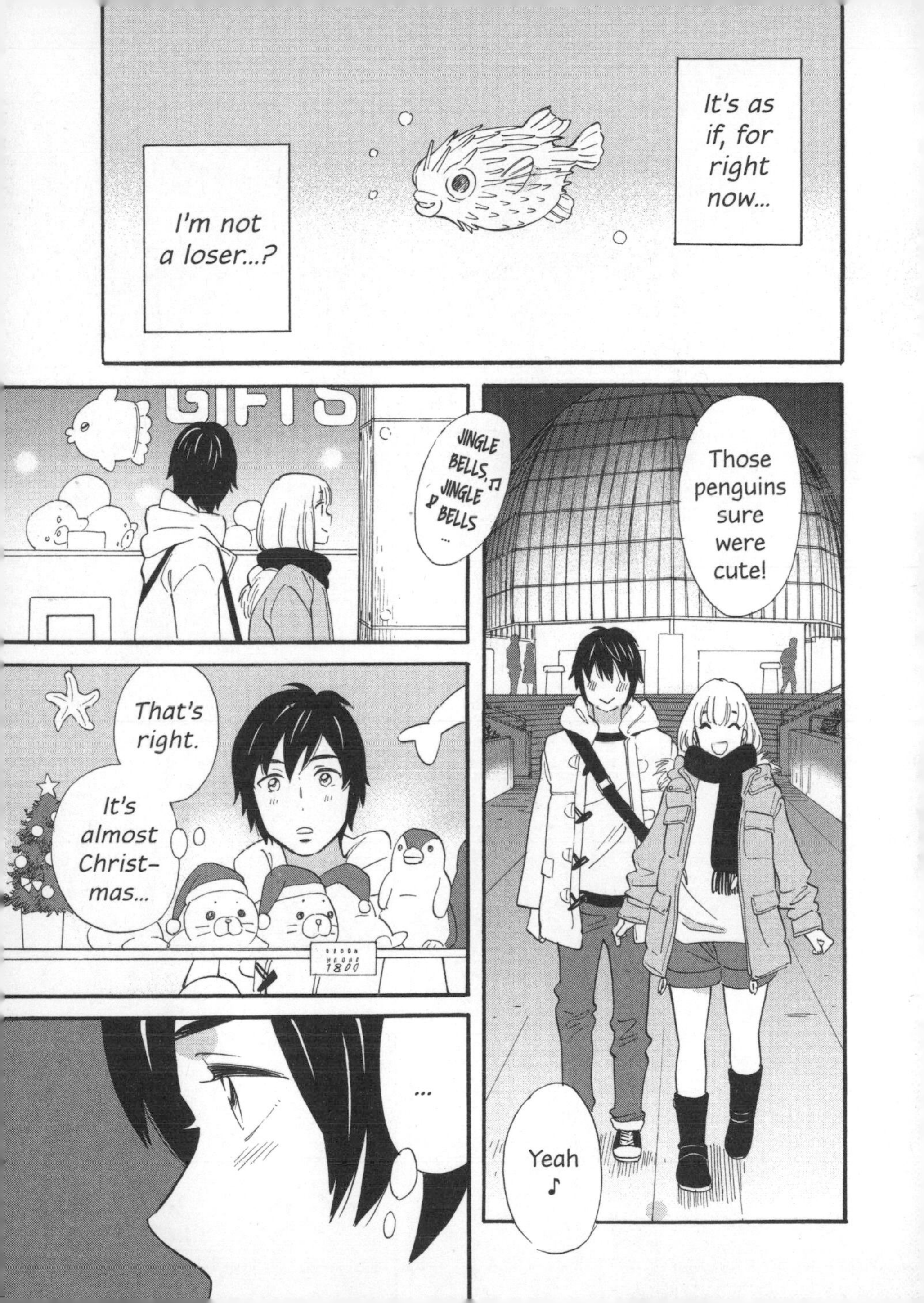
It's as if, for right now...
I'm not a loser...?
Those penguins sure were cute!
Yeah ♪
JINGLE BELLS, JINGLE BELLS ...
That's right.
It's almost Christ-mas...
...

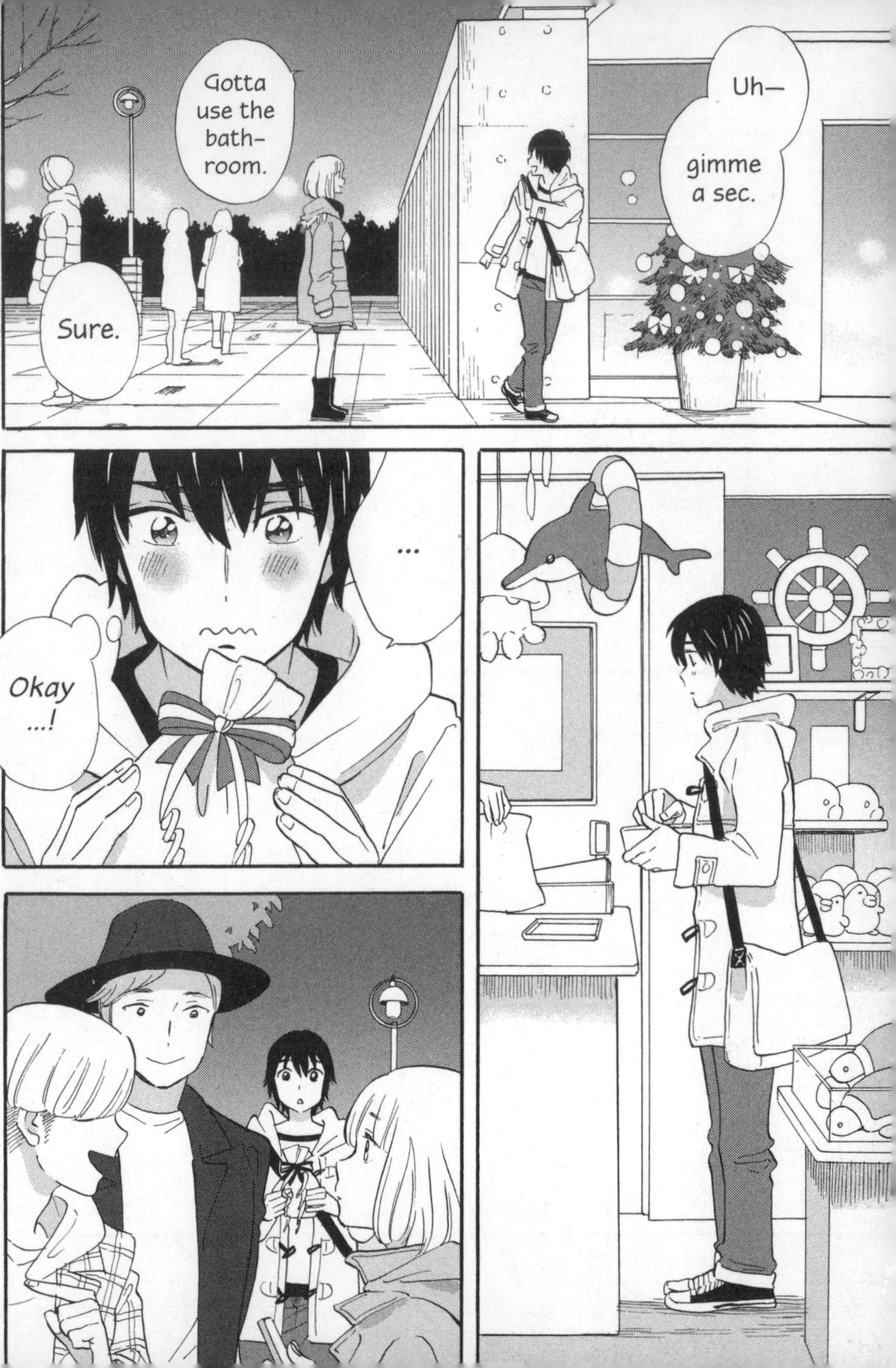
Uh—
gimme a sec.
Gotta use the bath-room.
Sure.
...
Okay ...!

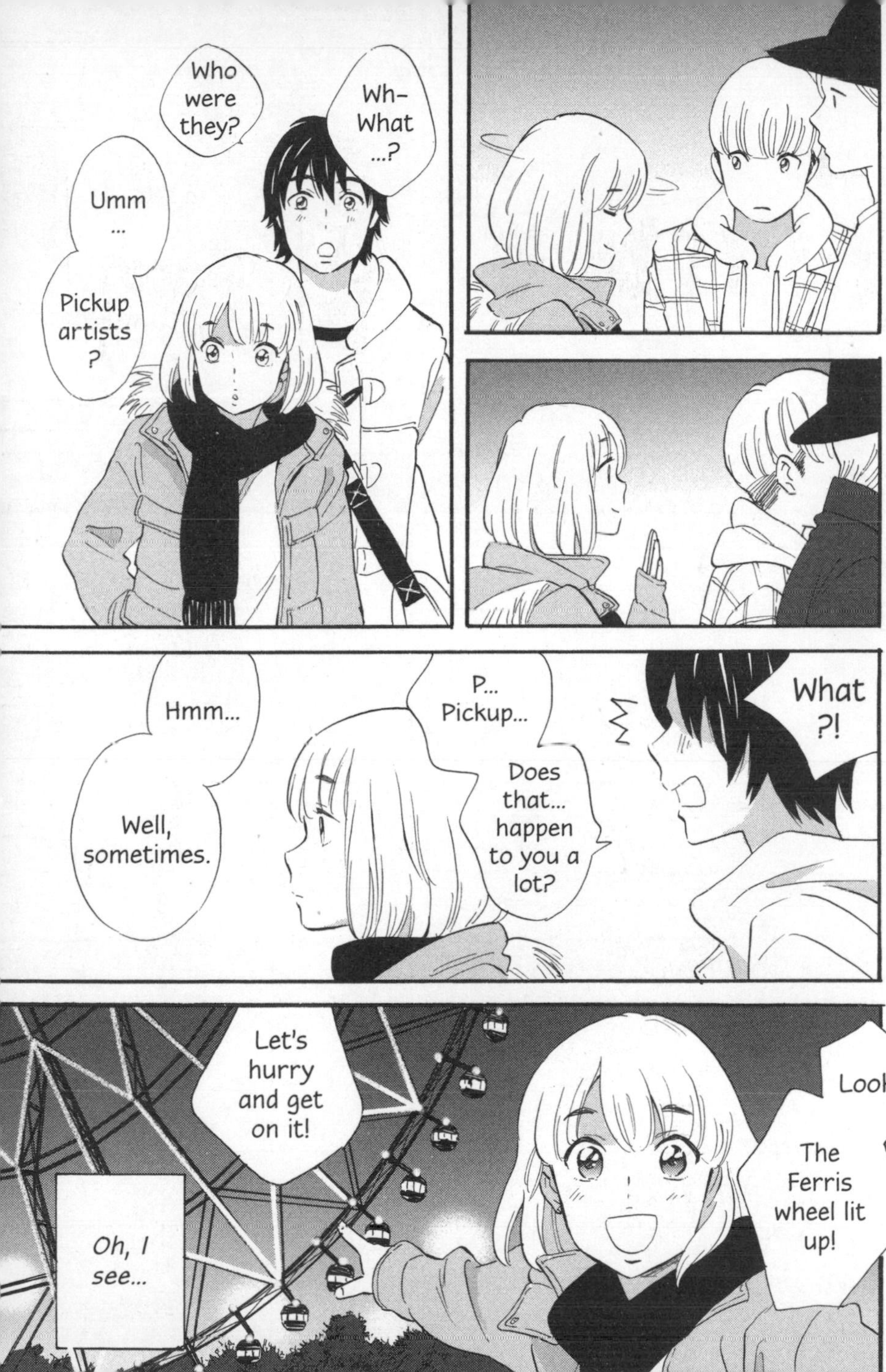
Wh- What ...?
Who were they?
Umm ...
Pickup artists ?
What ?!
P... Pickup...
Does that... happen to you a lot?
Hmm...
Well, sometimes.
Look!
The Ferris wheel lit up!
Let's hurry and get on it!
Oh, I see...

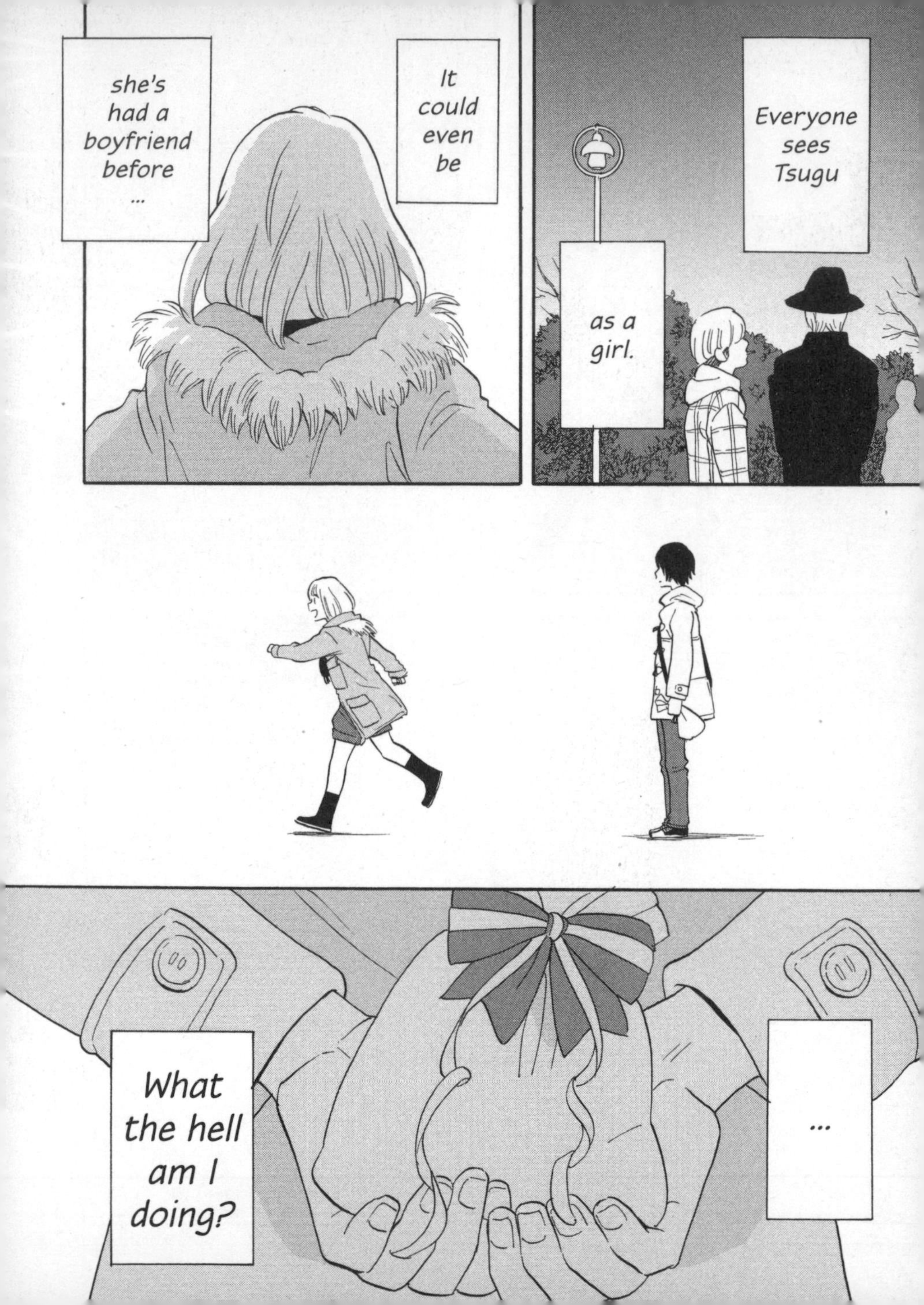
Everyone sees Tsugu
as a girl.
It could even be
she's had a boyfriend before ...
...
What the hell am I doing?

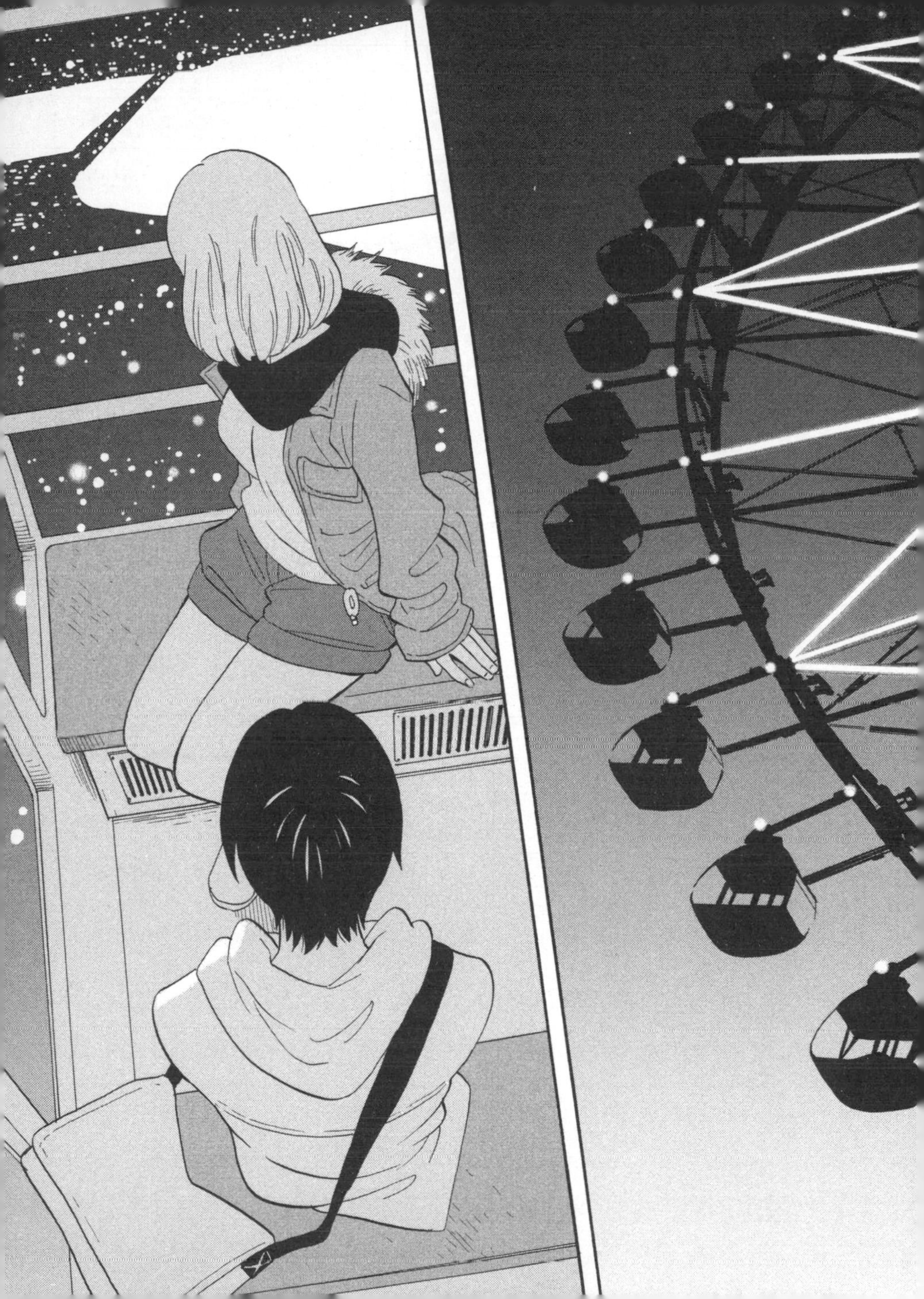

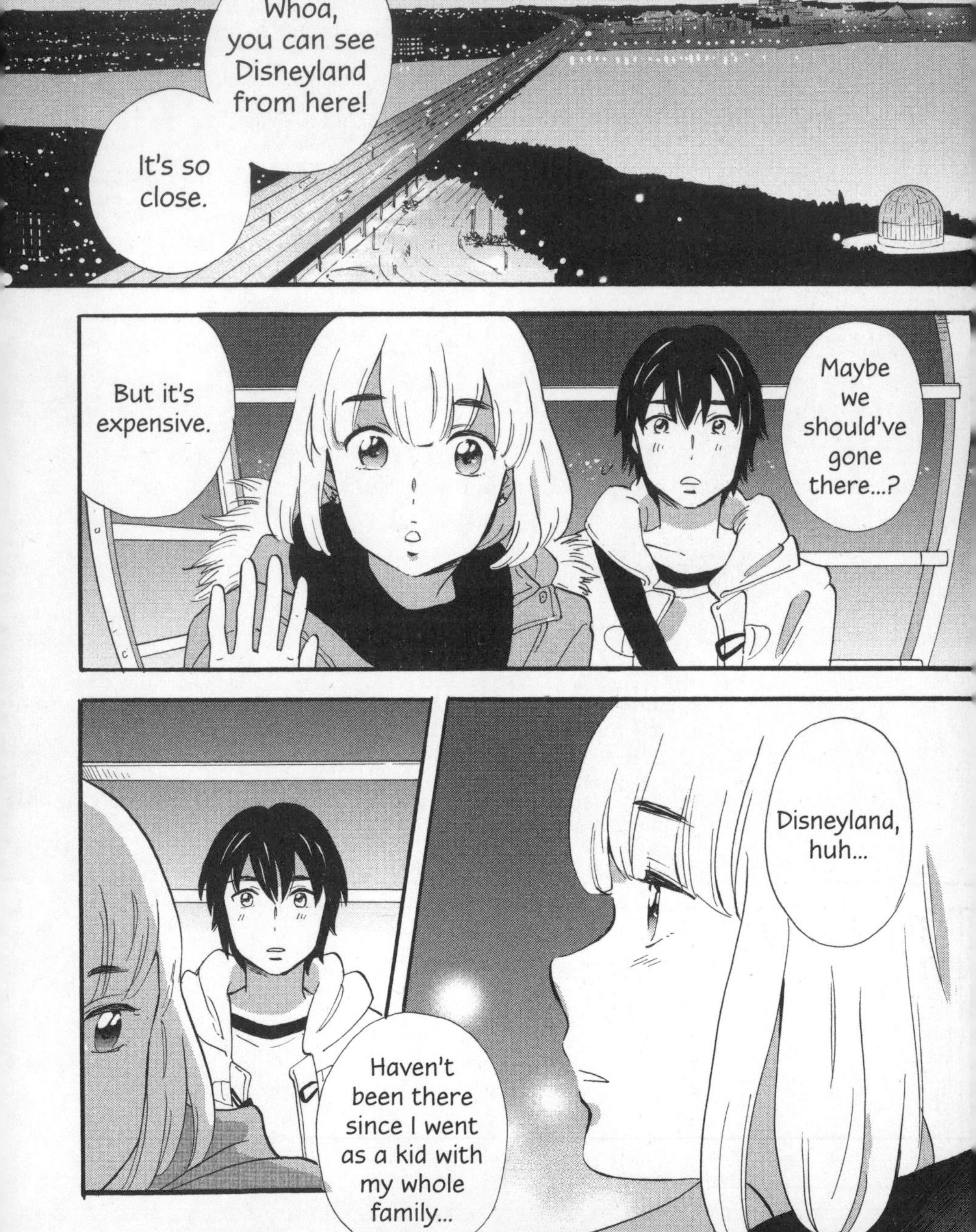
Whoa, you can see Disneyland from here!
It's so close.
Maybe we should've gone there...?
But it's expensive.
Disneyland, huh...
Haven't been there since I went as a kid with my whole family...

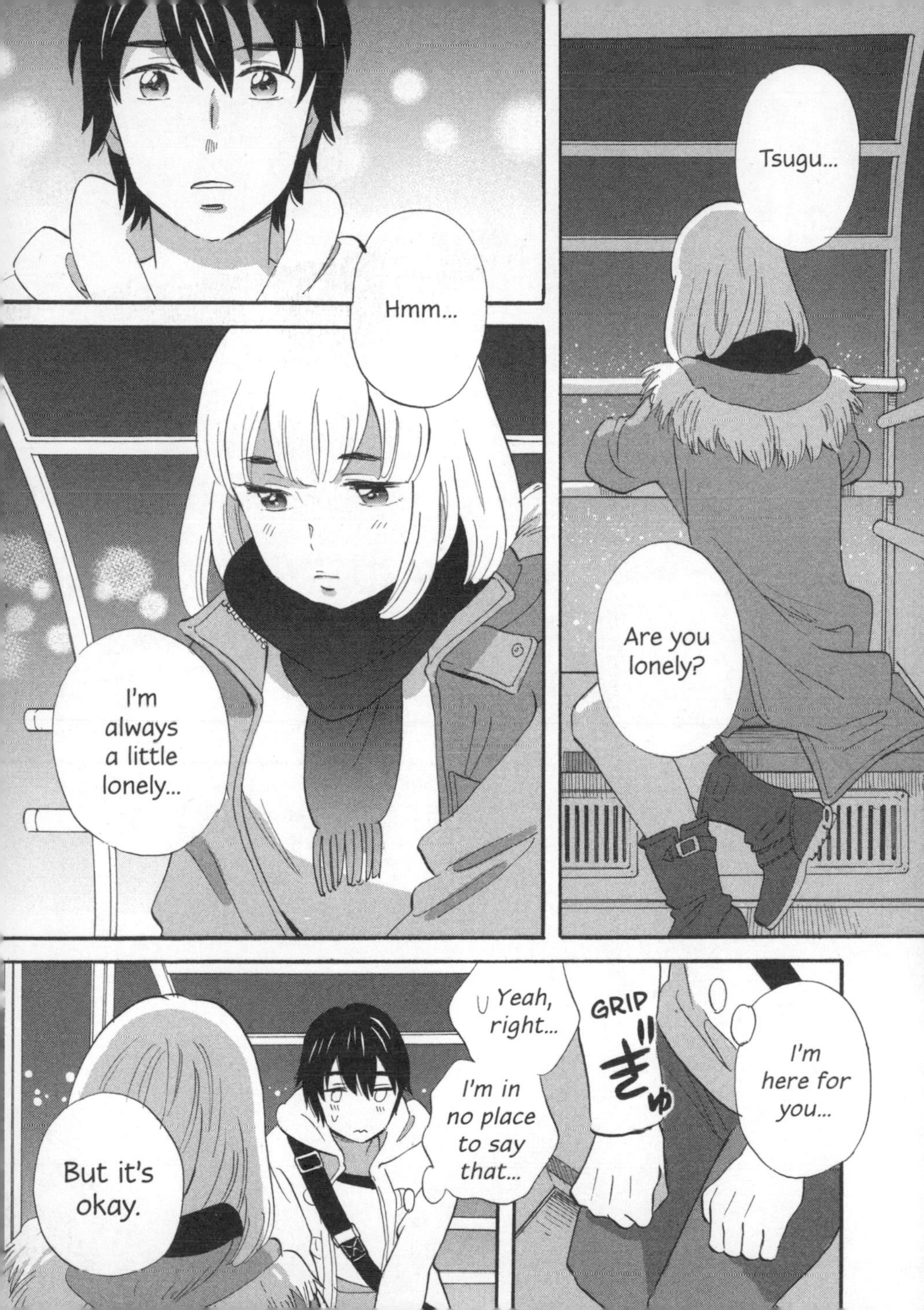
Tsugu...
Are you lonely?
Hmm...
I'm always a little lonely...
I'm here for you...
GRIP
ぎゅ
Yeah, right...
I'm in no place to say that...
But it's okay.

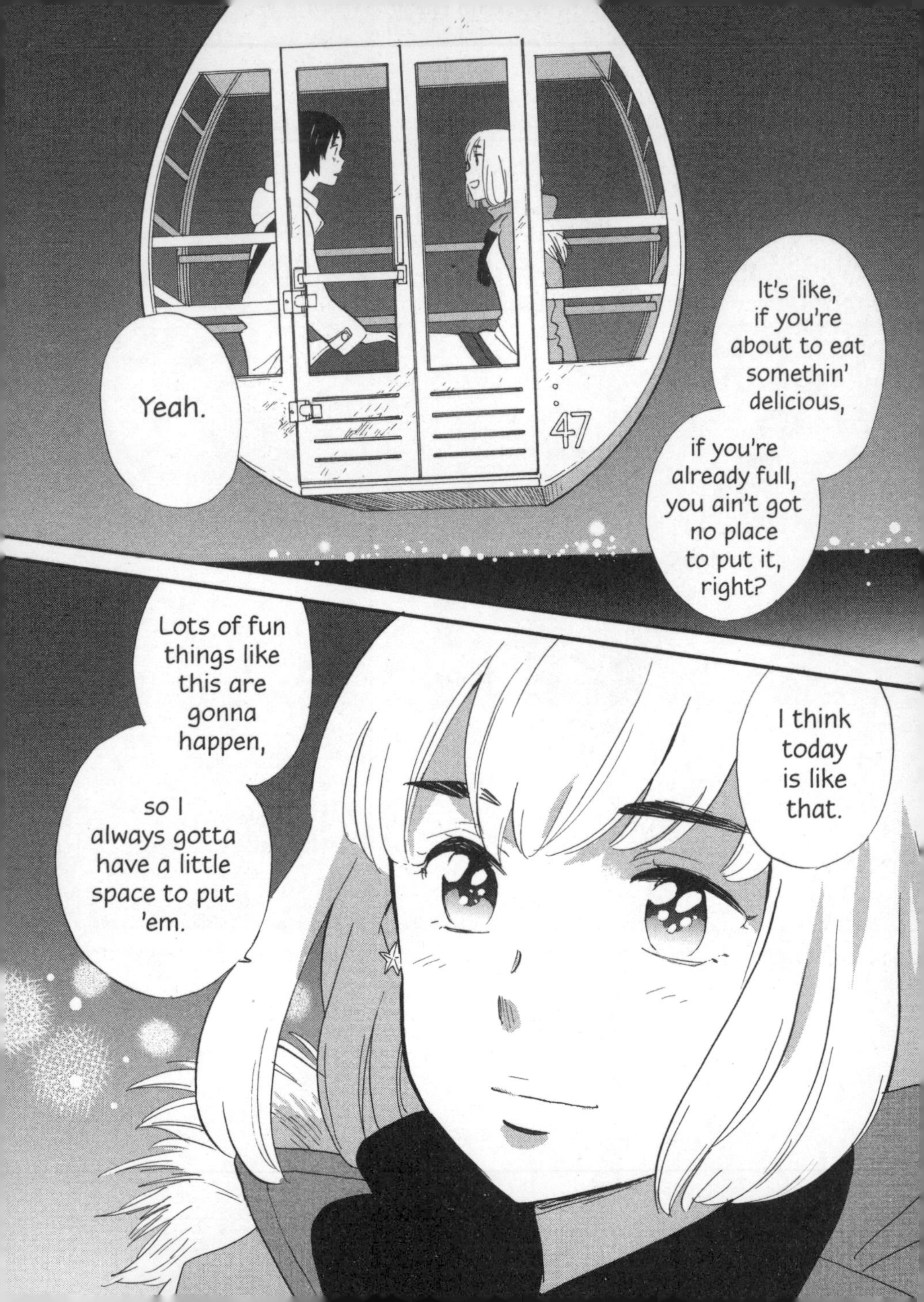
It's like, if you're about to eat somethin' delicious,
if you're already full, you ain't got no place to put it, right?
Yeah.
I think today is like that.
Lots of fun things like this are gonna happen,
so I always gotta have a little space to put 'em.

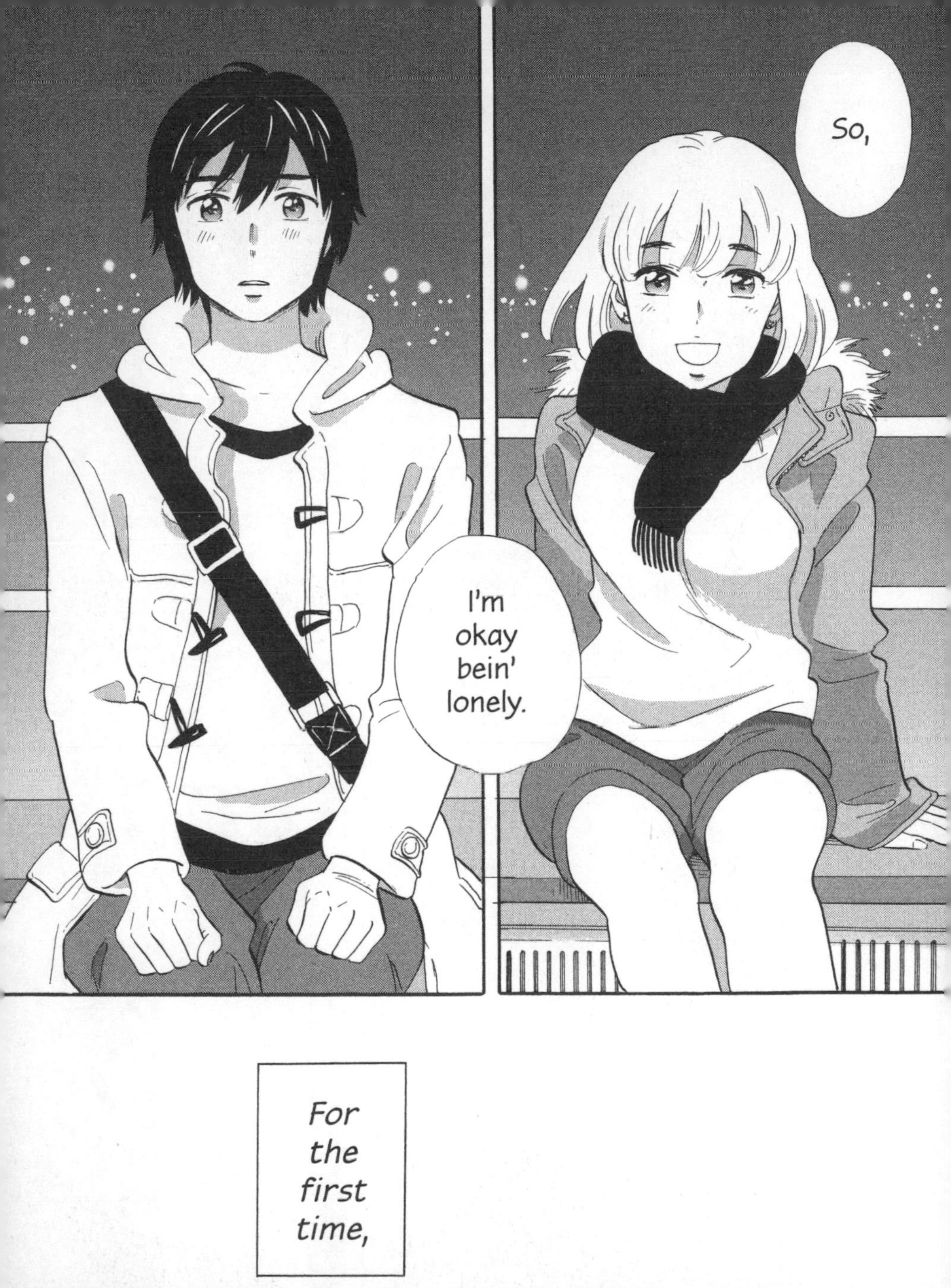
So,
I'm okay bein' lonely.
For the first time,

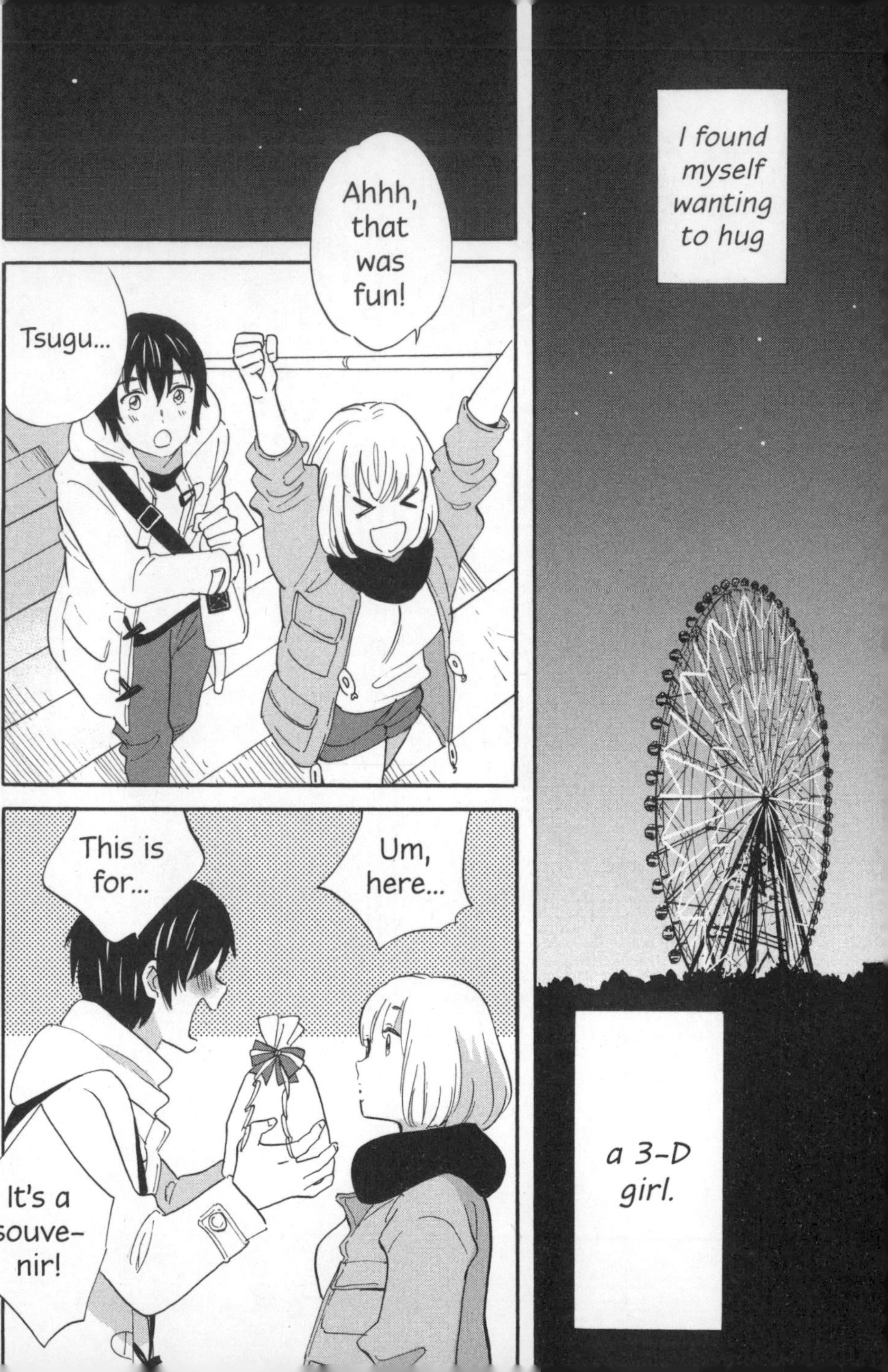
I found myself wanting to hug
a 3-D girl.
Ahhh, that was fun!
Tsugu...
Um, here...
This is for...
It's a souve-nir!

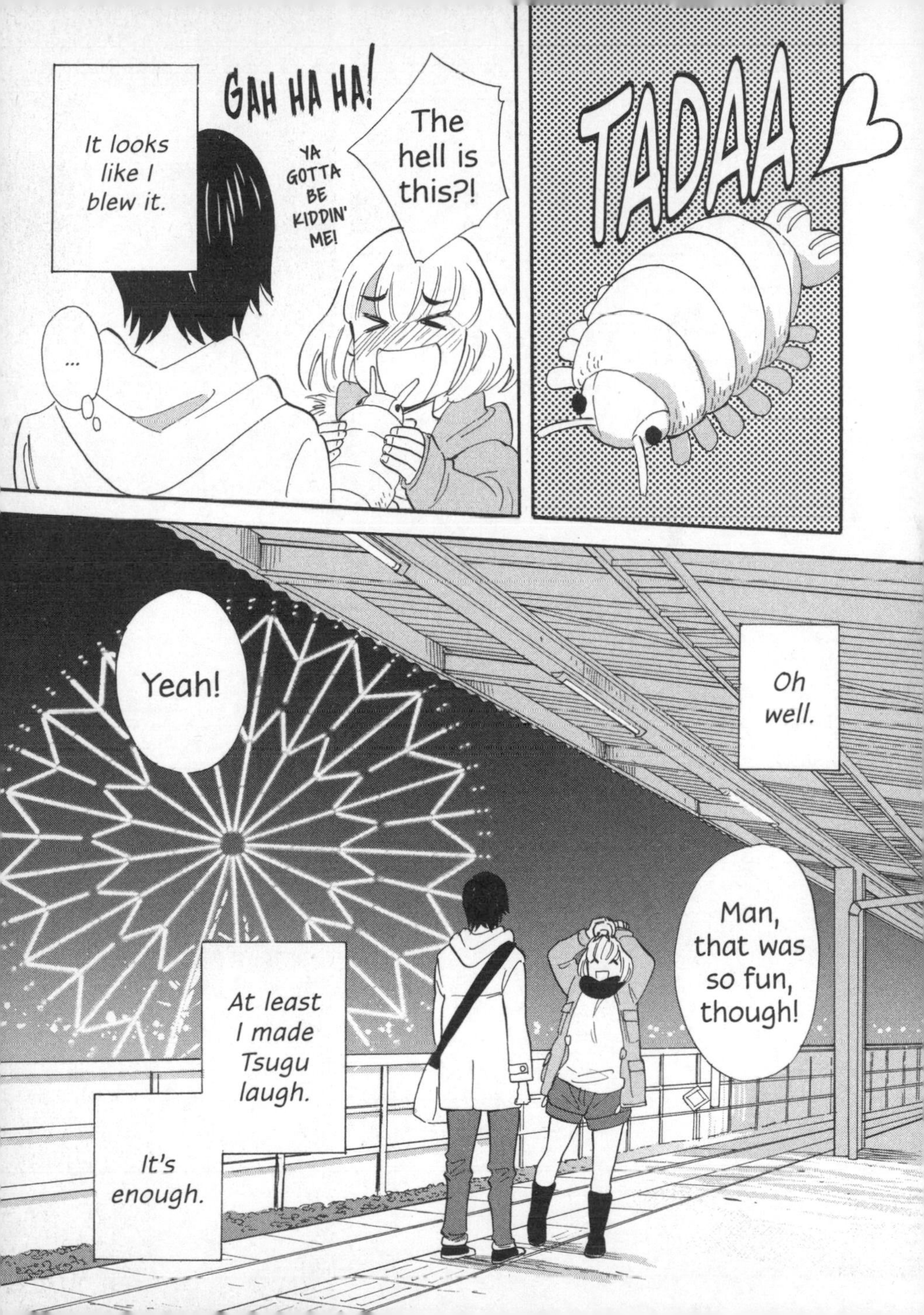
TADAA
GAH HA HA!
The hell is this?!
YA GOTTA BE KIDDIN' ME!
It looks like I blew it.
...
Oh well.
Yeah!
Man, that was so fun, though!
At least I made Tsugu laugh.
It's enough.

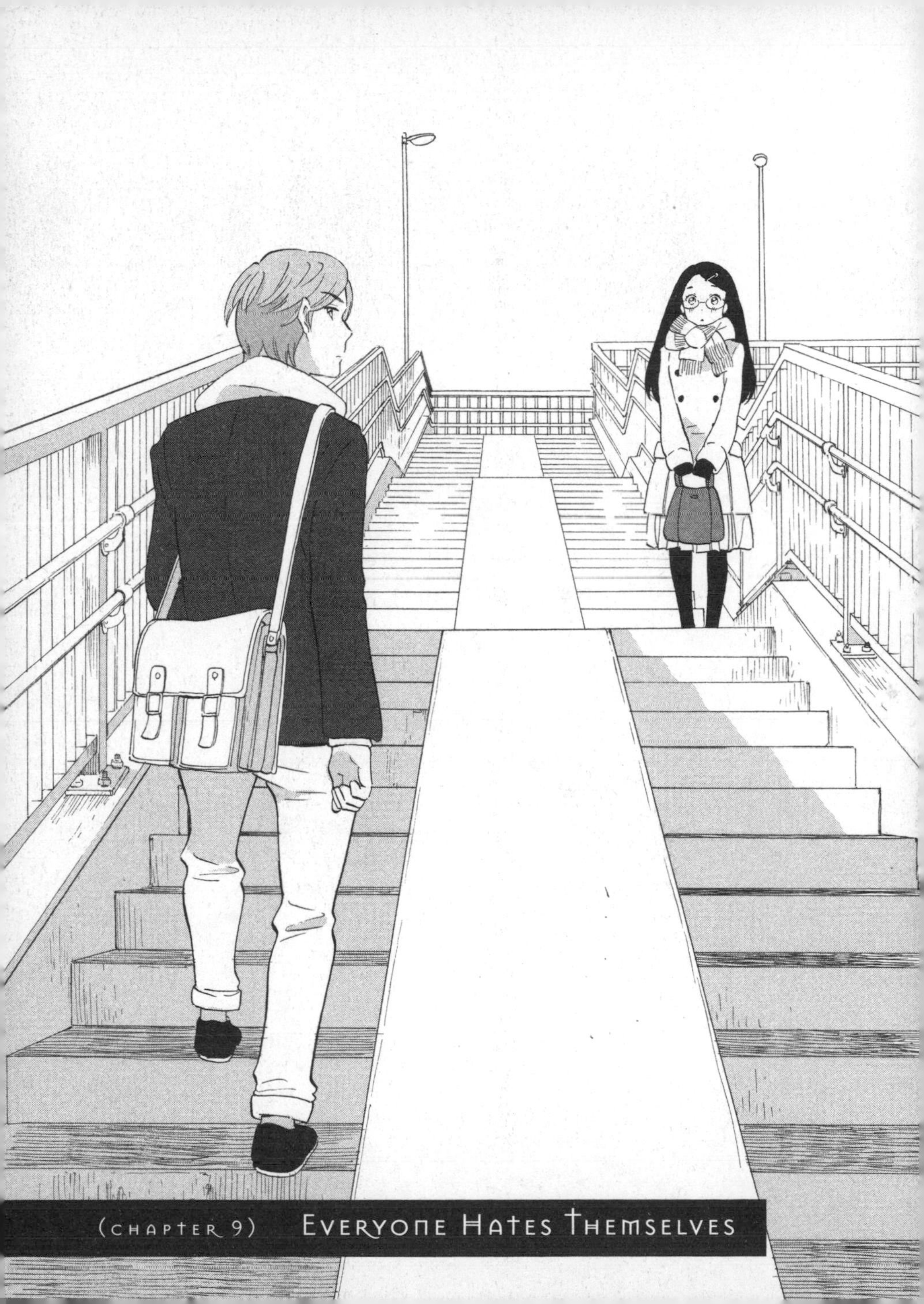

(CHAPTER 9) EVERYONE HATES THEMSELVES

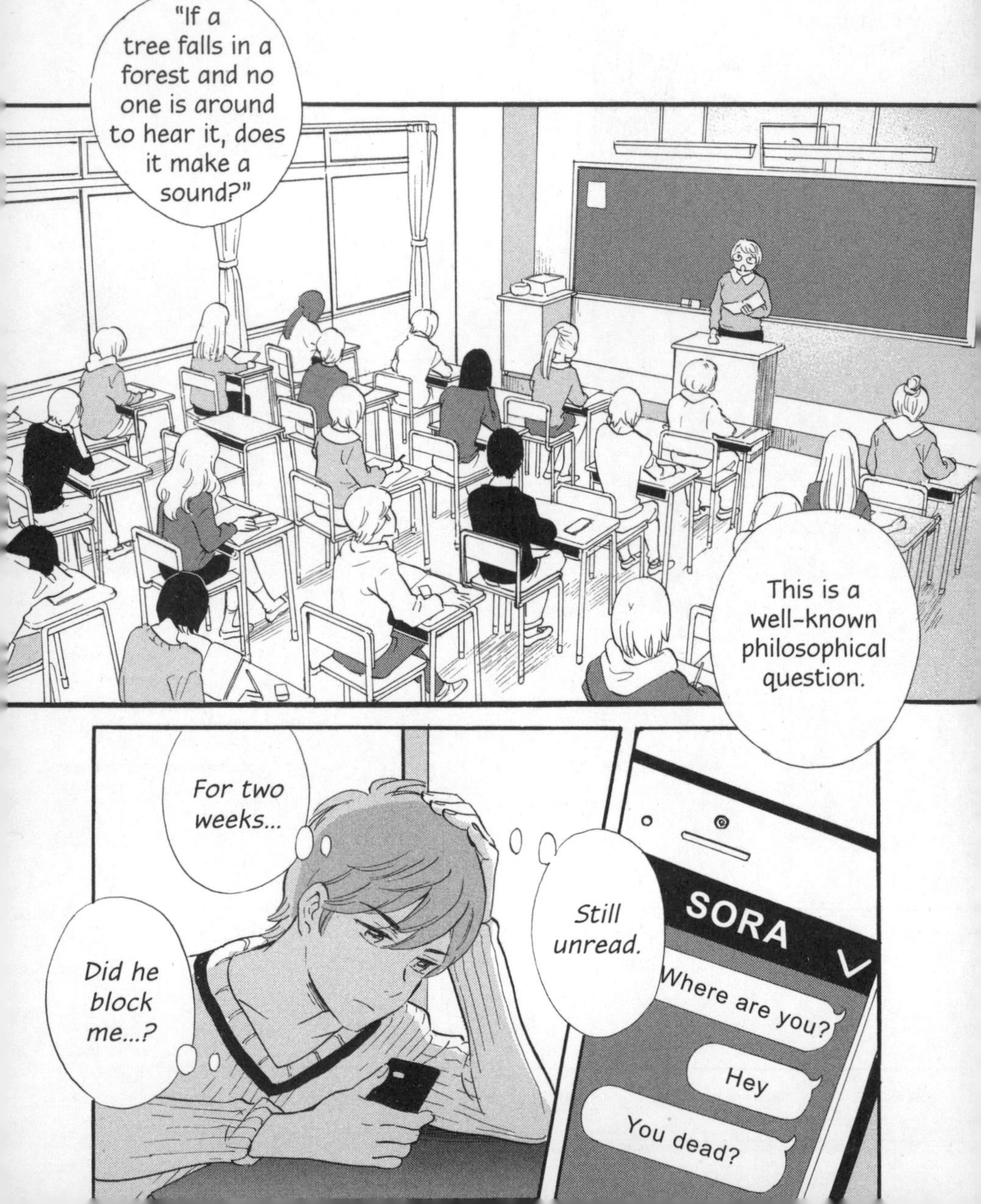
"If a tree falls in a forest and no one is around to hear it, does it make a sound?"
This is a well-known philosophical question.
SORA
Where are you?
Hey
You dead?
For two weeks...
Still unread.
Did he block me...?

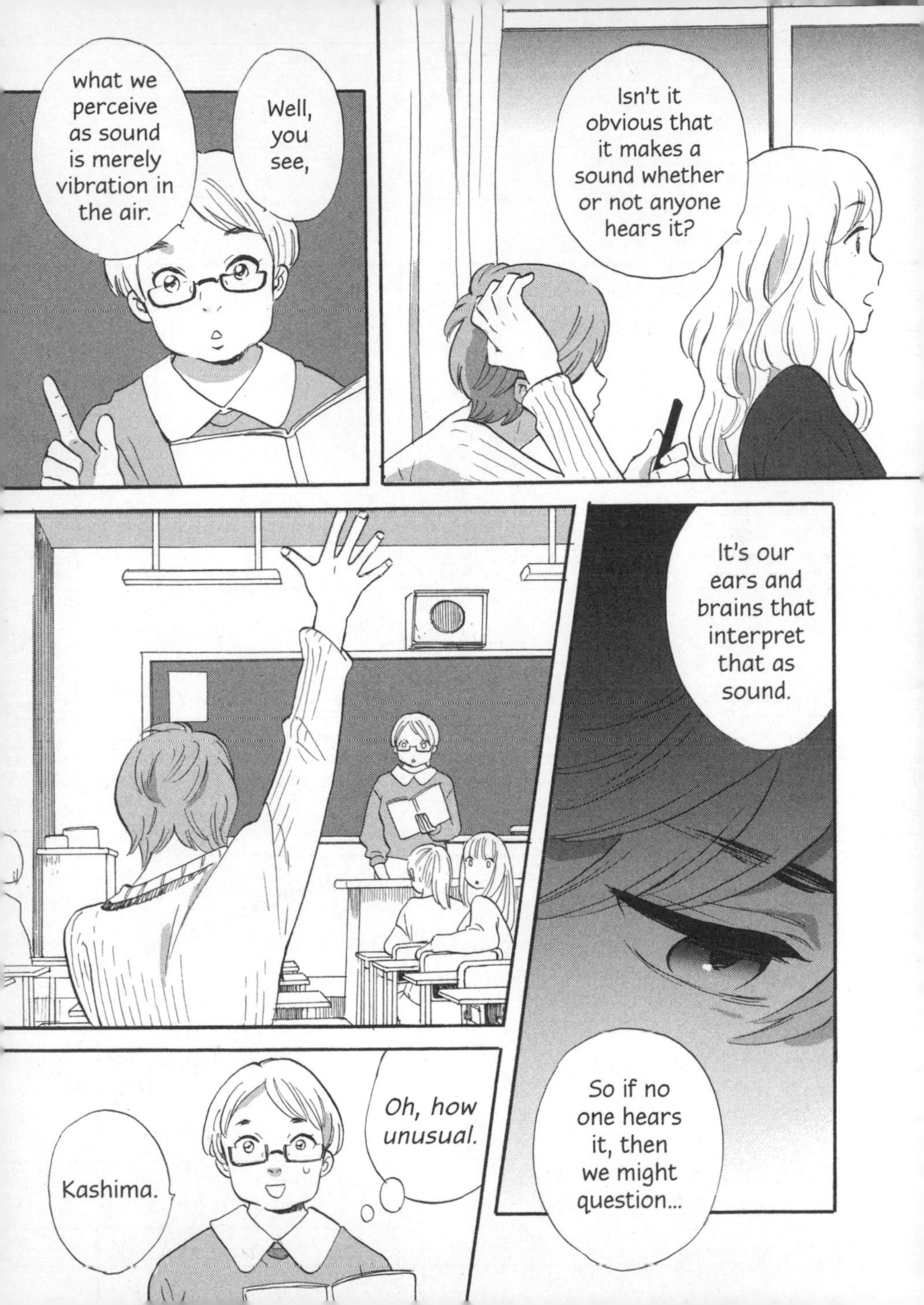
Isn't it obvious that it makes a sound whether or not anyone hears it?
Well, you see,
what we perceive as sound is merely vibration in the air.
It's our ears and brains that interpret that as sound.
So if no one hears it, then we might question...
Oh, how unusual.
Kashima.

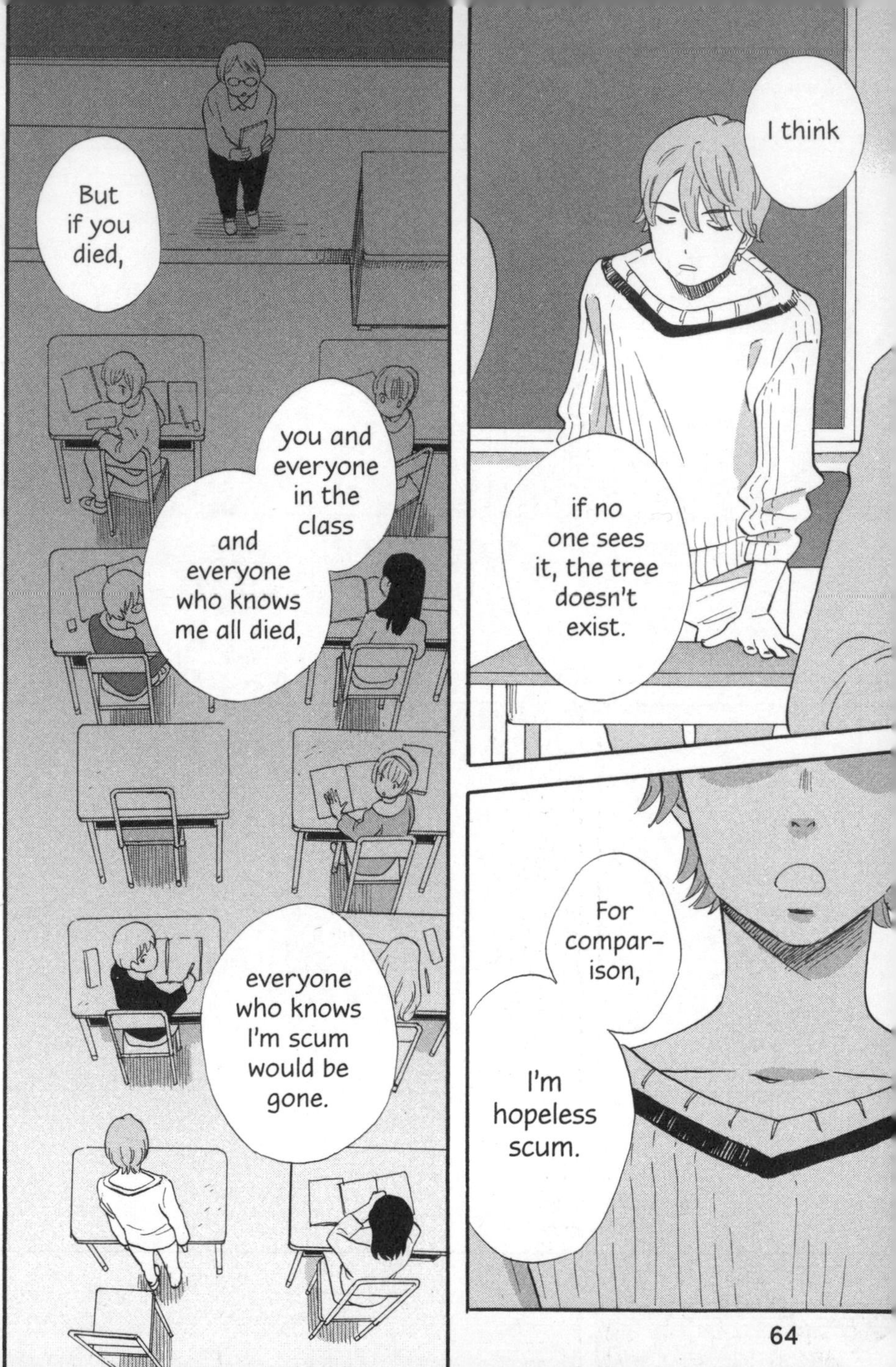
I think
if no one sees it, the tree doesn't exist.
For compar-ison,
I'm hopeless scum.
But if you died,
you and everyone in the class
and everyone who knows me all died,
everyone who knows I'm scum would be gone.

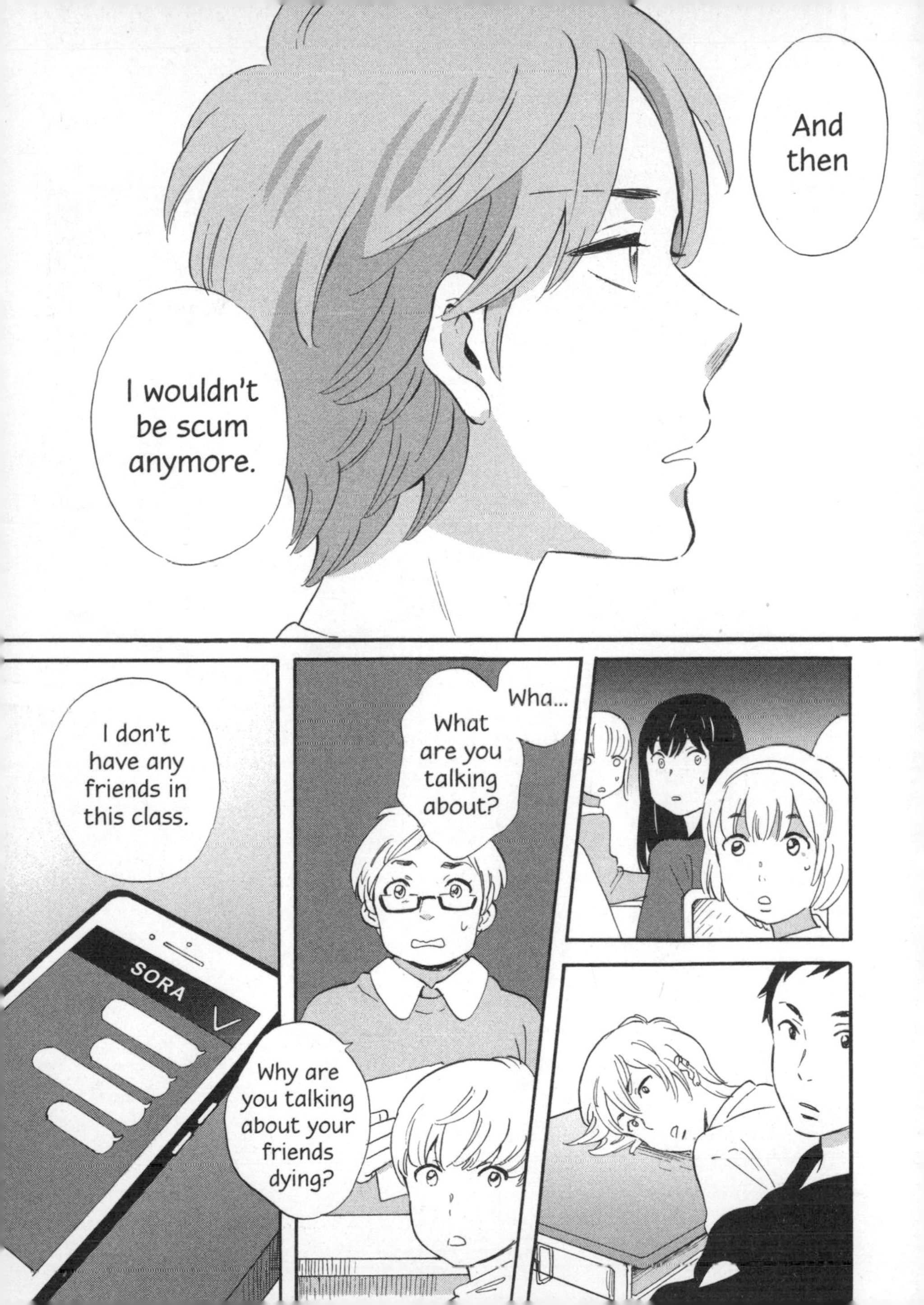
And then
I wouldn't be scum anymore.
Wha... What are you talking about?
Why are you talking about your friends dying?
I don't have any friends in this class.
SORA

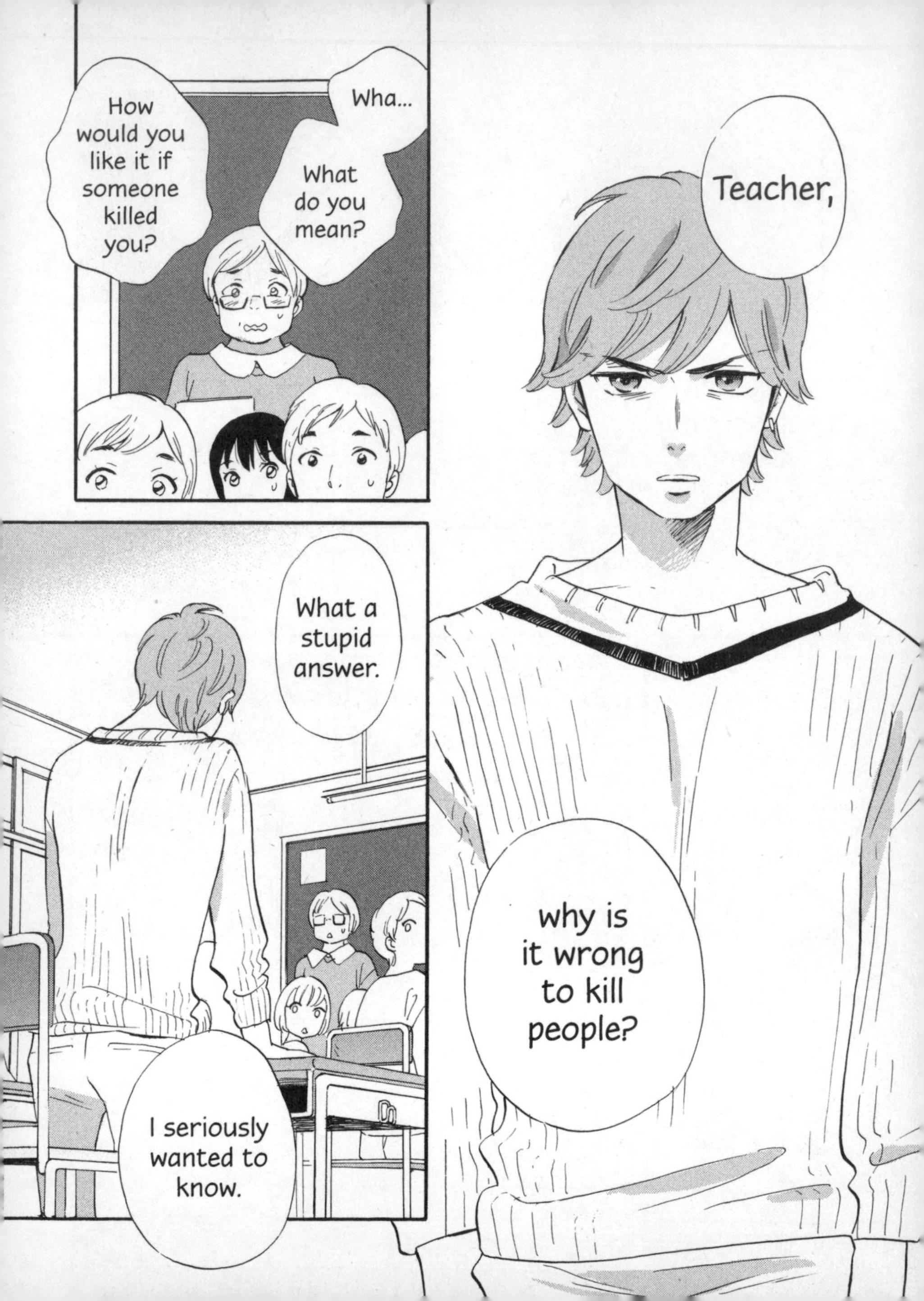
Teacher,
why is it wrong to kill people?
Wha...
What do you mean?
How would you like it if someone killed you?
What a stupid answer.
I seriously wanted to know.

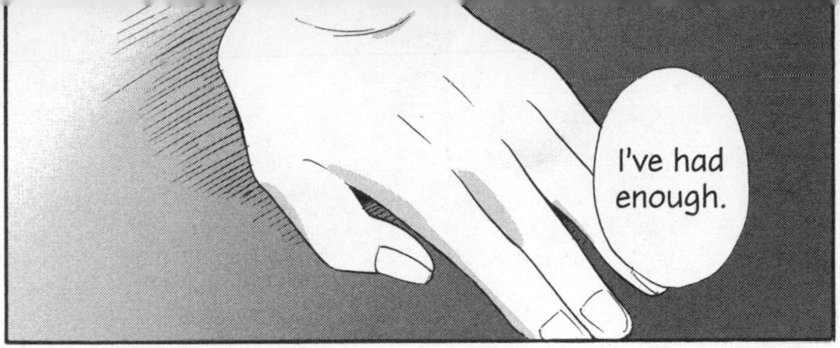
I've had enough.
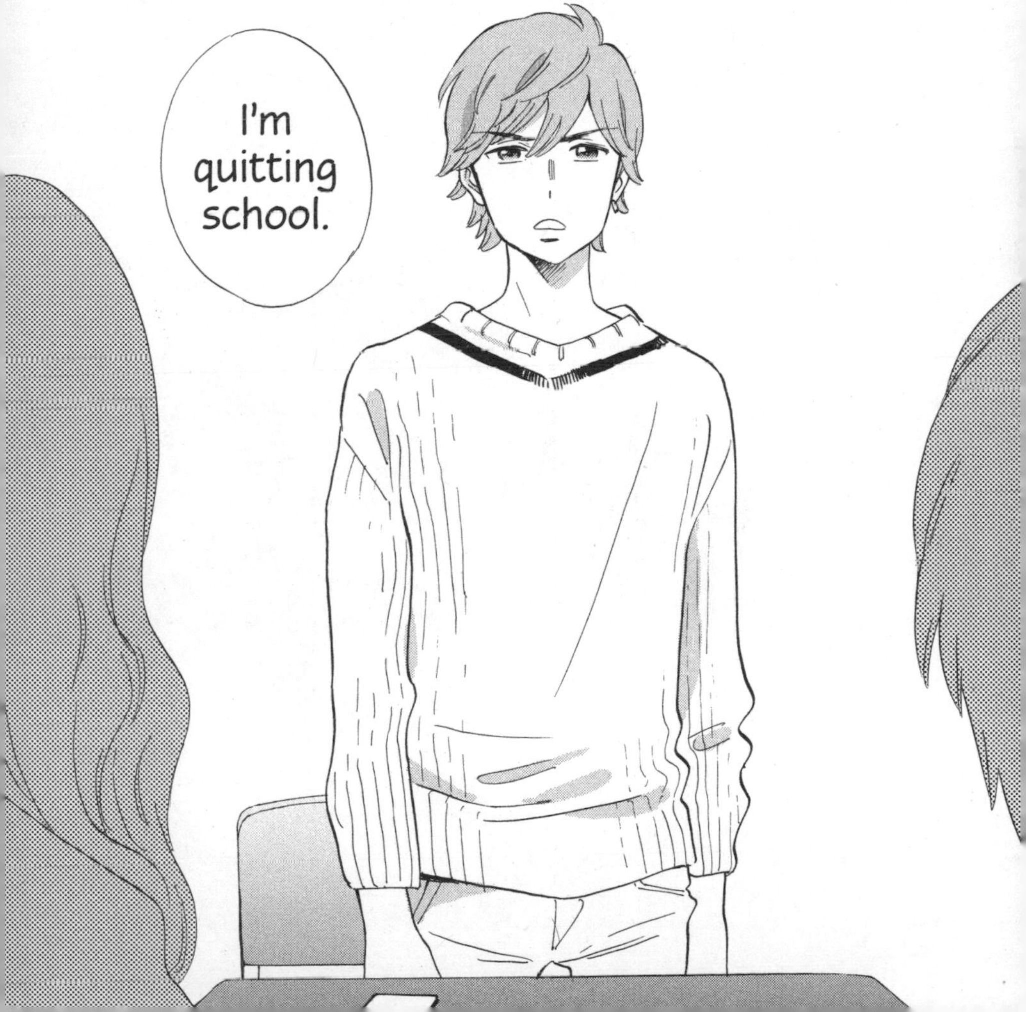
I'm quitting school.

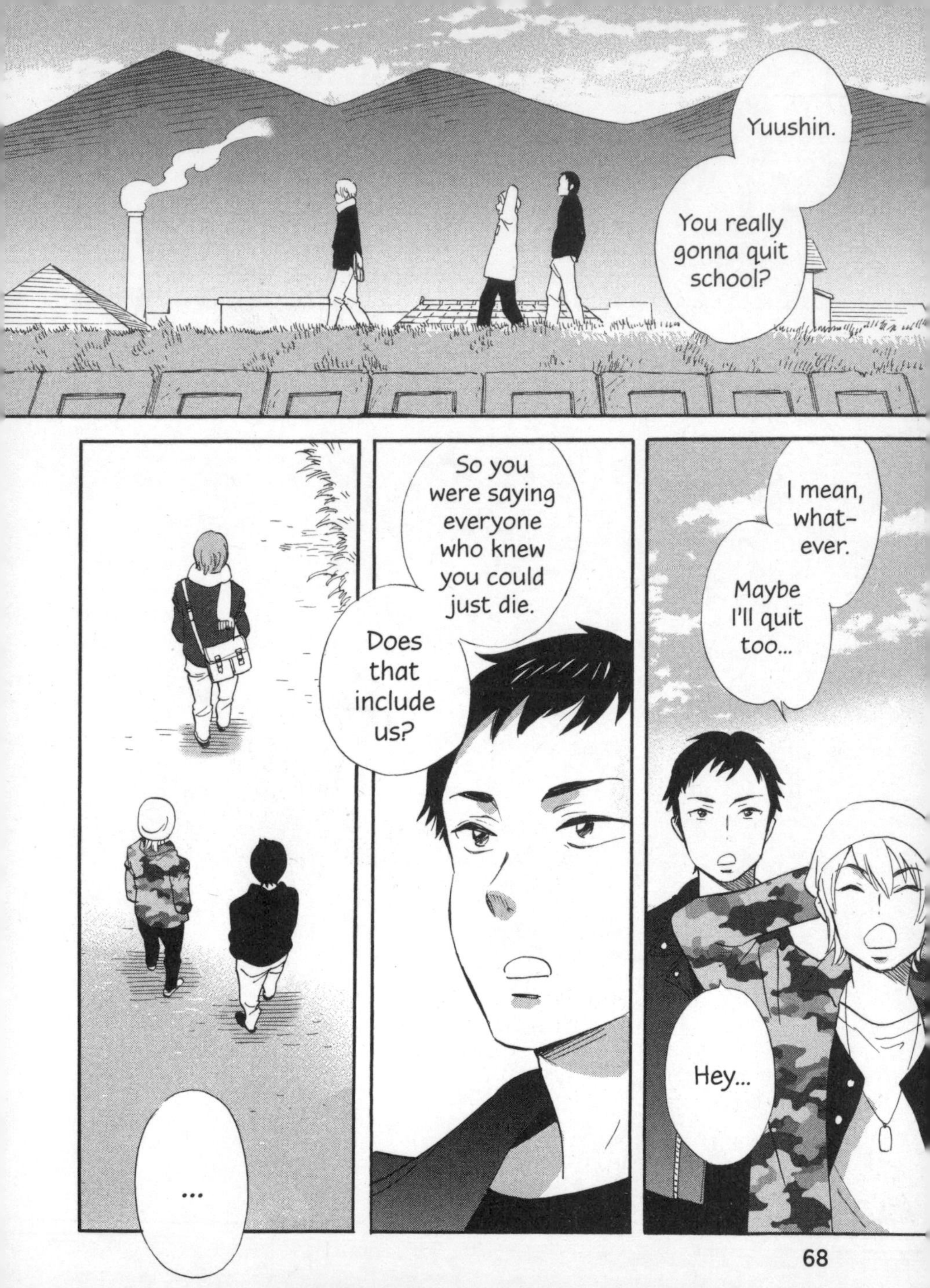
Yuushin.
You really gonna quit school?
I mean, what-ever.
Maybe I'll quit too...
Hey...
So you were saying everyone who knew you could just die.
Does that include us?
...

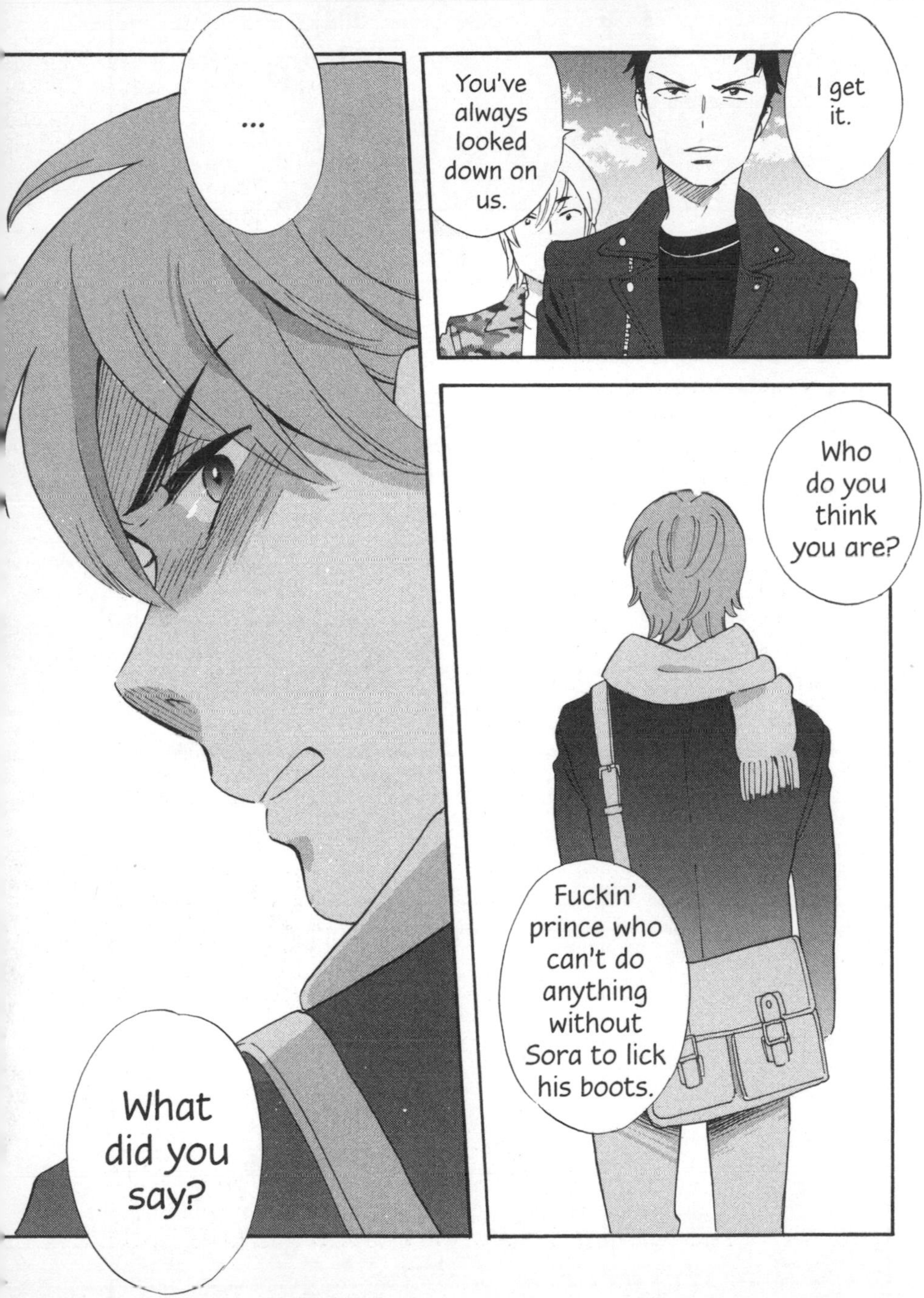
I get it.
You've always looked down on us.
Who do you think you are?
Fuckin' prince who can't do anything without Sora to lick his boots.
...
What did you say?

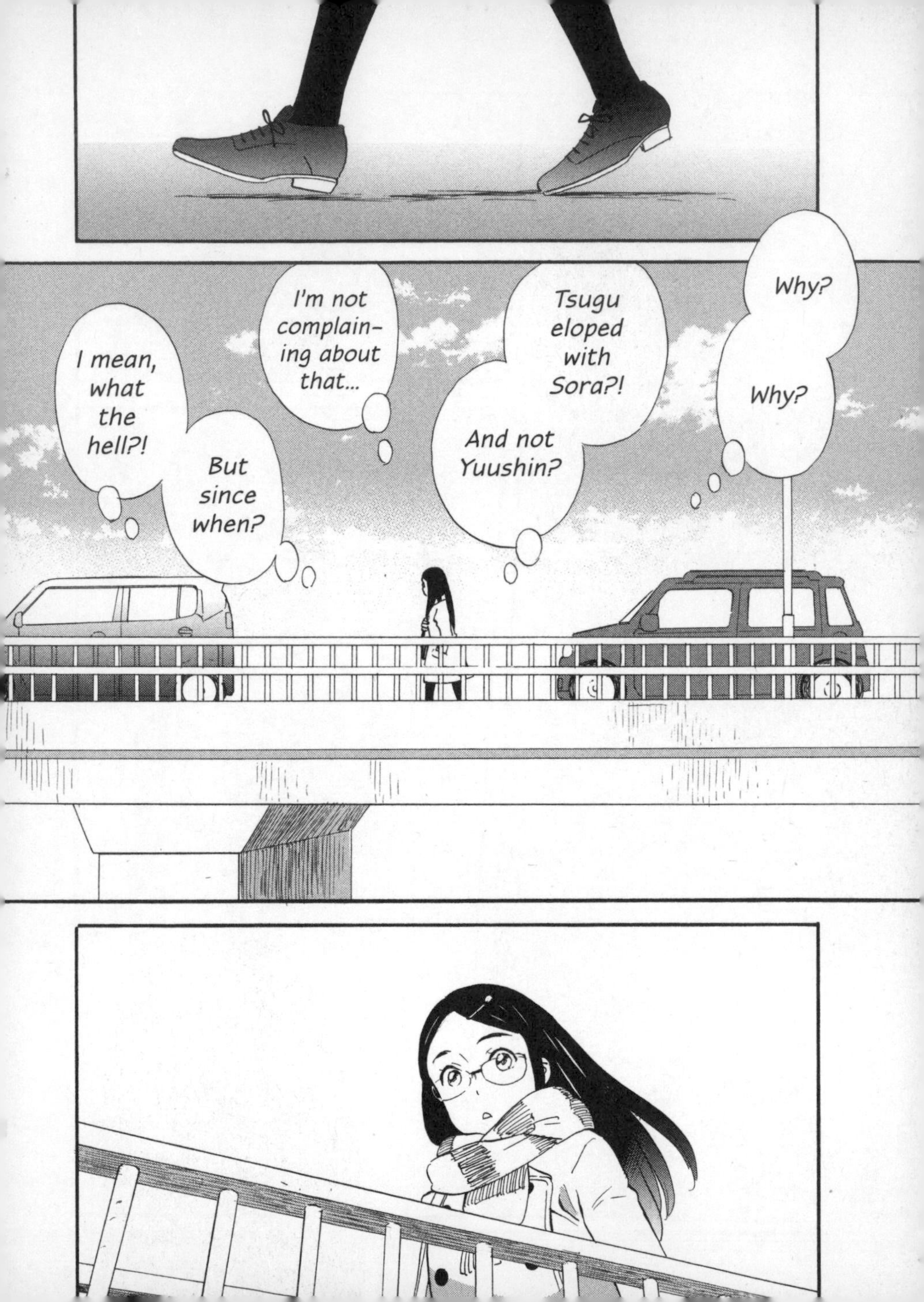
Why?
Why?
Tsugu eloped with Sora?!
And not Yuushin?
I'm not complaining about that...
But since when?
I mean, what the hell?!

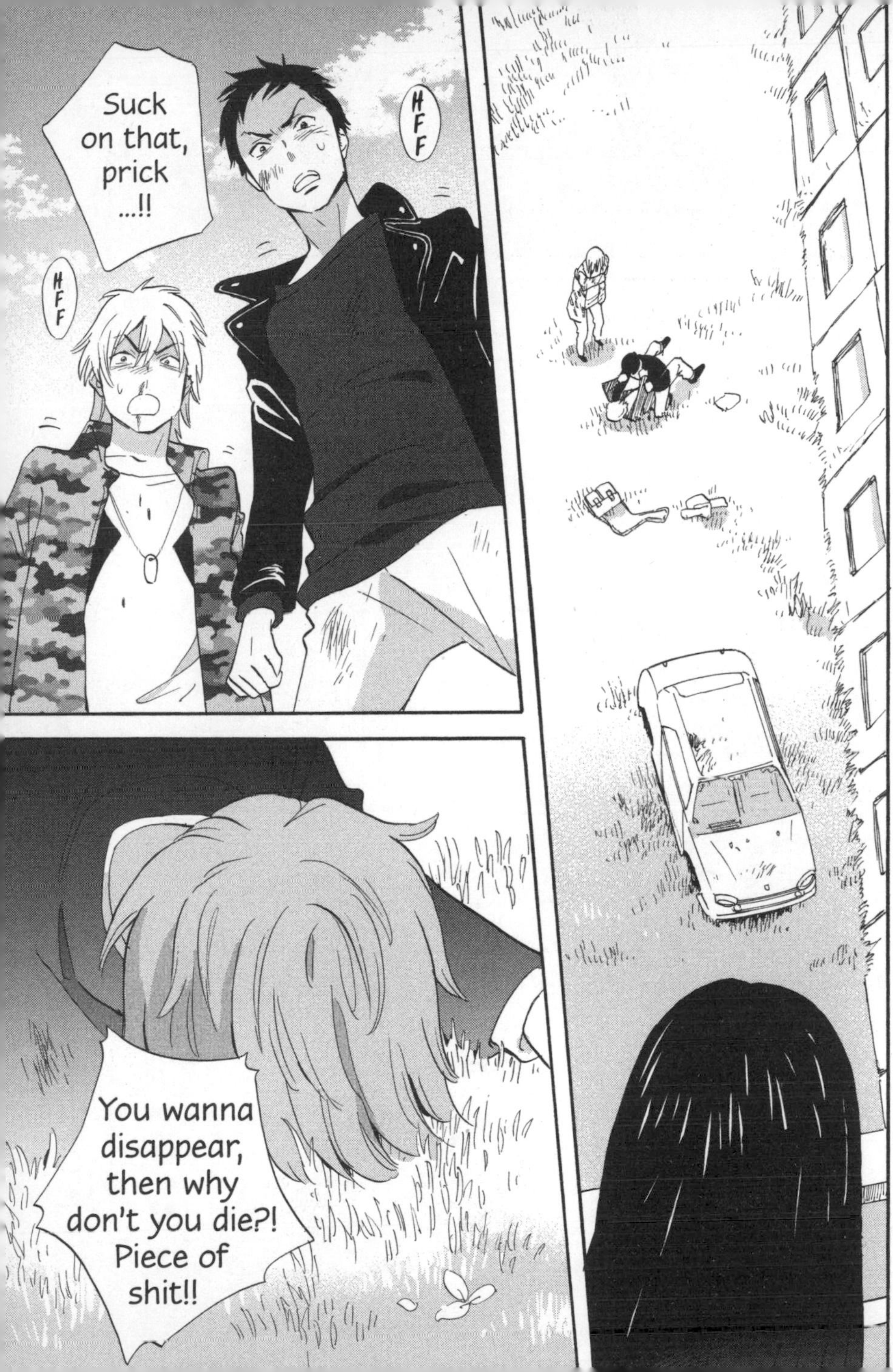
HFF
Suck on that, prick ...!!
HFF
You wanna disappear, then why don't you die?! Piece of shit!!

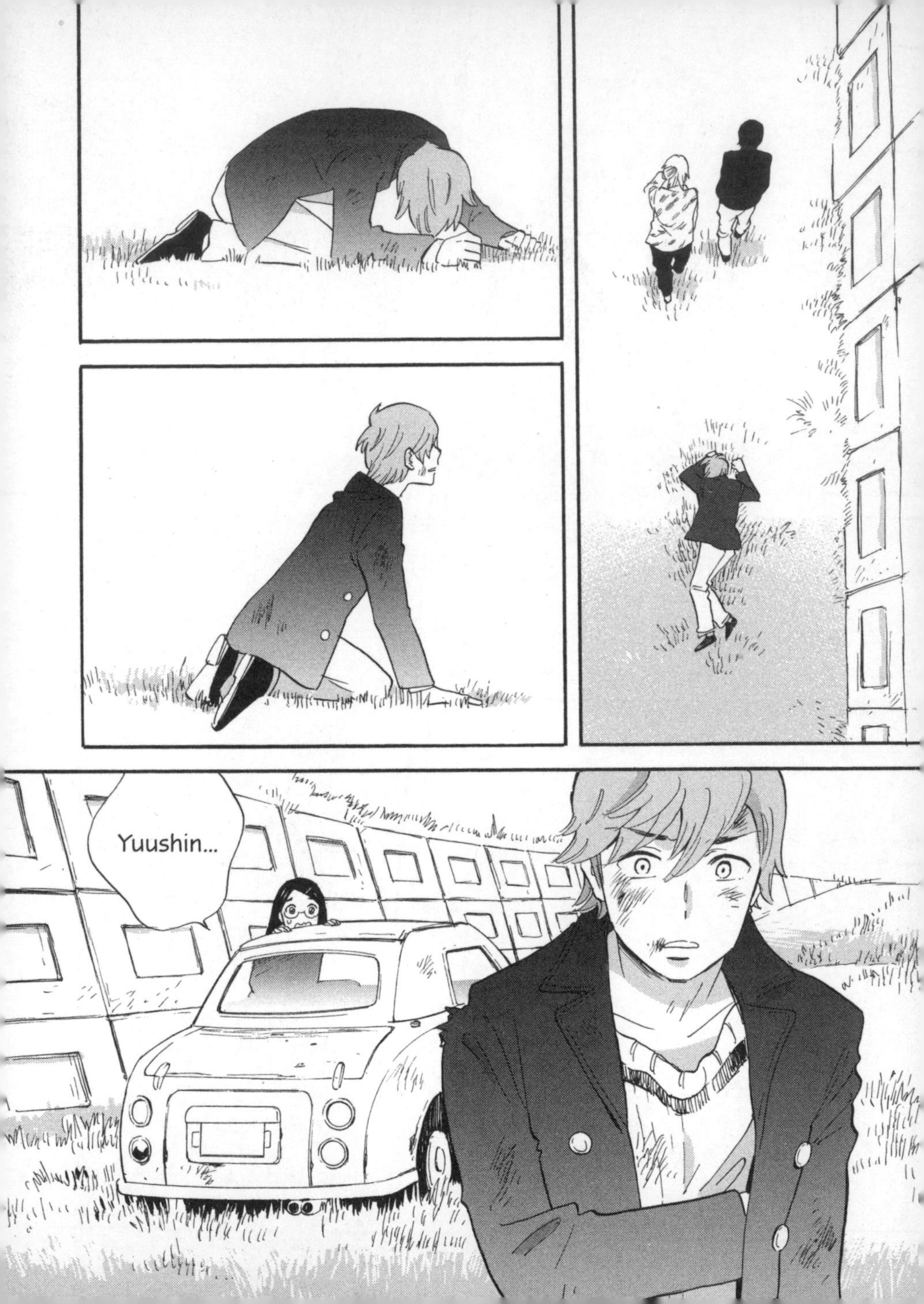
Yuushin...

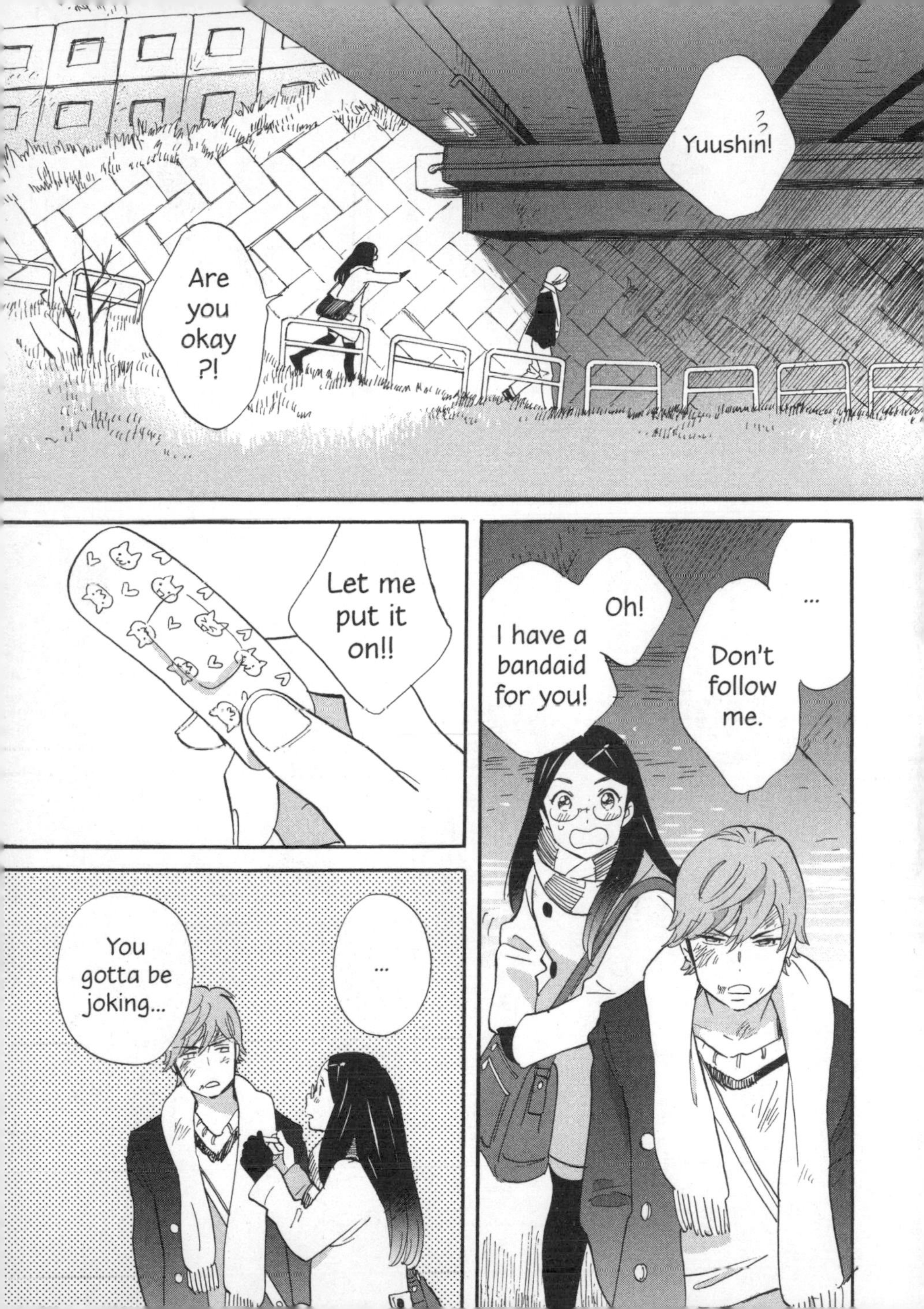
Yuushin!
Are you okay?!
... Don't follow me.
Oh! I have a bandaid for you!
Let me put it on!!
...
You gotta be joking...

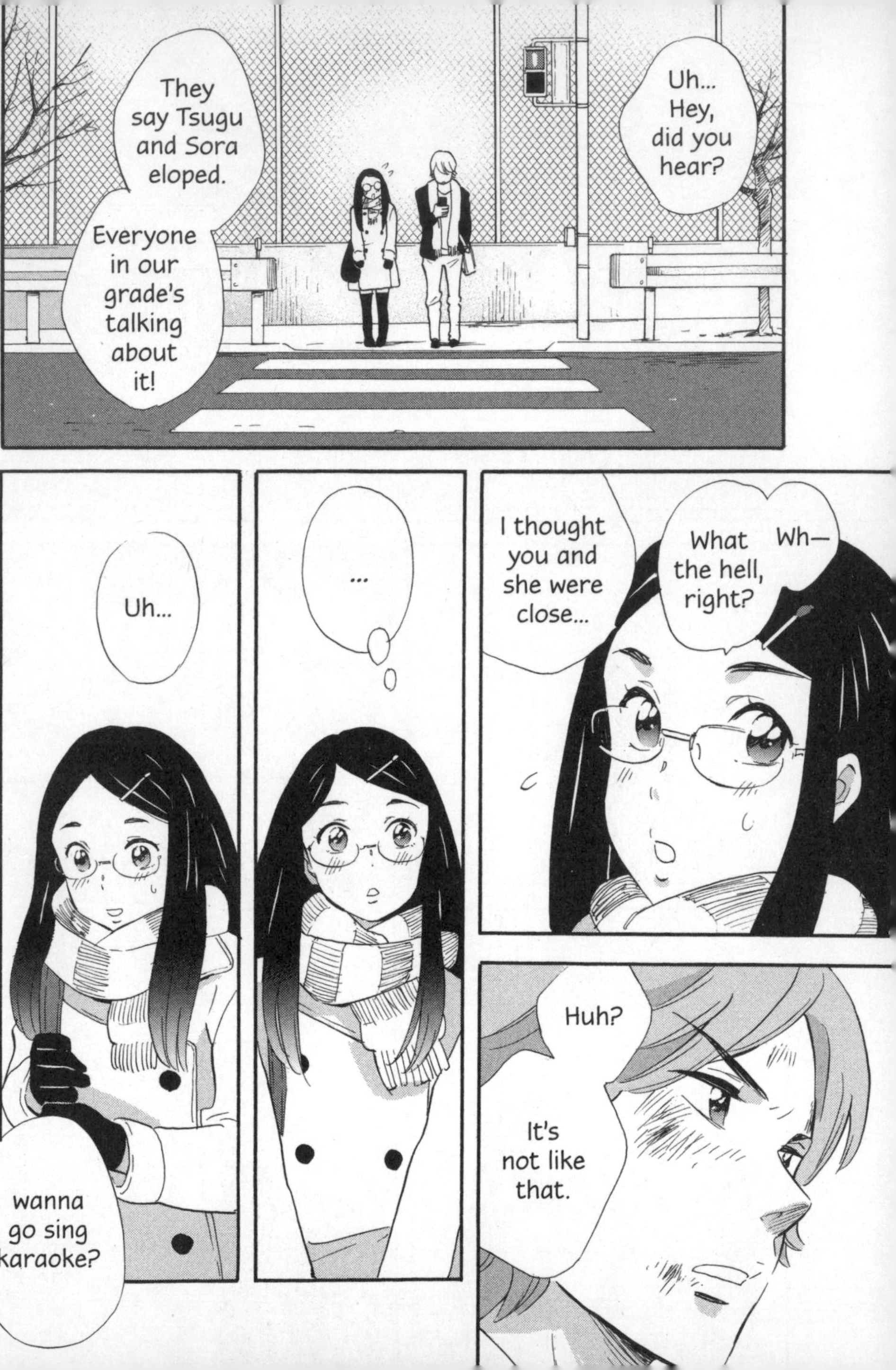
Uh... Hey, did you hear?
They say Tsugu and Sora eloped.
Everyone in our grade's talking about it!
Wh—
What the hell, right?
I thought you and she were close...
Huh?
It's not like that.
...
Uh...
wanna go sing karaoke?

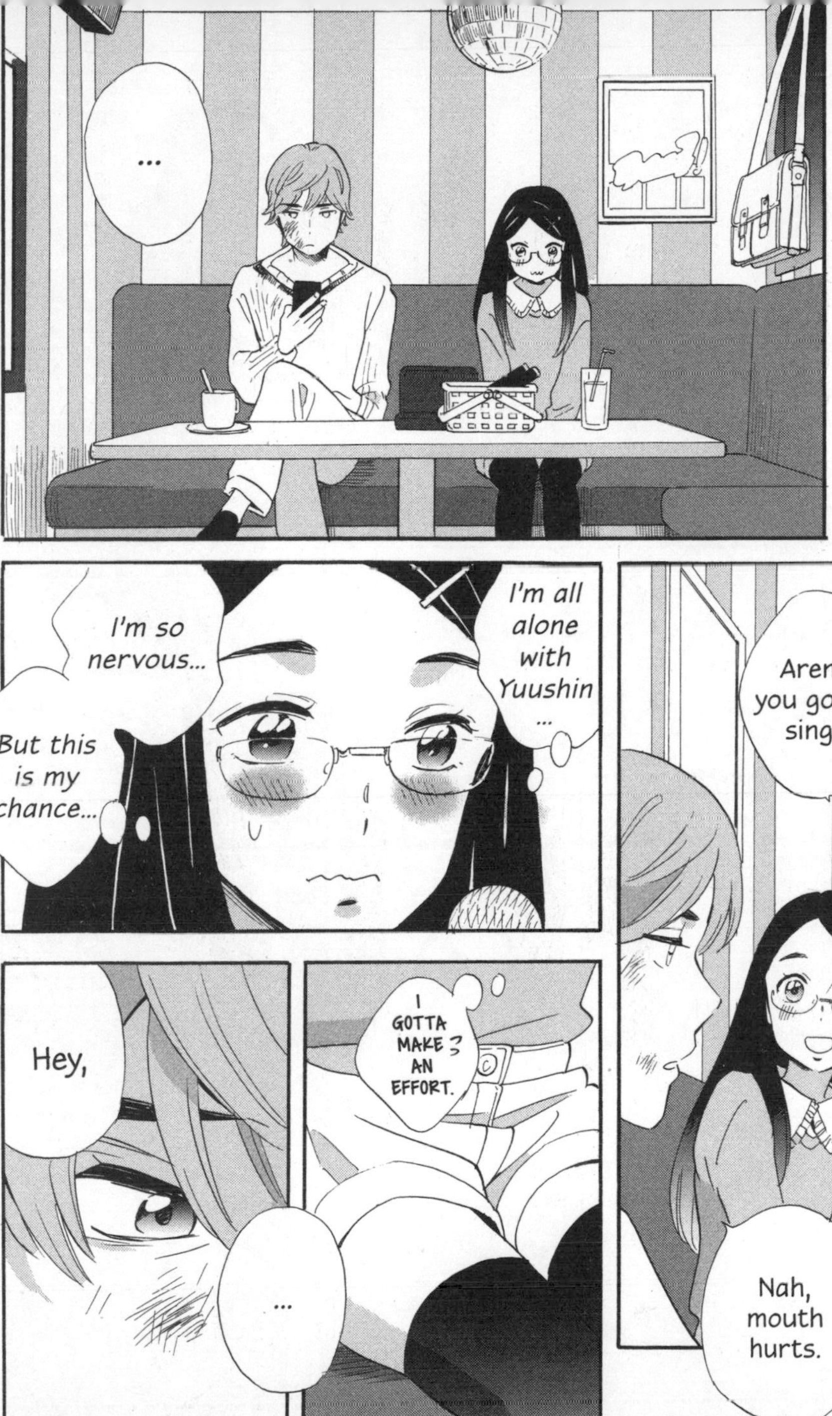
...
Aren't you gonna sing?
Nah, mouth hurts.
I'm all alone with Yuushin ...
I'm so nervous...
But this is my chance...
I GOTTA MAKE AN EFFORT.
...
Hey,

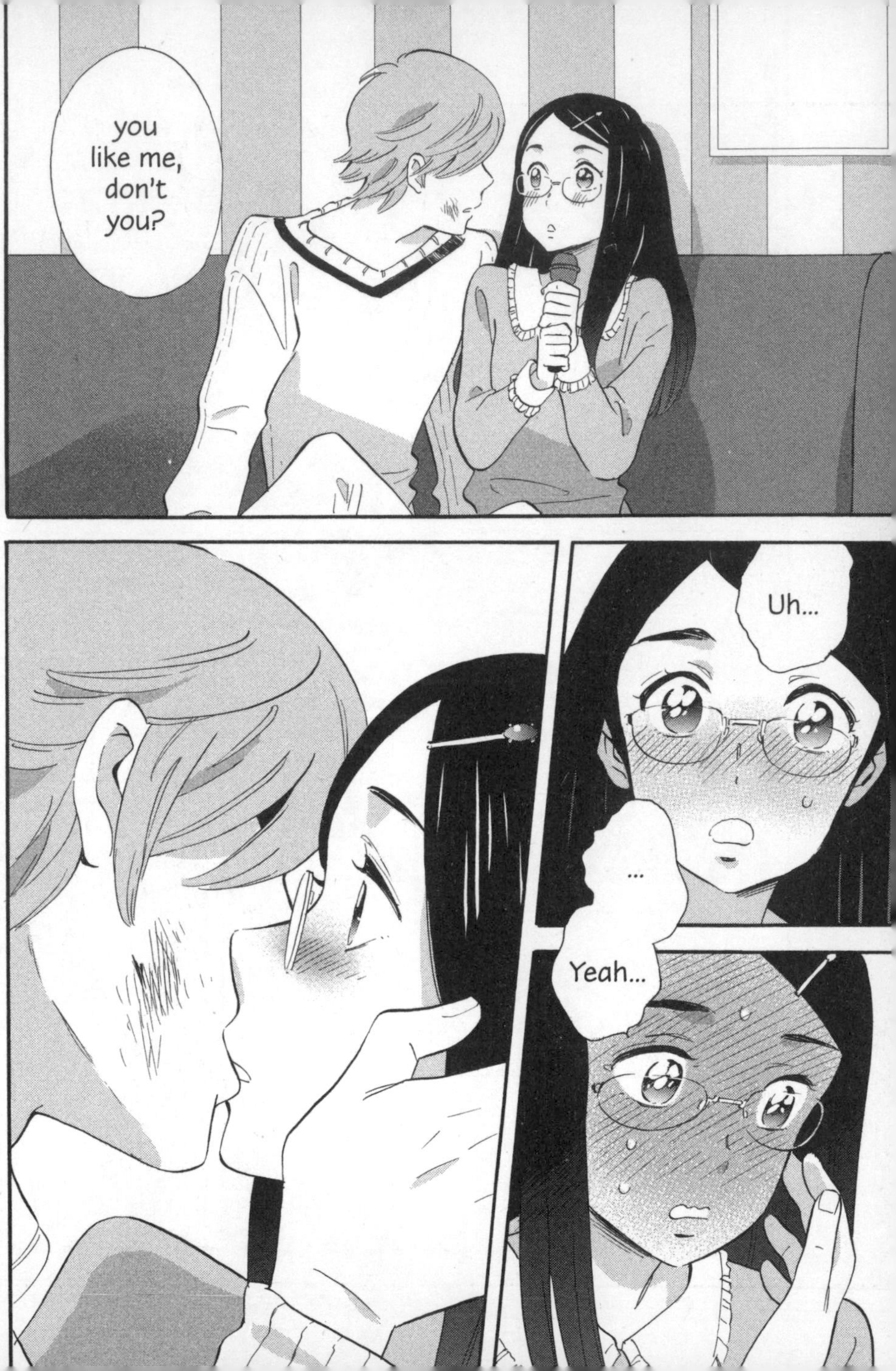
you like me, don't you?
Uh...
...
Yeah...

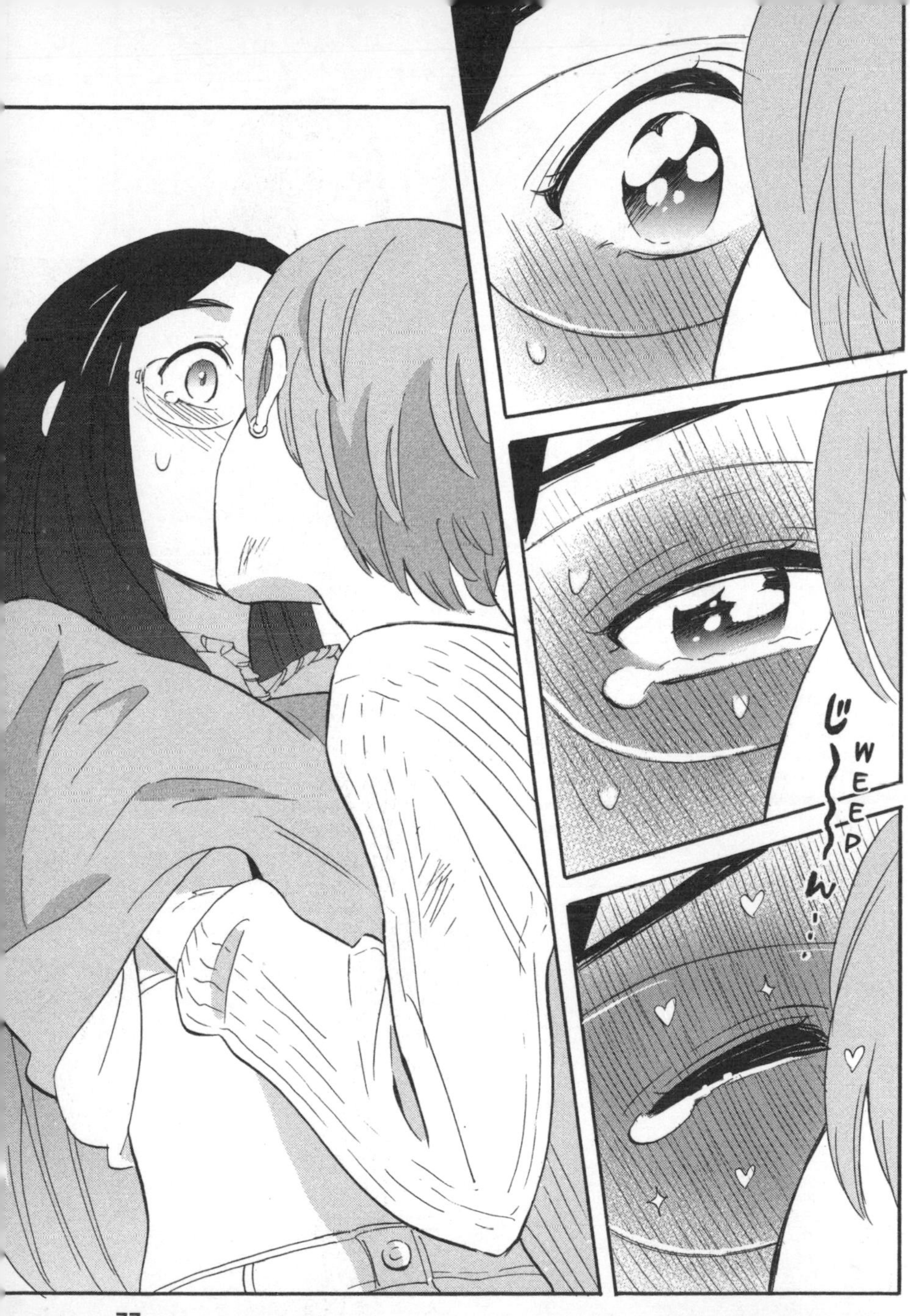
じ～ん
WEEP

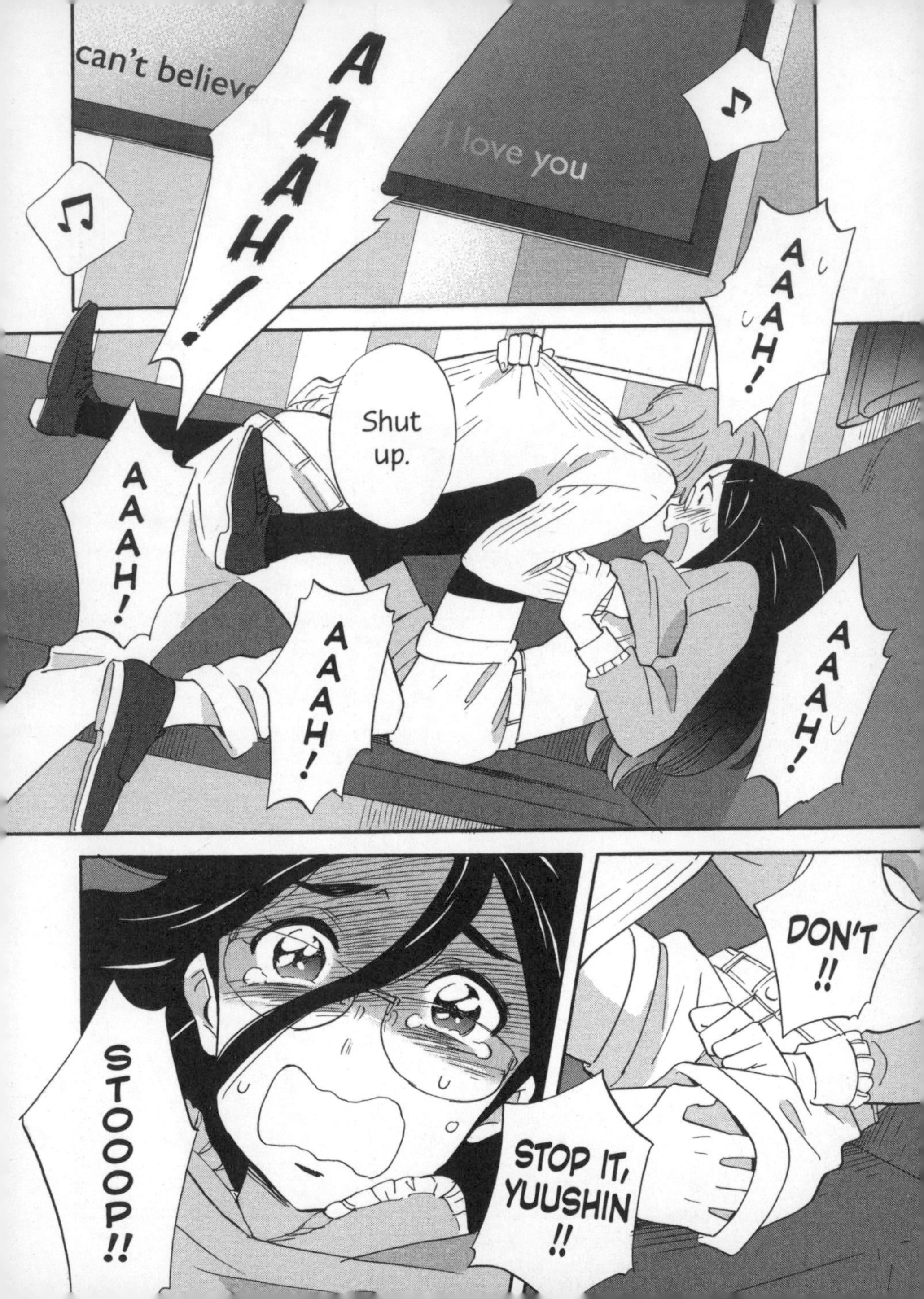
♪
I love you
AAAAH!!
can't believe
♫
AAAH!
AAAH!
Shut up.
AAAH!
AAAH!
DON'T !!
STOP IT, YUUSHIN !!
STOOOOP!!

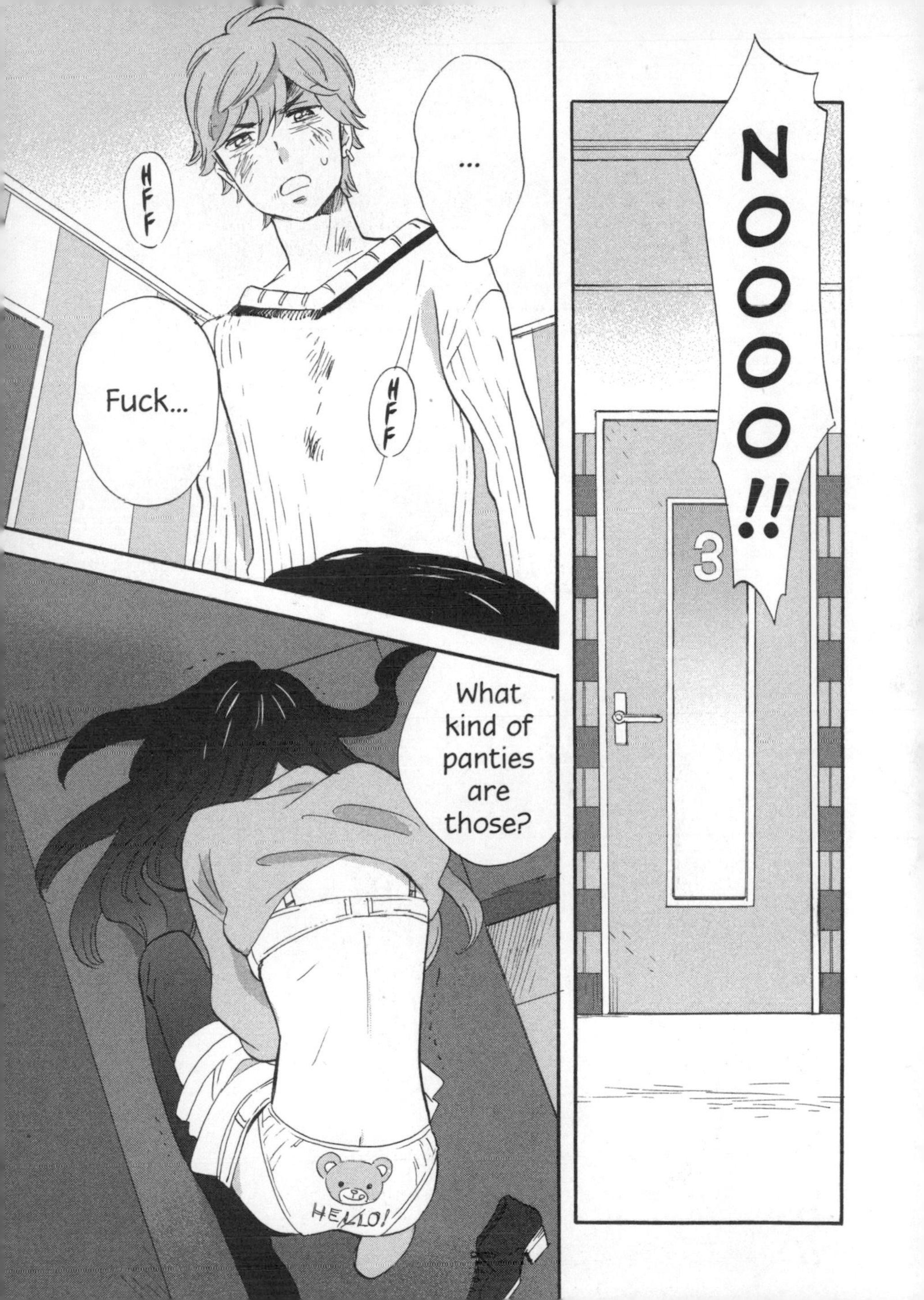
NOOOO!!
...
HFF
HFF
Fuck...
What kind of panties are those?
HELLO!

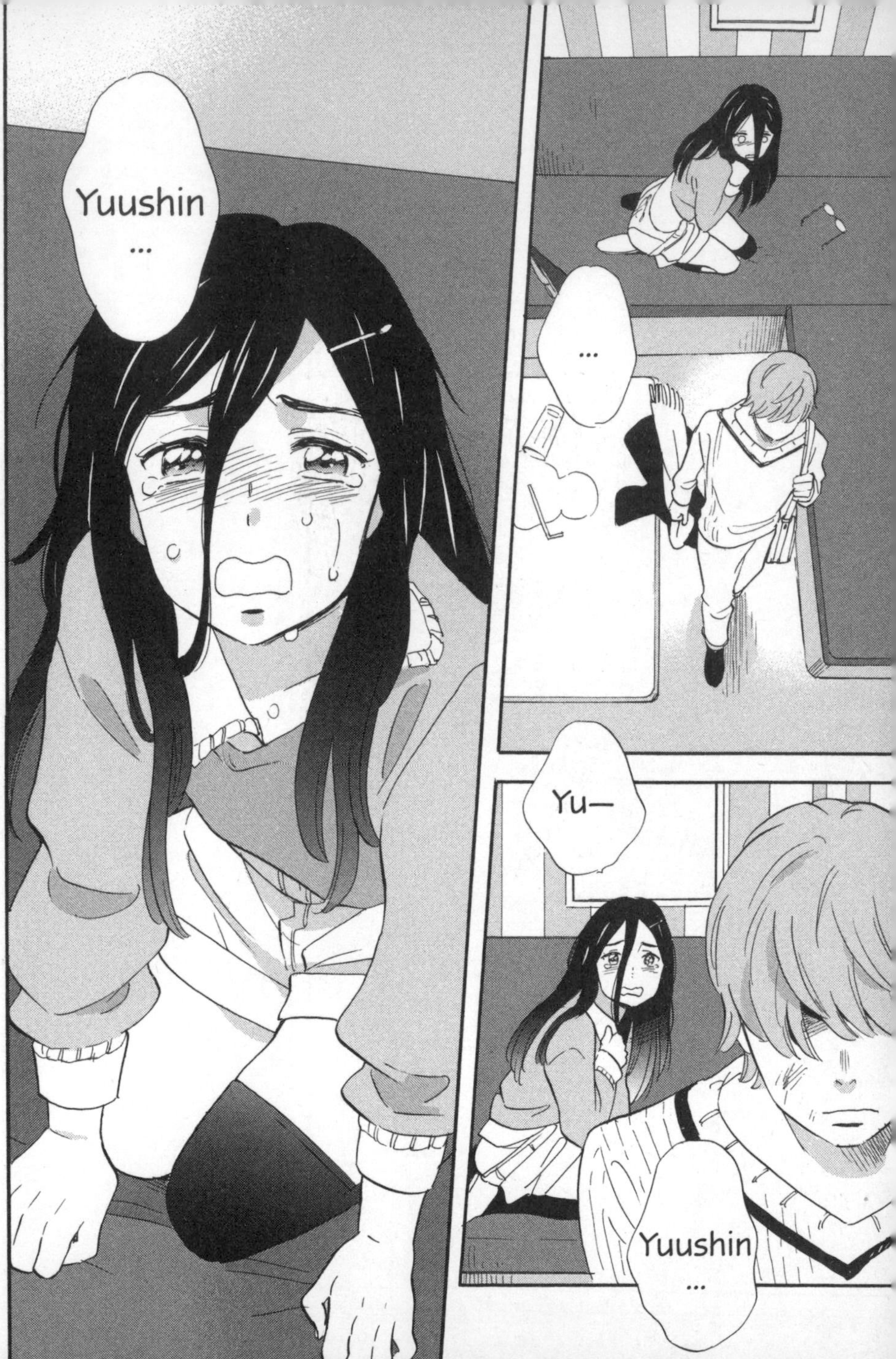
...
Yu—
Yuushin ...
Yuushin ...

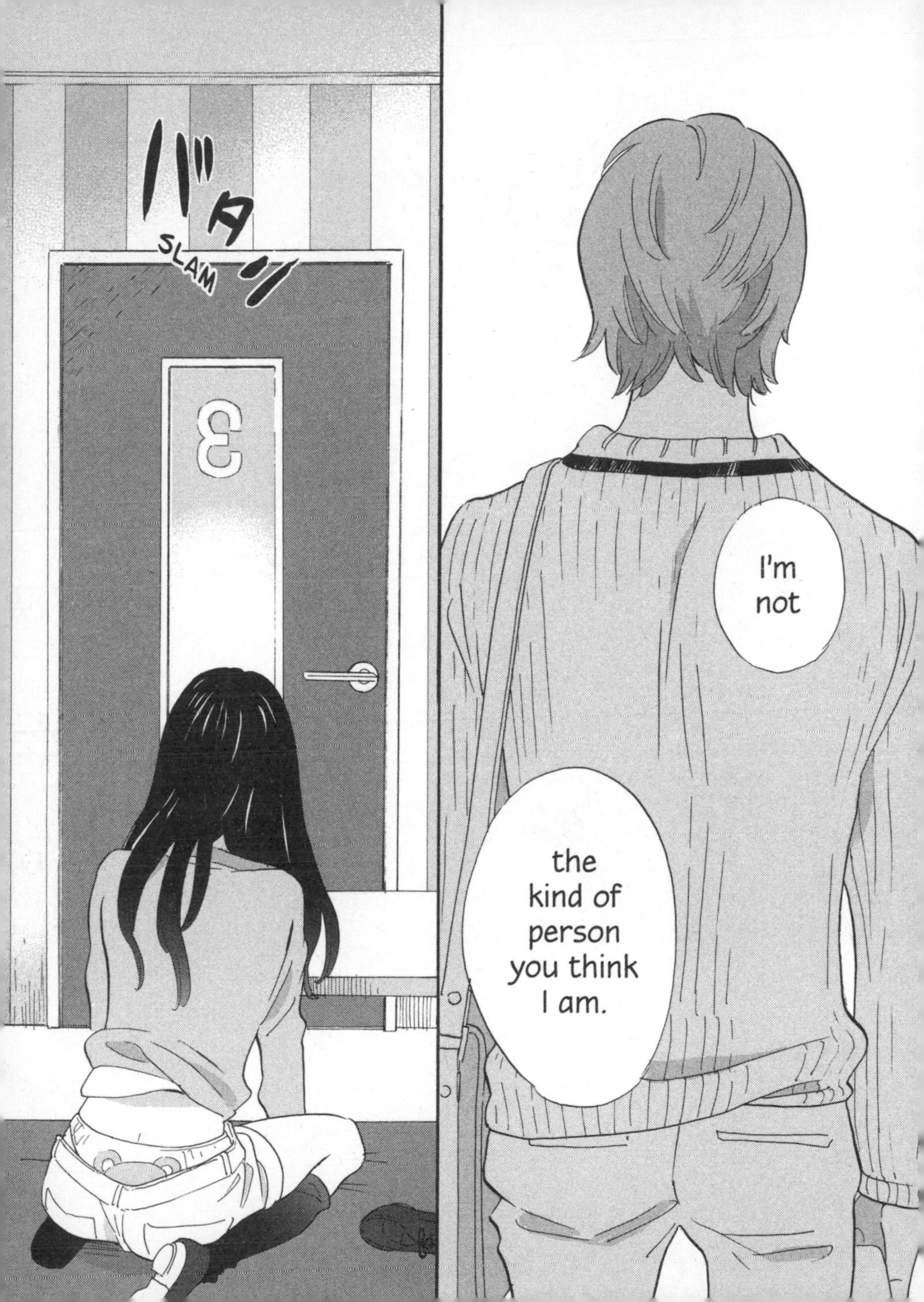
I'm not
the kind of person you think I am.
バタッ
SLAM

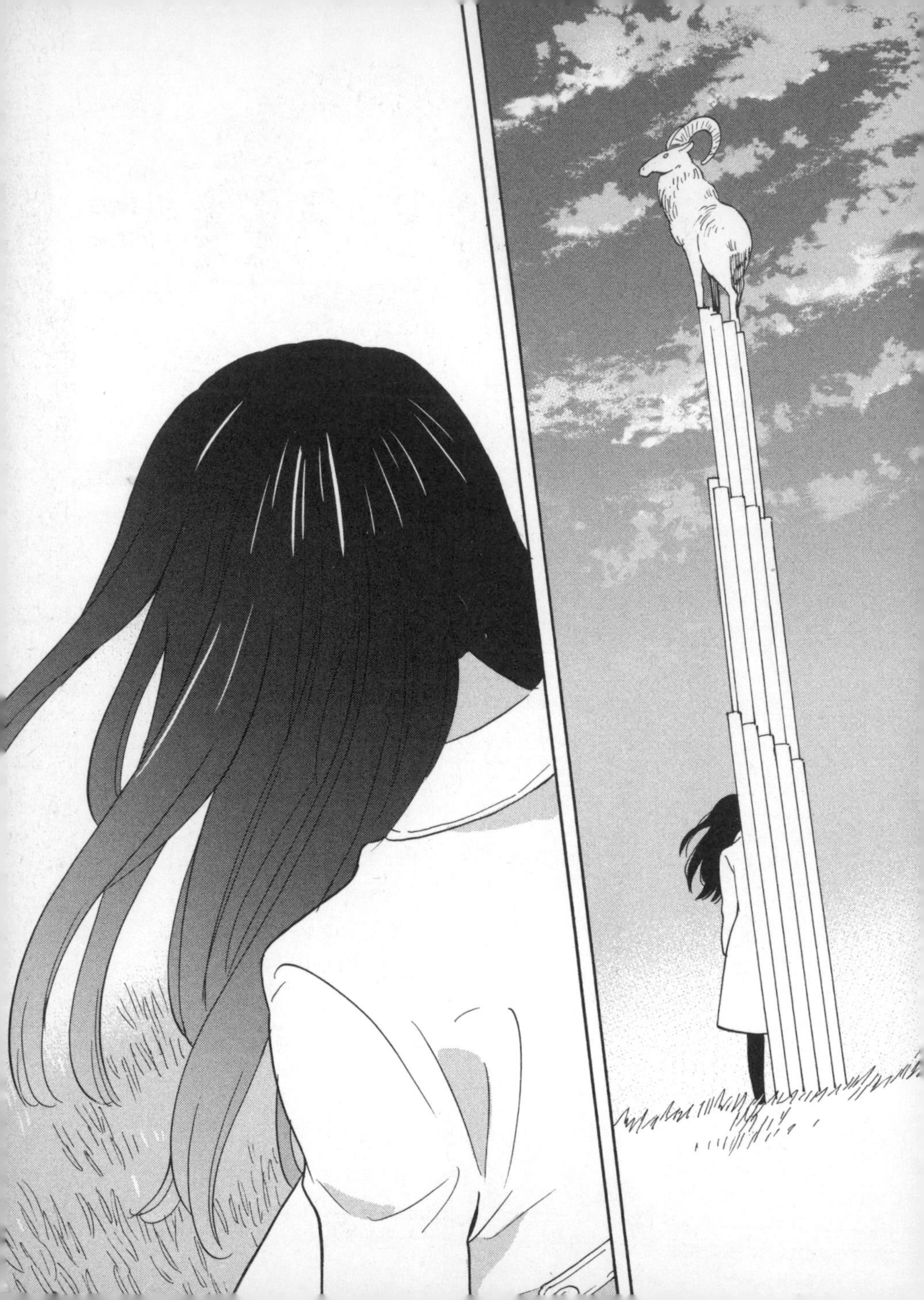

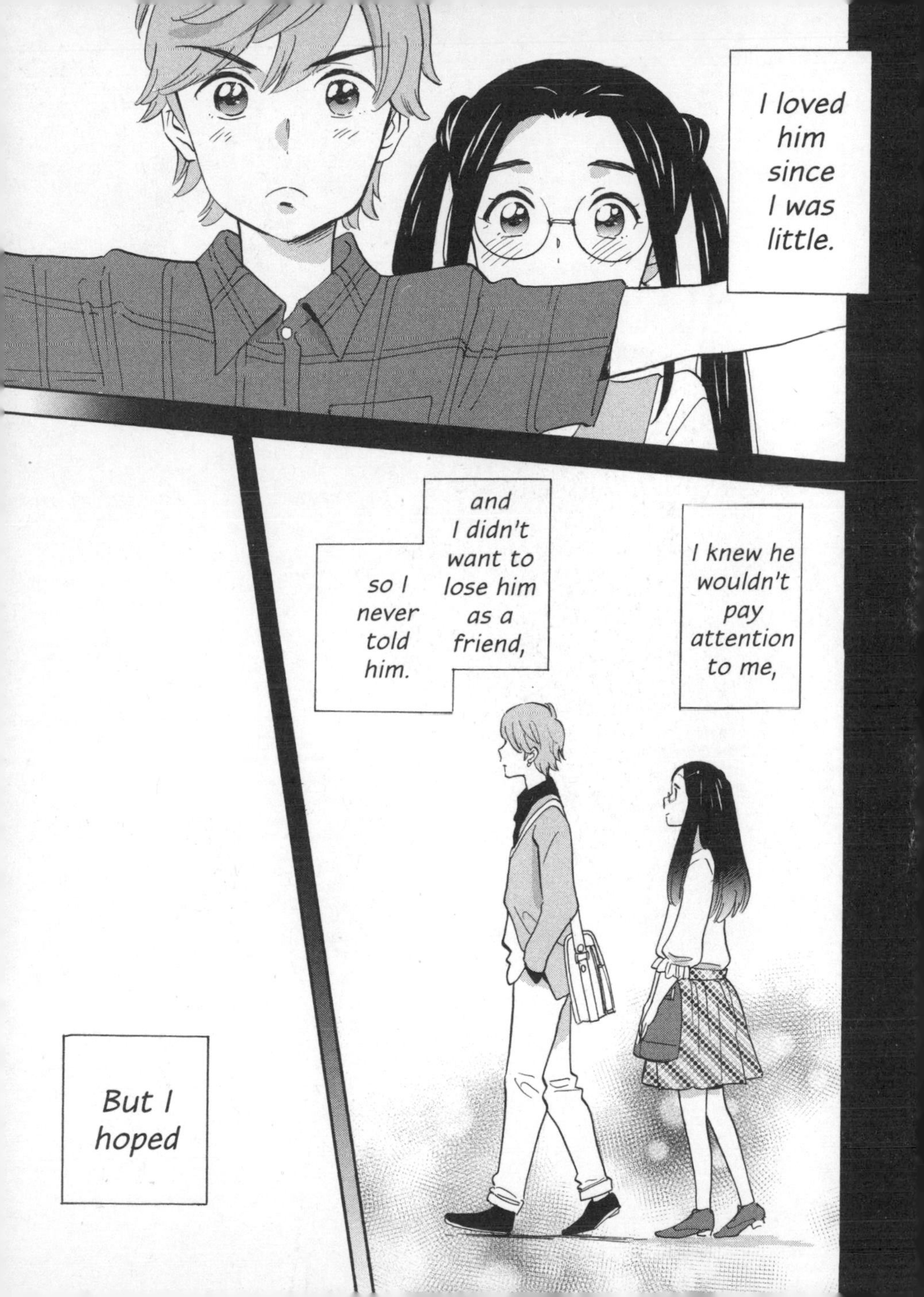
I loved him since I was little.
I knew he wouldn't pay attention to me,
and I didn't want to lose him as a friend,
so I never told him.
But I hoped

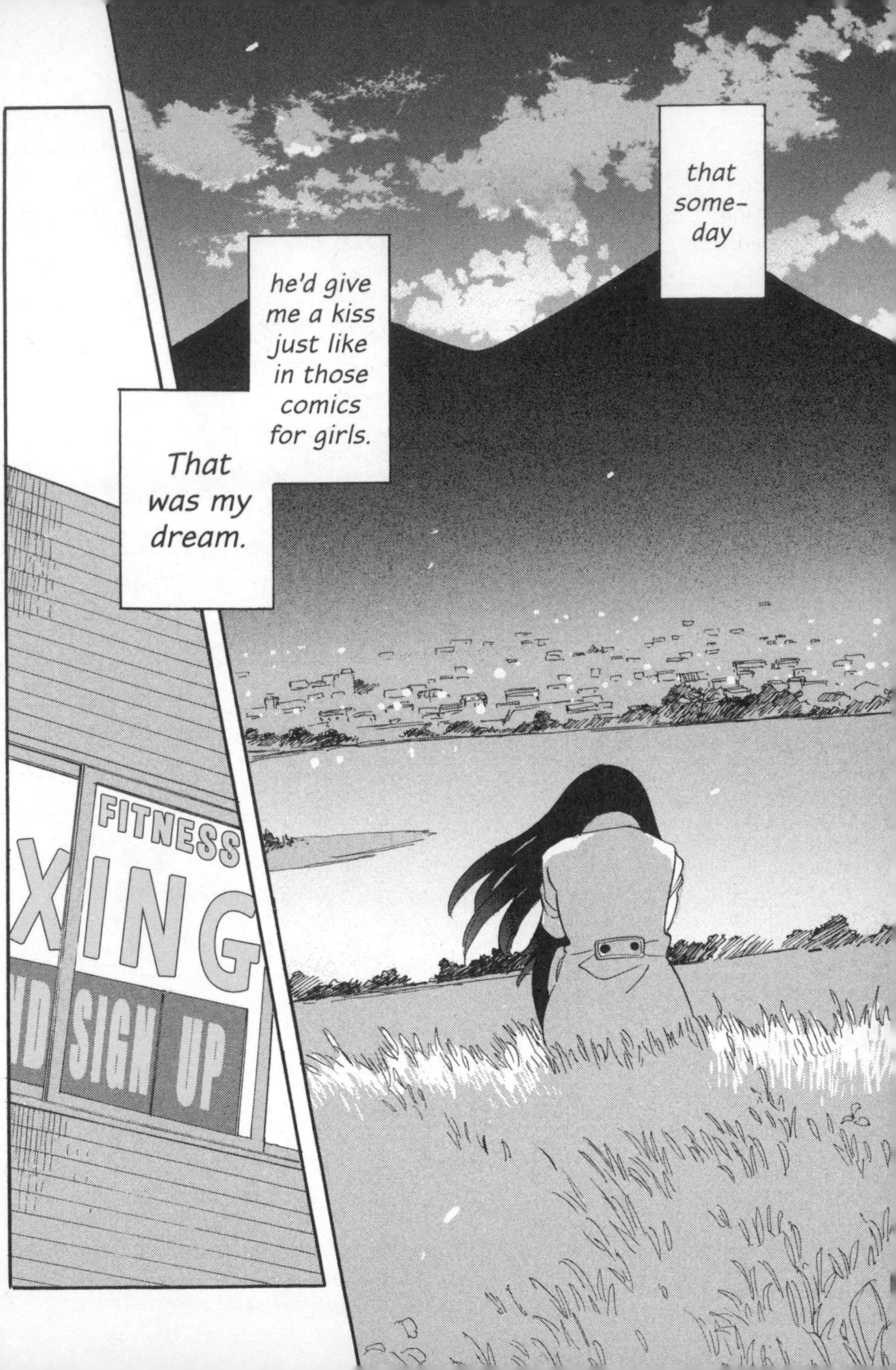
that some-day
he'd give me a kiss just like in those comics for girls.
That was my dream.
FITNESS
XING
SIGN UP

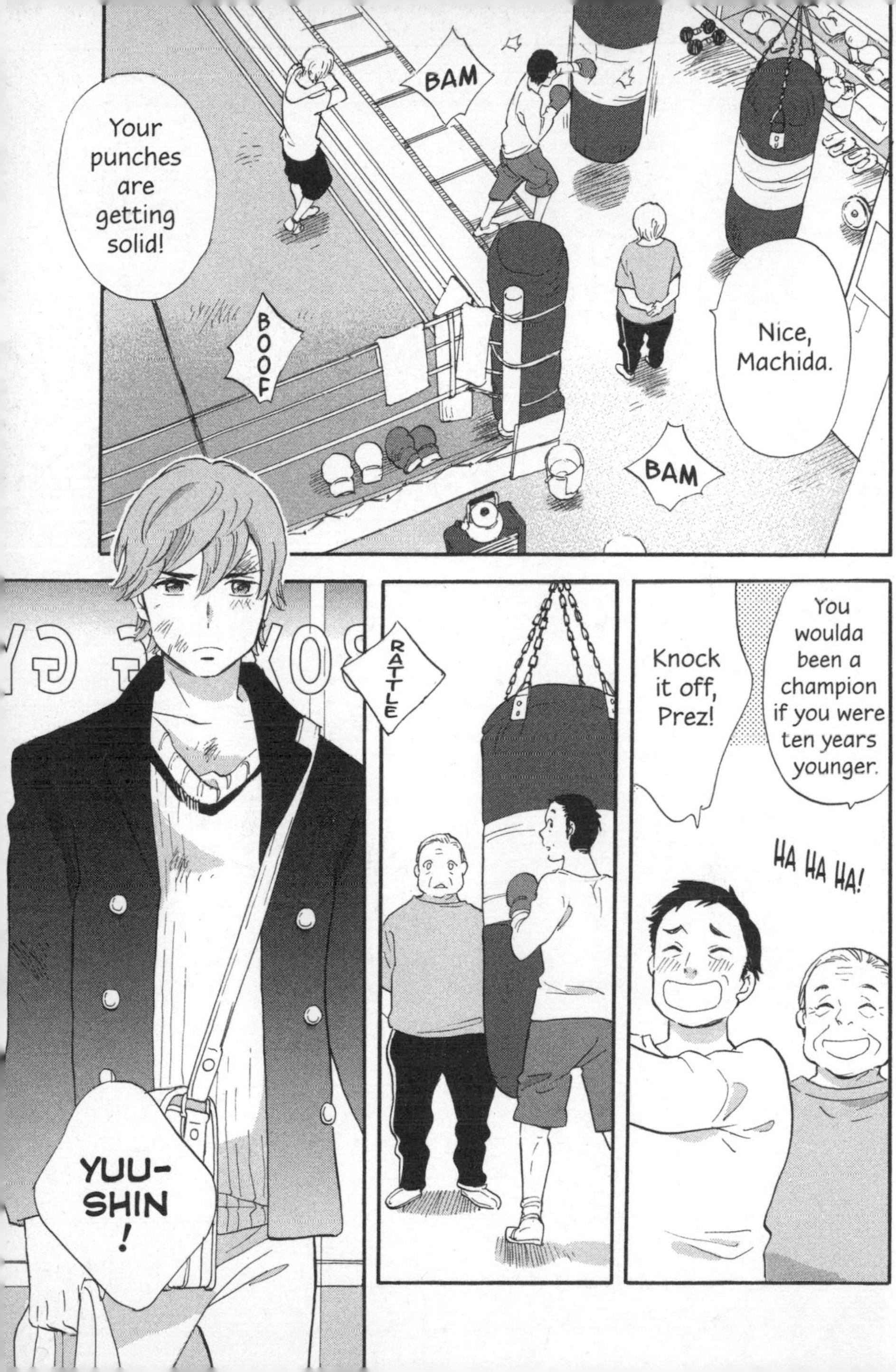
BAM
Nice, Machida.
Your punches are getting solid!
BOOF
BAM
You woulda been a champion if you were ten years younger.
Knock it off, Prez!
HA HA HA!
RATTLE
YUU-SHIN!

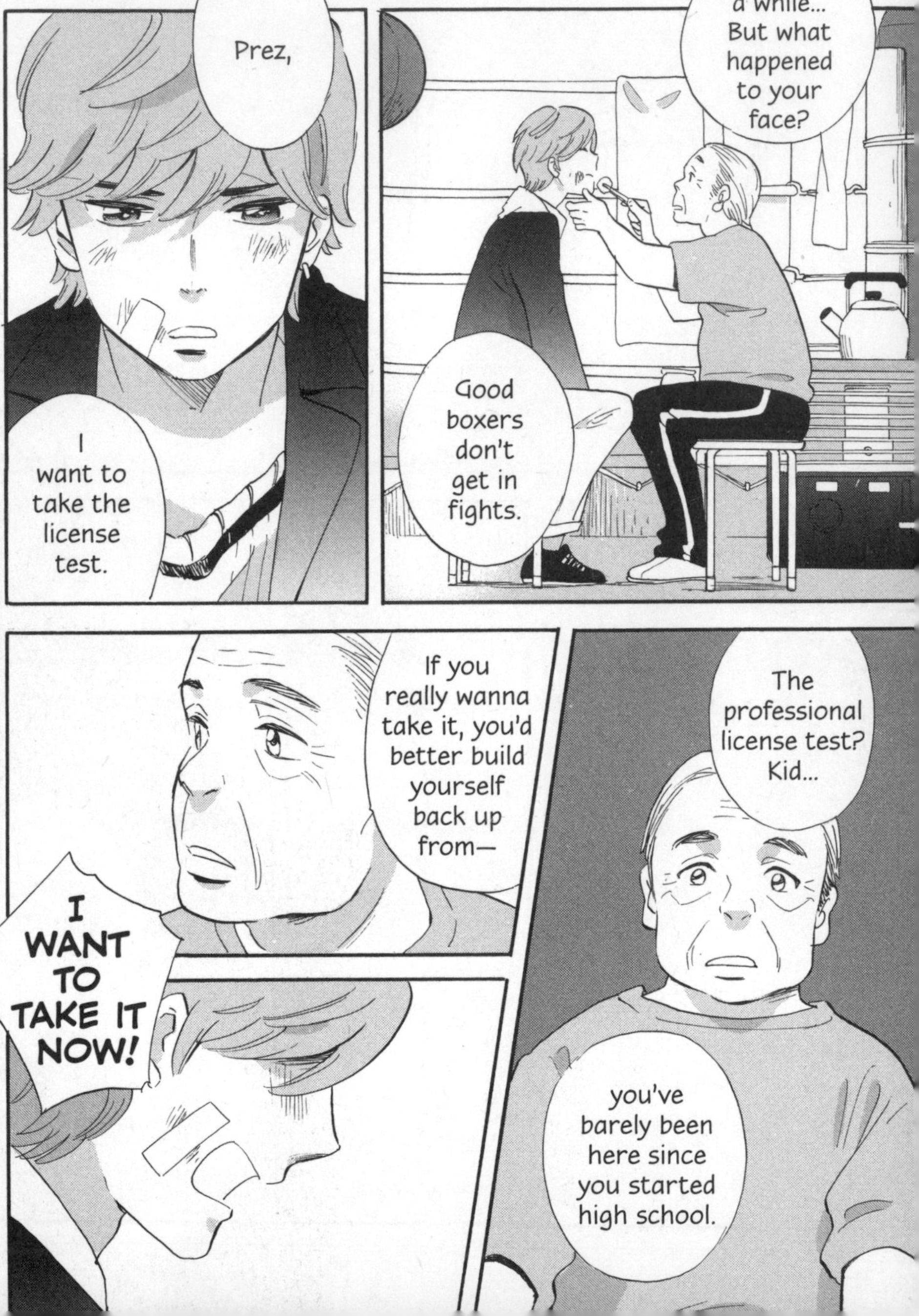
It's been a while... But what happened to your face?
Good boxers don't get in fights.
Prez,
I want to take the license test.
The professional license test? Kid...
you've barely been here since you started high school.
If you really wanna take it, you'd better build yourself back up from—
I WANT TO TAKE IT NOW!

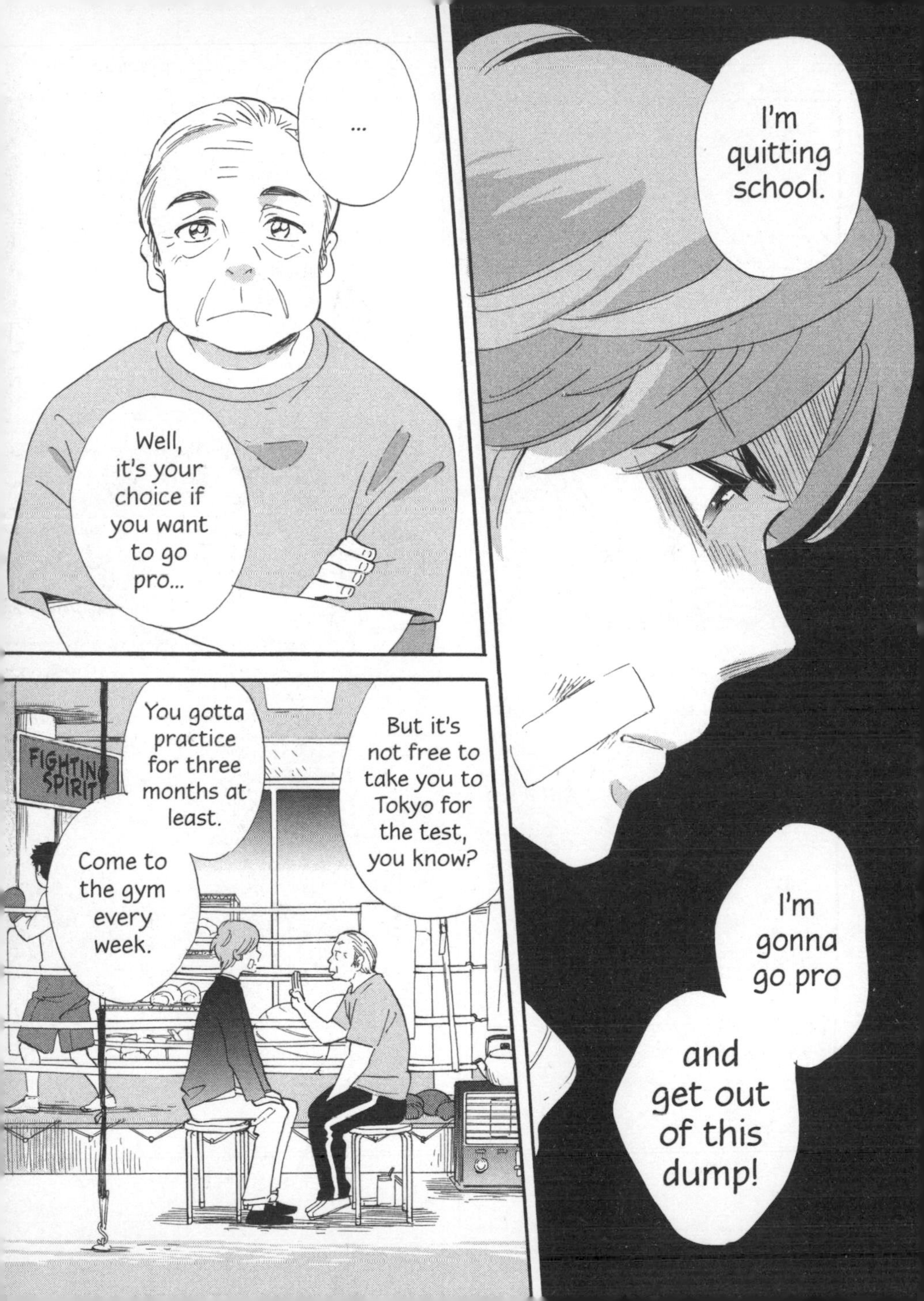
I'm quitting school.
I'm gonna go pro
and get out of this dump!
...
Well, it's your choice if you want to go pro...
But it's not free to take you to Tokyo for the test, you know?
You gotta practice for three months at least.
FIGHTING SPIRIT
Come to the gym every week.

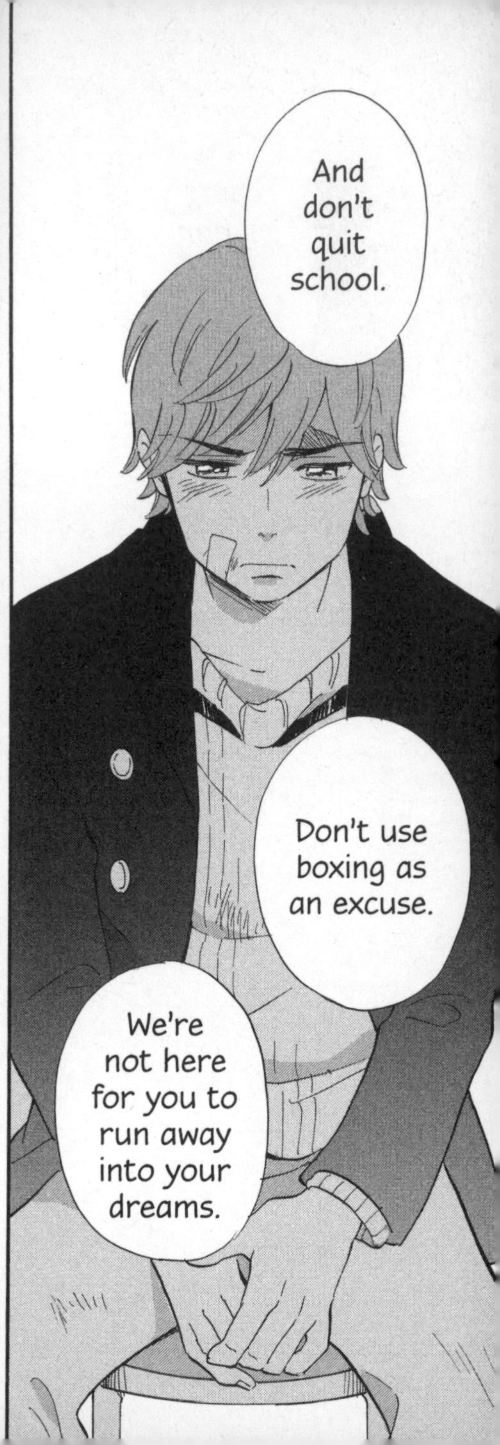
And don't quit school.
Don't use boxing as an excuse.
We're not here for you to run away into your dreams.

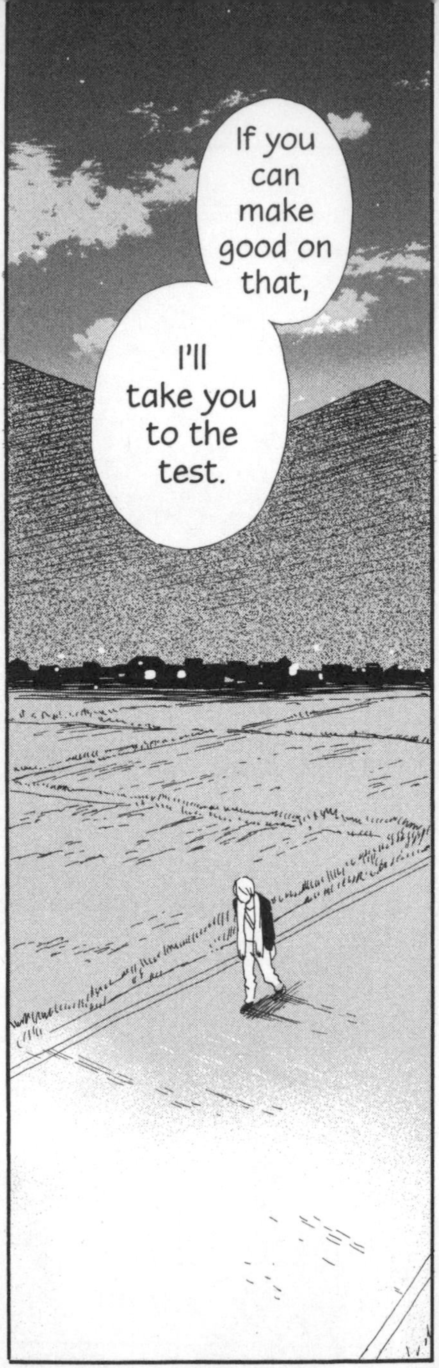
If you can make good on that,
I'll take you to the test.

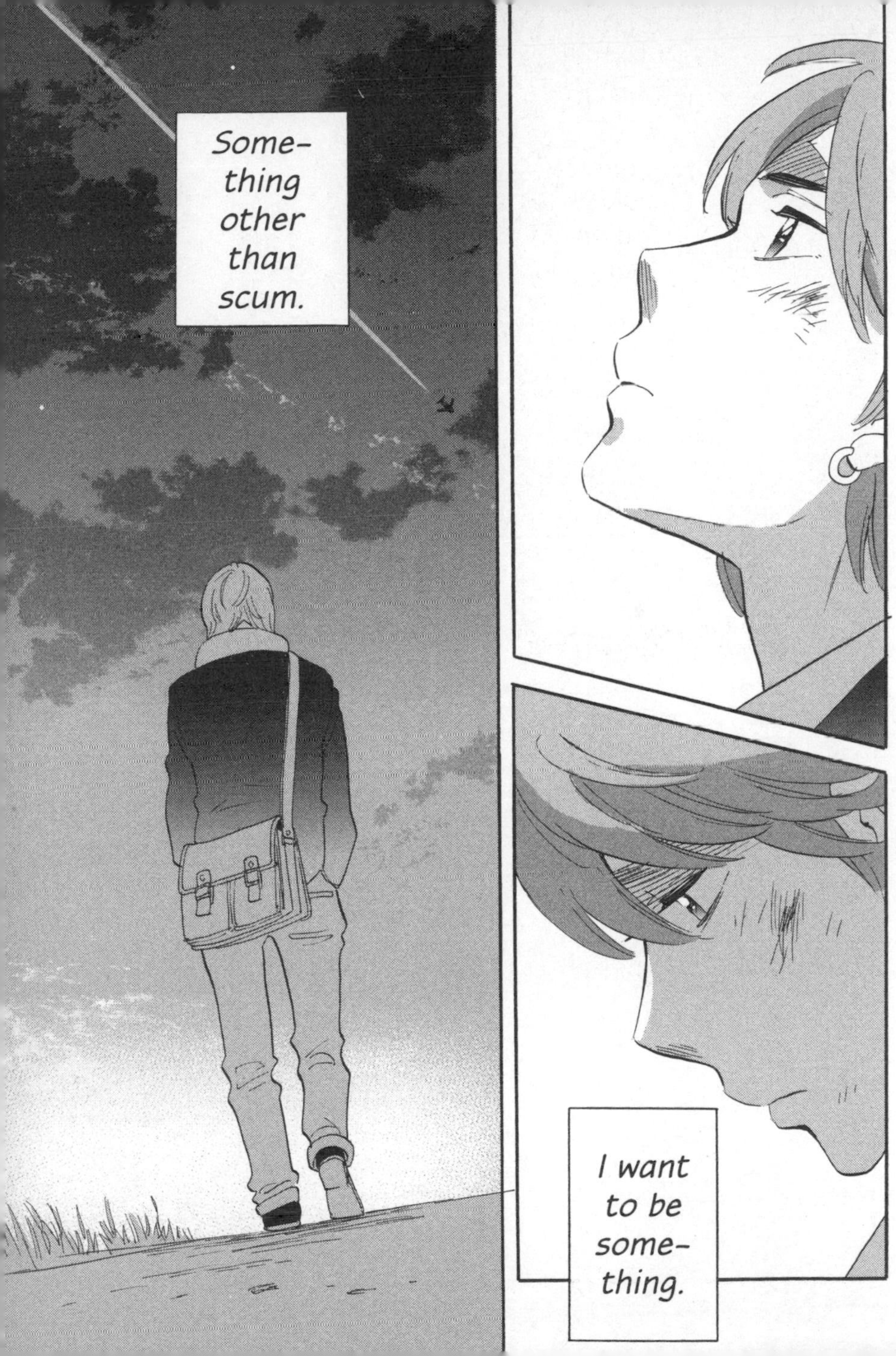
I want to be some-thing.
Some-thing other than scum.

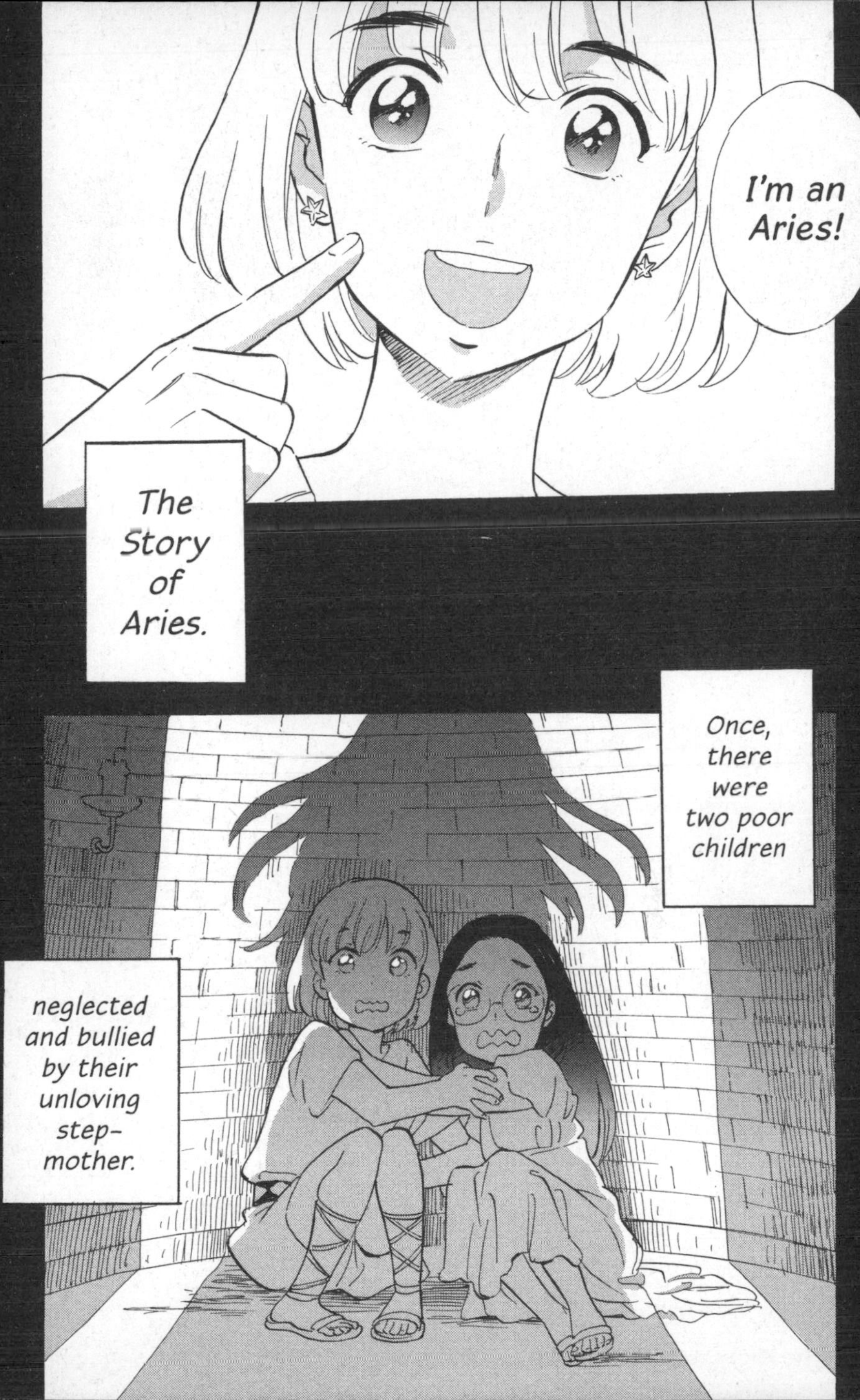
I'm an Aries!
The Story of Aries.
Once, there were two poor children
neglected and bullied by their unloving step-mother.

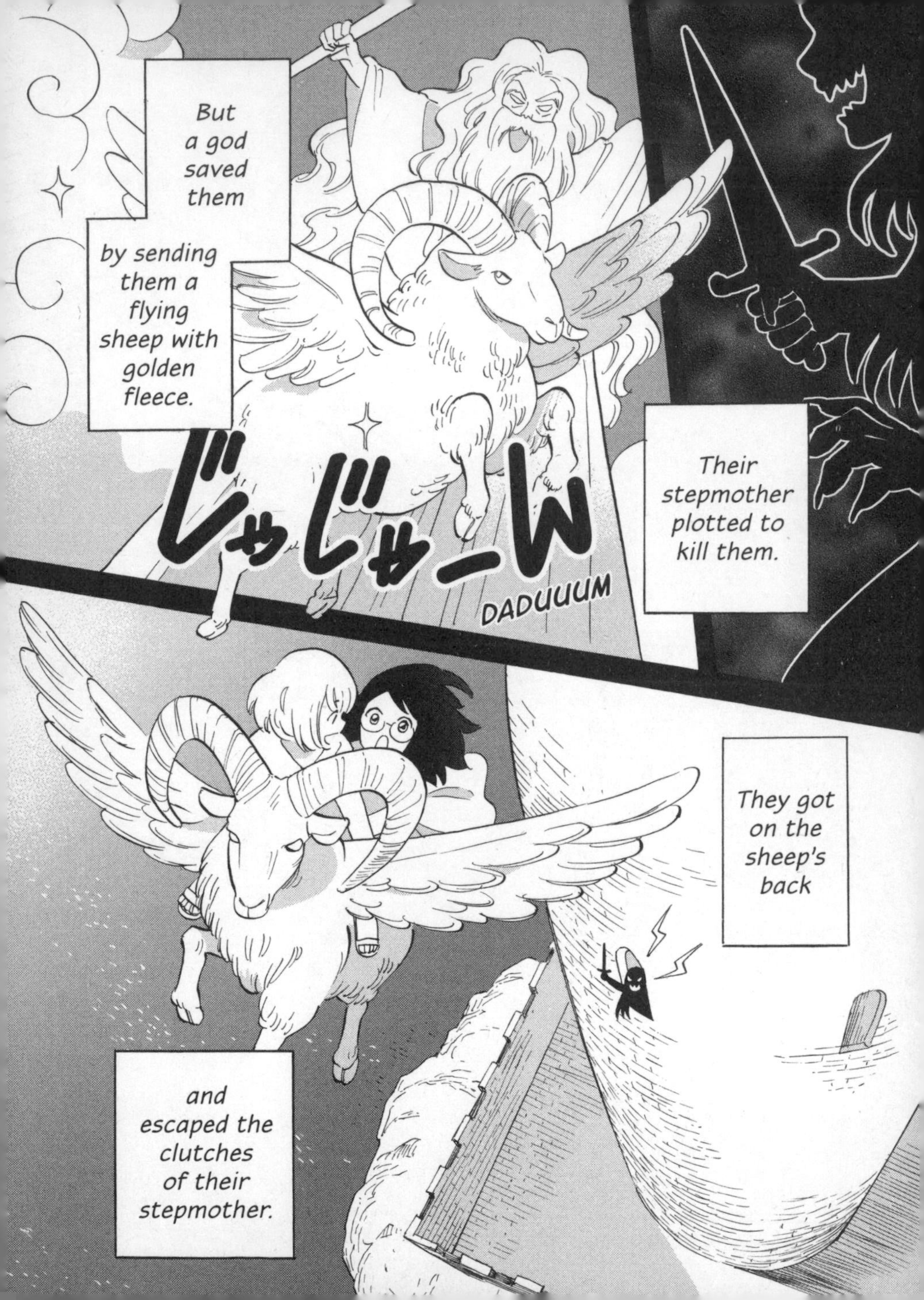
Their stepmother plotted to kill them.
But a god saved them
by sending them a flying sheep with golden fleece.
じゃじゃーん
DADUUUM
They got on the sheep's back
and escaped the clutches of their stepmother.

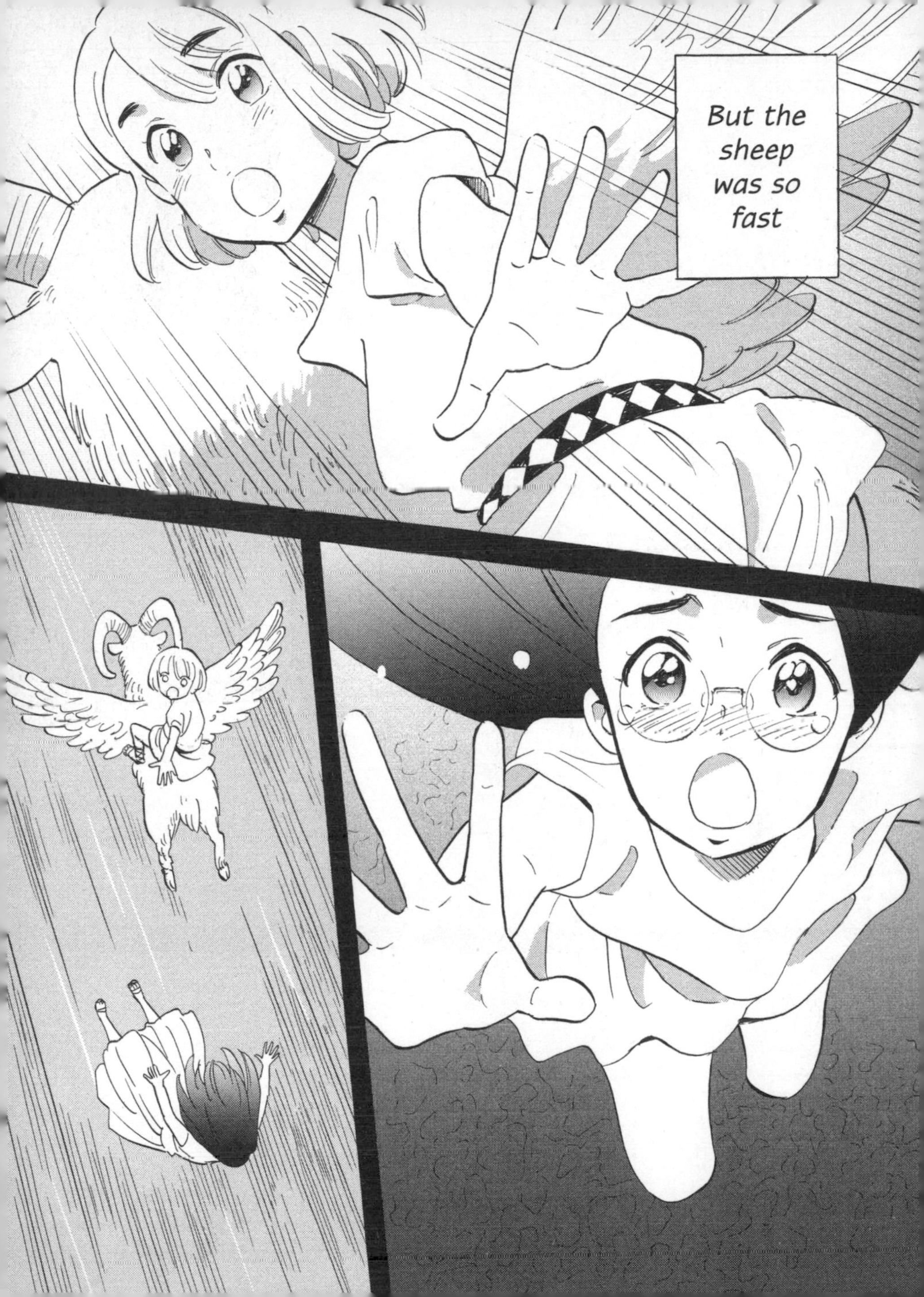
But the sheep was so fast

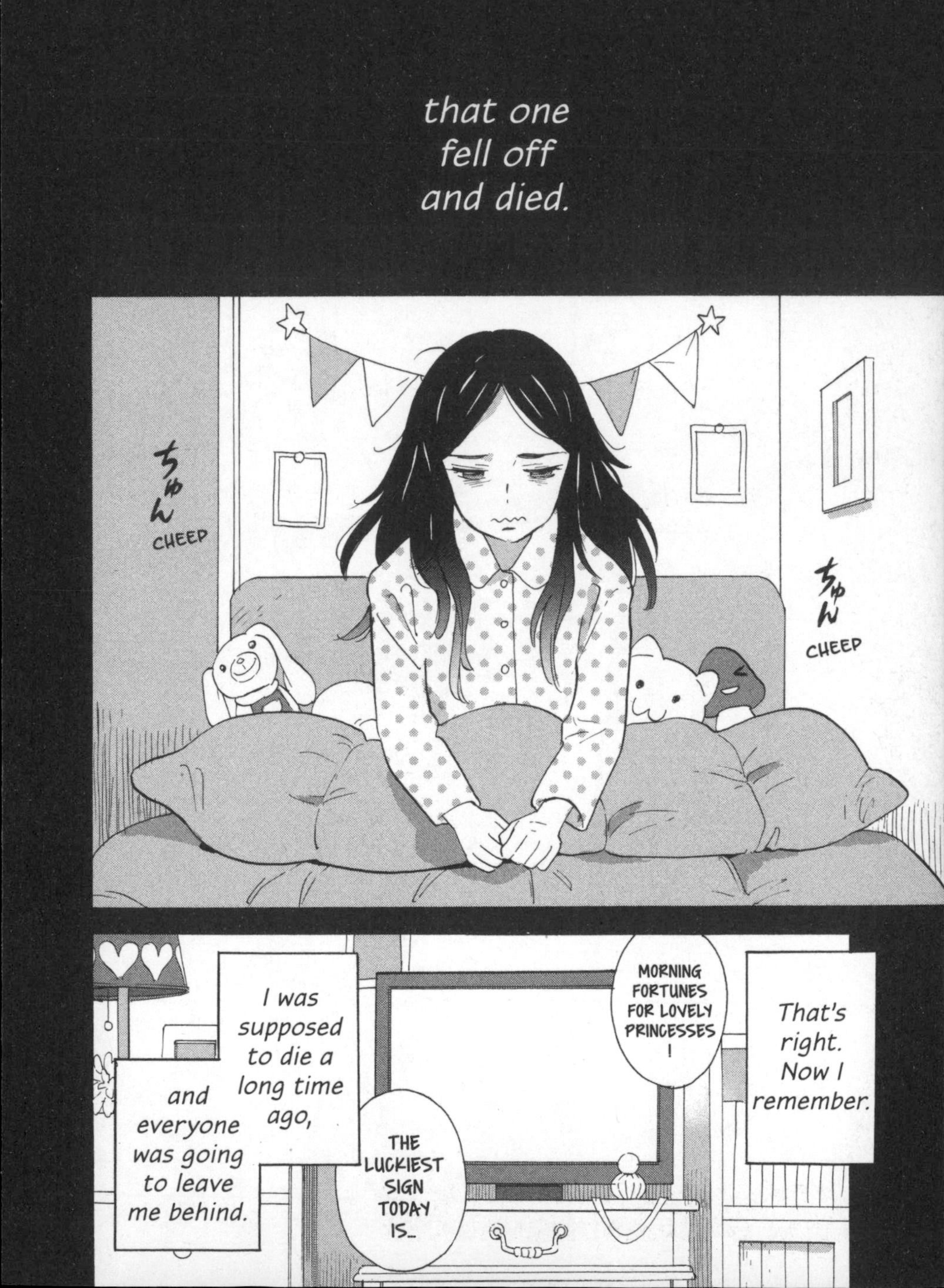
that one fell off and died.
ちゅん CHEEP
ちゅん CHEEP
That's right. Now I remember.
MORNING FORTUNES FOR LOVELY PRINCESSES!
I was supposed to die a long time ago,
THE LUCKIEST SIGN TODAY IS…
and everyone was going to leave me behind.

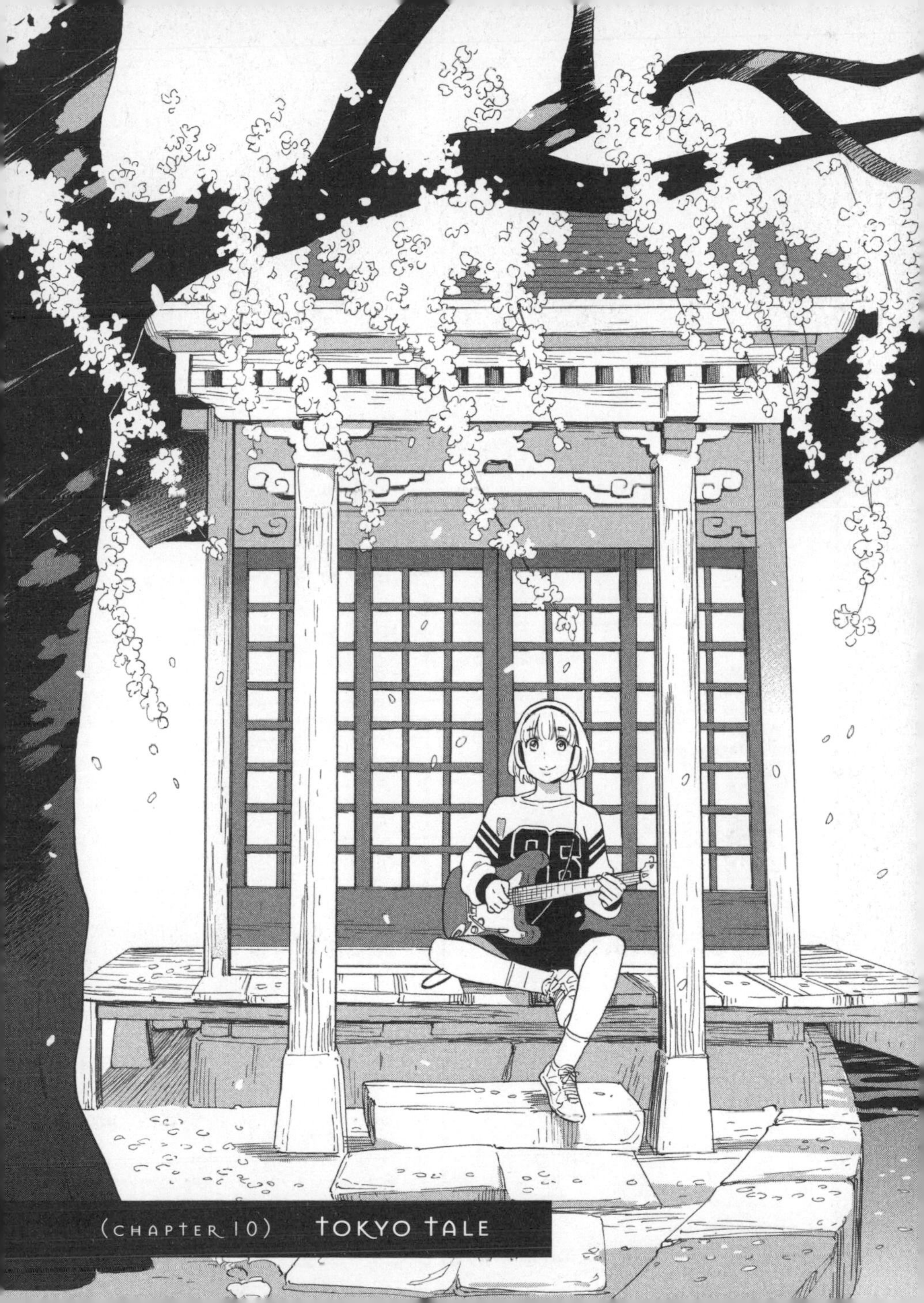

(CHAPTER 10) TOKYO TALE

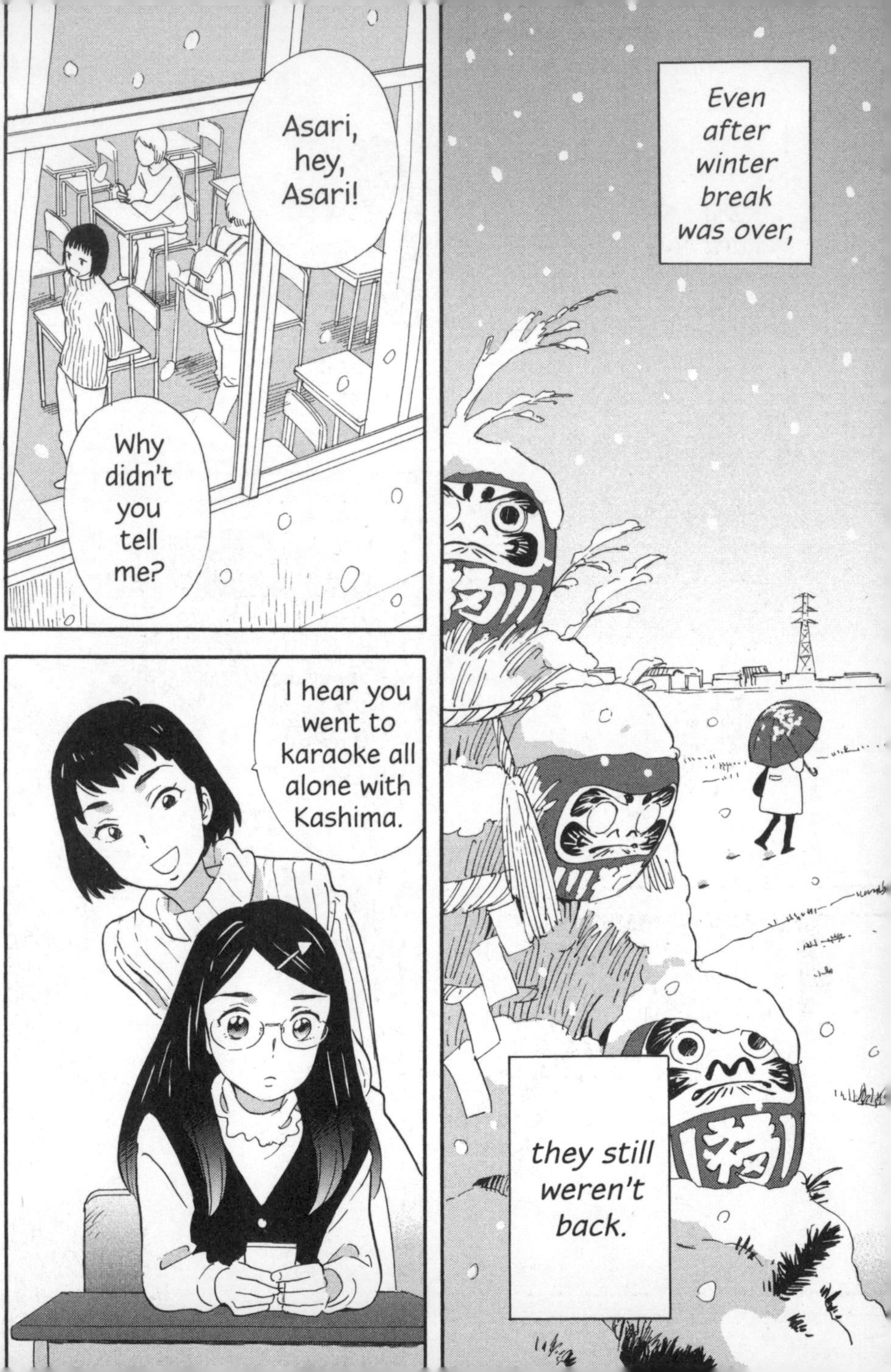
Even after winter break was over,
they still weren't back.
Asari, hey, Asari!
Why didn't you tell me?
I hear you went to karaoke all alone with Kashima.

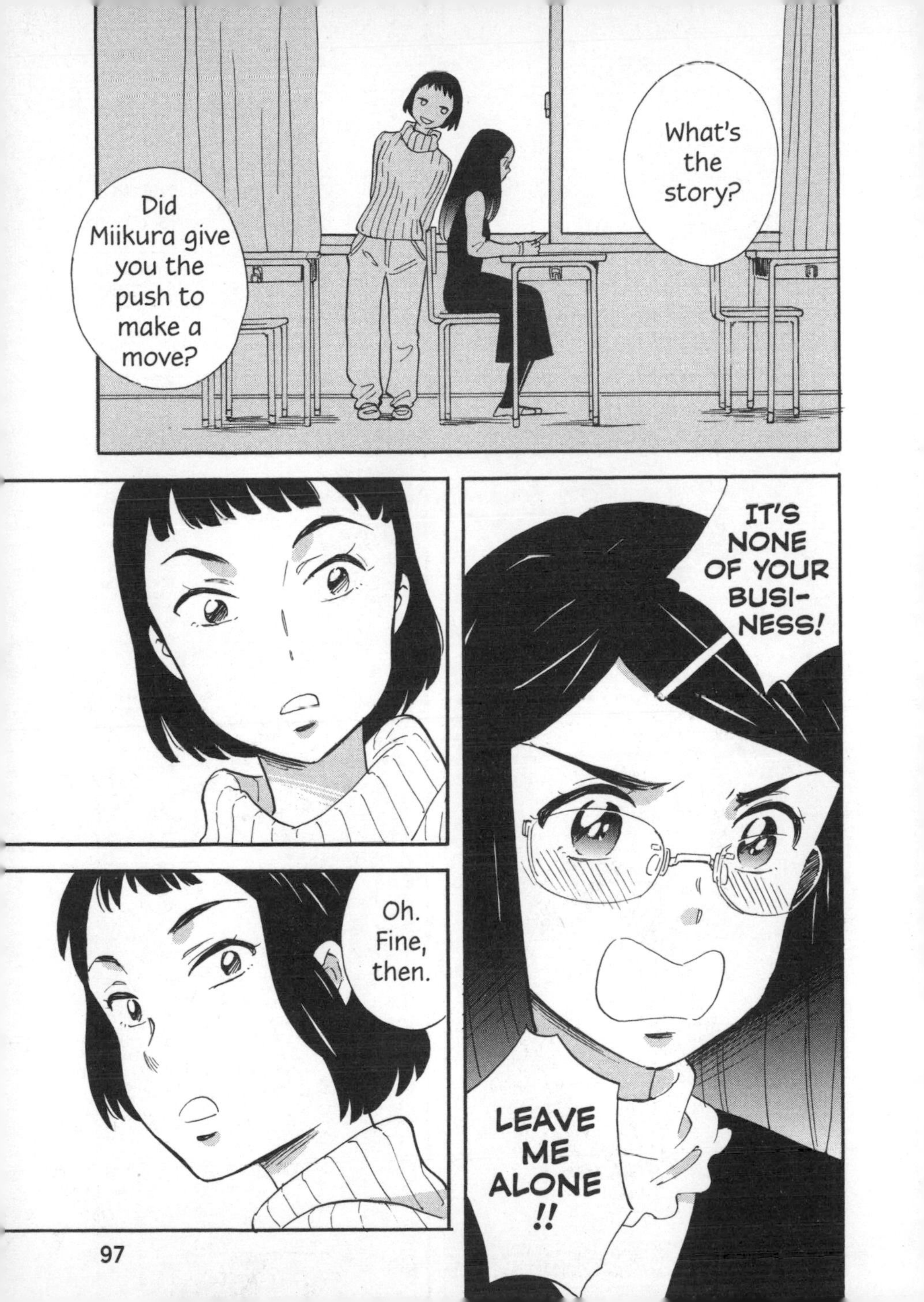
What's the story?
Did Miikura give you the push to make a move?
IT'S NONE OF YOUR BUSI-NESS!
LEAVE ME ALONE!!
Oh. Fine, then.

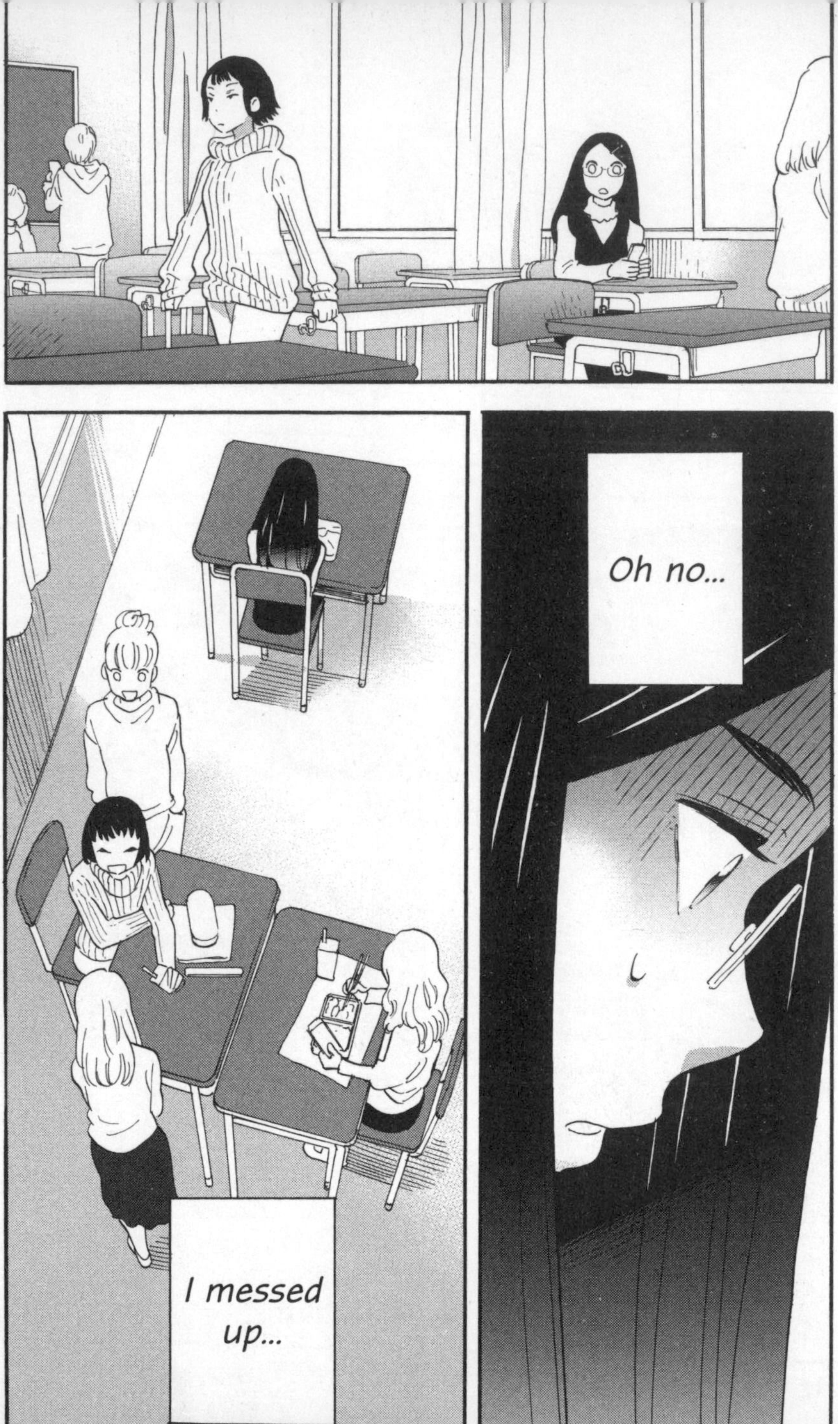
Oh no...
I messed up...

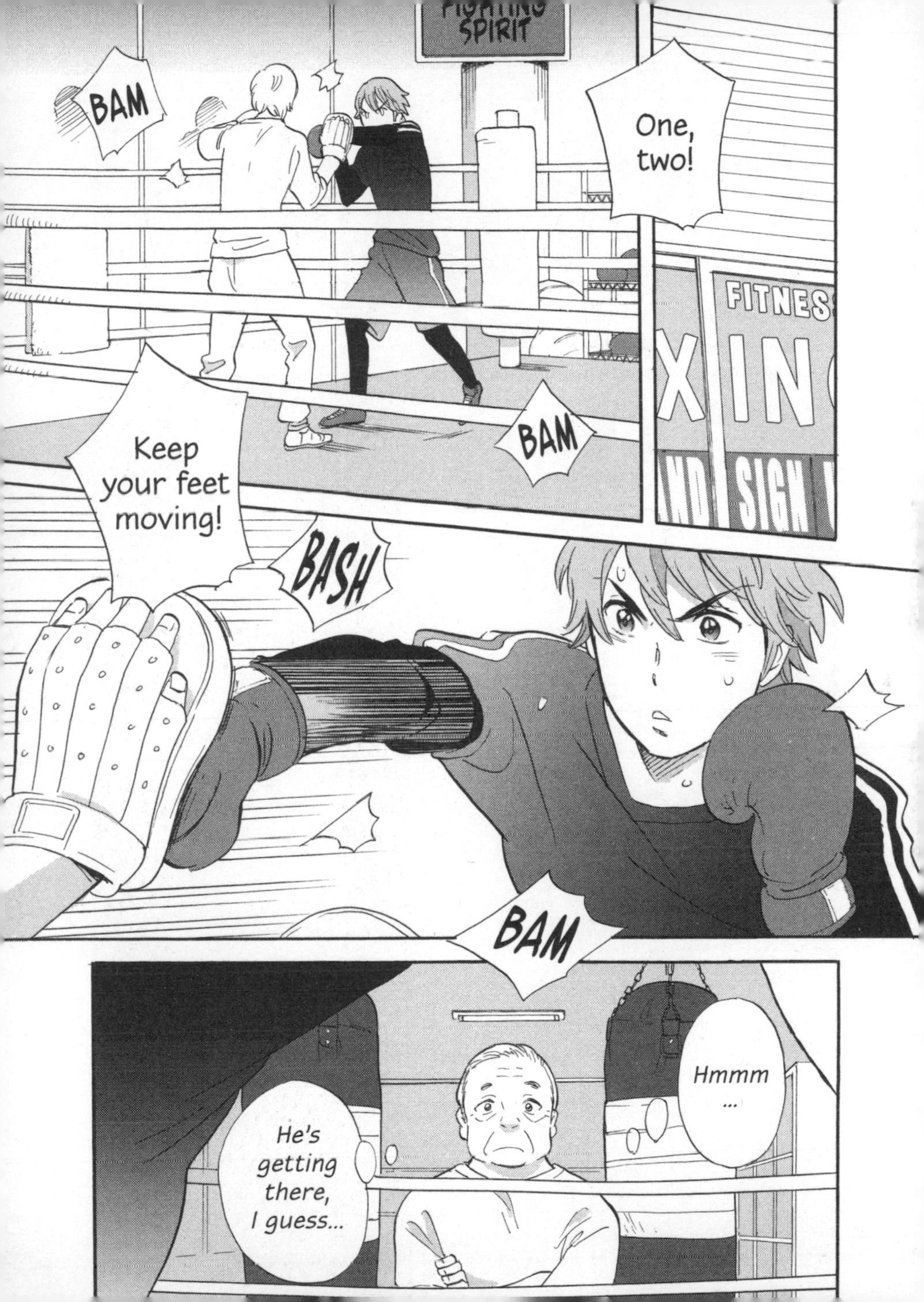
One, two!
SPIRIT
BAM
BAM
Keep your feet moving!
BASH
BAM
Hmmm ...
He's getting there, I guess...

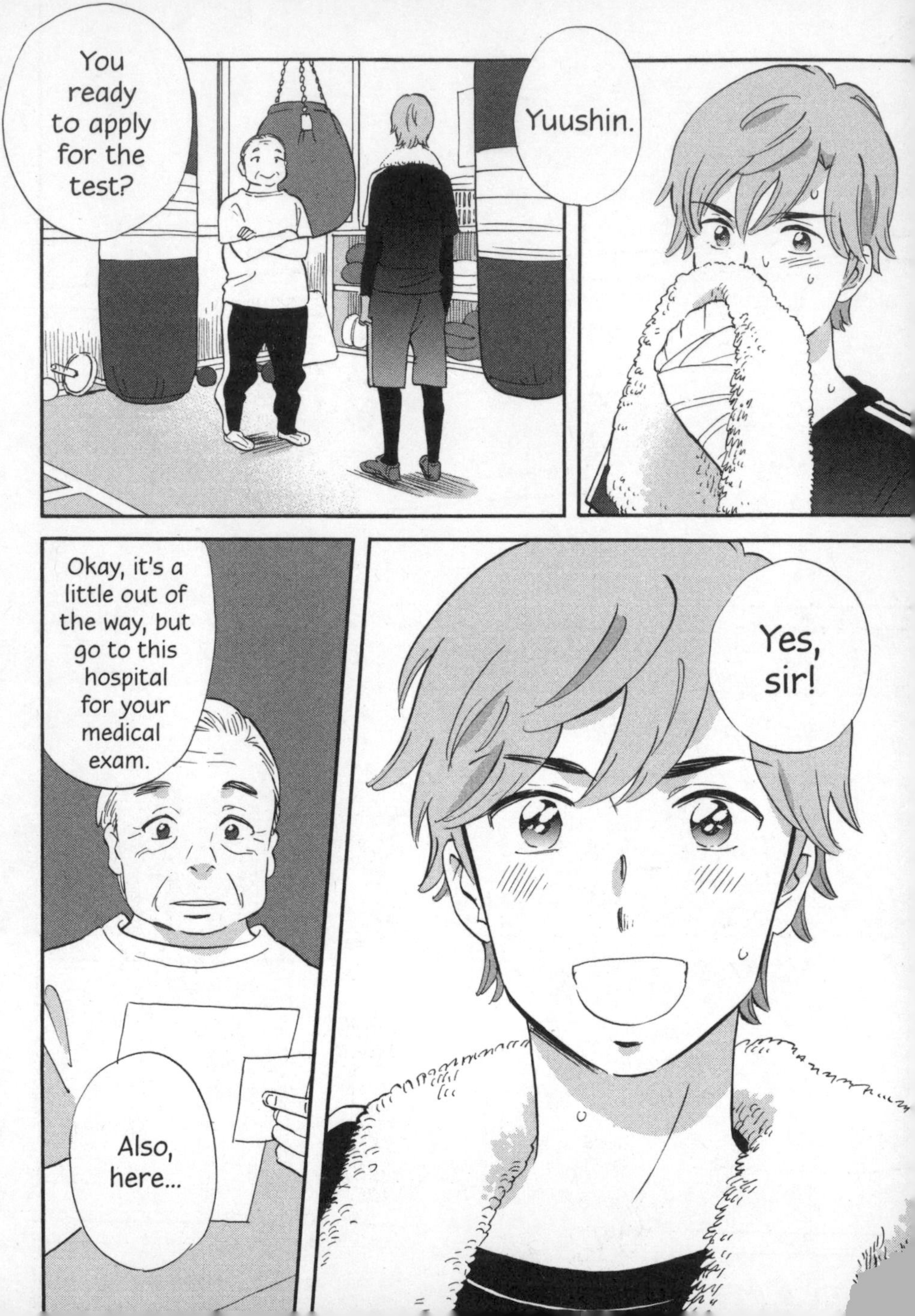
Yuushin.
You ready to apply for the test?
Yes, sir!
Okay, it's a little out of the way, but go to this hospital for your medical exam.
Also, here...

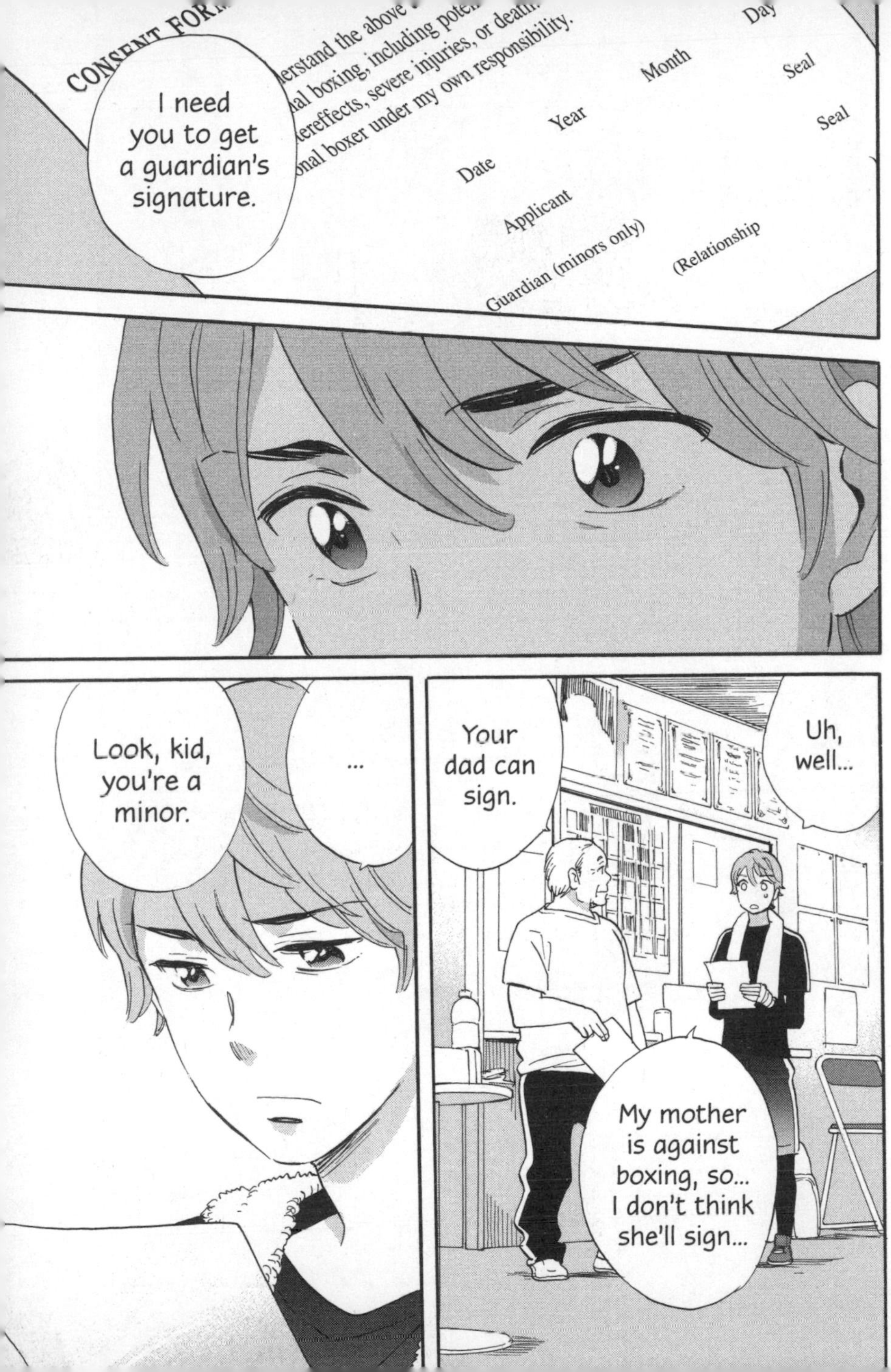
CONSENT FOR
erstand the above
al boxing, including pote
ereffects, severe injuries, or deat
nal boxer under my own responsibility.
Date
Year
Month
Day
Seal
Applicant
Seal
Guardian (minors only)
(Relationship)
I need you to get a guardian's signature.
Uh, well...
Your dad can sign.
My mother is against boxing, so... I don't think she'll sign...
...
Look, kid, you're a minor.

You need
your parents'
permission
to do
anything.

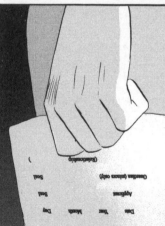

Yuushin,
welcome
home...

...

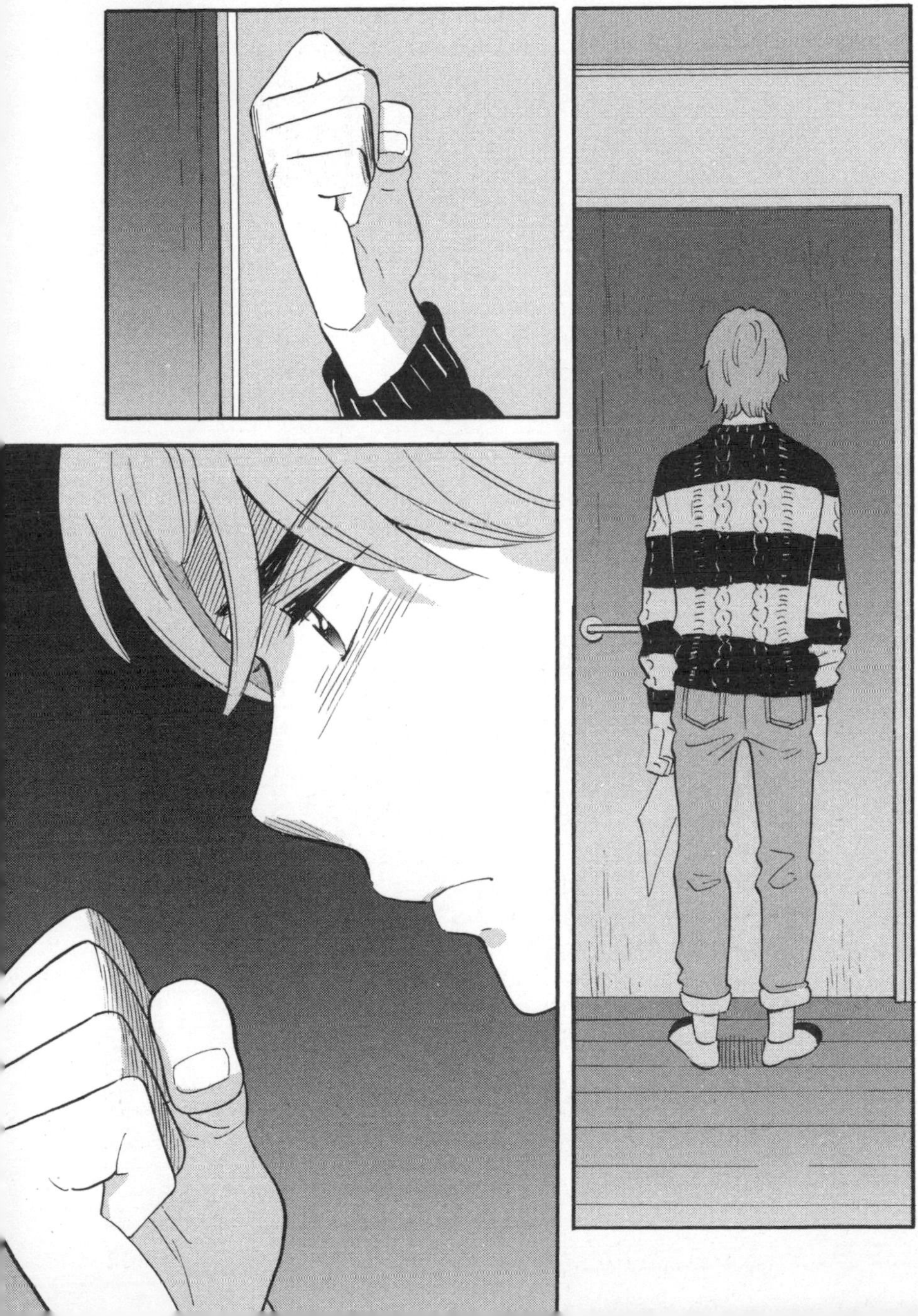

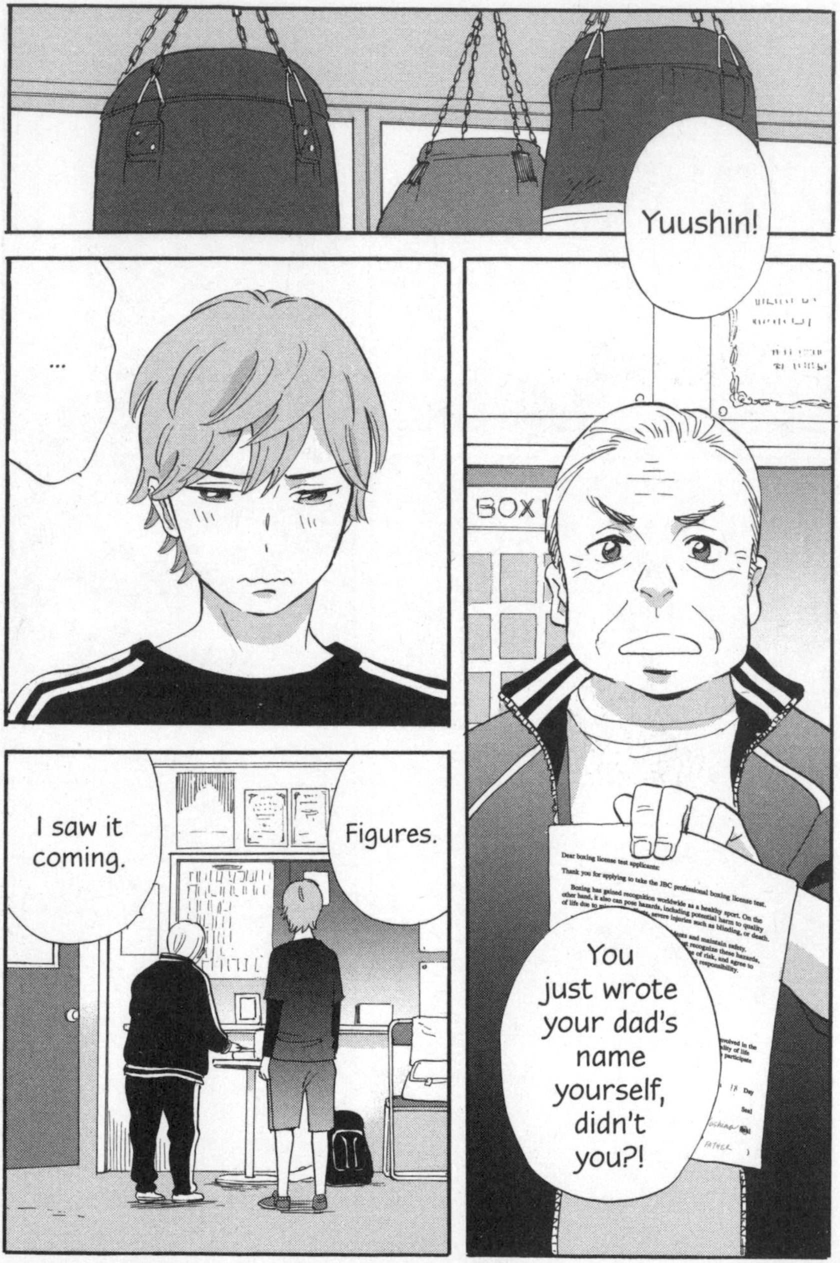
Yuushin!
Dear boxing license test applicants:
Thank you for applying to take the JBC professional boxing license test.
Boxing has gained recognition worldwide as a healthy sport. On the other hand, it also can pose hazards, including potential harm to quality
You just wrote your dad's name yourself, didn't you?!
...
Figures.
I saw it coming.
BOX

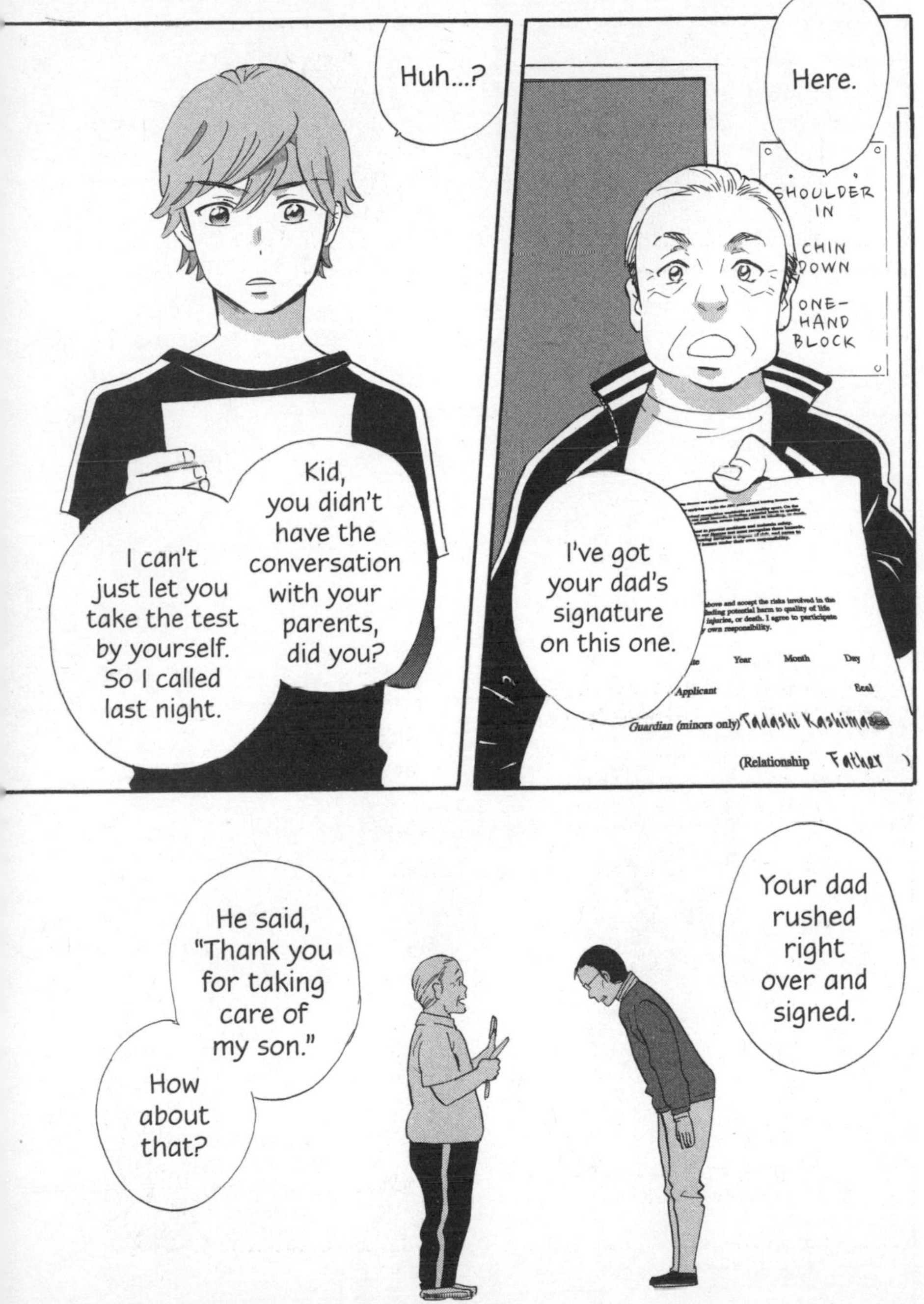

Here.
SHOULDER IN
CHIN DOWN
ONE-HAND BLOCK
I've got your dad's signature on this one.
Year Month Day
Applicant Seal
Guardian (minors only) Tadashi Kashima
(Relationship Father)
Huh...?
Kid, you didn't have the conversation with your parents, did you?
I can't just let you take the test by yourself. So I called last night.
Your dad rushed right over and signed.
He said, "Thank you for taking care of my son."
How about that?

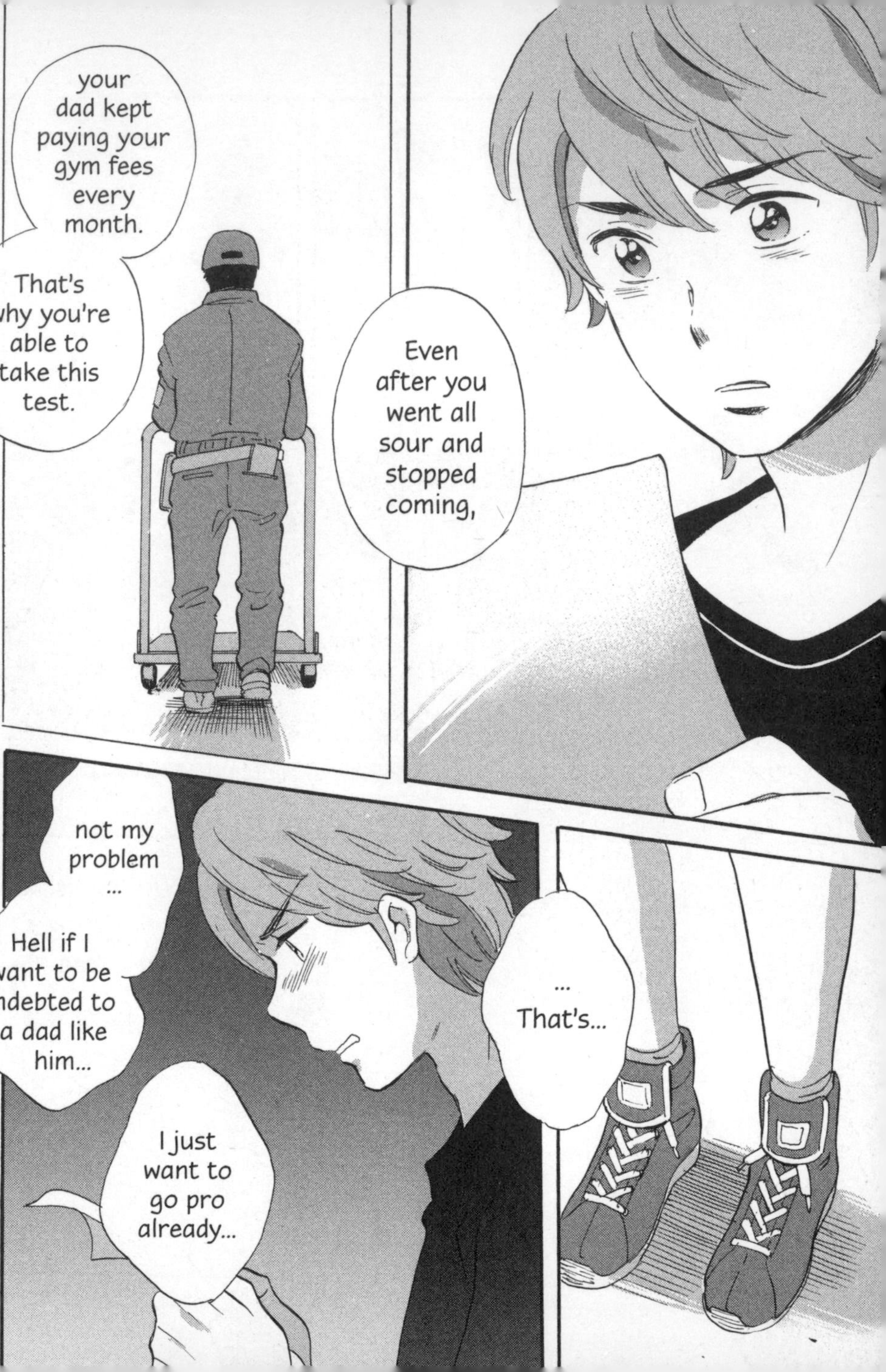
Even after you went all sour and stopped coming,
your dad kept paying your gym fees every month.
That's why you're able to take this test.
... That's...
not my problem ...
Hell if I want to be indebted to a dad like him...
I just want to go pro already...

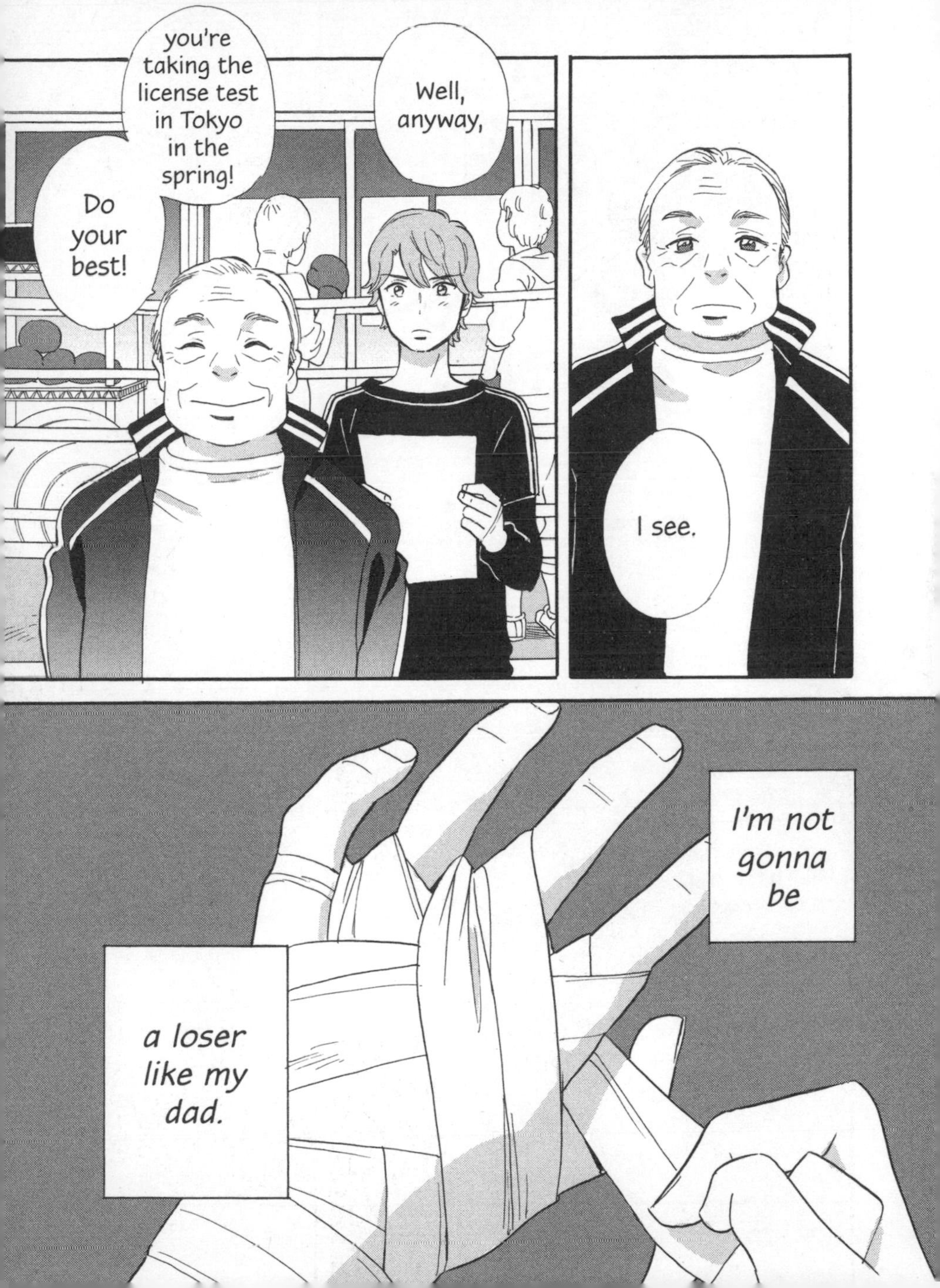
I see.
Well, anyway,
you're taking the license test in Tokyo in the spring!
Do your best!
I'm not gonna be
a loser like my dad.

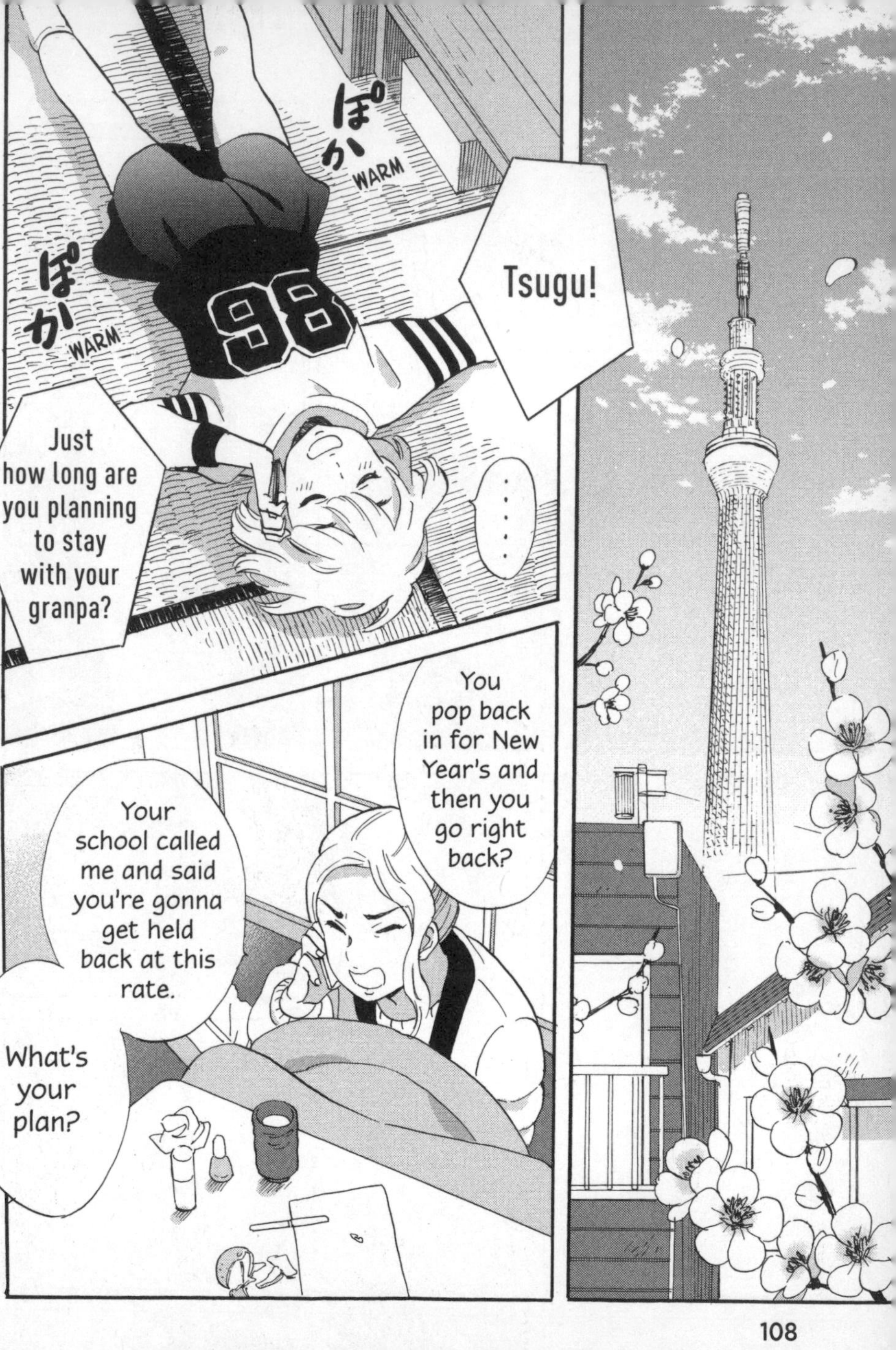

Tsugu!
ぽか WARM
ぽか WARM
......
Just how long are you planning to stay with your granpa?
You pop back in for New Year's and then you go right back?
Your school called me and said you're gonna get held back at this rate.
What's your plan?

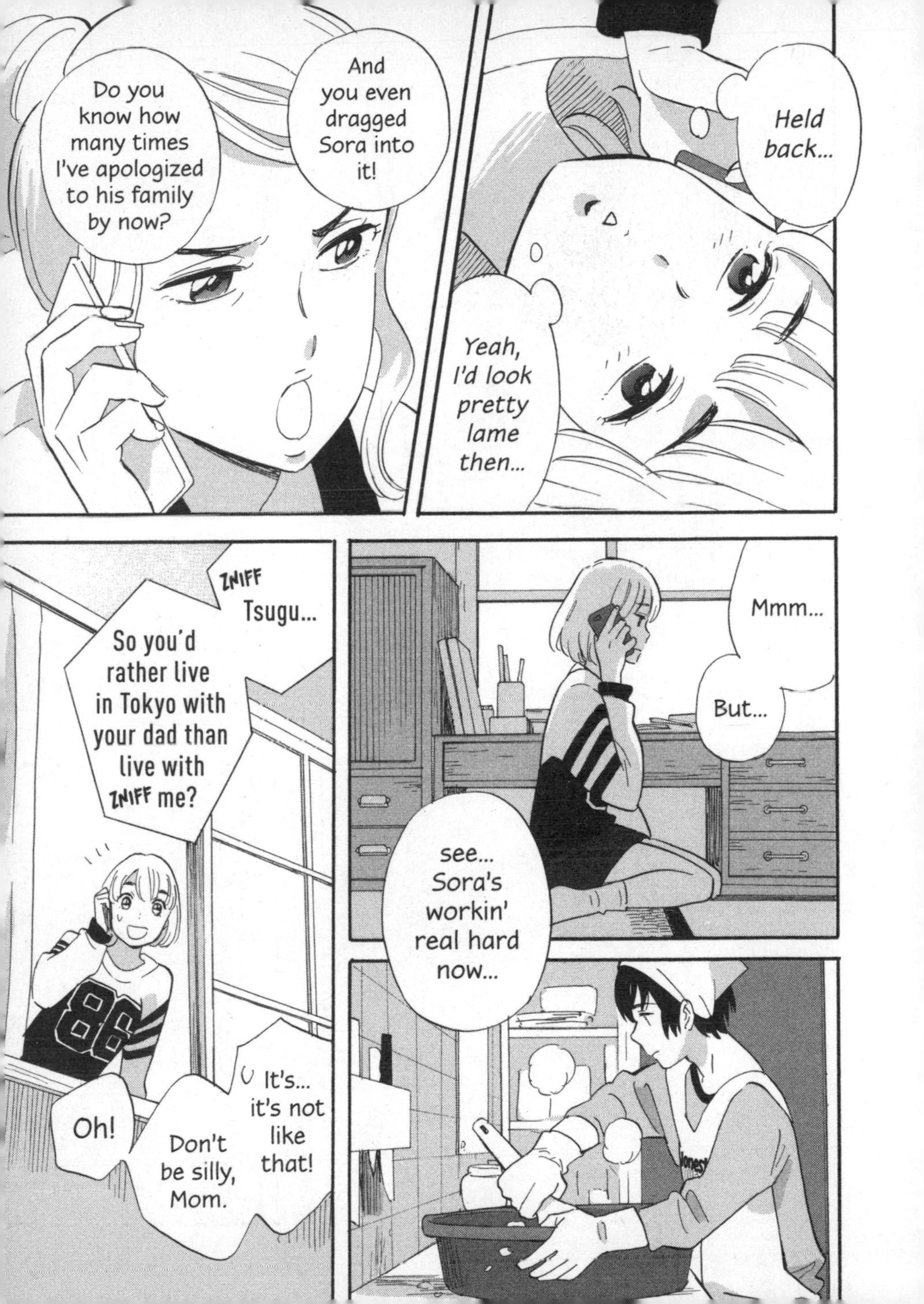
Held back...
Yeah, I'd look pretty lame then...
And you even dragged Sora into it!
Do you know how many times I've apologized to his family by now?
Mmm...
But...
see... Sora's workin' real hard now...
ZNIFF
Tsugu...
So you'd rather live in Tokyo with your dad than live with ZNIFF me?
It's... it's not like that!
Don't be silly, Mom.
Oh!

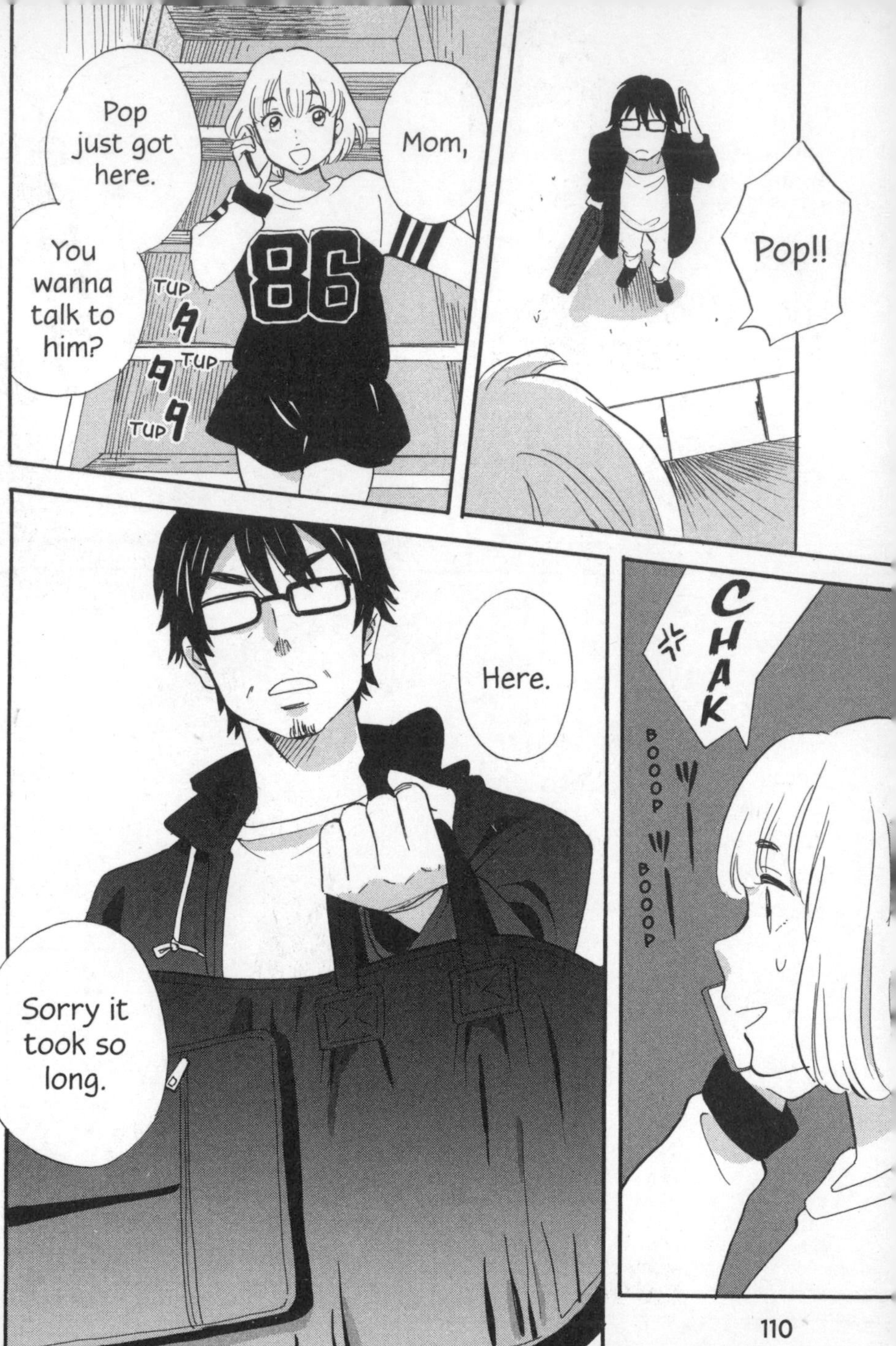
Pop!!
Mom,
Pop just got here.
You wanna talk to him?
TUP
TUP
TUP
CHAK
BOOOP
BOOOP
Here.
Sorry it took so long.

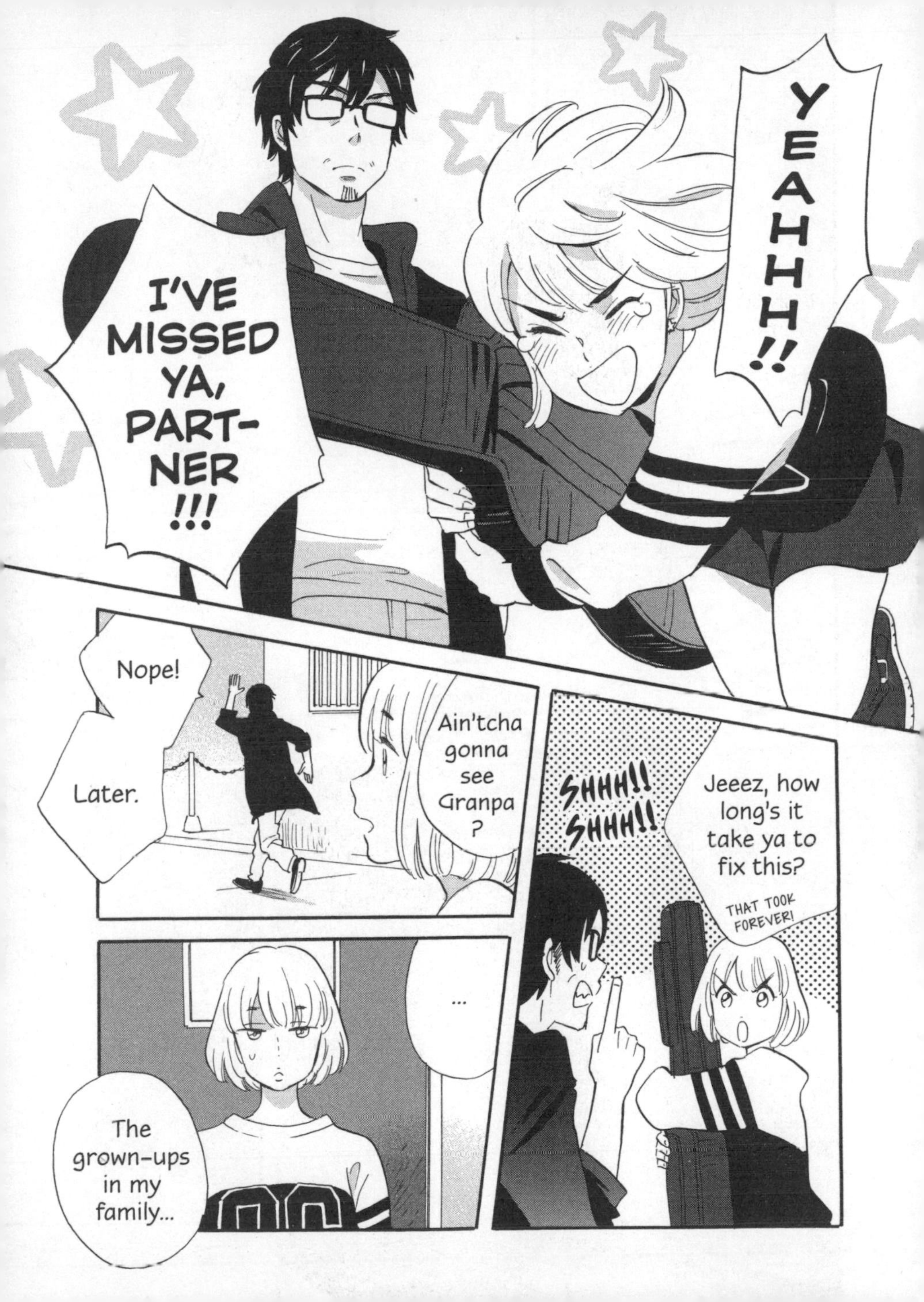
YEAHHH!!
I'VE MISSED YA, PARTNER!!!
Jeeez, how long's it take ya to fix this?
SHHH!! SHHH!!
THAT TOOK FOREVER!
Ain'tcha gonna see Granpa?
Nope!
Later.
...
The grown-ups in my family...

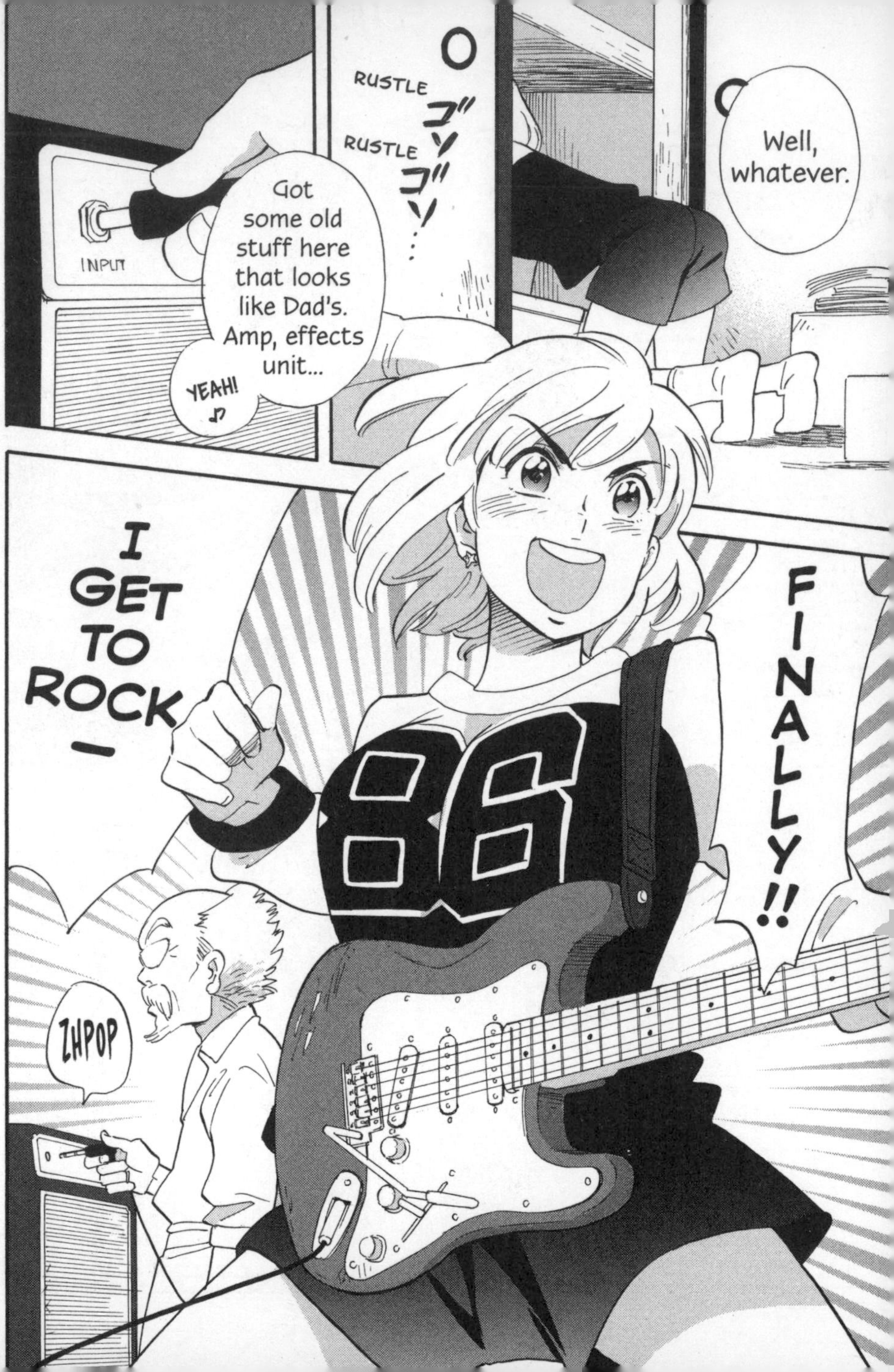
Well, whatever.
RUSTLE ゴソ
RUSTLE ゴソ...
INPUT
Got some old stuff here that looks like Dad's. Amp, effects unit...
YEAH! ♪
I GET TO ROCK—
FINALLY!!
ZHPOP

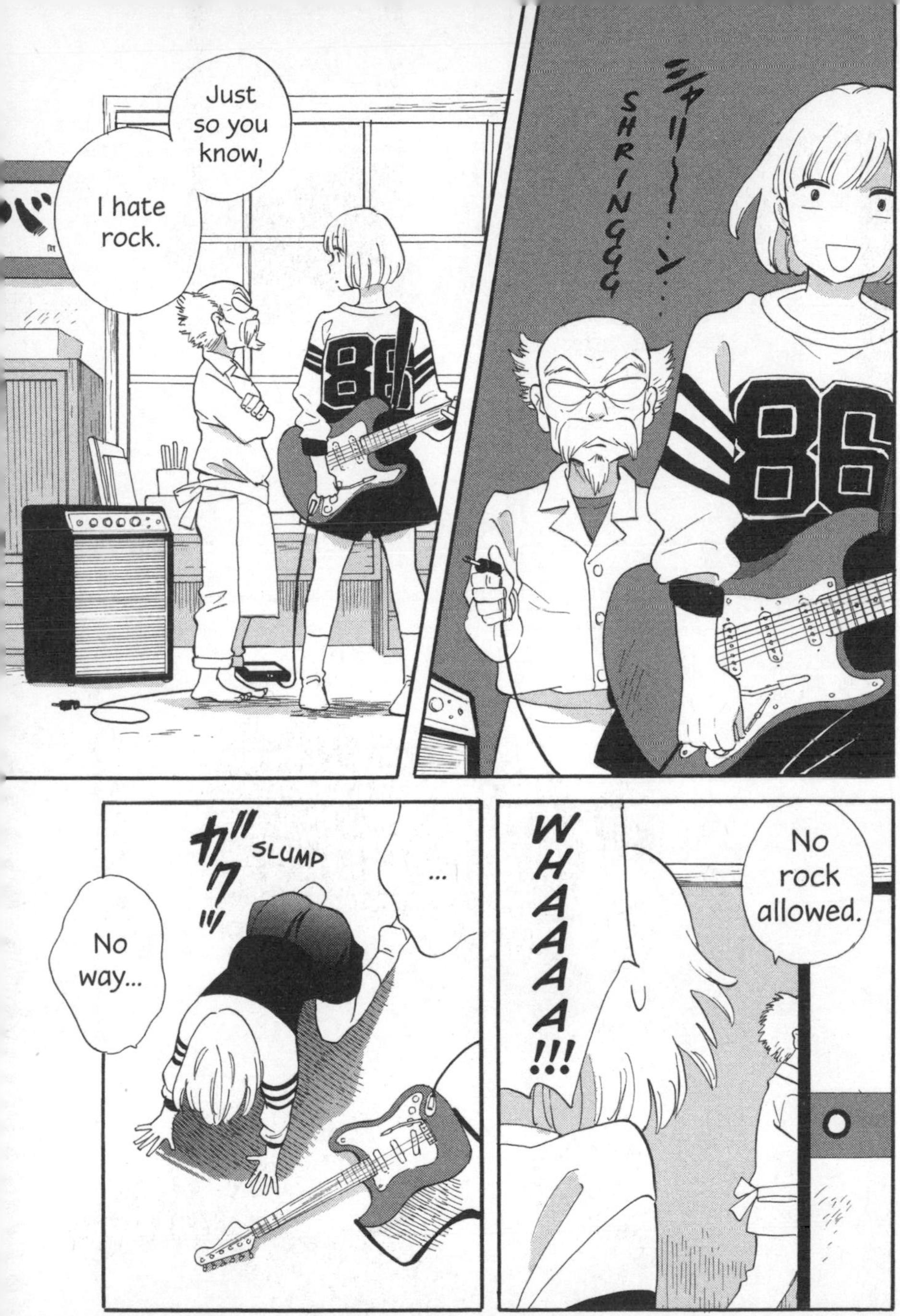
SHRINGGG
Just so you know,
I hate rock.
WHAAAAA!!!
No rock allowed.
SLUMP
...
No way...

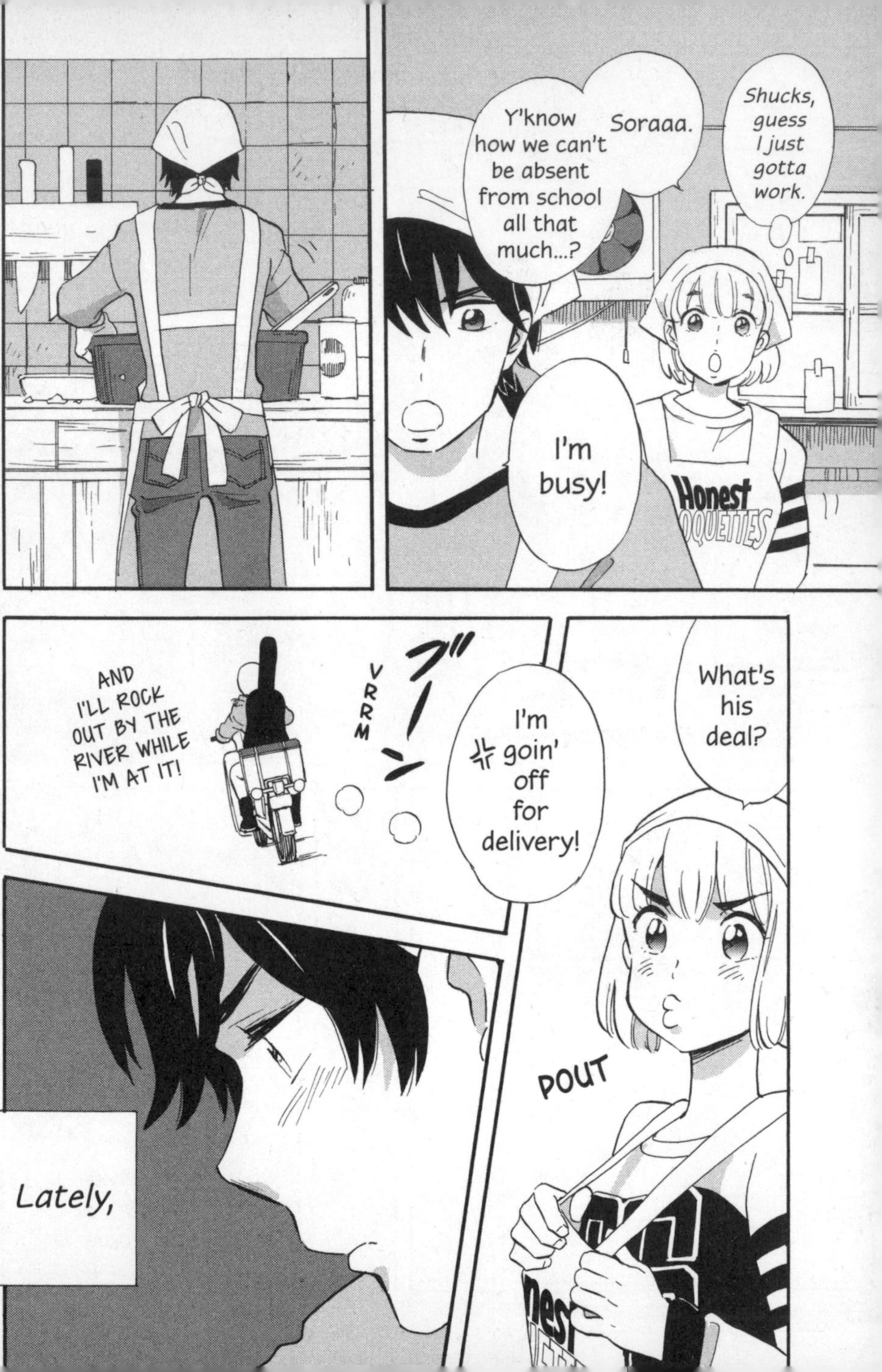
Shucks, guess I just gotta work.
Soraaa.
Y'know how we can't be absent from school all that much...?
I'm busy!
What's his deal?
I'm goin' off for delivery!
VRRM
AND I'LL ROCK OUT BY THE RIVER WHILE I'M AT IT!
POUT
Lately,

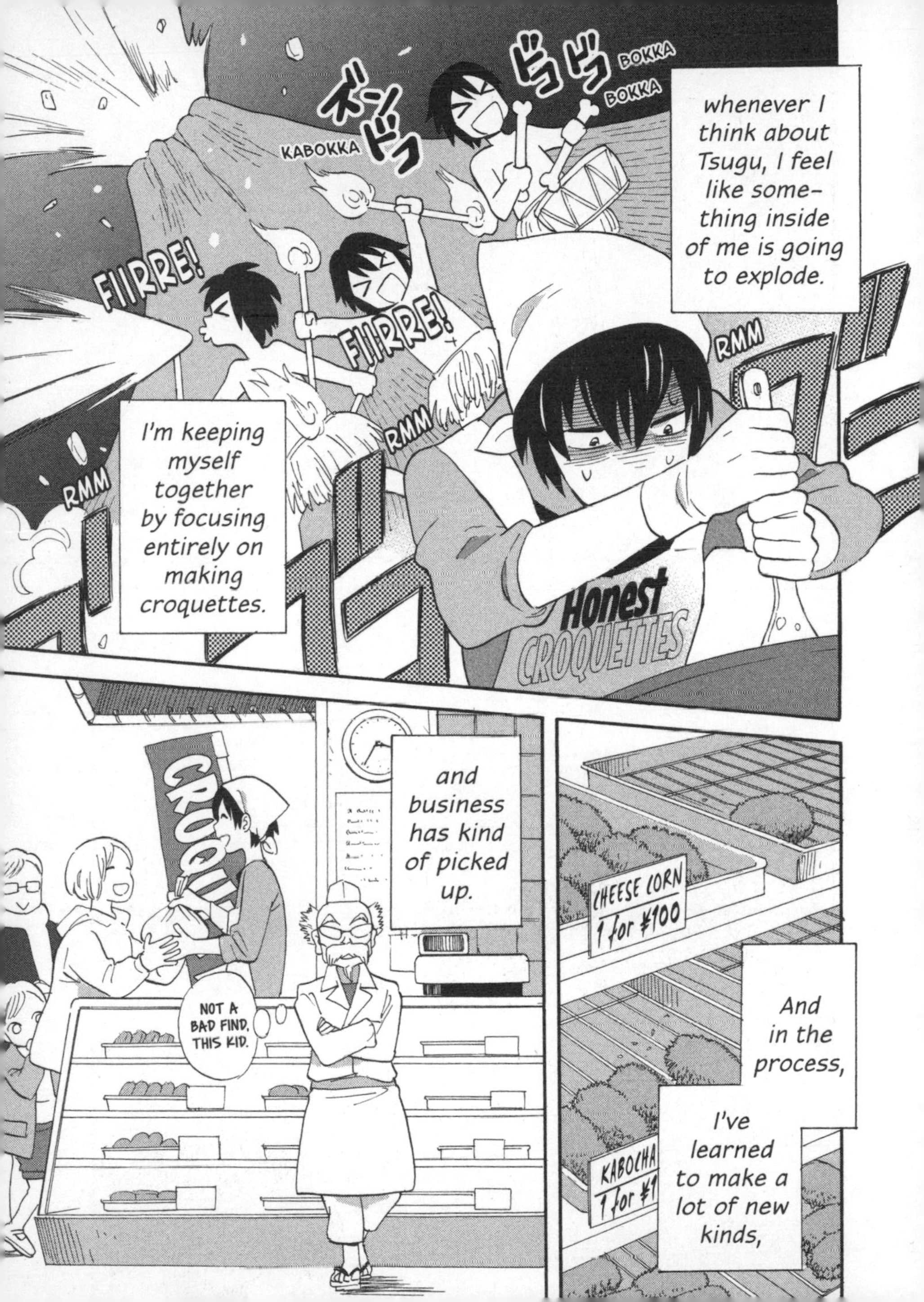
whenever I think about Tsugu, I feel like something inside of me is going to explode.
BOKKA
BOKKA
KABOKKA
FIIRRE!
FIIRRE!
RMM
RMM
RMM
I'm keeping myself together by focusing entirely on making croquettes.
Honest CROQUETTES
CROQU
and business has kind of picked up.
NOT A BAD FIND, THIS KID.
CHEESE CORN 1 for ¥100
KABOCHA 1 for ¥1
And in the process,
I've learned to make a lot of new kinds,

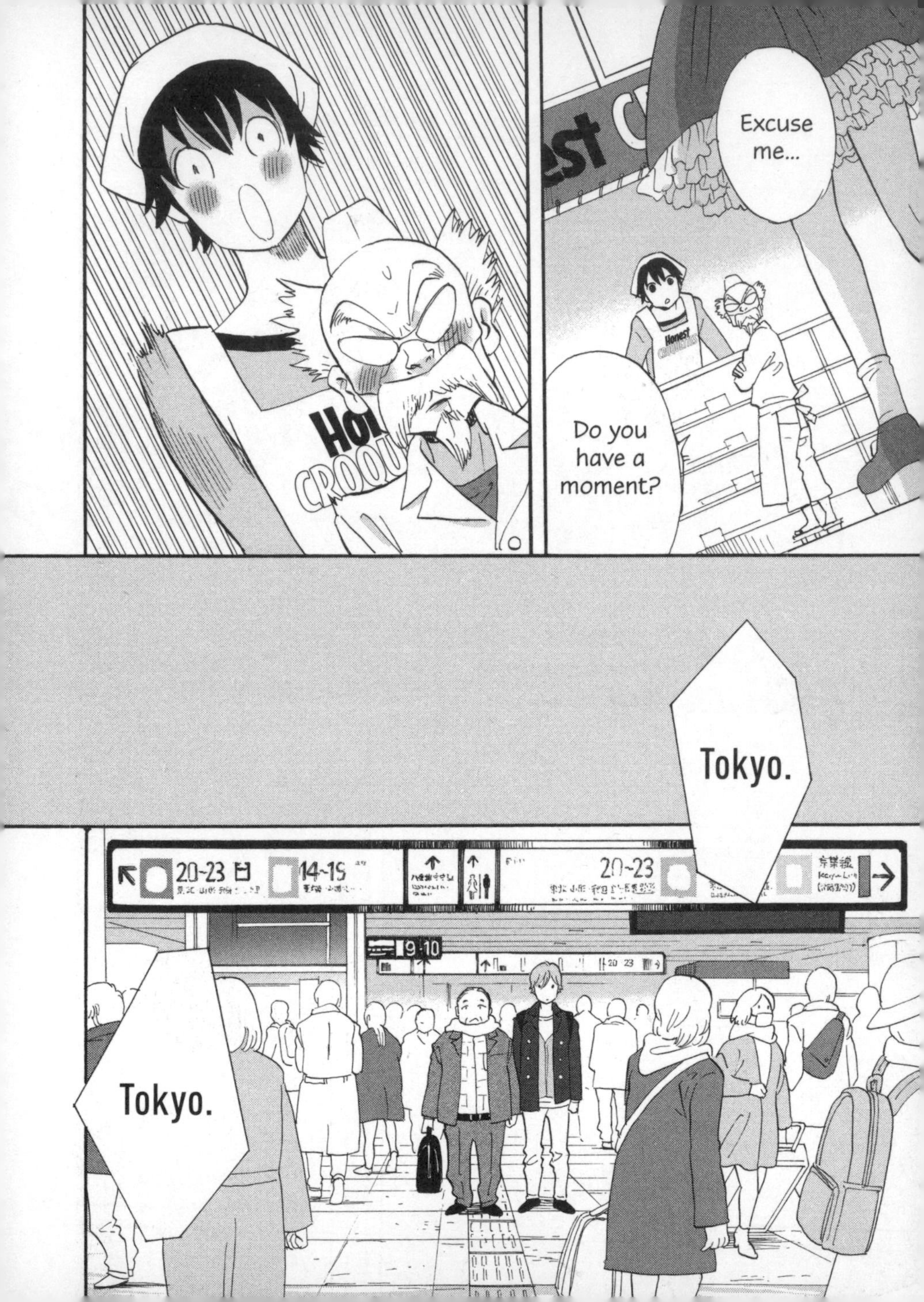

Excuse me...
Do you have a moment?
Tokyo.
Tokyo.

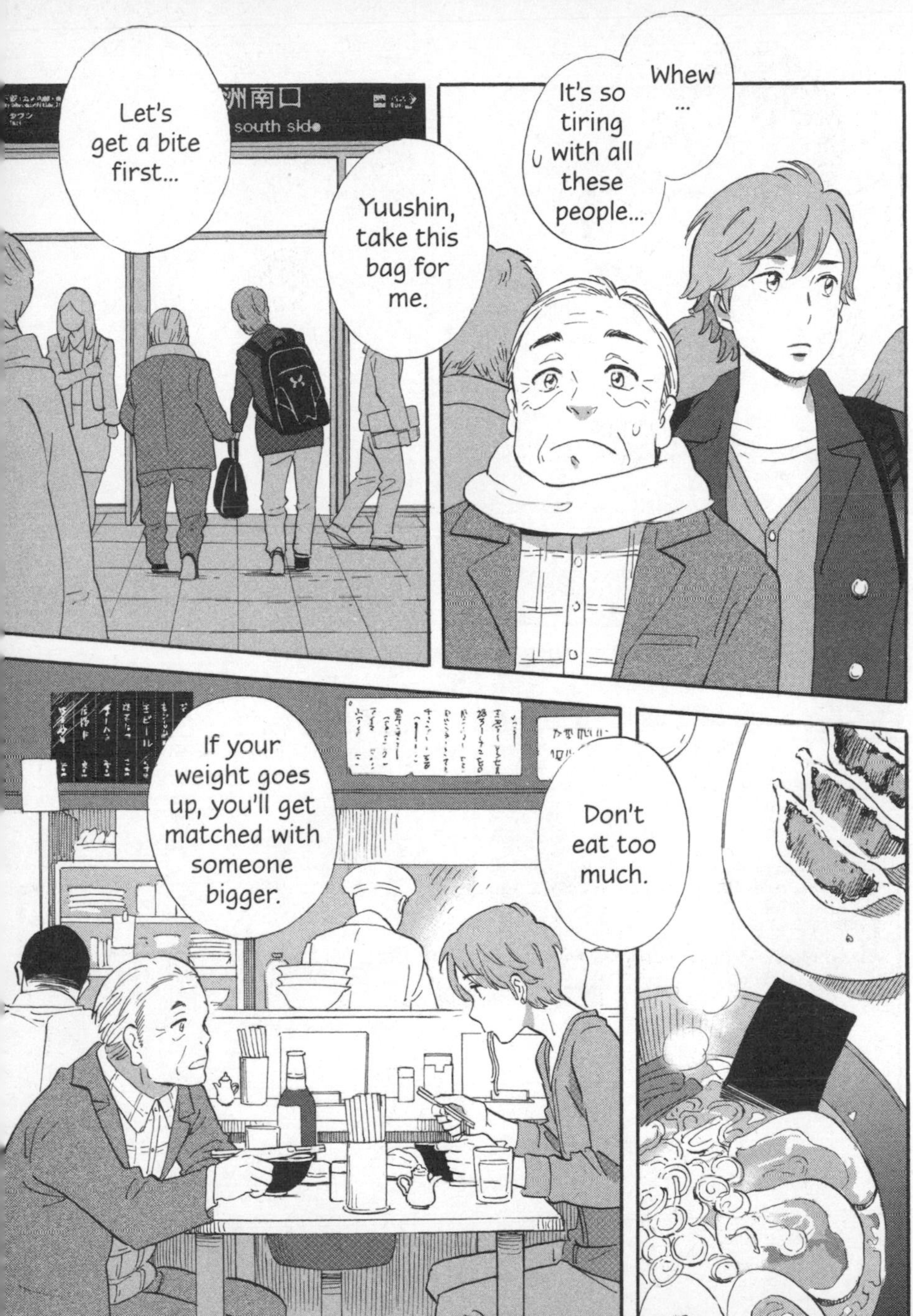
Whew ...
It's so tiring with all these people...
洲南口
south side
Let's get a bite first...
Yuushin, take this bag for me.
Don't eat too much.
If your weight goes up, you'll get matched with someone bigger.

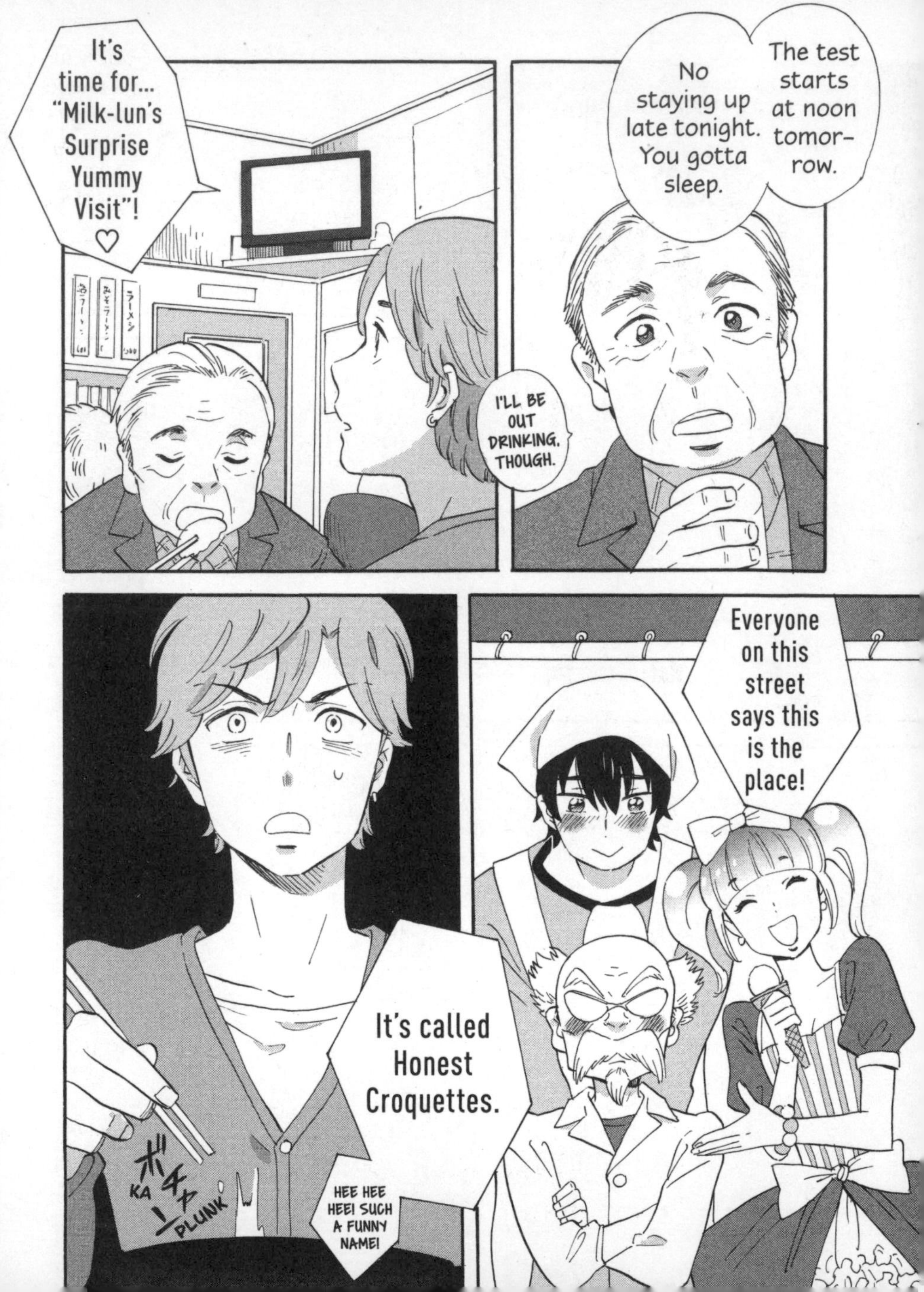
The test starts at noon tomorrow.
No staying up late tonight. You gotta sleep.
I'LL BE OUT DRINKING, THOUGH.
It's time for... "Milk-lun's Surprise Yummy Visit"! ♡
Everyone on this street says this is the place!
It's called Honest Croquettes.
HEE HEE HEE! SUCH A FUNNY NAME!
ポチャ
KA-PLUNK

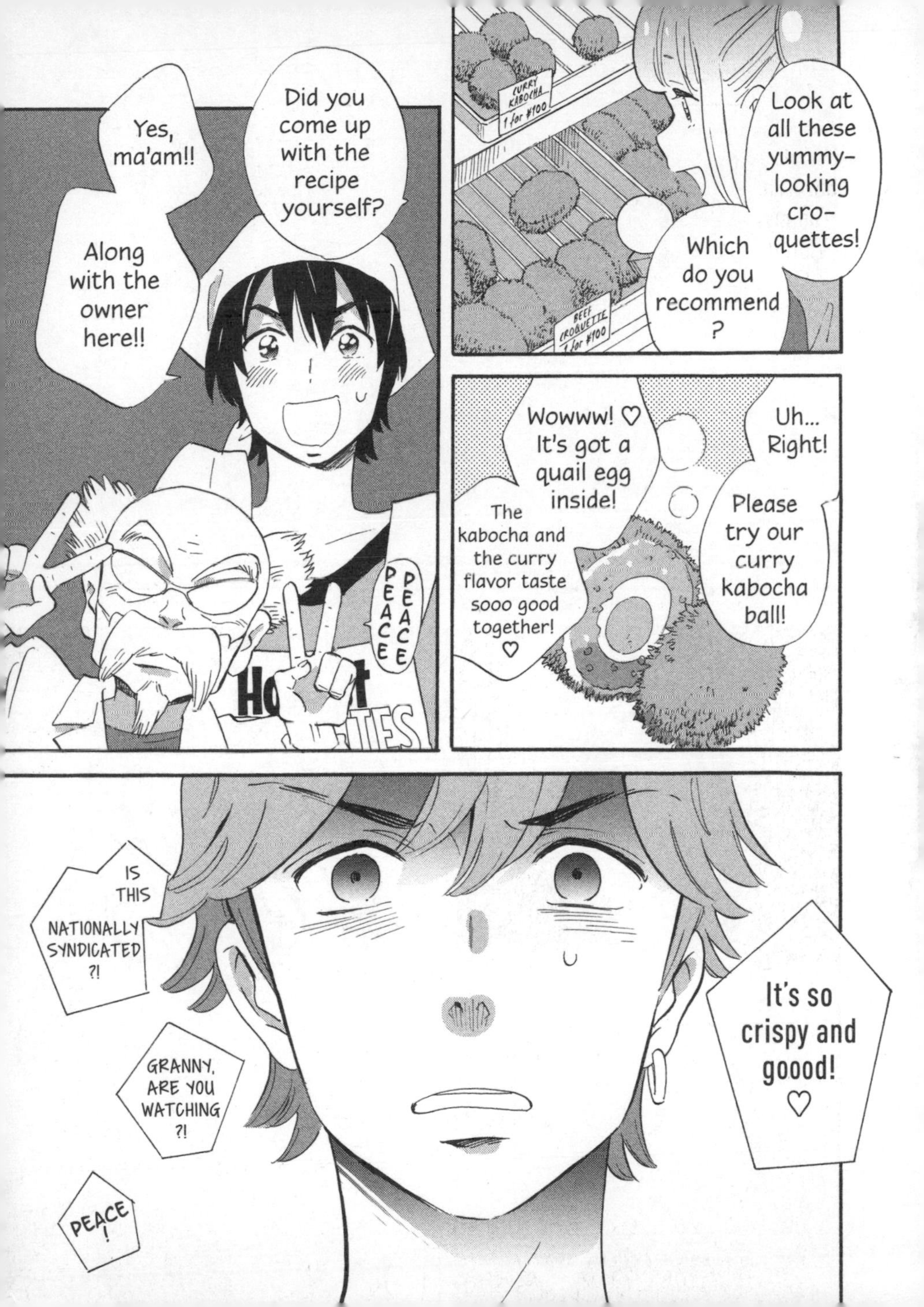
CURRY KABOCHA 1 for ¥100
Look at all these yummy-looking cro-quettes!
Which do you recommend?
BEEF CROQUETTE 1 for ¥100
Uh... Right!
Please try our curry kabocha ball!
Wowww! ♡ It's got a quail egg inside!
The kabocha and the curry flavor taste sooo good together! ♡
Did you come up with the recipe yourself?
Yes, ma'am!!
Along with the owner here!!
PEACE
PEACE
It's so crispy and goood! ♡
IS THIS NATIONALLY SYNDICATED?!
GRANNY, ARE YOU WATCHING?!
PEACE!

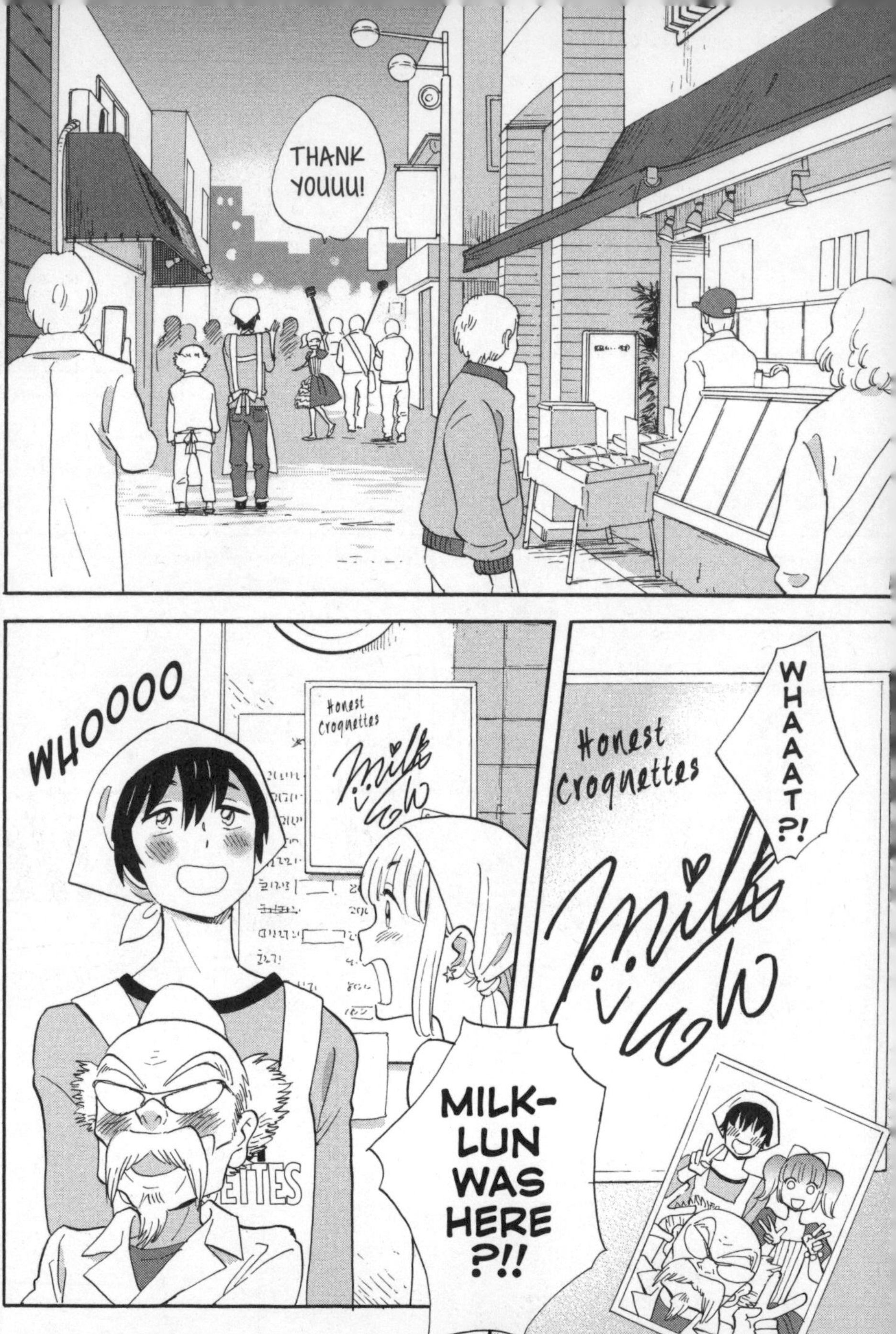
THANK YOUUU!
WHAAAT?!
Honest Croquettes
MILK-LUN WAS HERE?!!
WHOOOO
Honest Croquettes

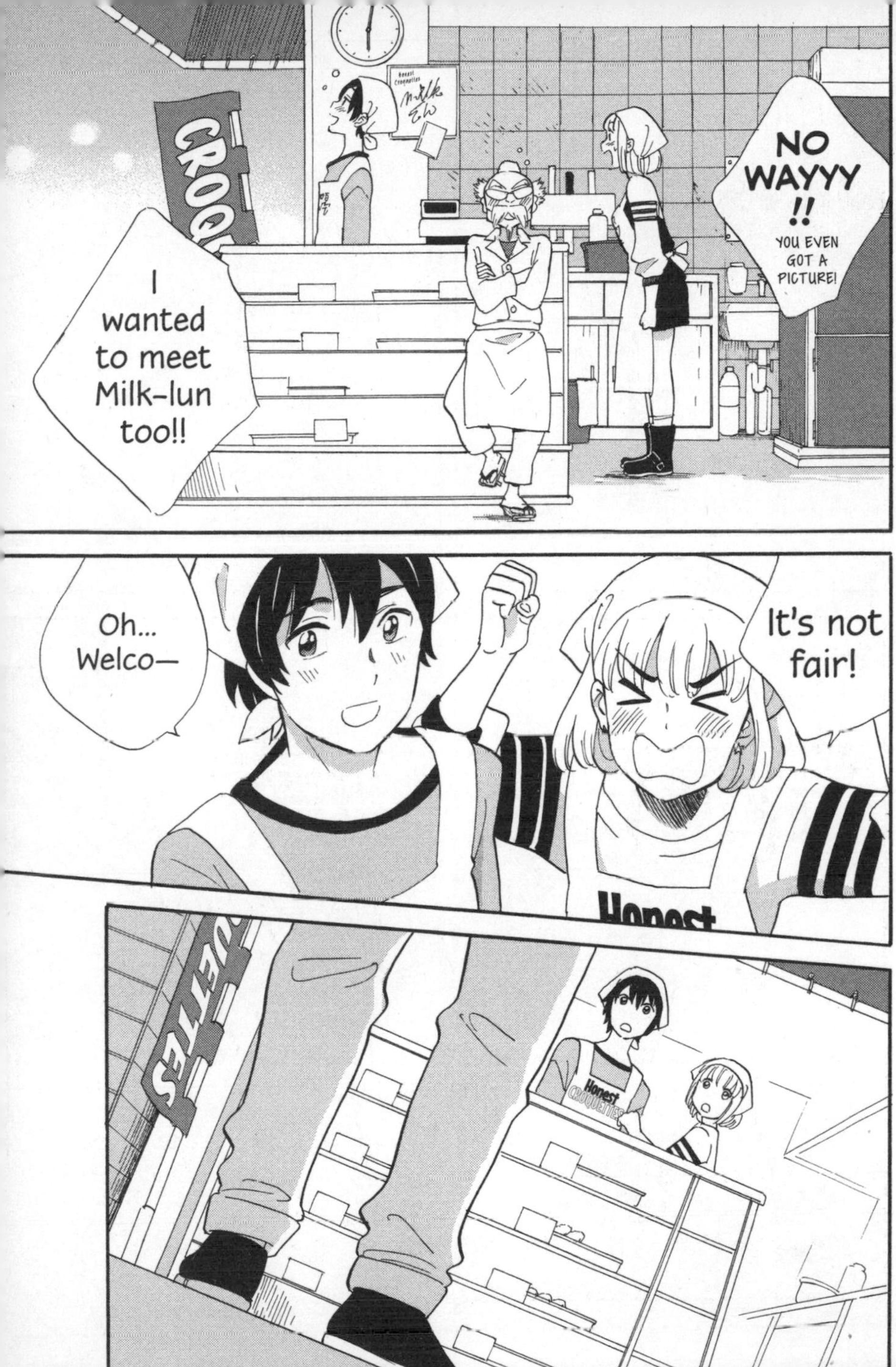
NO WAYYY!!
YOU EVEN GOT A PICTURE!
I wanted to meet Milk-lun too!!
CROQ
It's not fair!
Oh... Welco—
Honest
QUETTES
Honest CROQUETTES

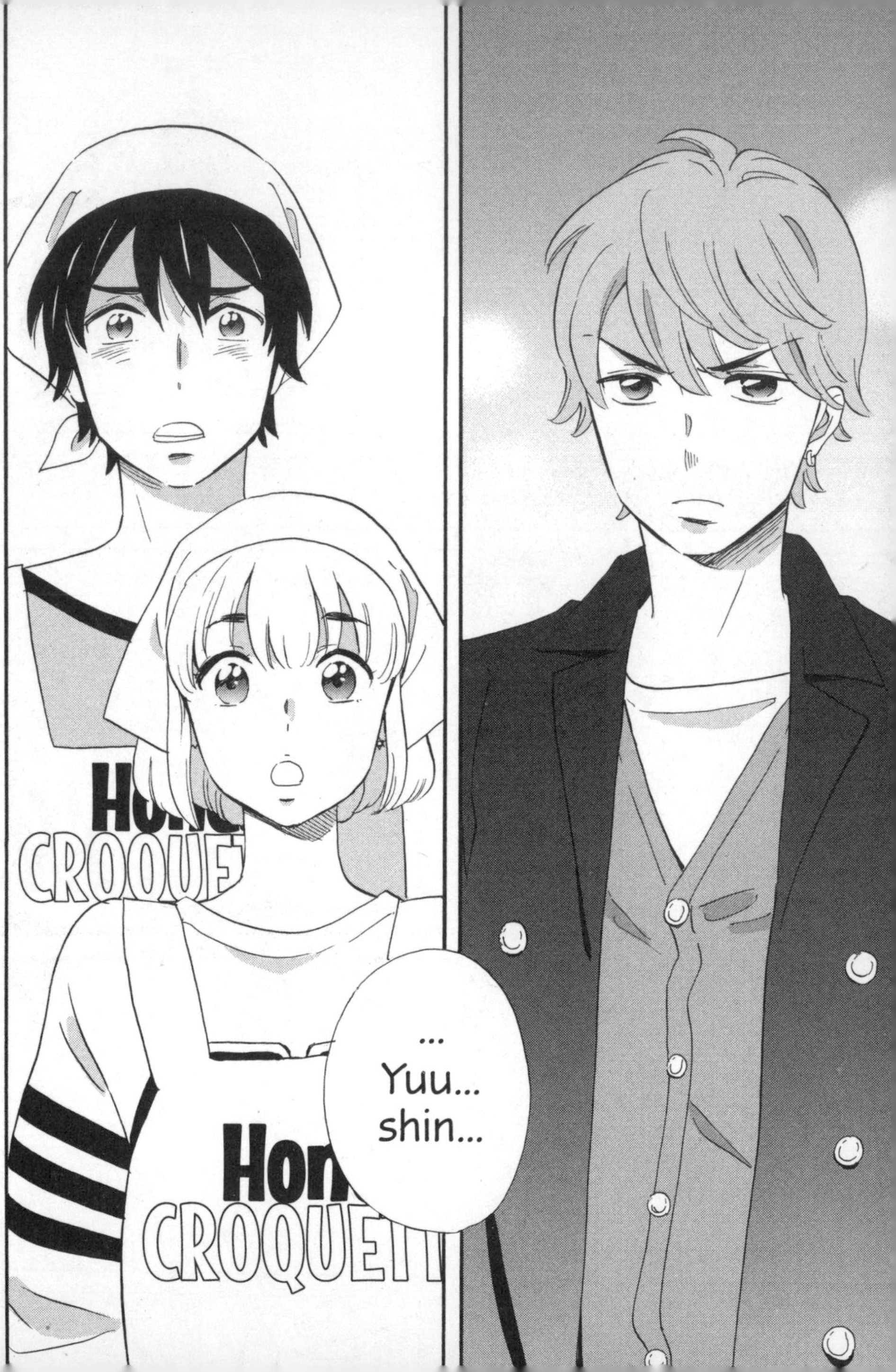
... Yuu... shin...

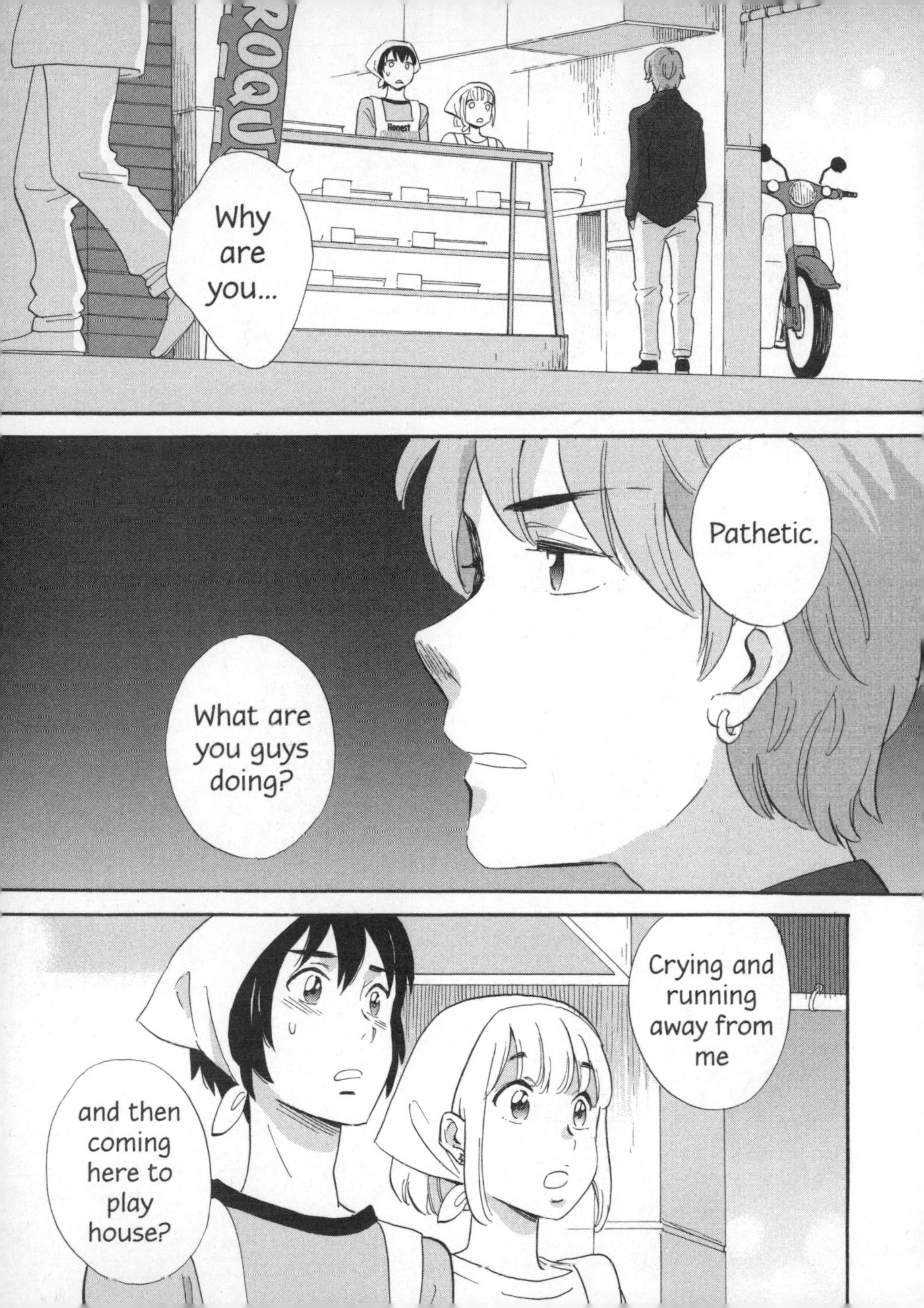
Honest
Why are you...
Pathetic.
What are you guys doing?
Crying and running away from me
and then coming here to play house?

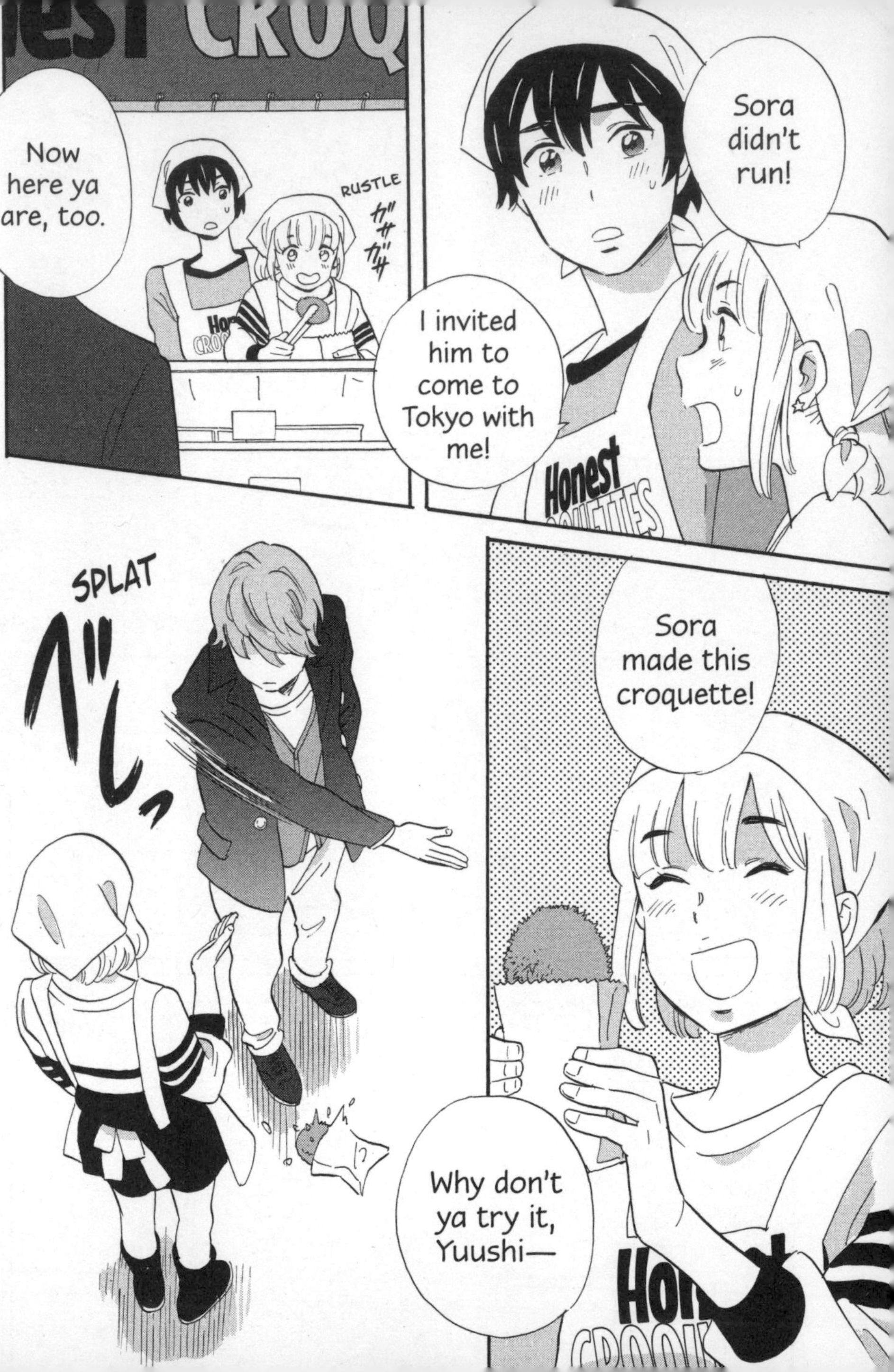
Sora didn't run!
I invited him to come to Tokyo with me!
Now here ya are, too.
RUSTLE
Sora made this croquette!
Why don't ya try it, Yuushi—
SPLAT
べしっ

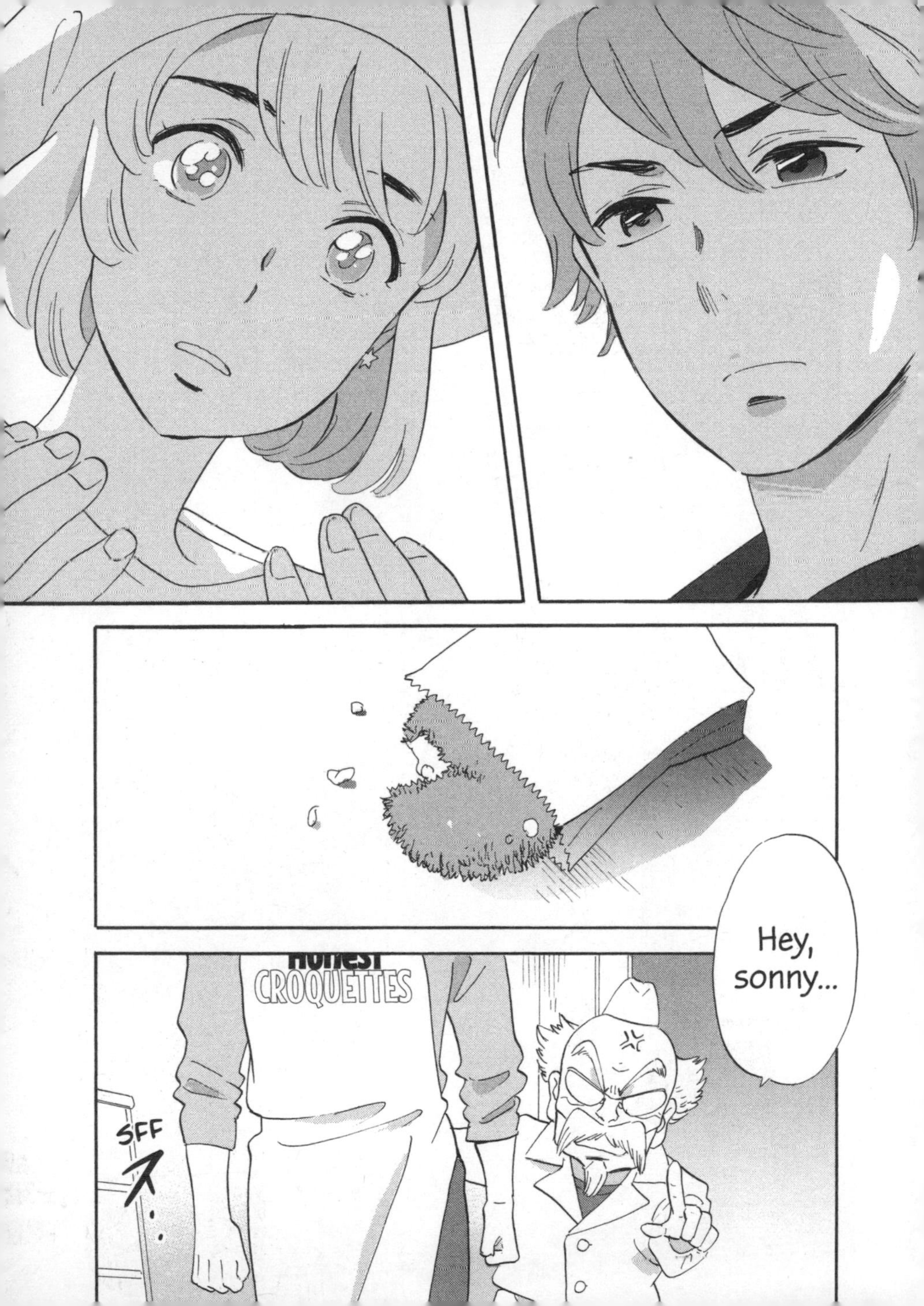
Hey, sonny...
CROQUETTES
SFF

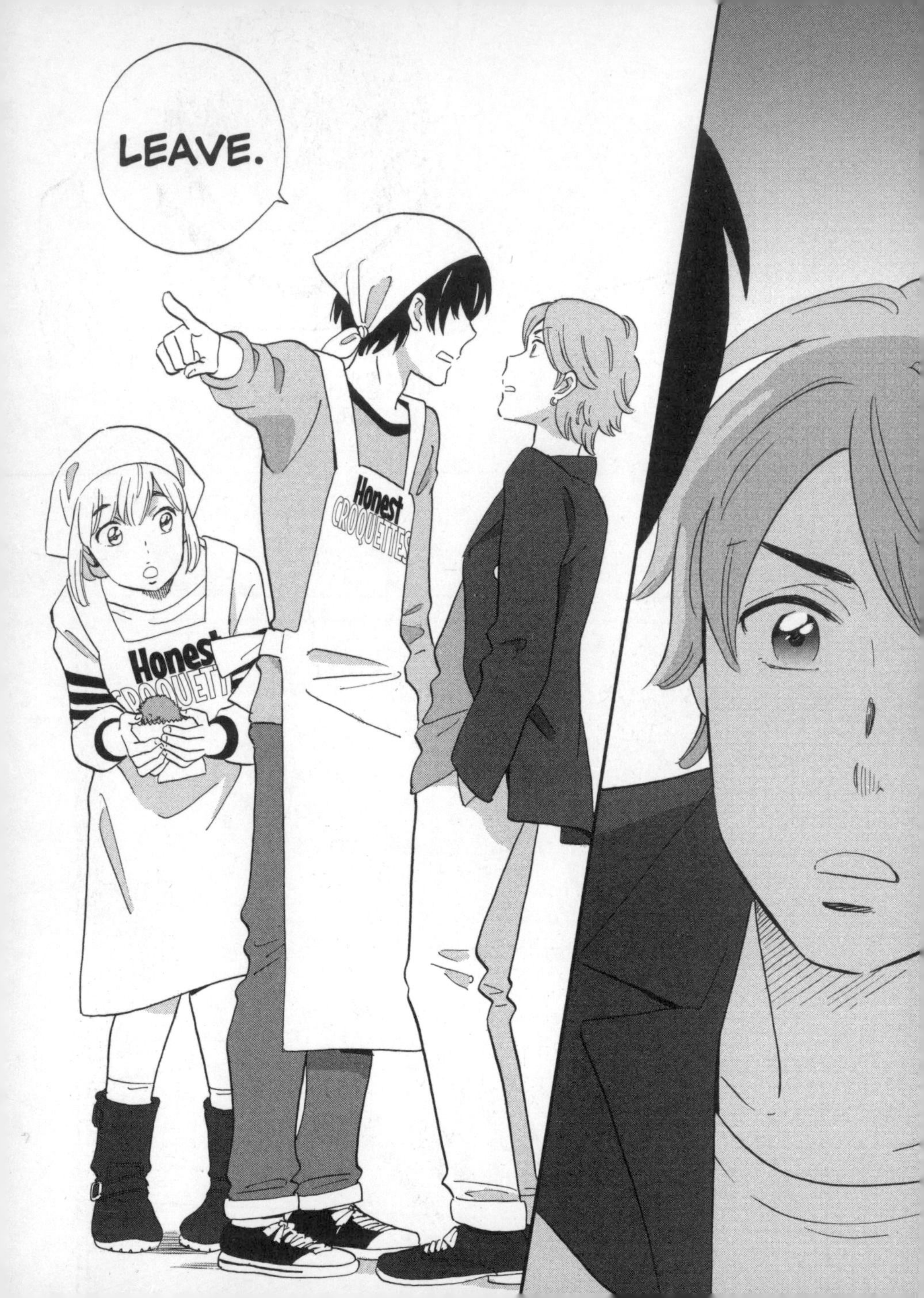
LEAVE.
Honest CROQUETTES
Honest CROQUETTES

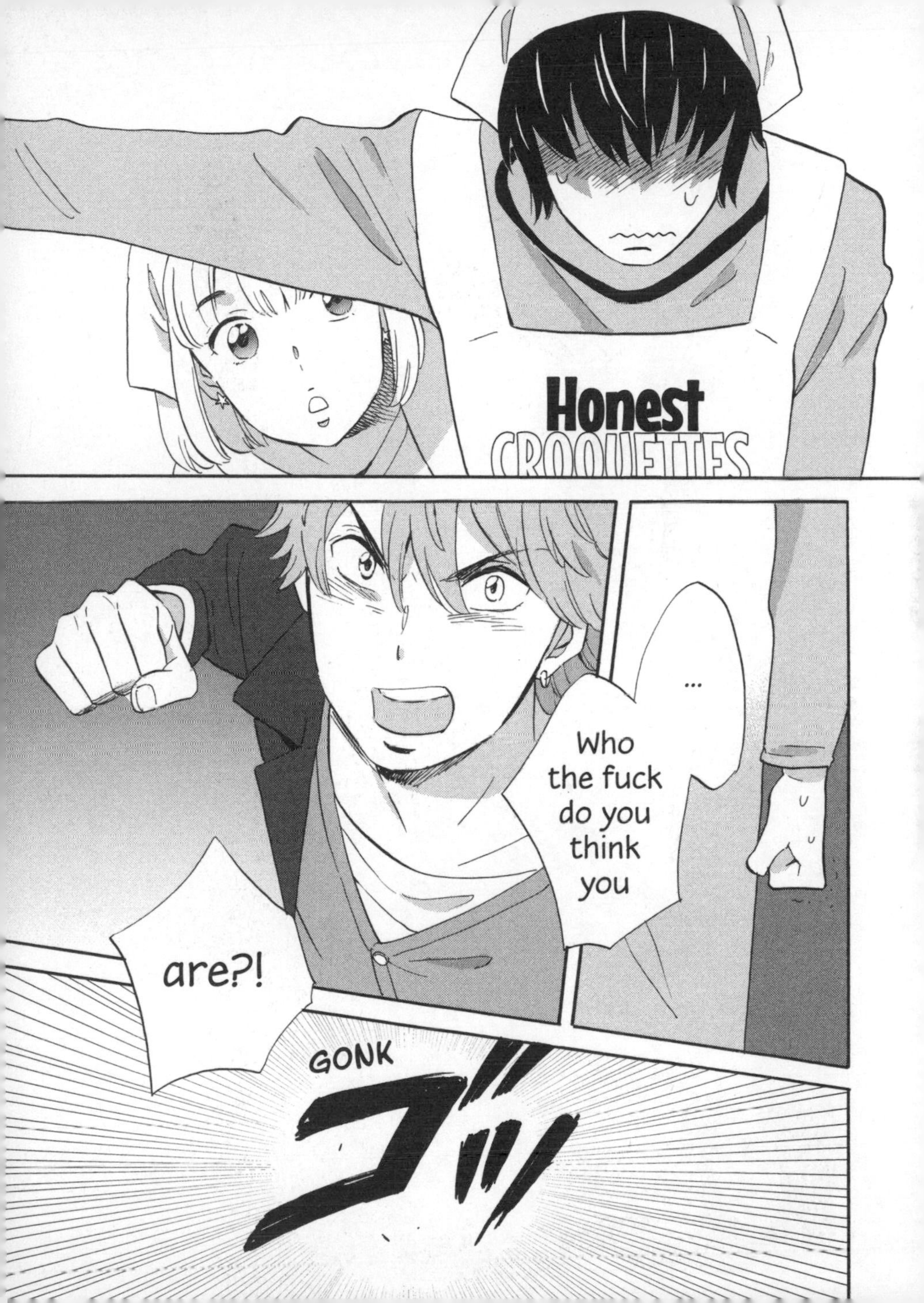
Honest
CROQUETTES
...
Who the fuck do you think you
are?!
GONK

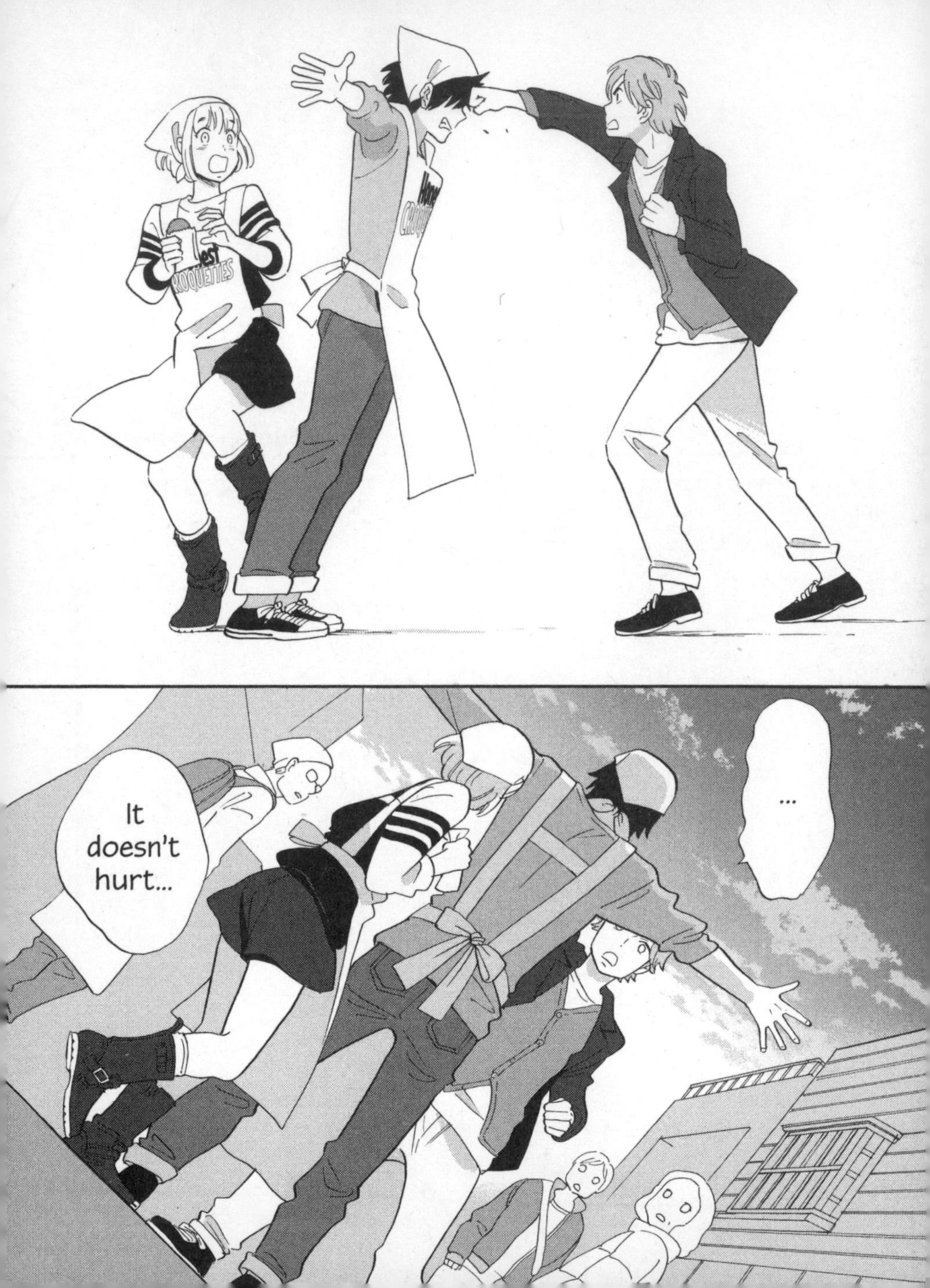
CROQUETTES
...
It doesn't hurt...

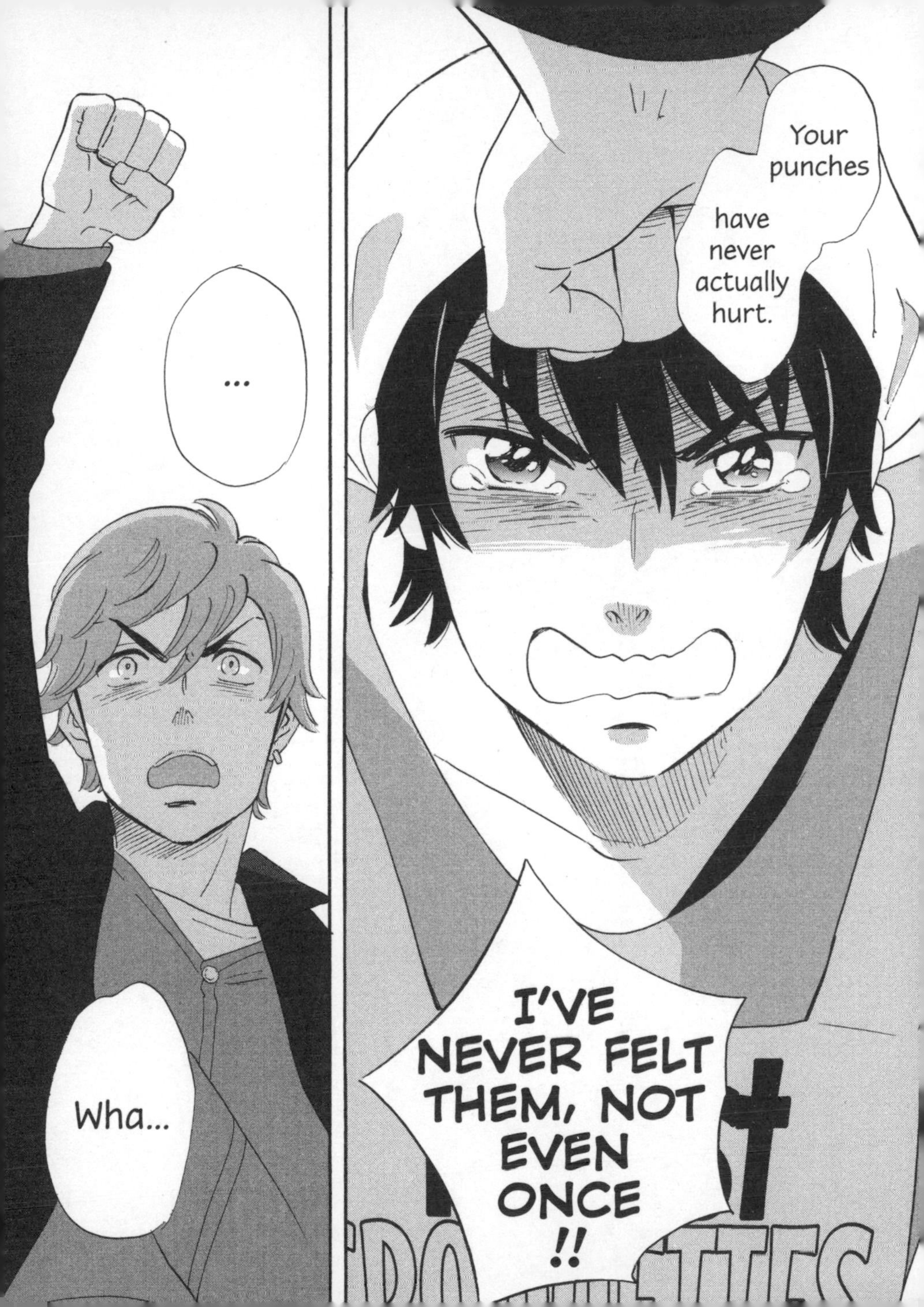
Your punches have never actually hurt.
I'VE NEVER FELT THEM, NOT EVEN ONCE !!
...
Wha...

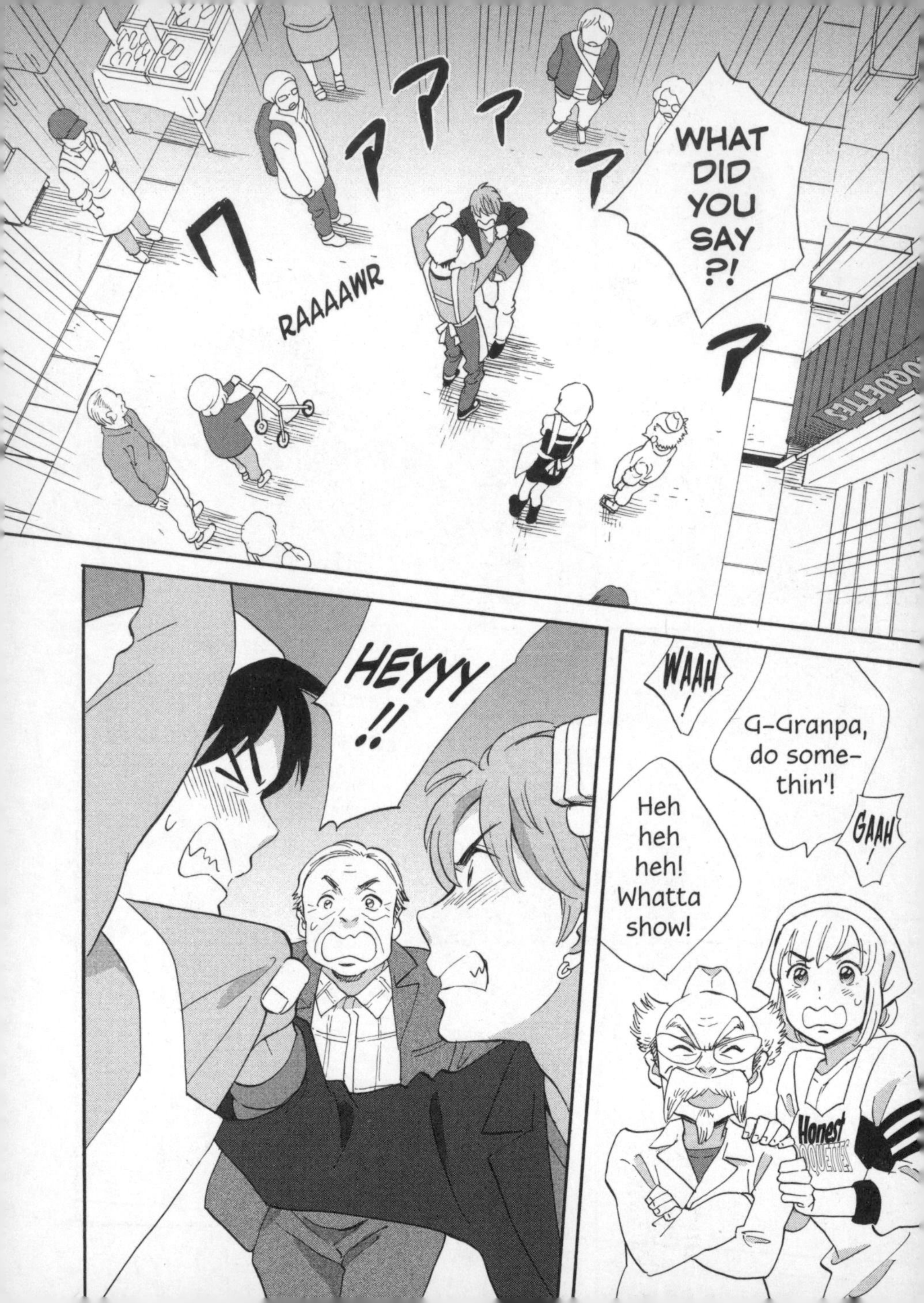
WHAT DID YOU SAY?!
RAAAAWR
WAAH!
G-Granpa, do some-thin'!
GAAH!
Heh heh heh! Whatta show!
Honest
HEYYY!!

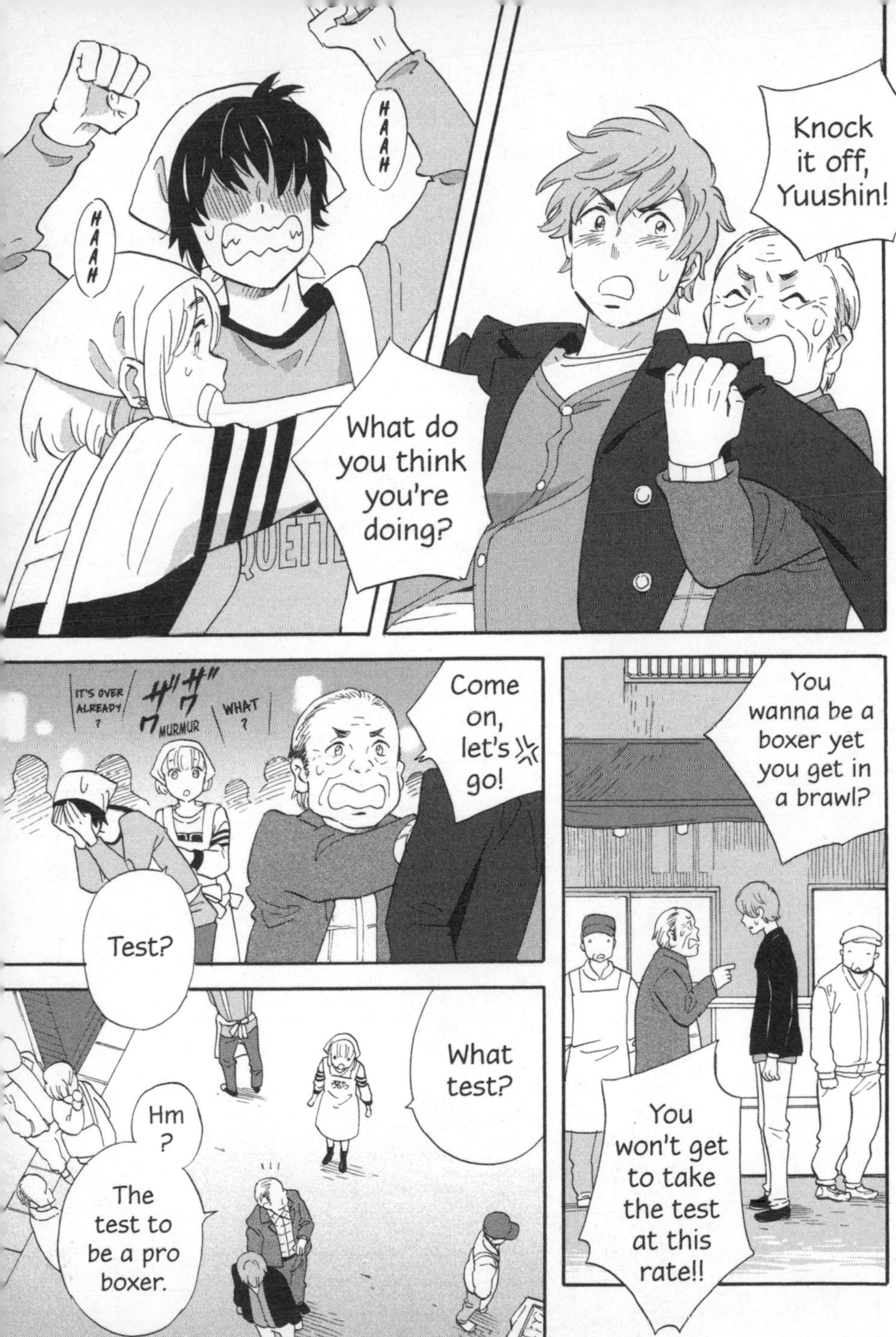
Knock it off, Yuushin!
What do you think you're doing?
HAAAH
HAAAH
You wanna be a boxer yet you get in a brawl?
You won't get to take the test at this rate!!
Come on, let's go!
WHAT?
ザワザワ MURMUR
IT'S OVER ALREADY?
Test?
What test?
Hm?
The test to be a pro boxer.

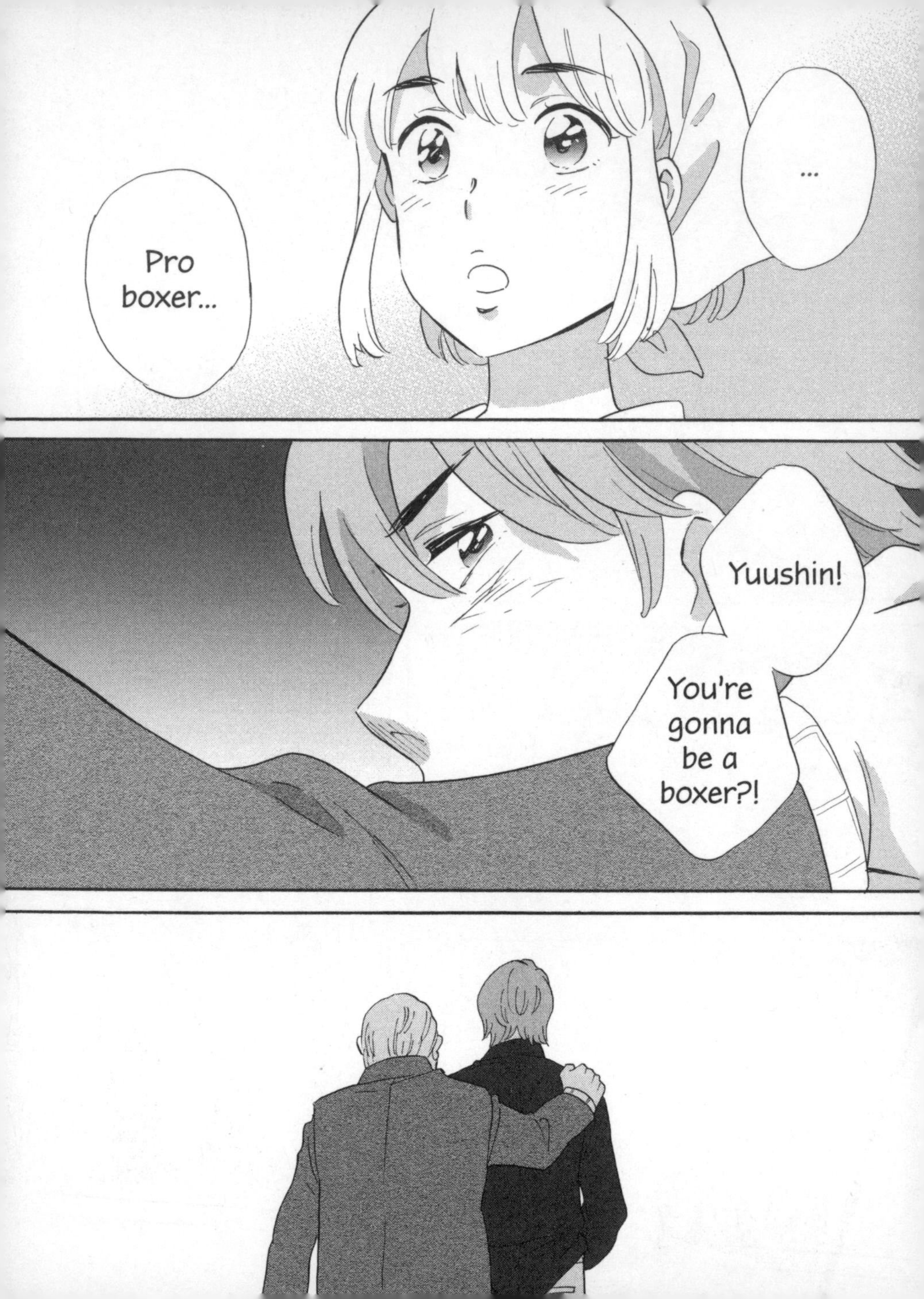
...
Pro boxer...
Yuushin!
You're gonna be a boxer?!

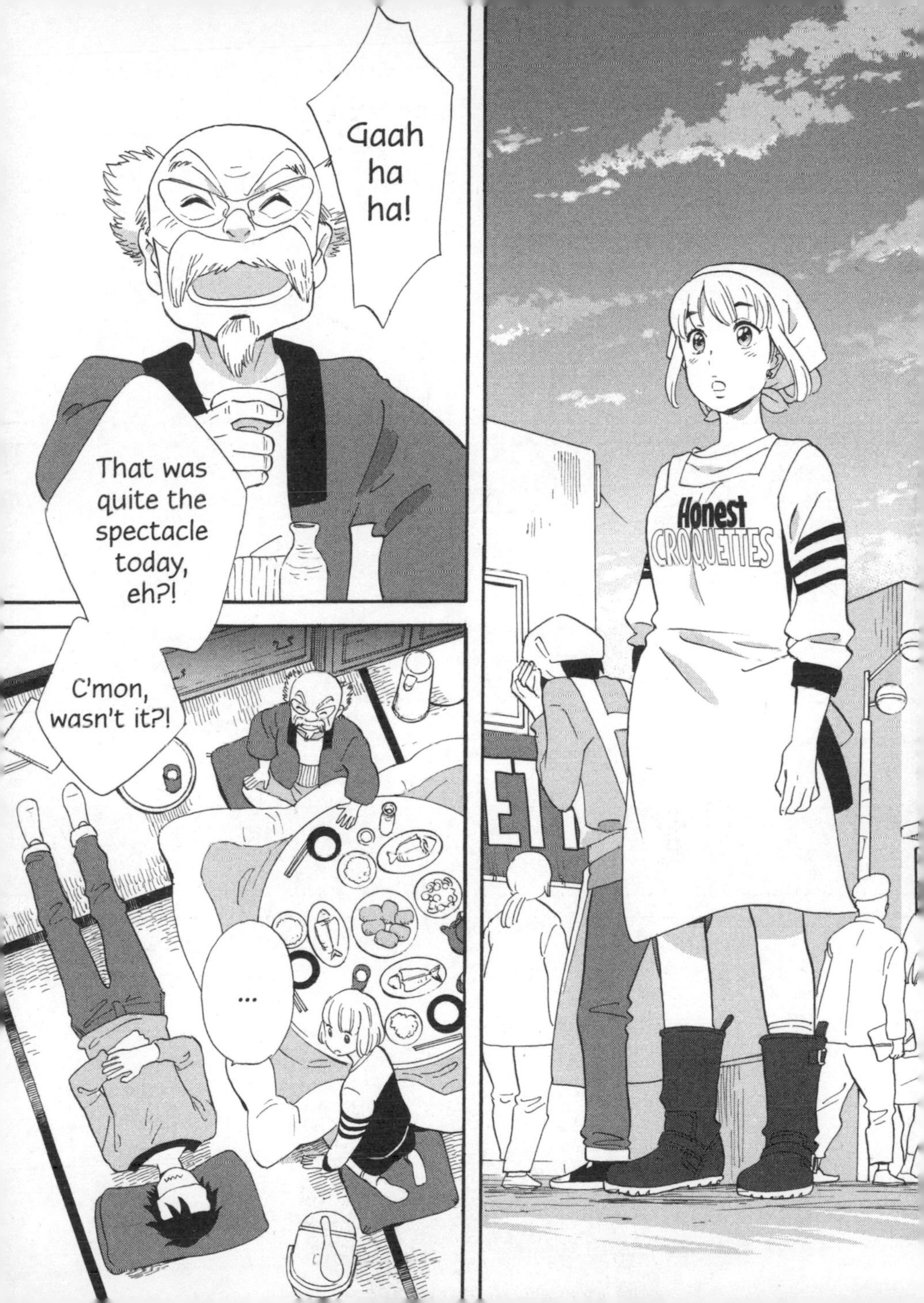
Honest
CROQUETTES
Gaah ha ha!
That was quite the spectacle today, eh?!
C'mon, wasn't it?!
...

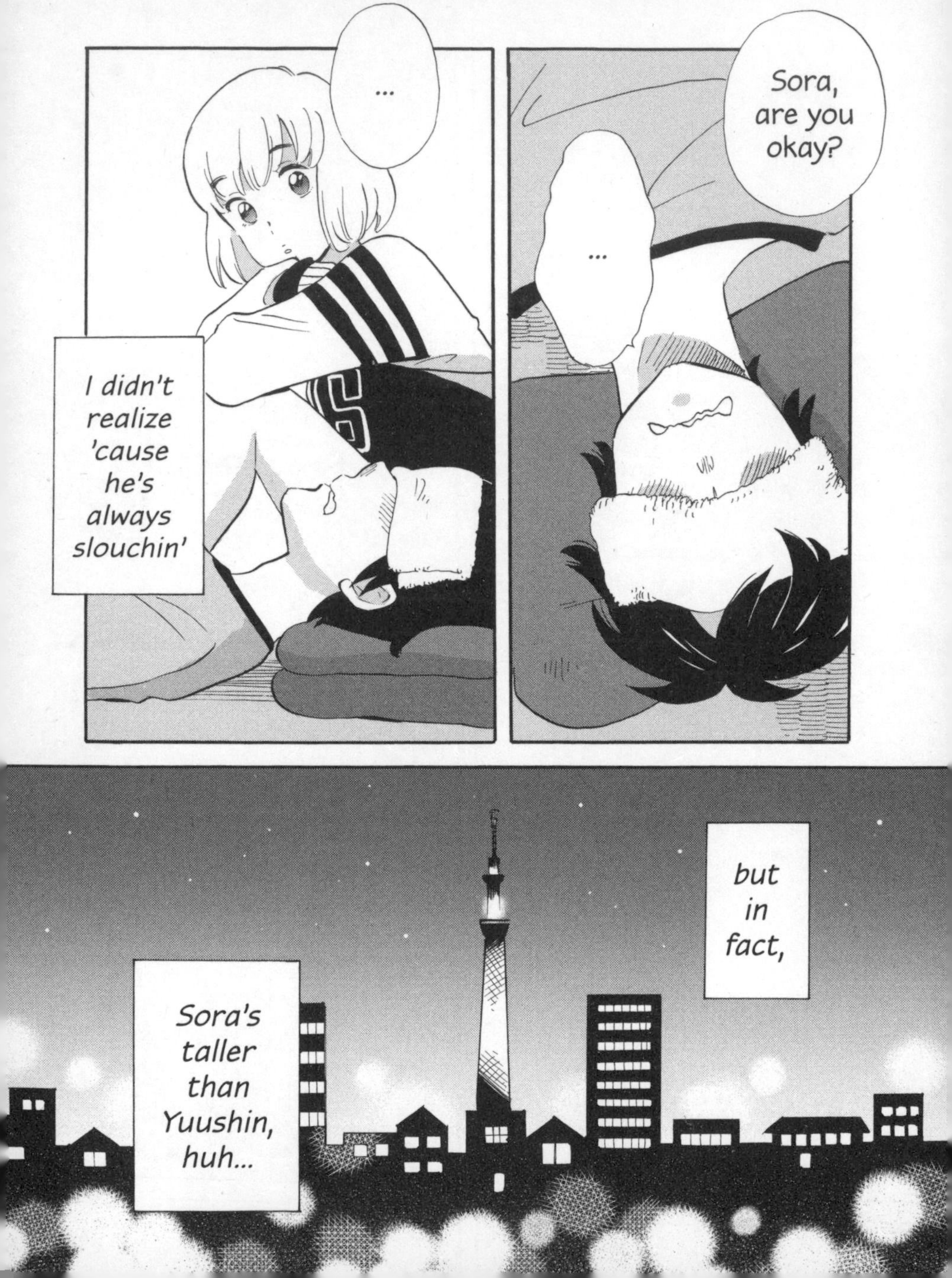
Sora, are you okay?
...
...
I didn't realize 'cause he's always slouchin'
but in fact,
Sora's taller than Yuushin, huh...

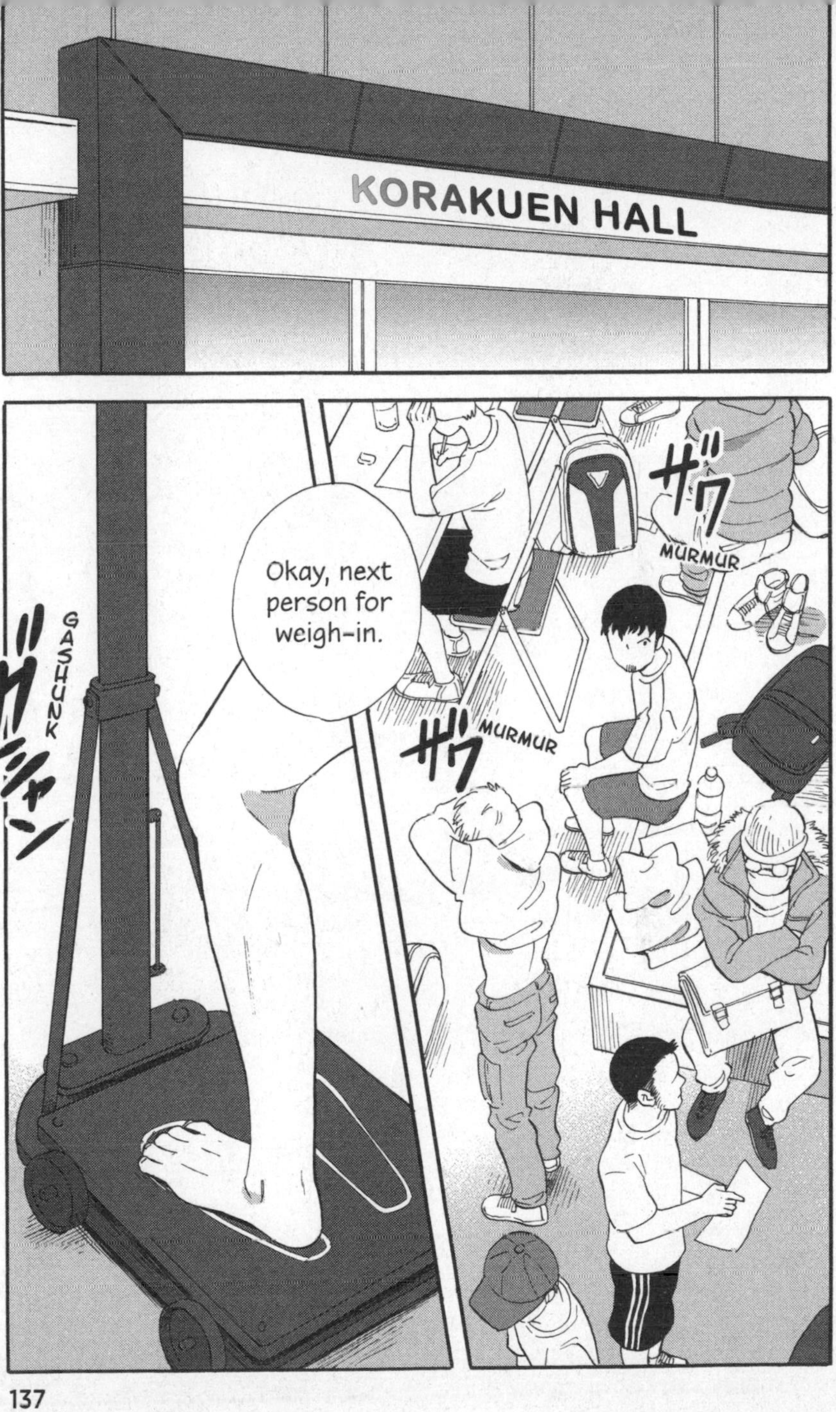
KORAKUEN HALL
ザワ
MURMUR
ザワ
MURMUR
Okay, next person for weigh-in.
ガシャン
GASHUNK

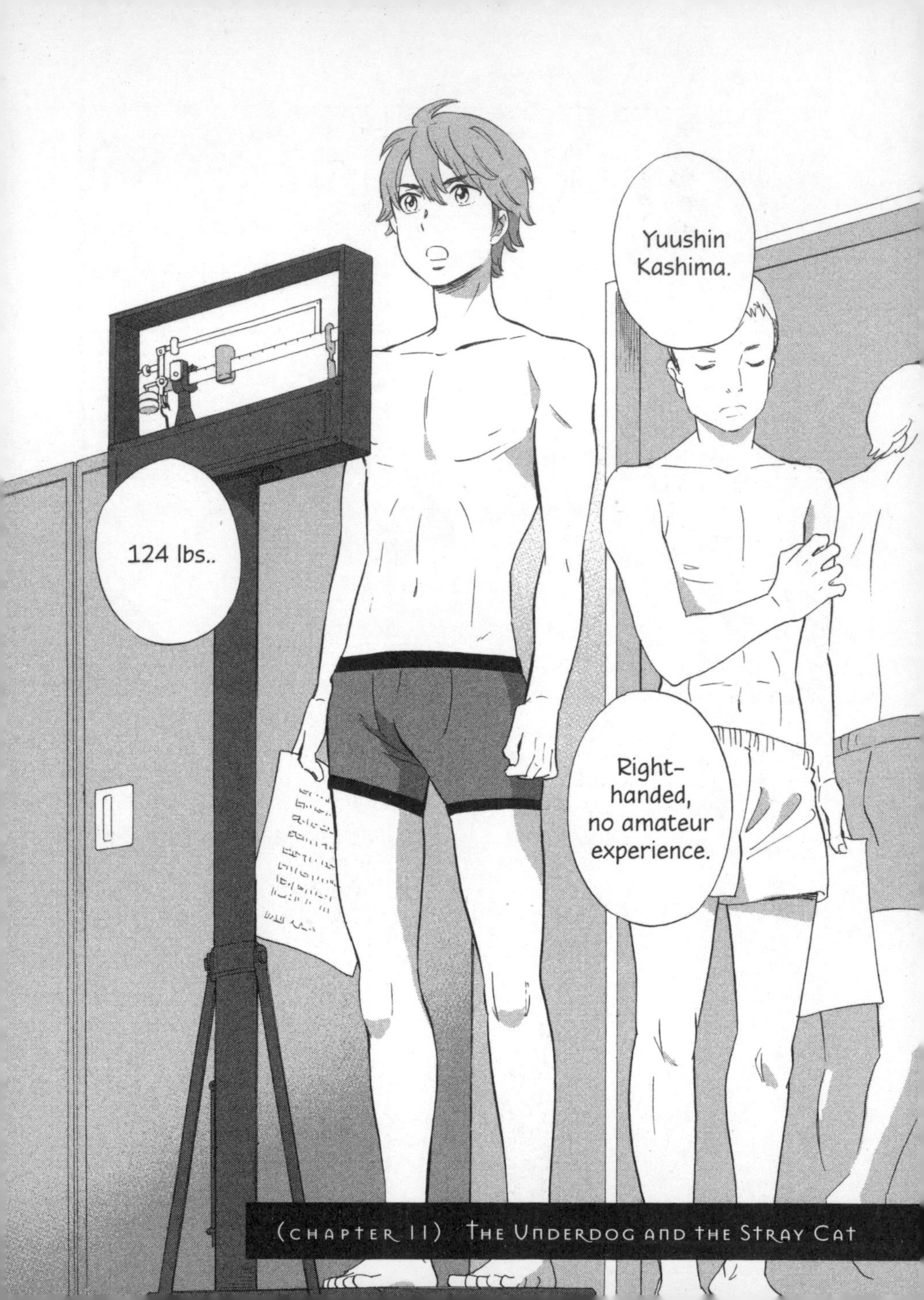
Yuushin Kashima.
124 lbs..
Right-handed, no amateur experience.

(Chapter 11) The Underdog and the Stray Cat

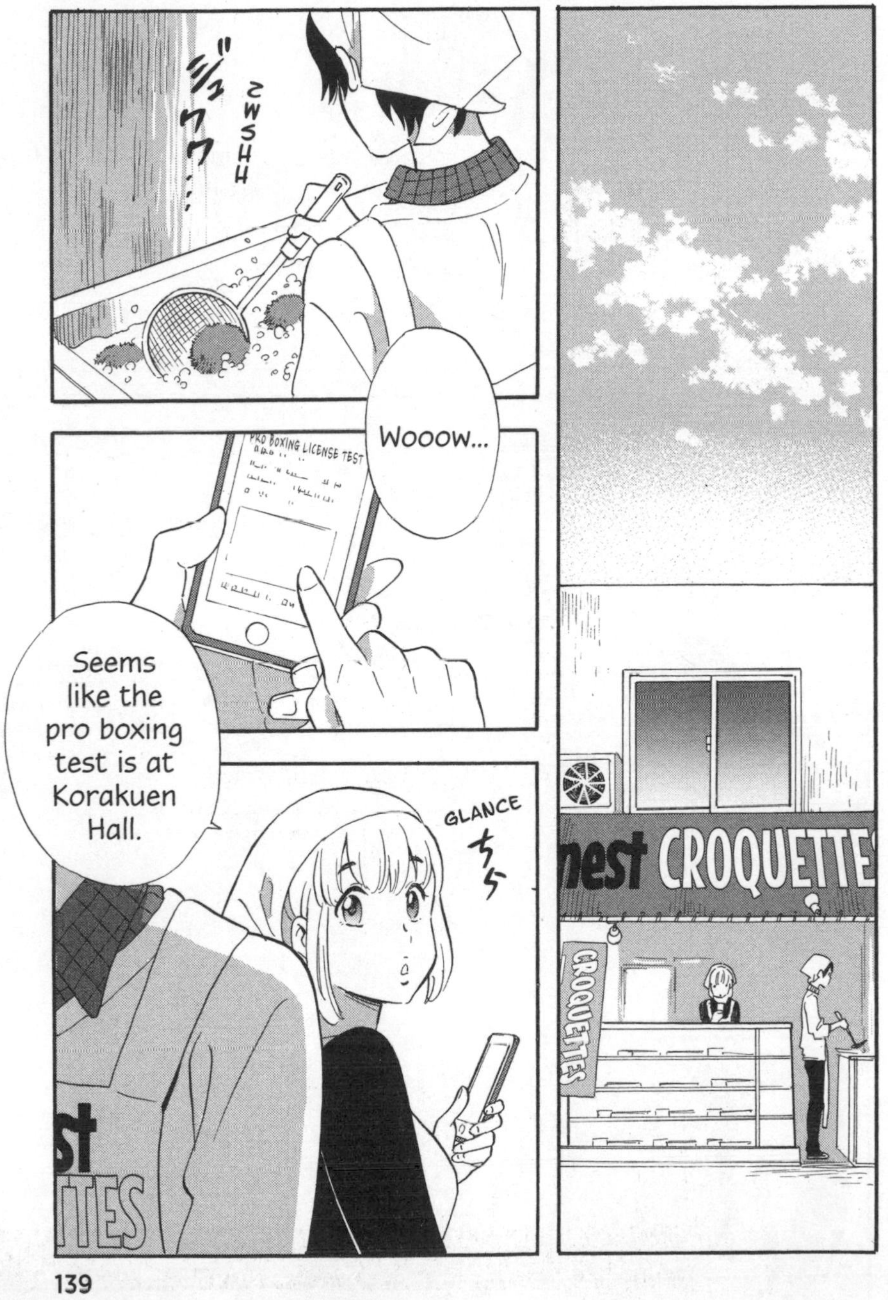
nest CROQUETTES
CROQUETTES
CROQUETTES
ジュワ…
ZWSHH
Wooow...
PRO BOXING LICENSE TEST
Seems like the pro boxing test is at Korakuen Hall.
GLANCE
ちら

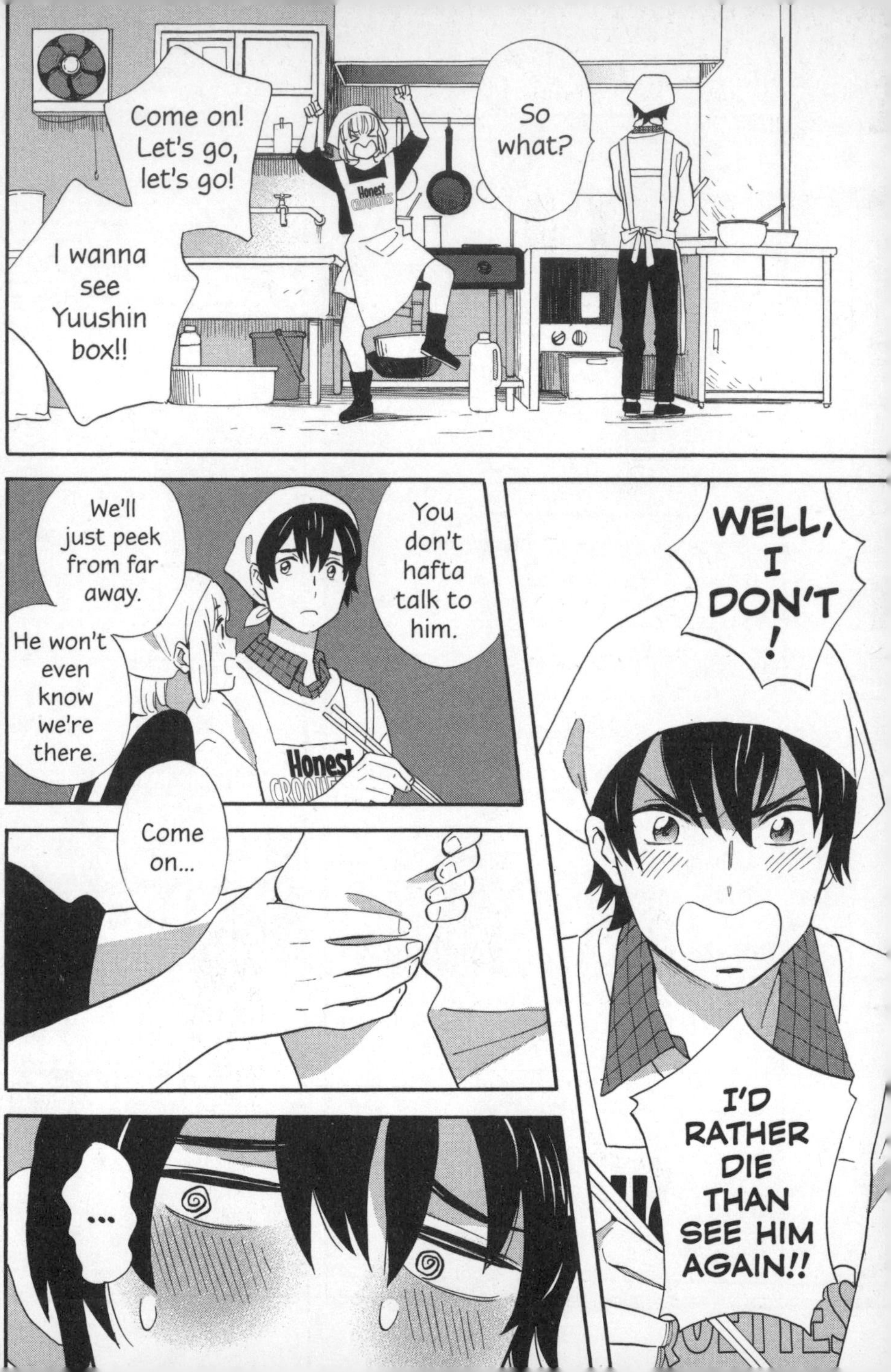
So what?
Come on! Let's go, let's go!
I wanna see Yuushin box!!
WELL, I DON'T!
I'D RATHER DIE THAN SEE HIM AGAIN!!
You don't hafta talk to him.
We'll just peek from far away.
He won't even know we're there.
Come on...
...

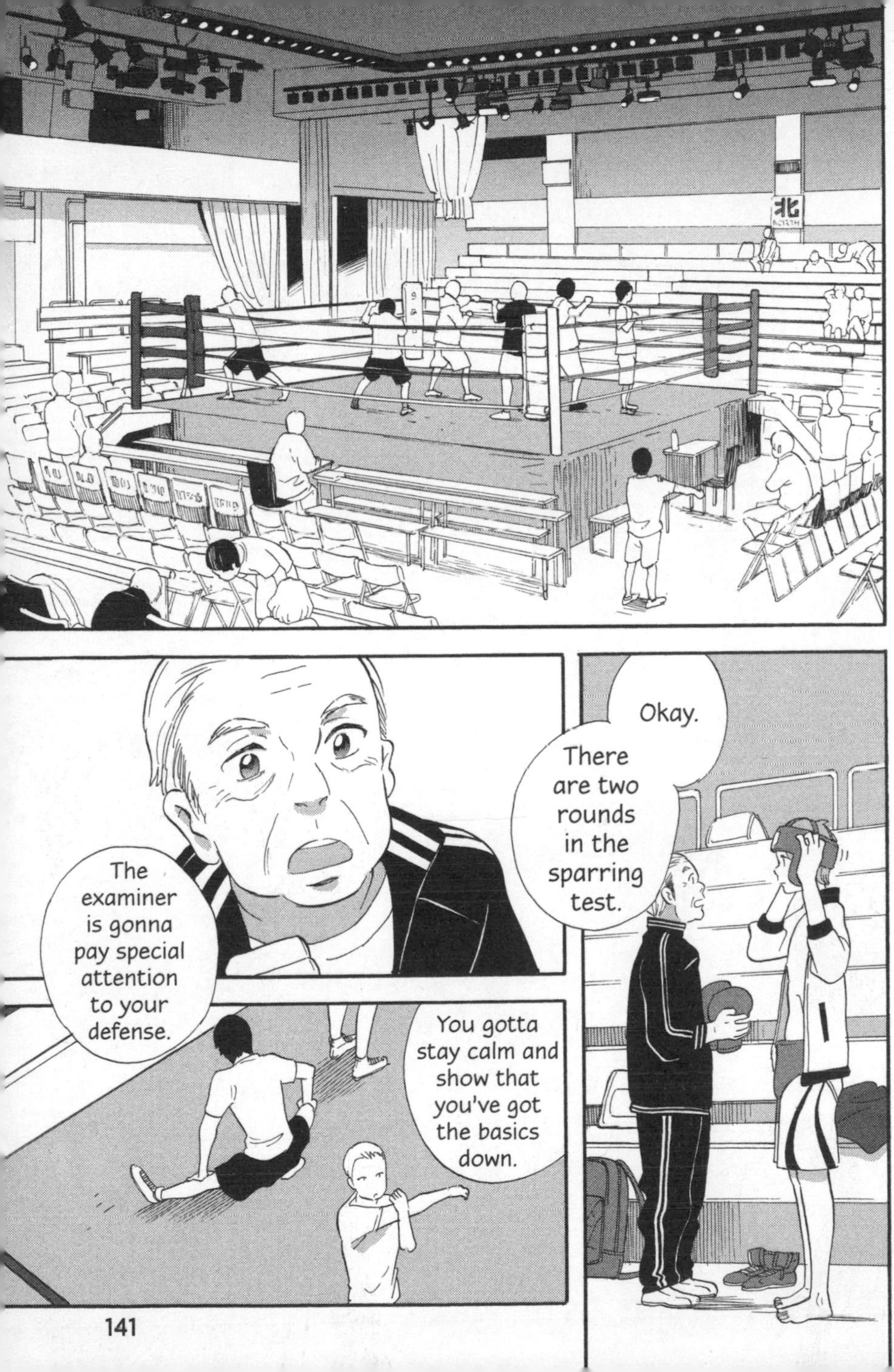
北
Okay.
There are two rounds in the sparring test.
The examiner is gonna pay special attention to your defense.
You gotta stay calm and show that you've got the basics down.

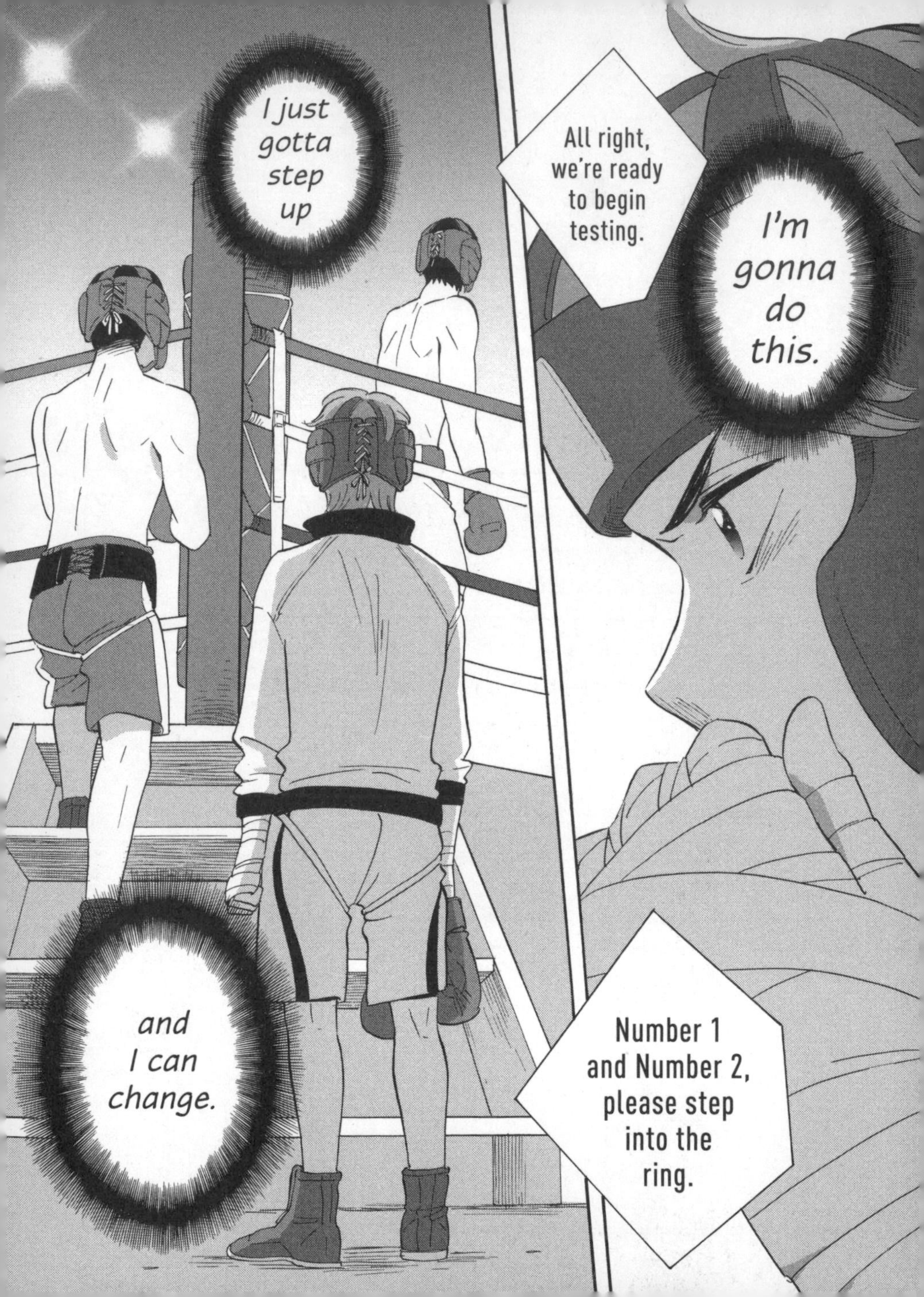
All right, we're ready to begin testing.
I'm gonna do this.
Number 1 and Number 2, please step into the ring.
I just gotta step up
and I can change.

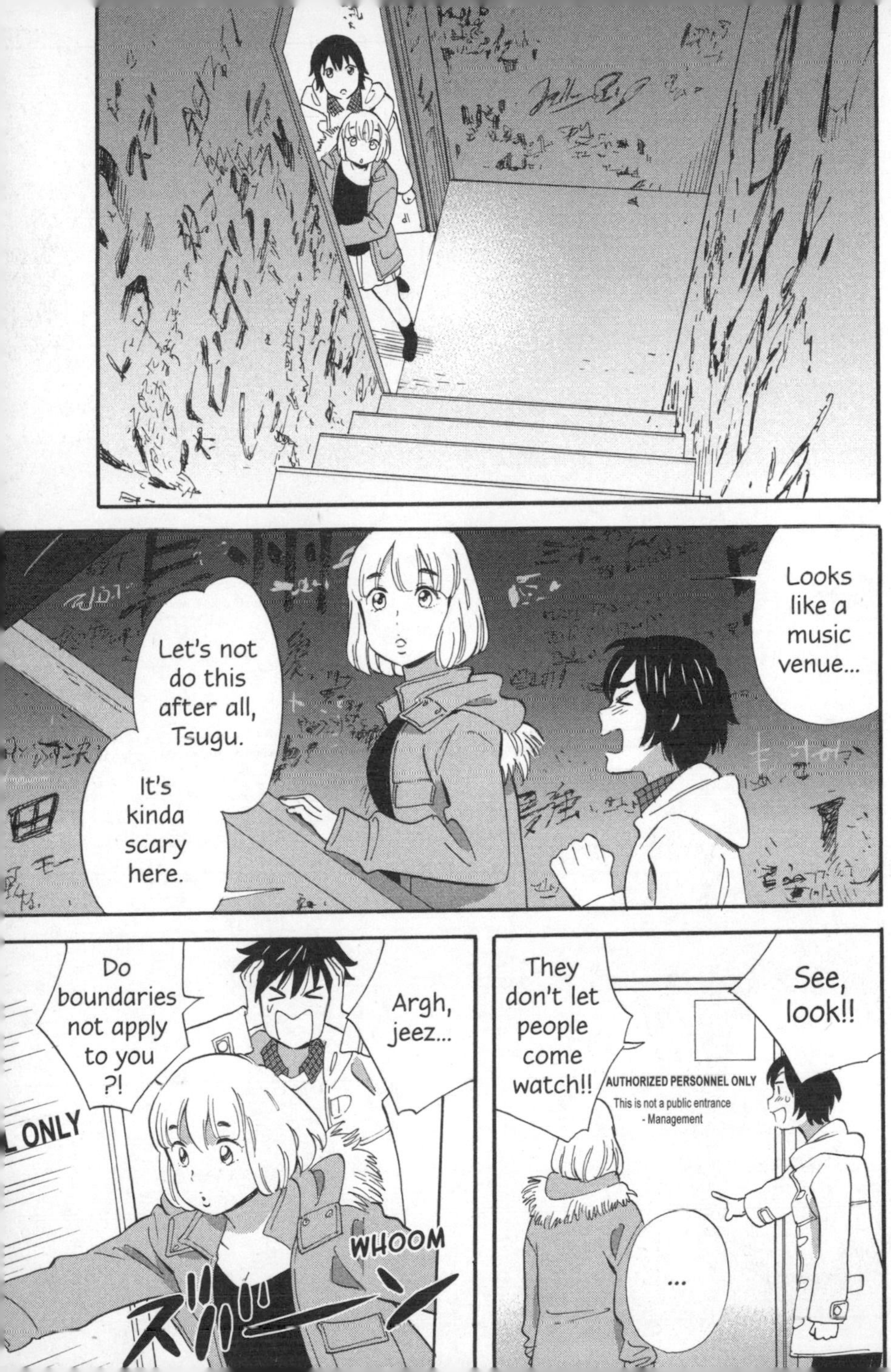
Looks like a music venue...
Let's not do this after all, Tsugu.
It's kinda scary here.
See, look!!
They don't let people come watch!!
AUTHORIZED PERSONNEL ONLY
This is not a public entrance
- Management
...
Argh, jeez...
Do boundaries not apply to you ?!
L ONLY
WHOOM

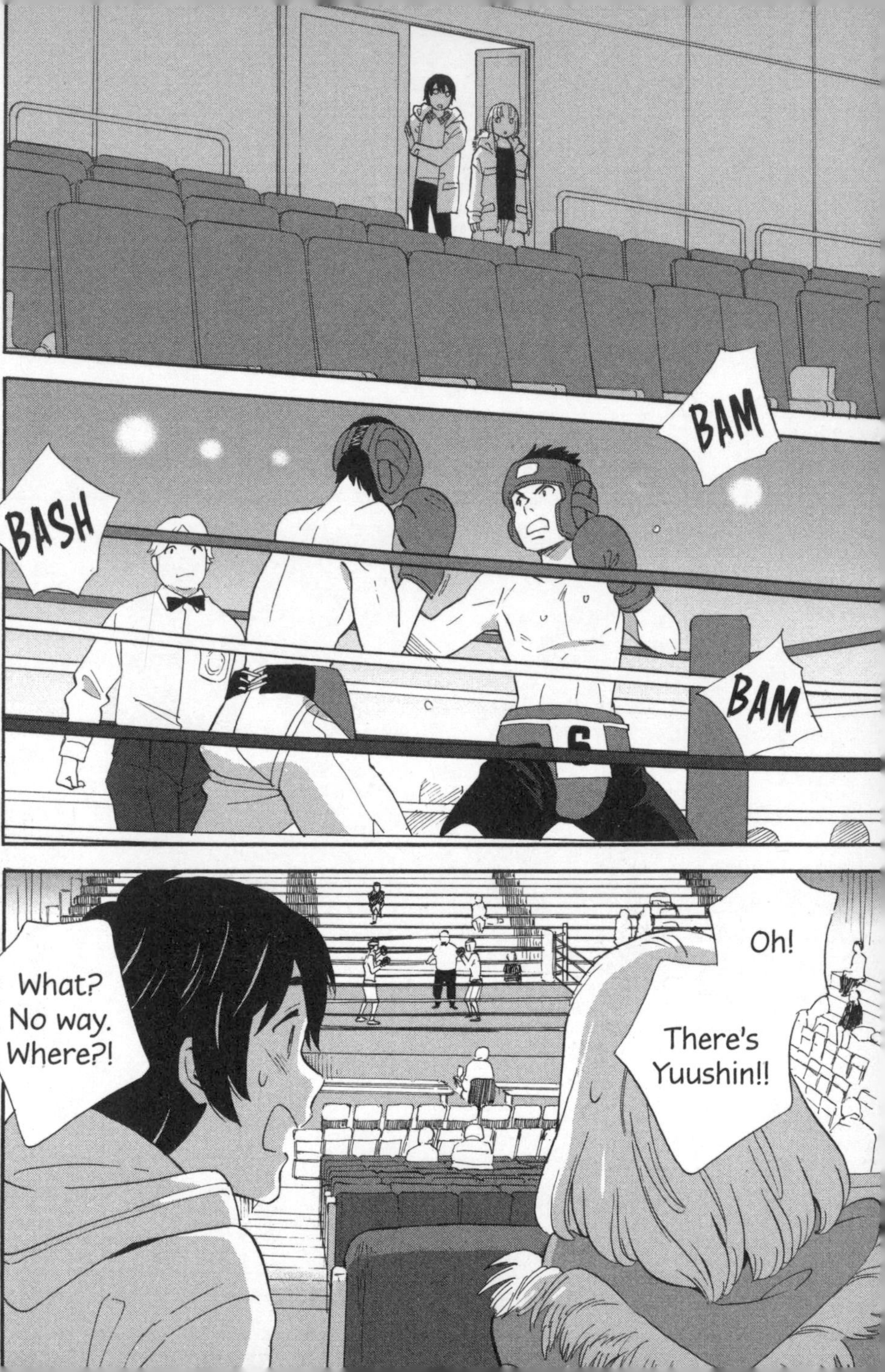
BAM
BASH
BAM
Oh!
There's Yuushin!!
What? No way. Where?!

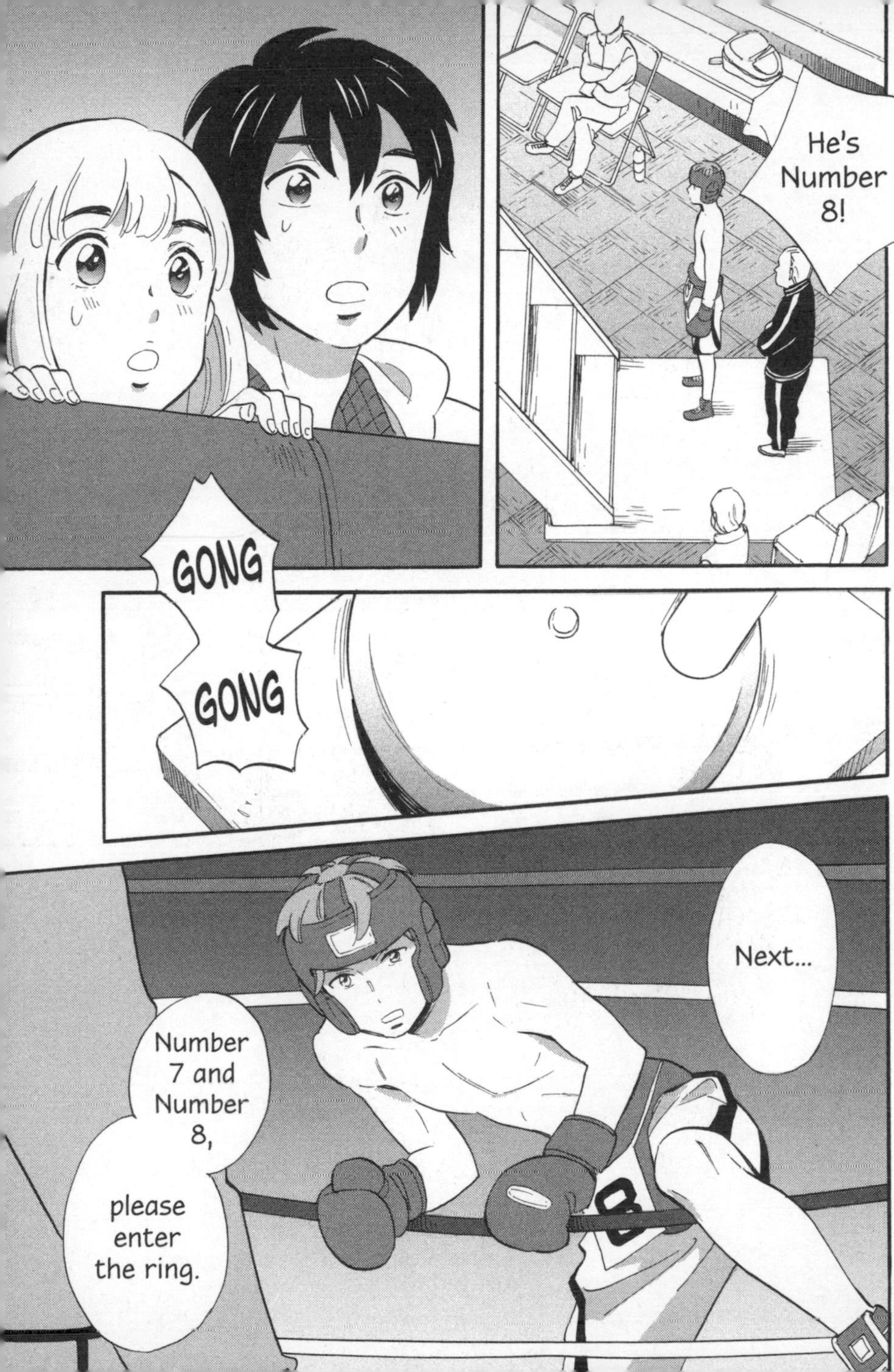
He's Number 8!
GONG
GONG
Next...
Number 7 and Number 8,
please enter the ring.

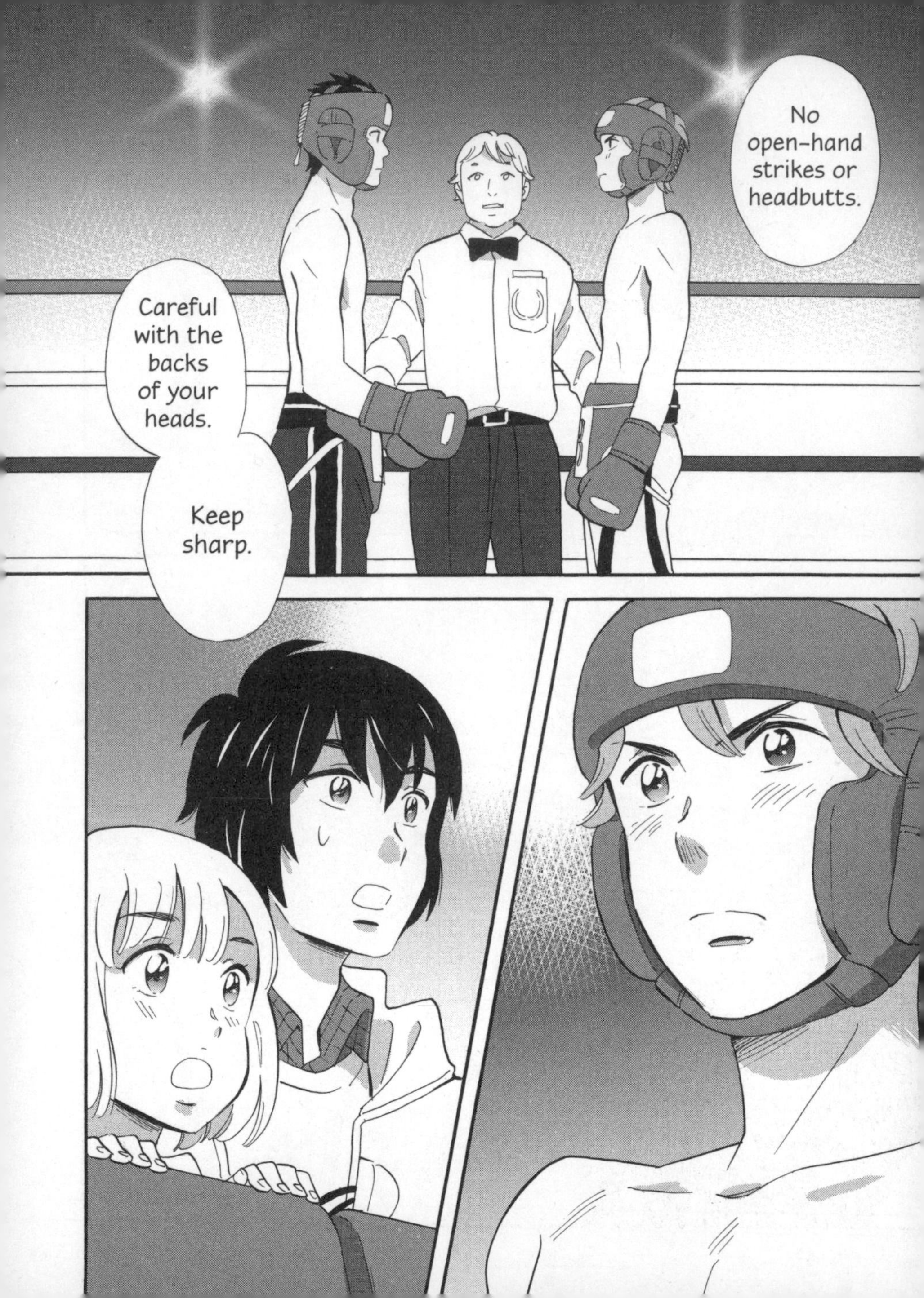
No open-hand strikes or headbutts.
Careful with the backs of your heads.
Keep sharp.

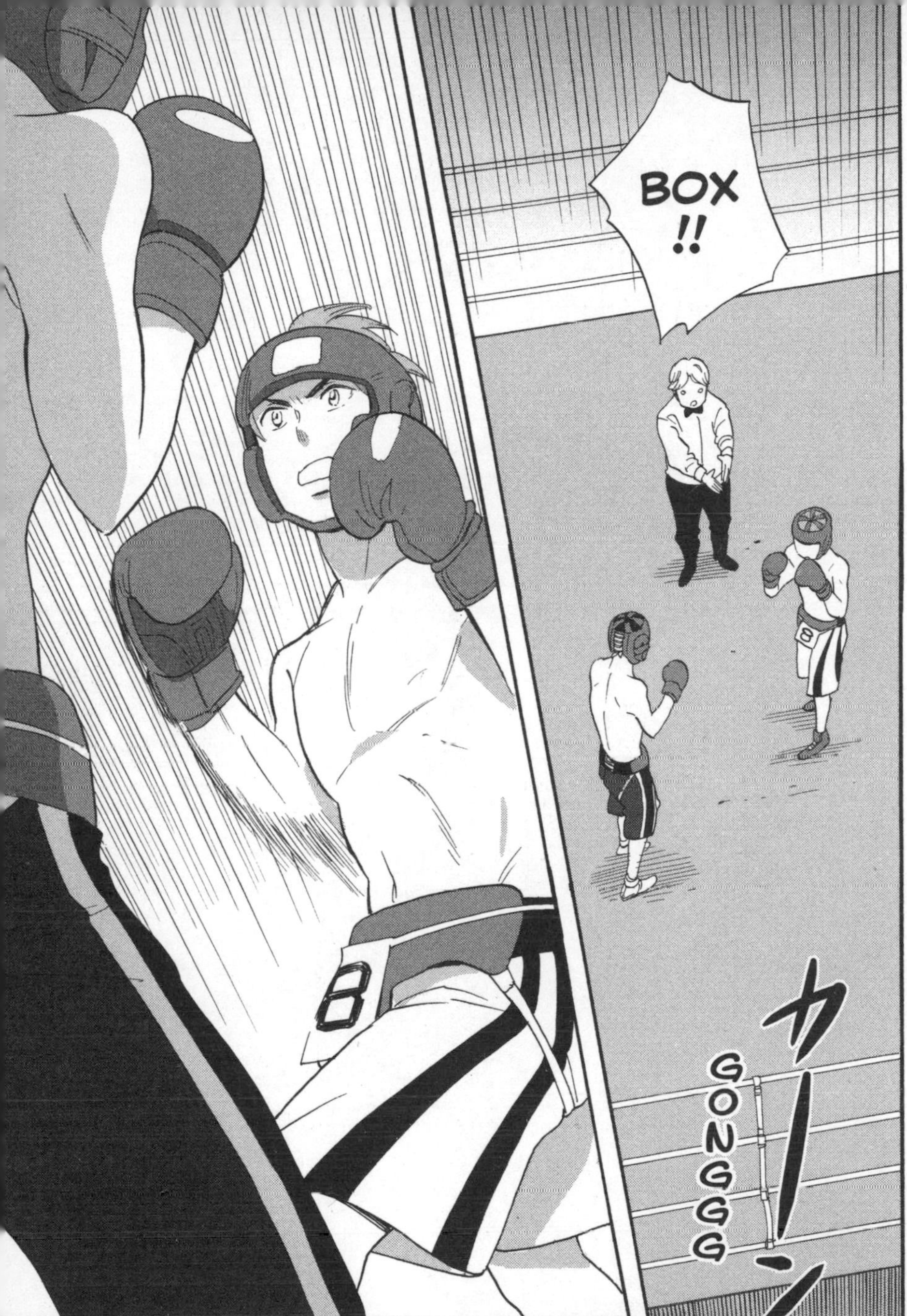
BOX !!
カーン
GONGGG

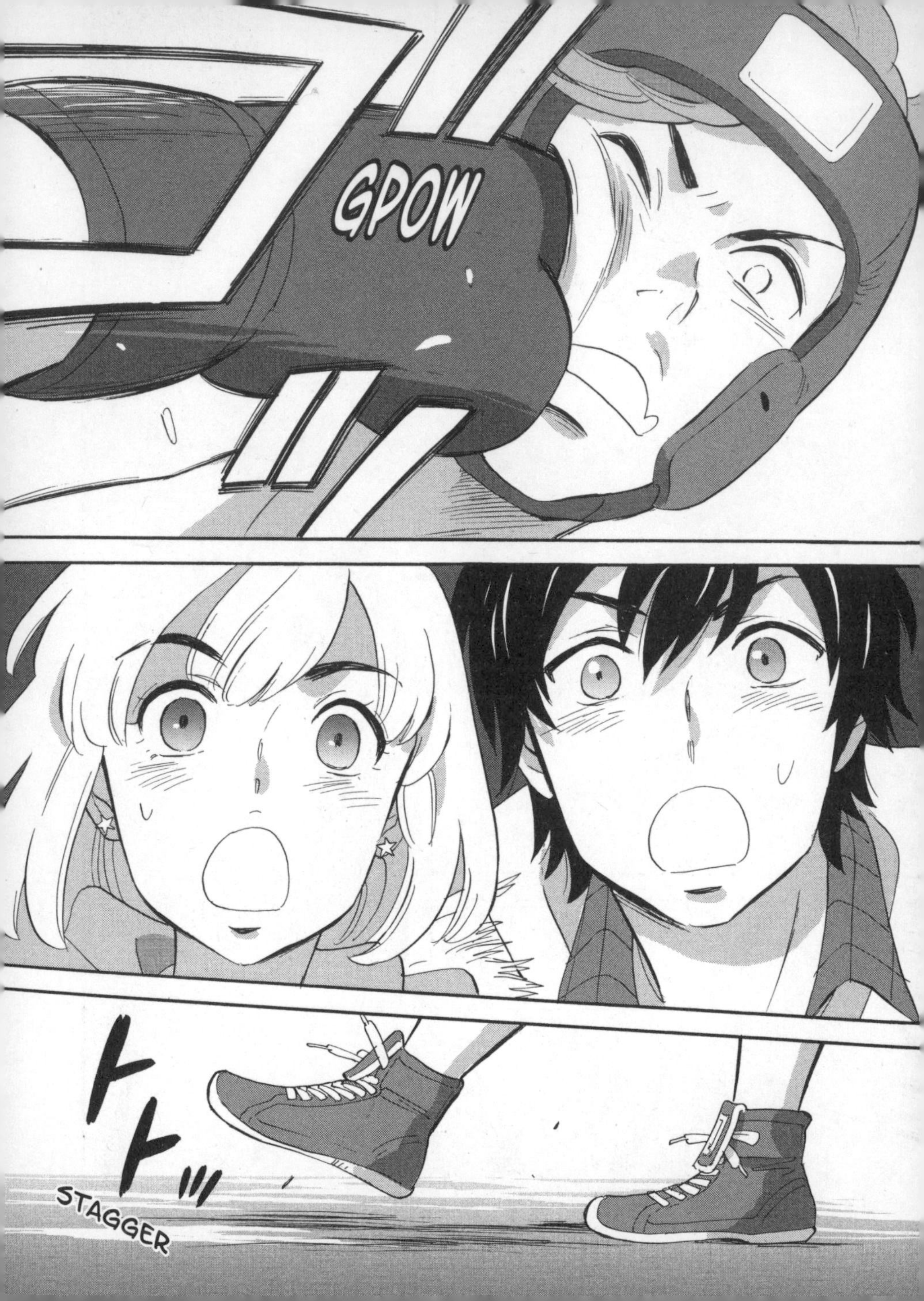
GPOW
STAGGER

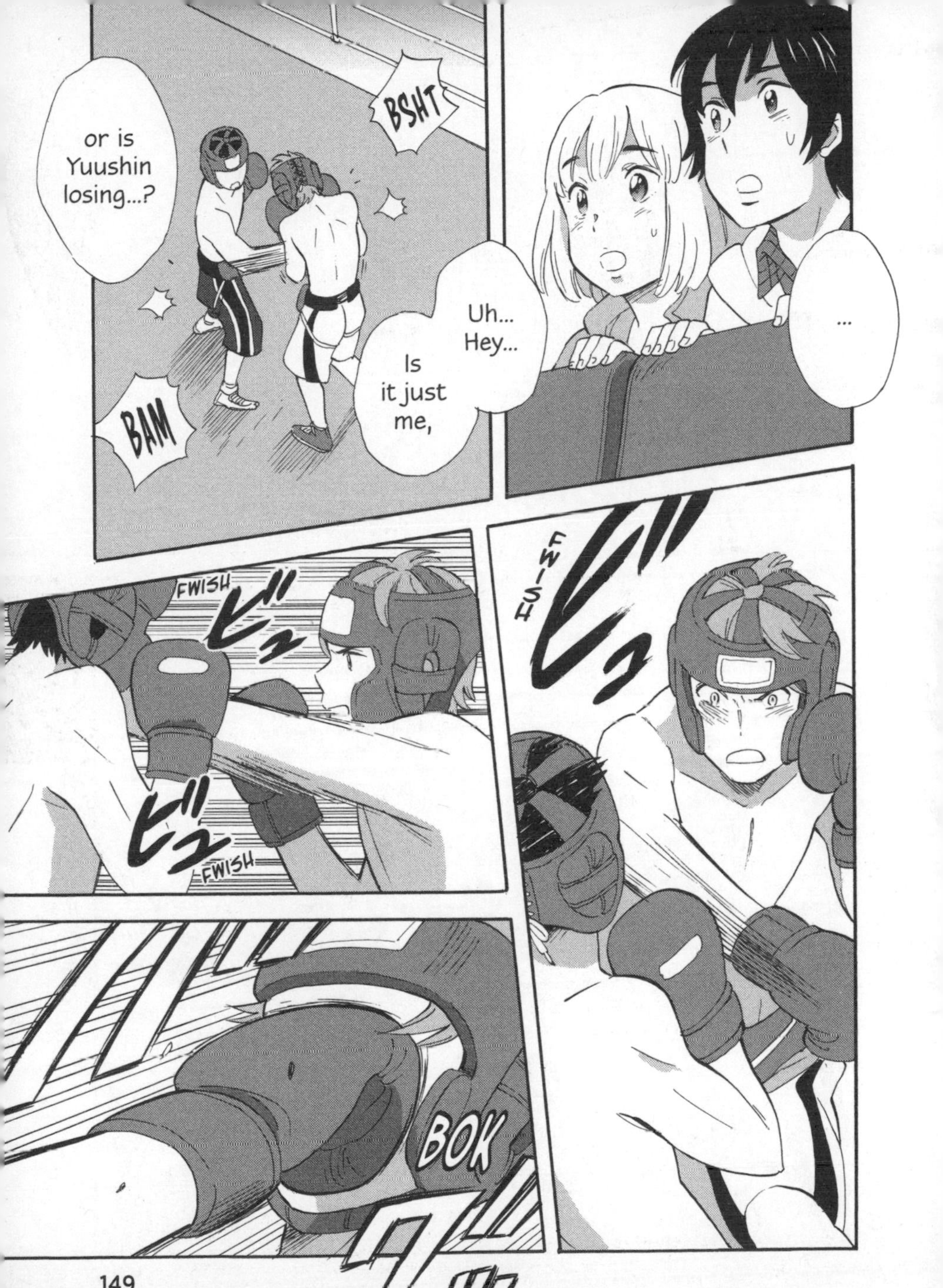
...
Uh... Hey...
Is it just me,
or is Yuushin losing...?
BSHT
BAM
FWISH
FWISH
FWISH
BOK

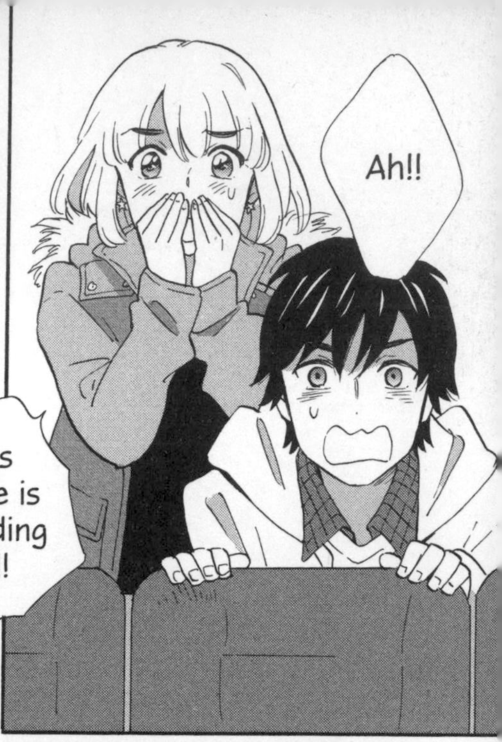
Ah!!
His nose is bleeding ...!!
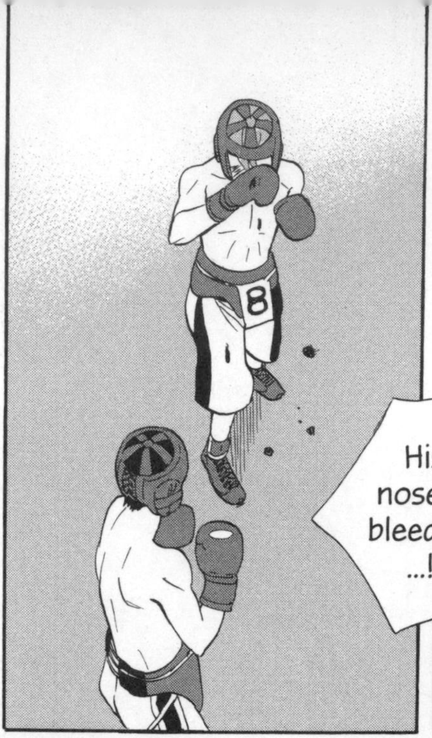
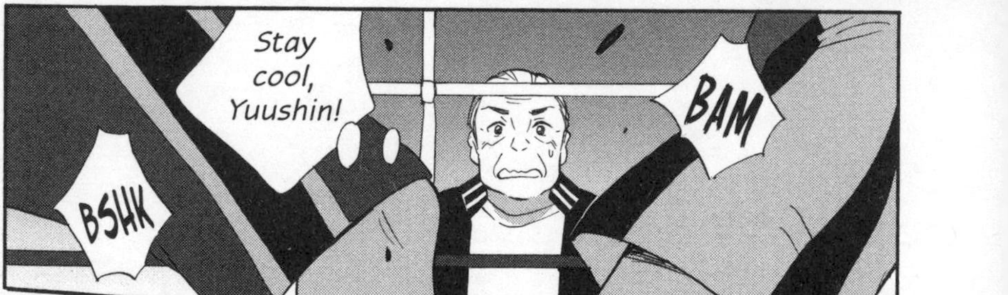
BAM
Stay cool, Yuushin!
BSHK
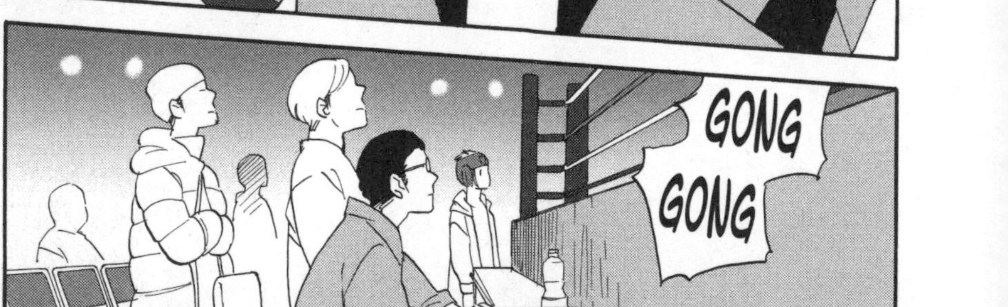
GONG GONG

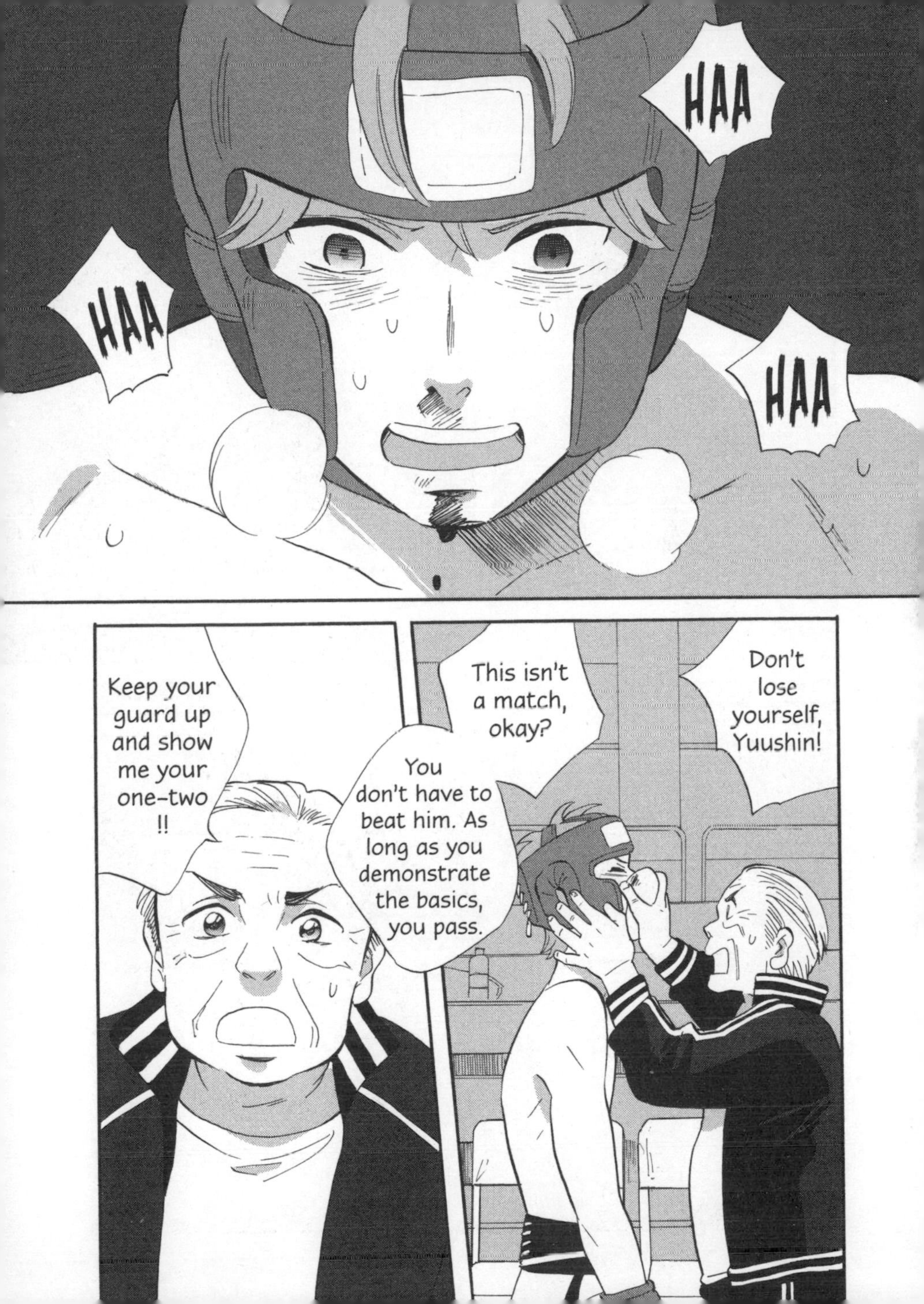
HAA
HAA
HAA
Don't lose yourself, Yuushin!
This isn't a match, okay?
You don't have to beat him. As long as you demonstrate the basics, you pass.
Keep your guard up and show me your one-two !!

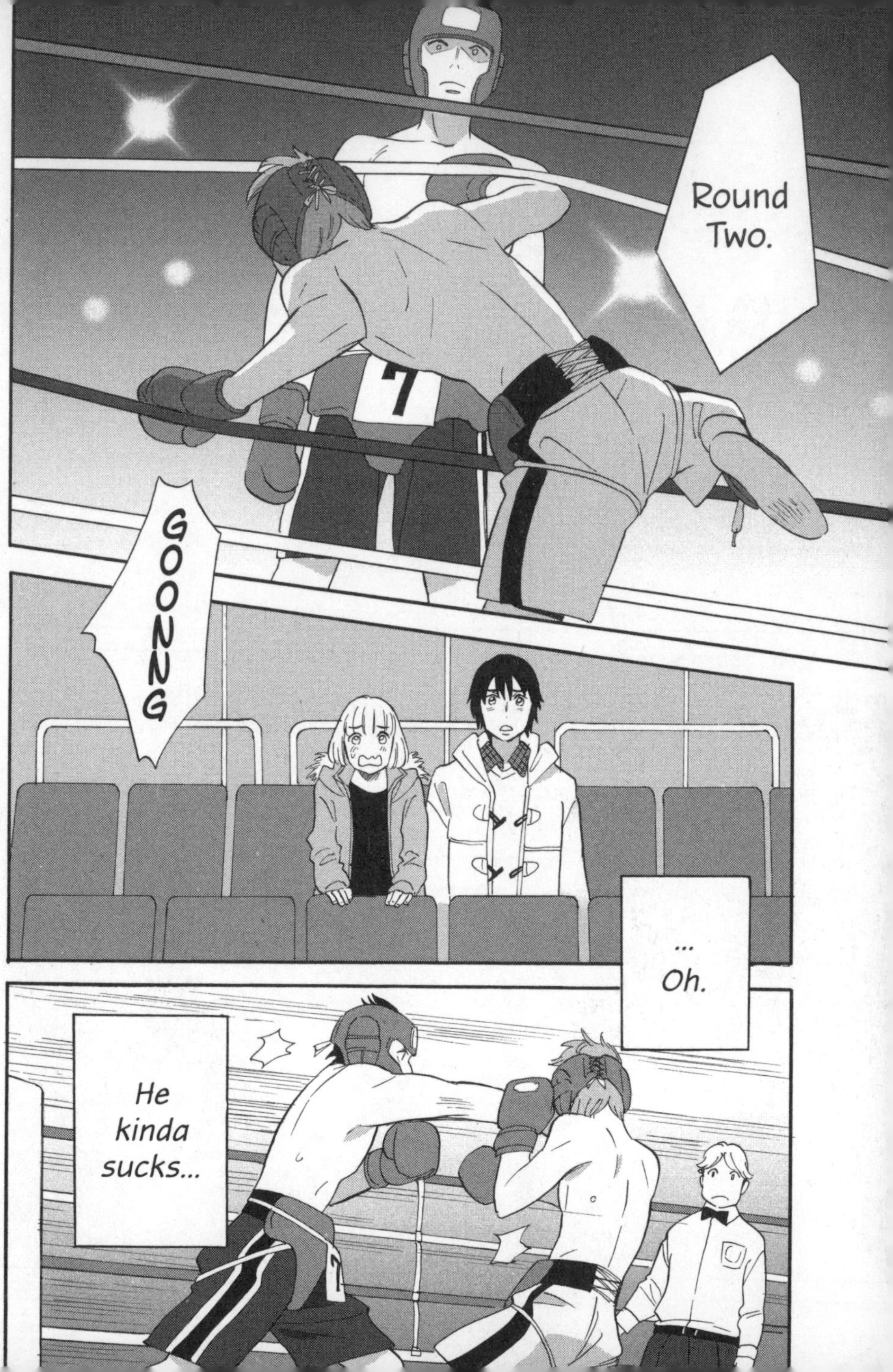
Round Two.
GOOONNG
... Oh.
He kinda sucks...

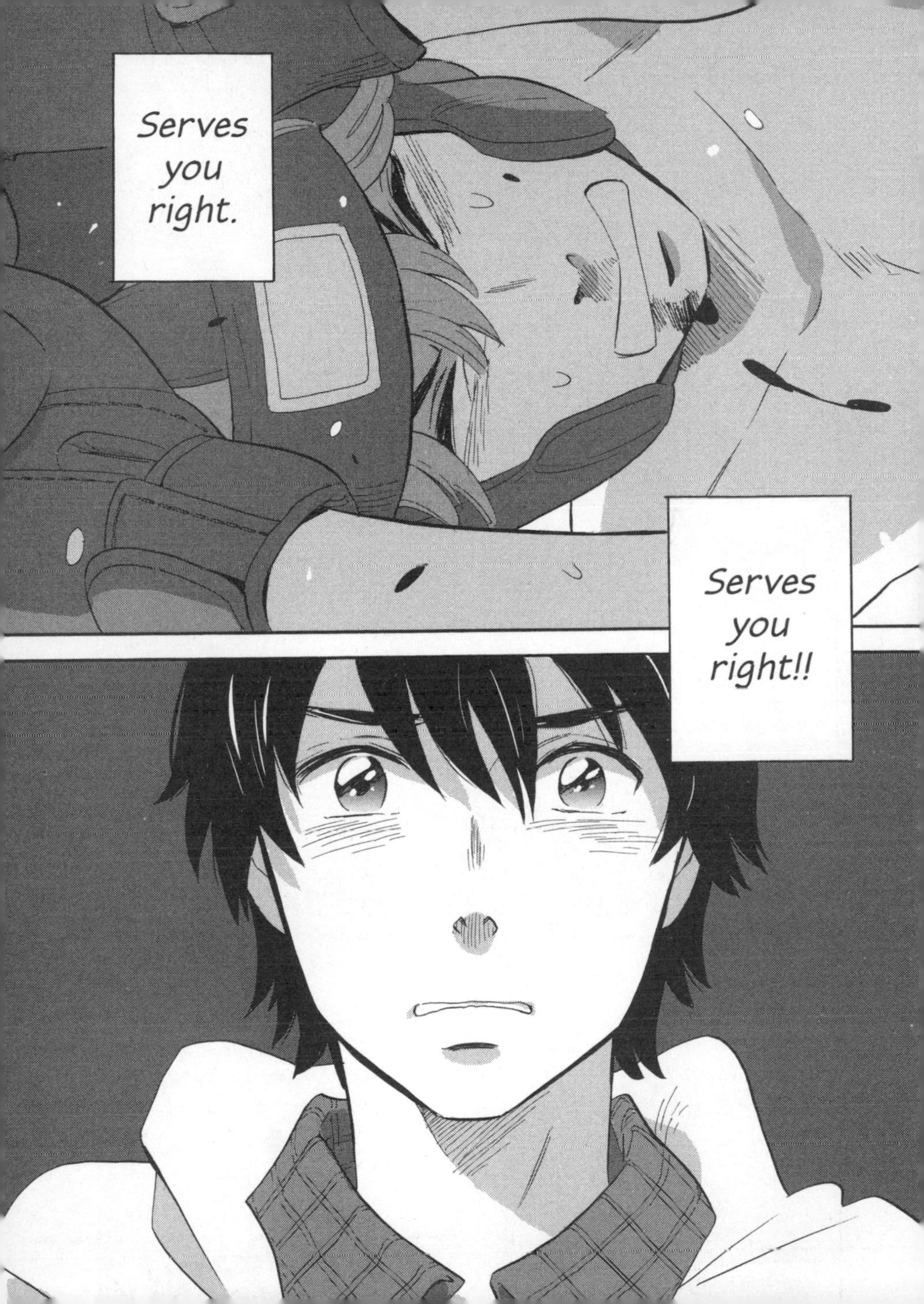
Serves you right.
Serves you right!!

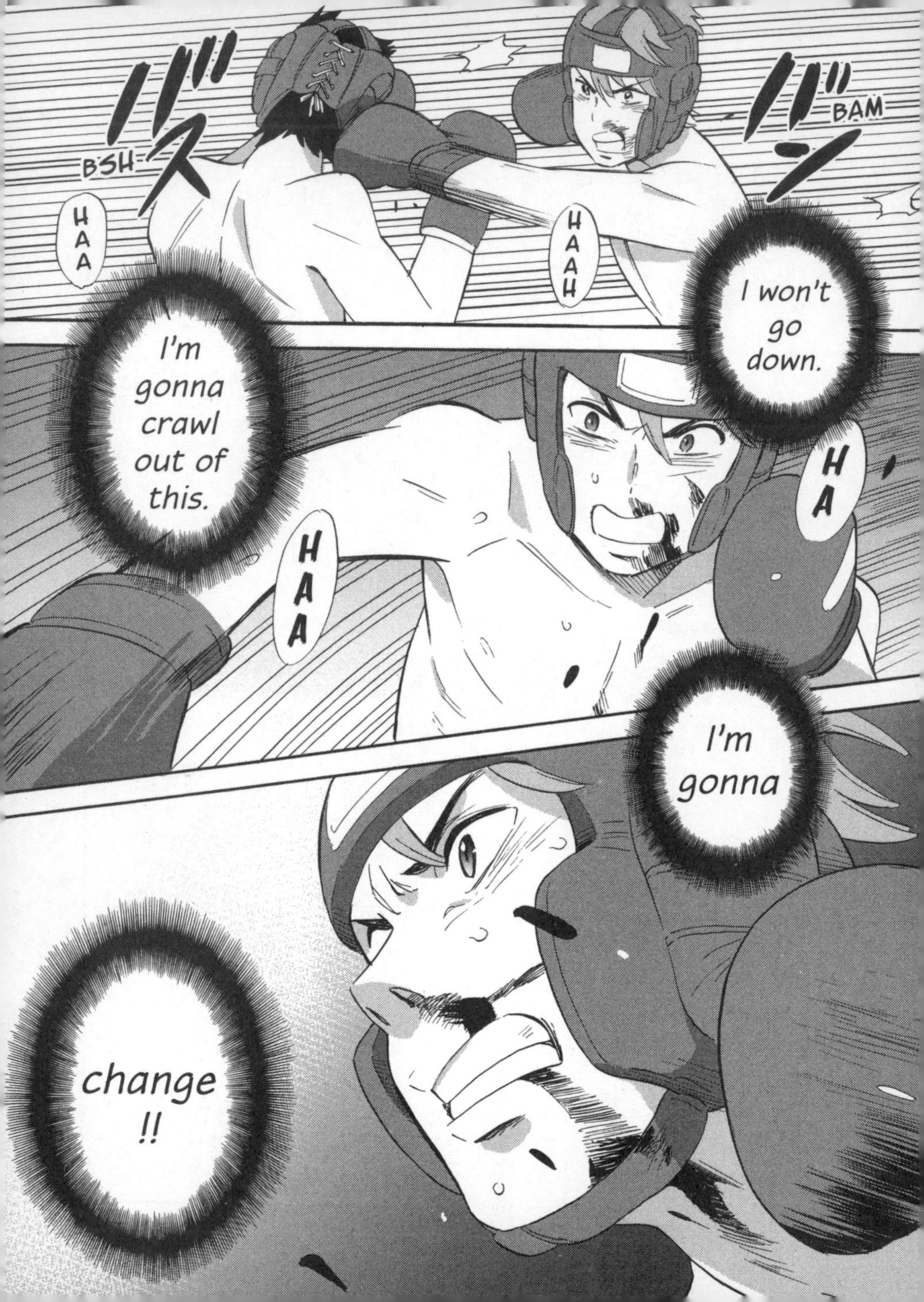
BAM
HAAH
BSH
HAA
I won't go down.
HA
I'm gonna crawl out of this.
HAA
I'm gonna
change !!

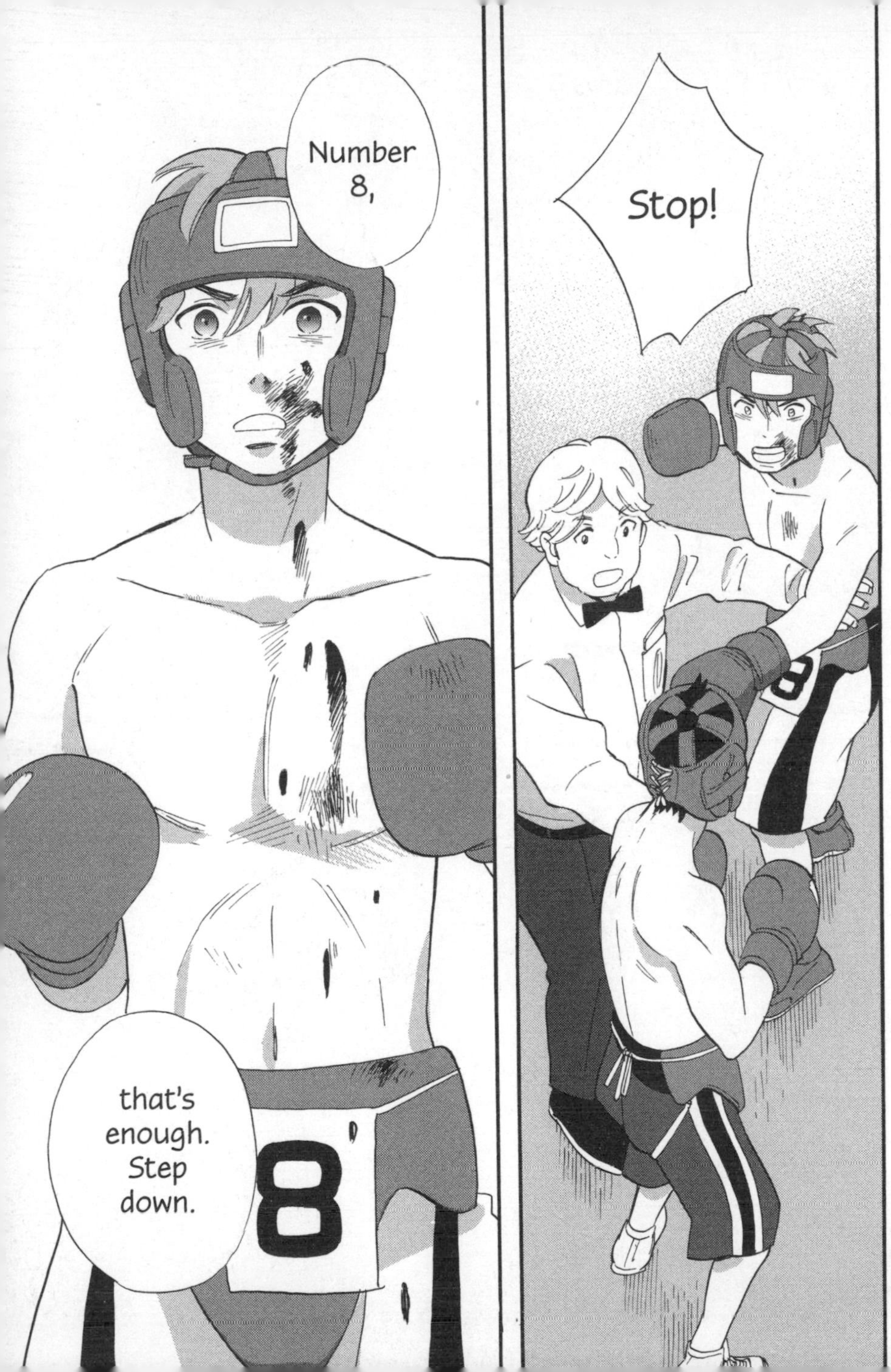
Stop!
Number 8,
that's enough. Step down.

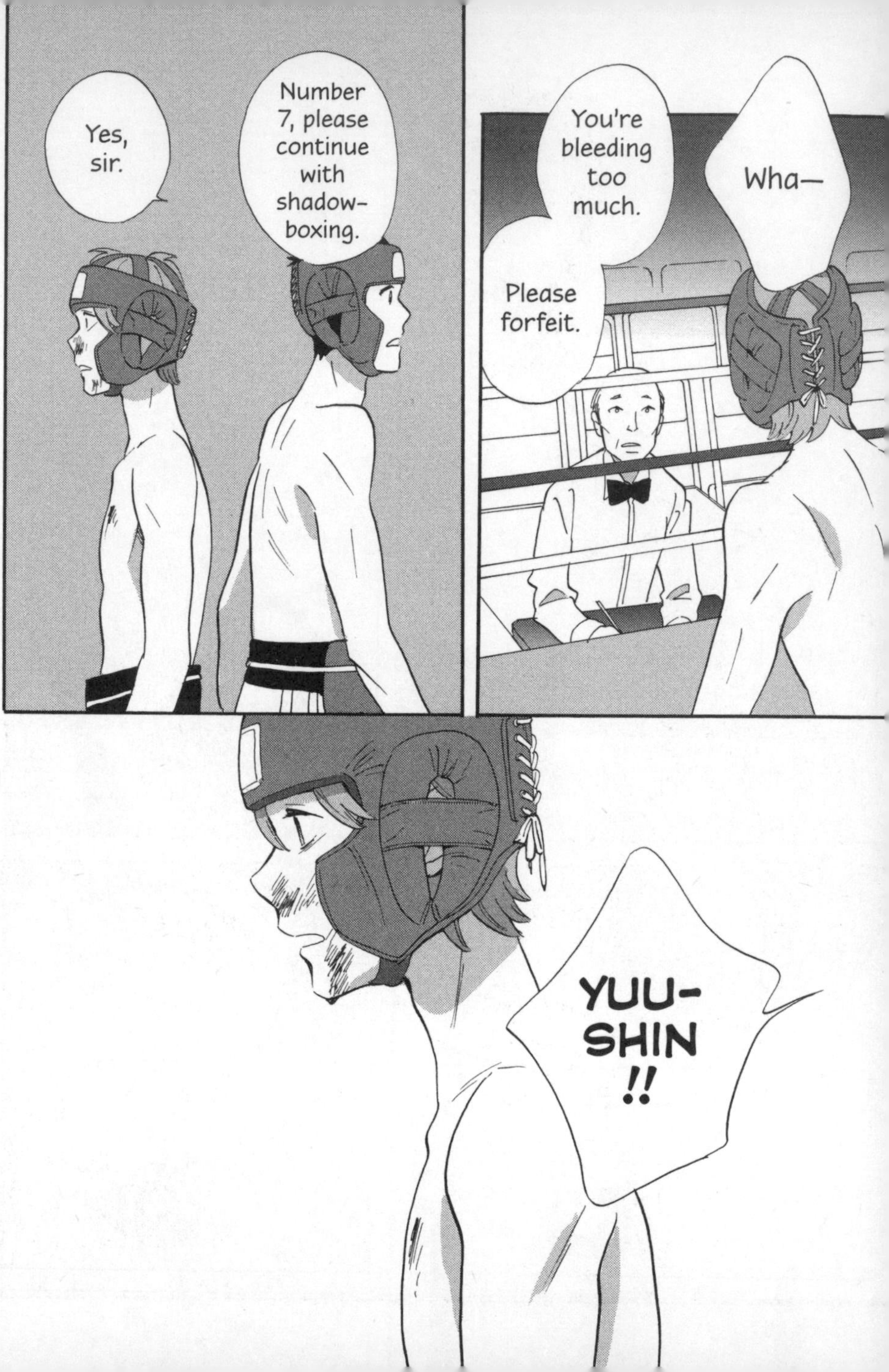
Wha—
You're bleeding too much.
Please forfeit.
Number 7, please continue with shadow-boxing.
Yes, sir.
YUU-SHIN!!

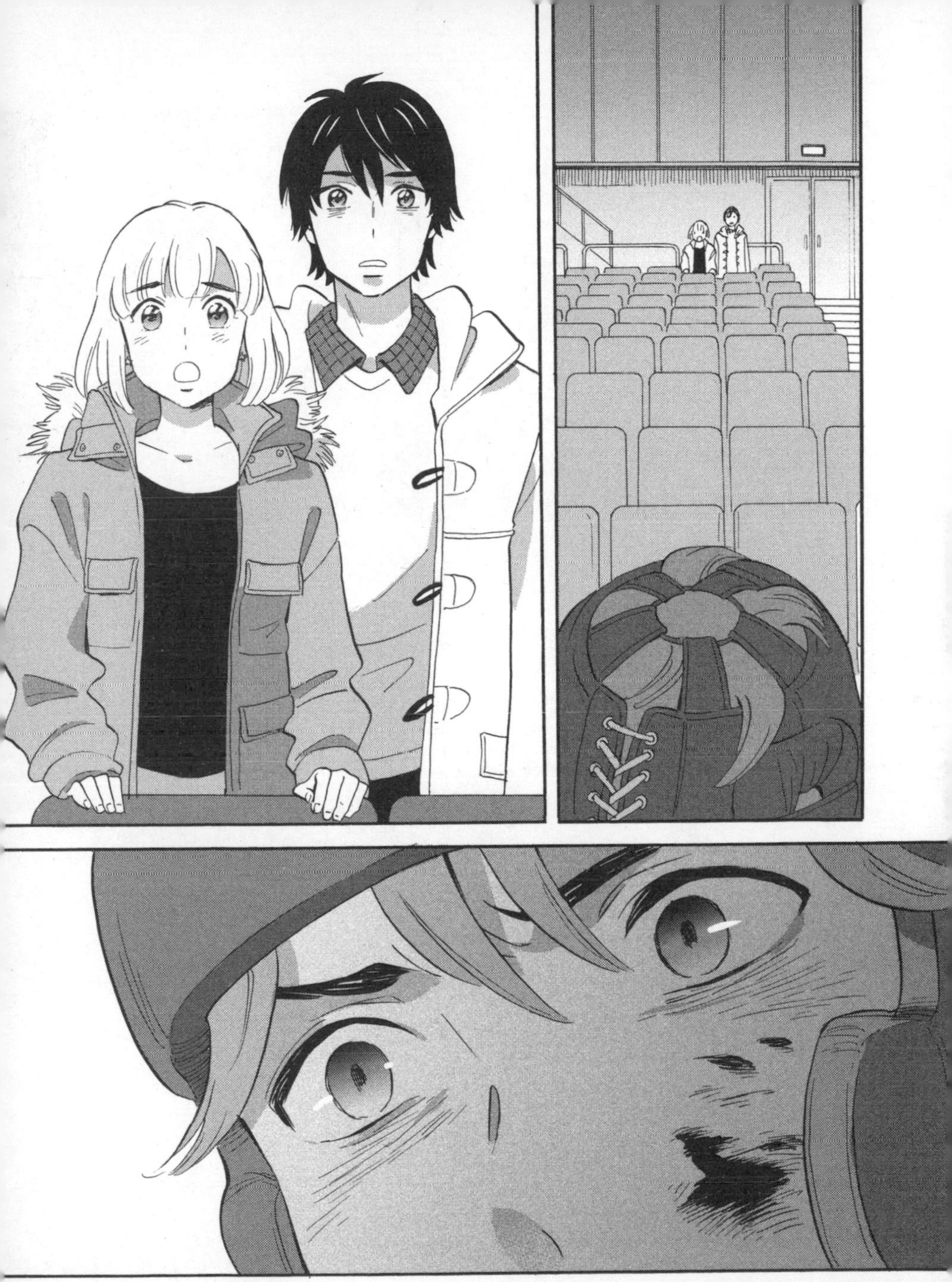

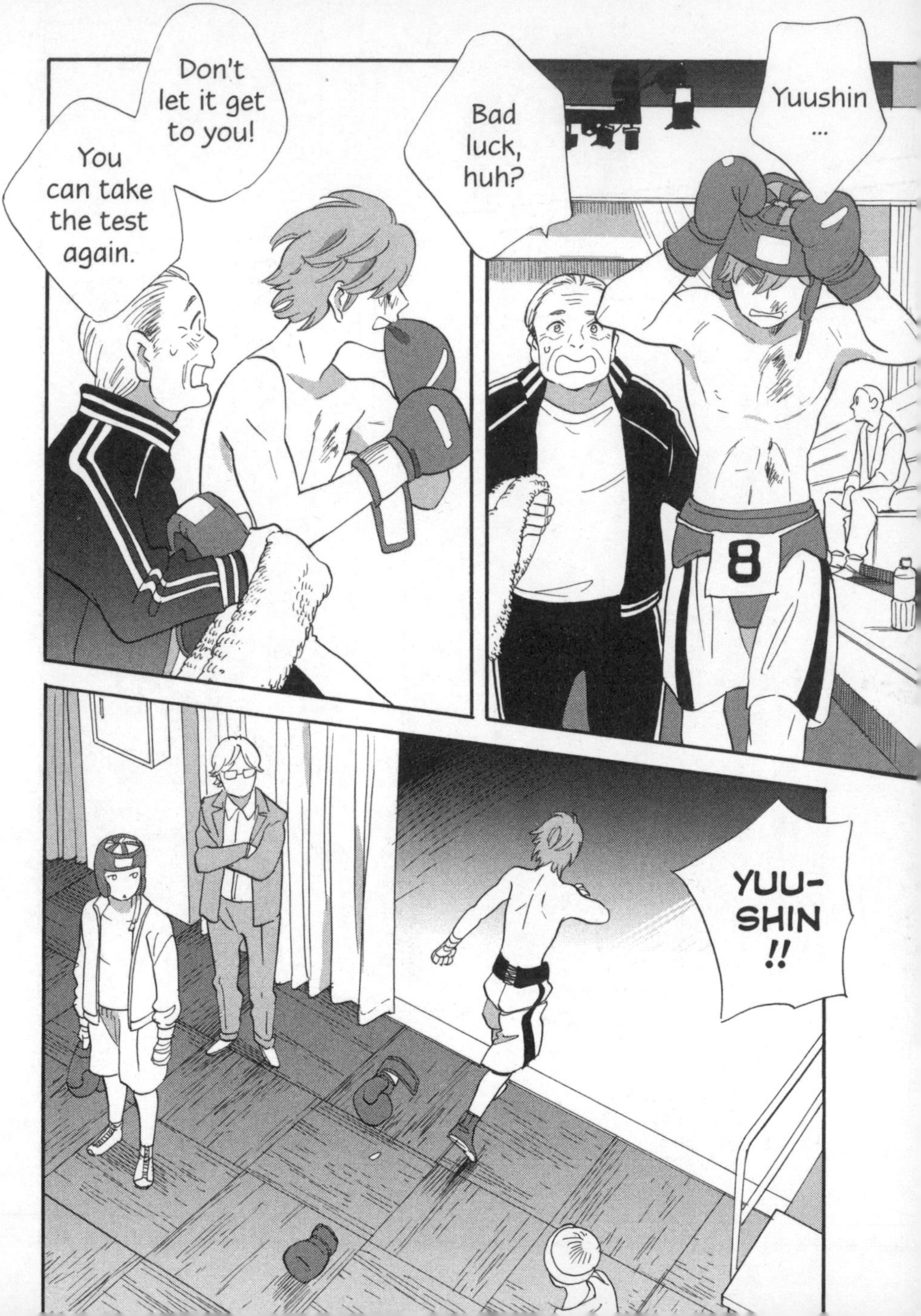
Yuushin
...
Bad luck, huh?
Don't let it get to you!
You can take the test again.
YUU-SHIN!!

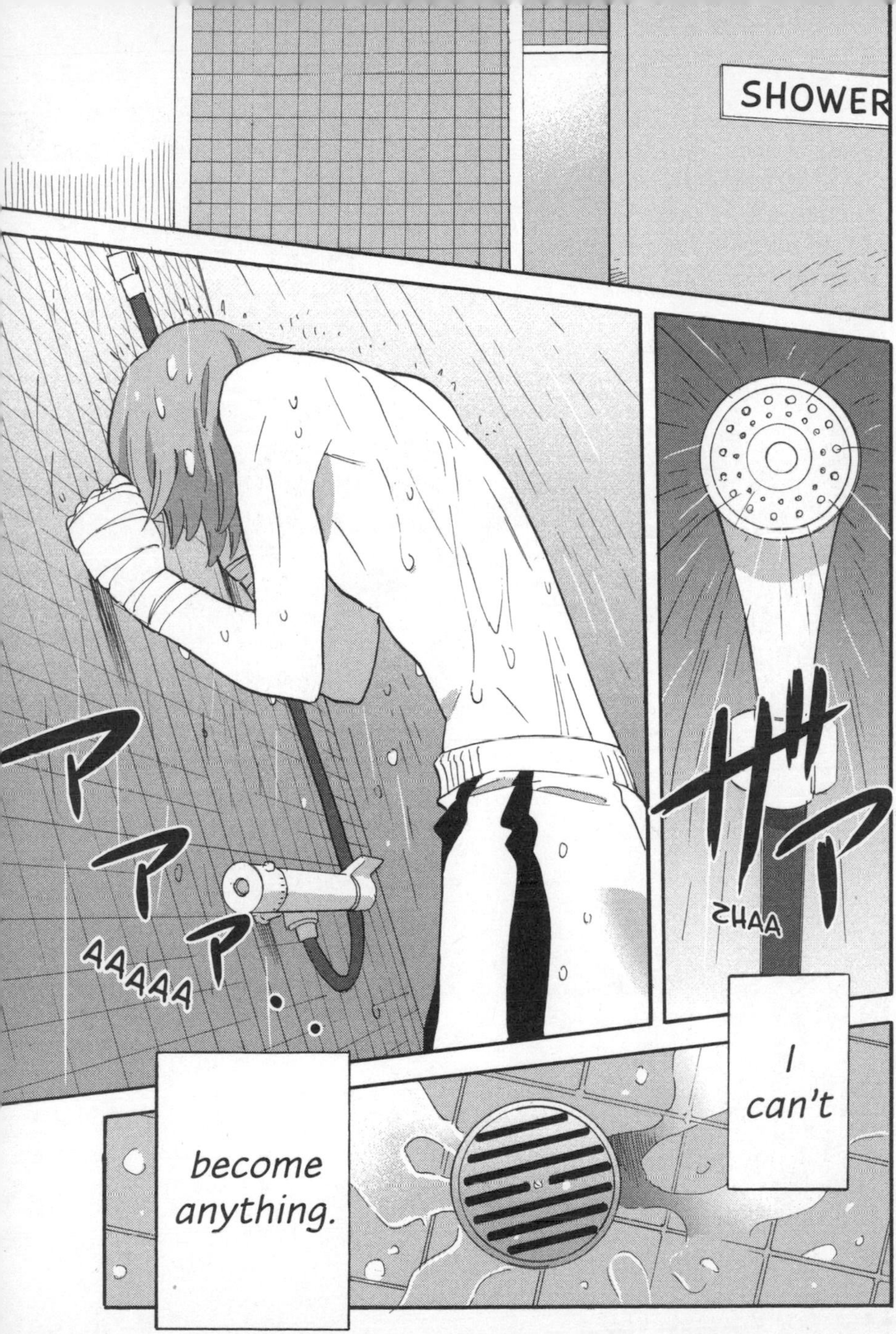
SHOWER
ザァ
ZHAA
アアア
AAAAA
I can't
become anything.

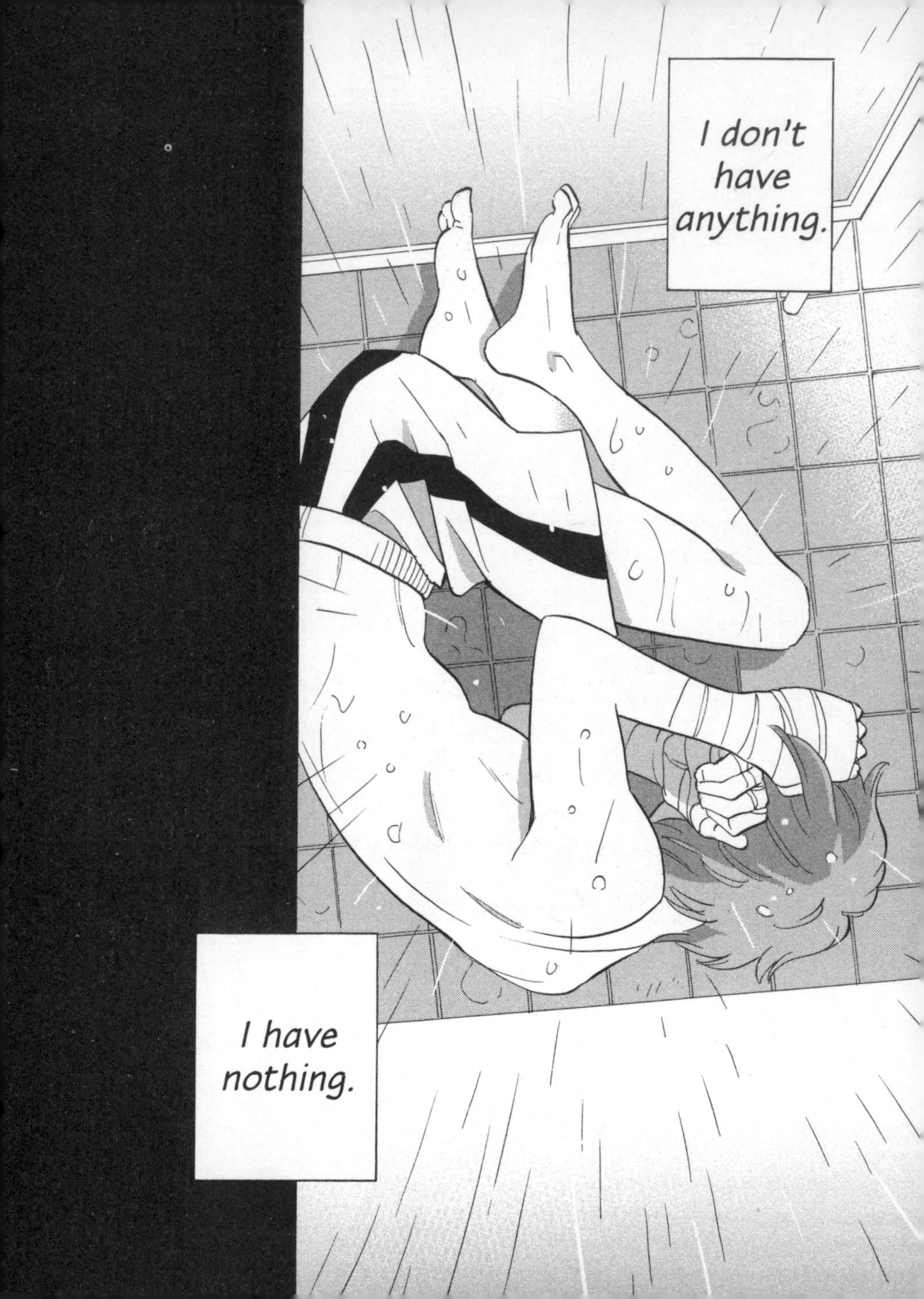
I don't have anything.
I have nothing.

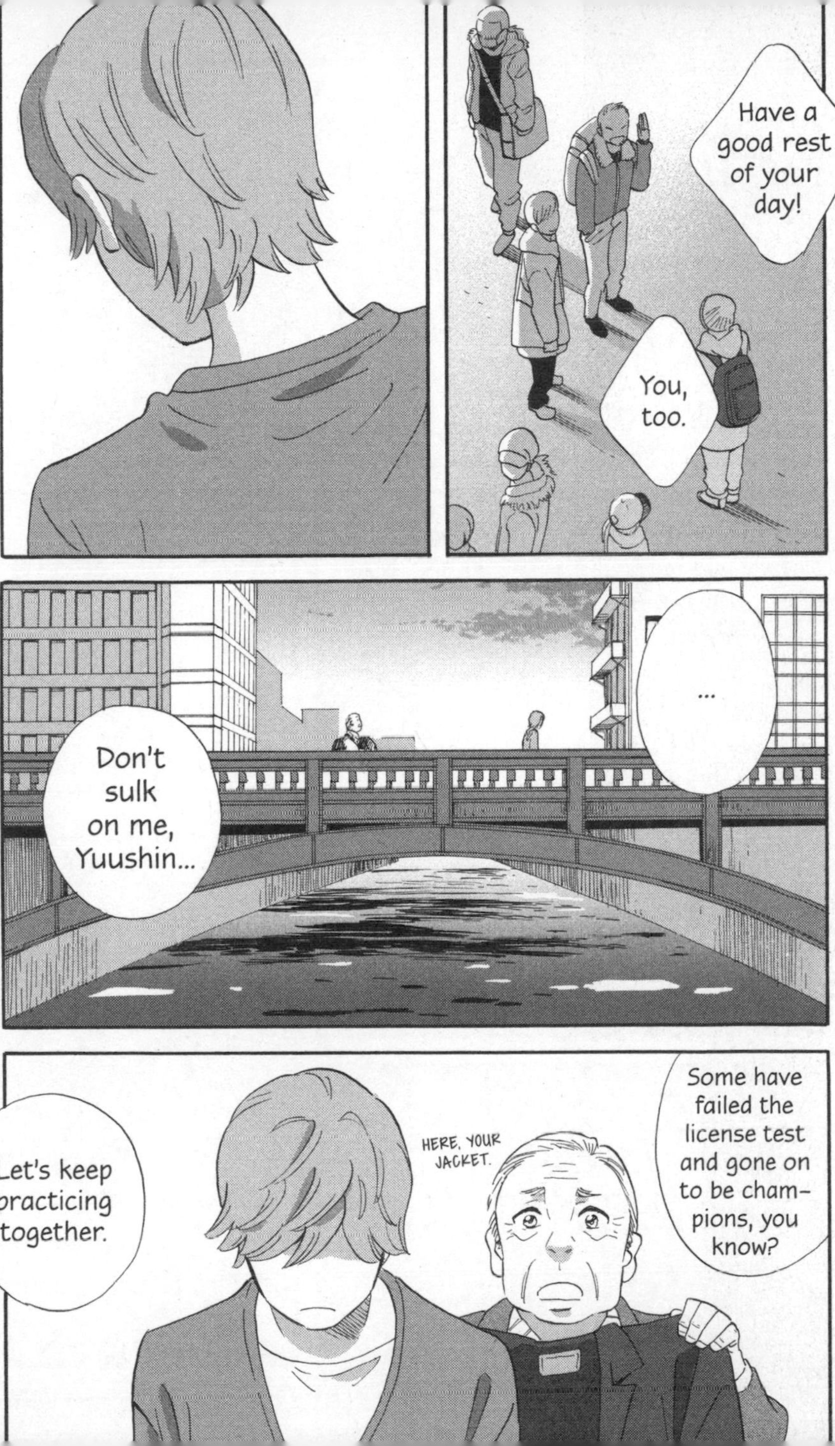
Have a good rest of your day!
You, too.
...
Don't sulk on me, Yuushin...
Some have failed the license test and gone on to be champions, you know?
HERE, YOUR JACKET.
Let's keep practicing together.

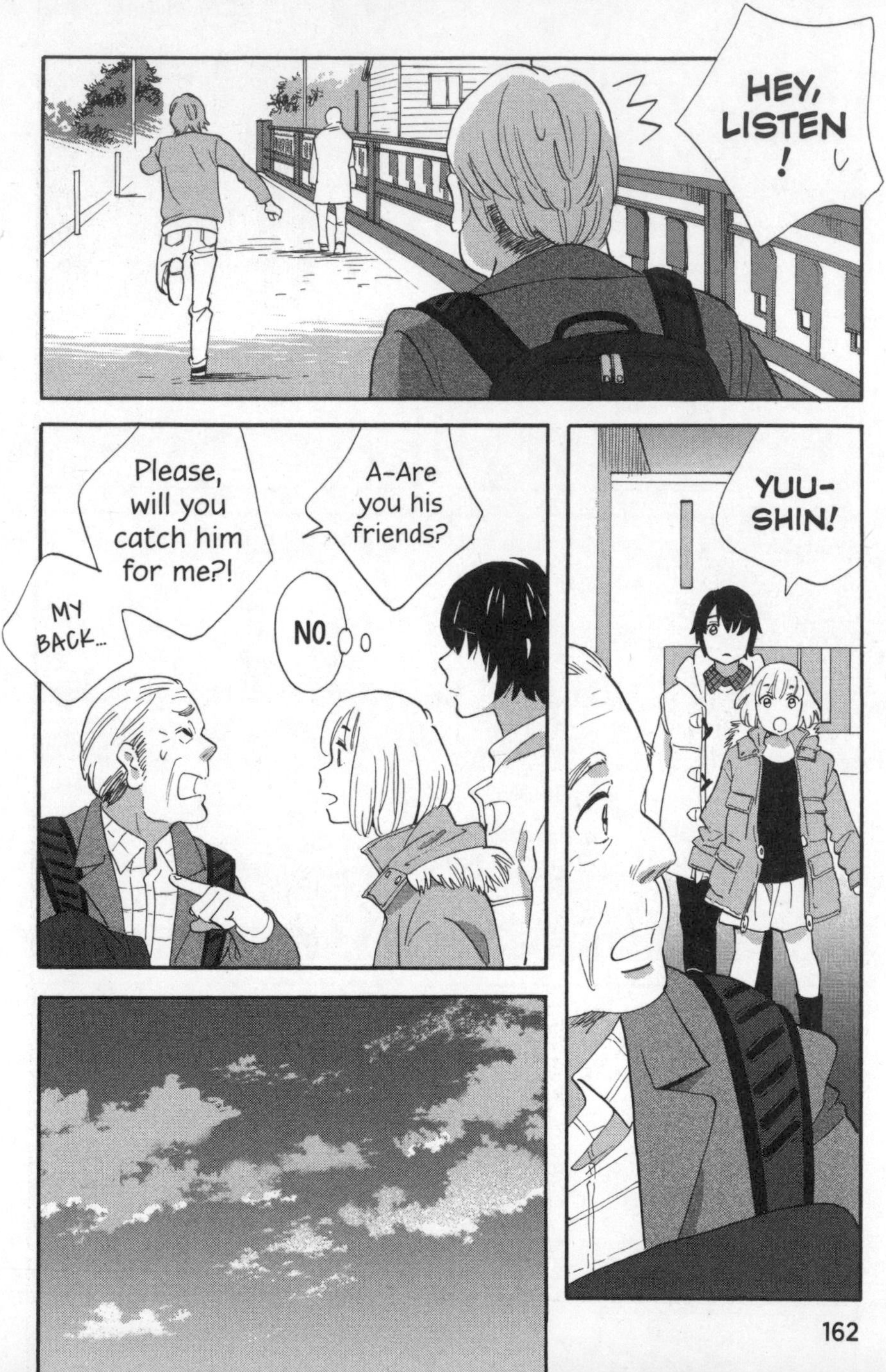
HEY, LISTEN!
YUU-SHIN!
A-Are you his friends?
Please, will you catch him for me?!
NO.
MY BACK...

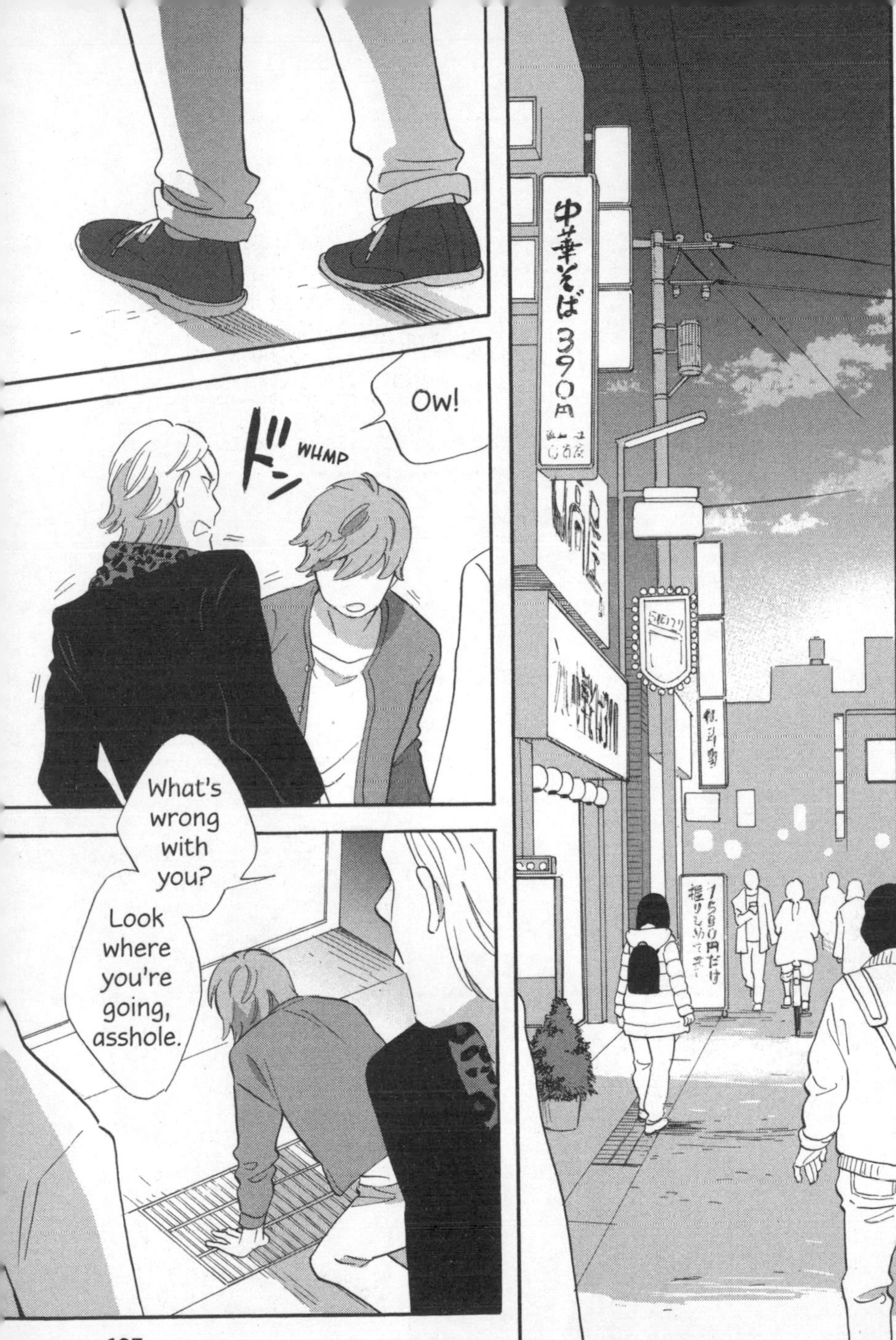
中華そば390円
Ow!
ドン
WHMP
What's wrong with you?
Look where you're going, asshole.

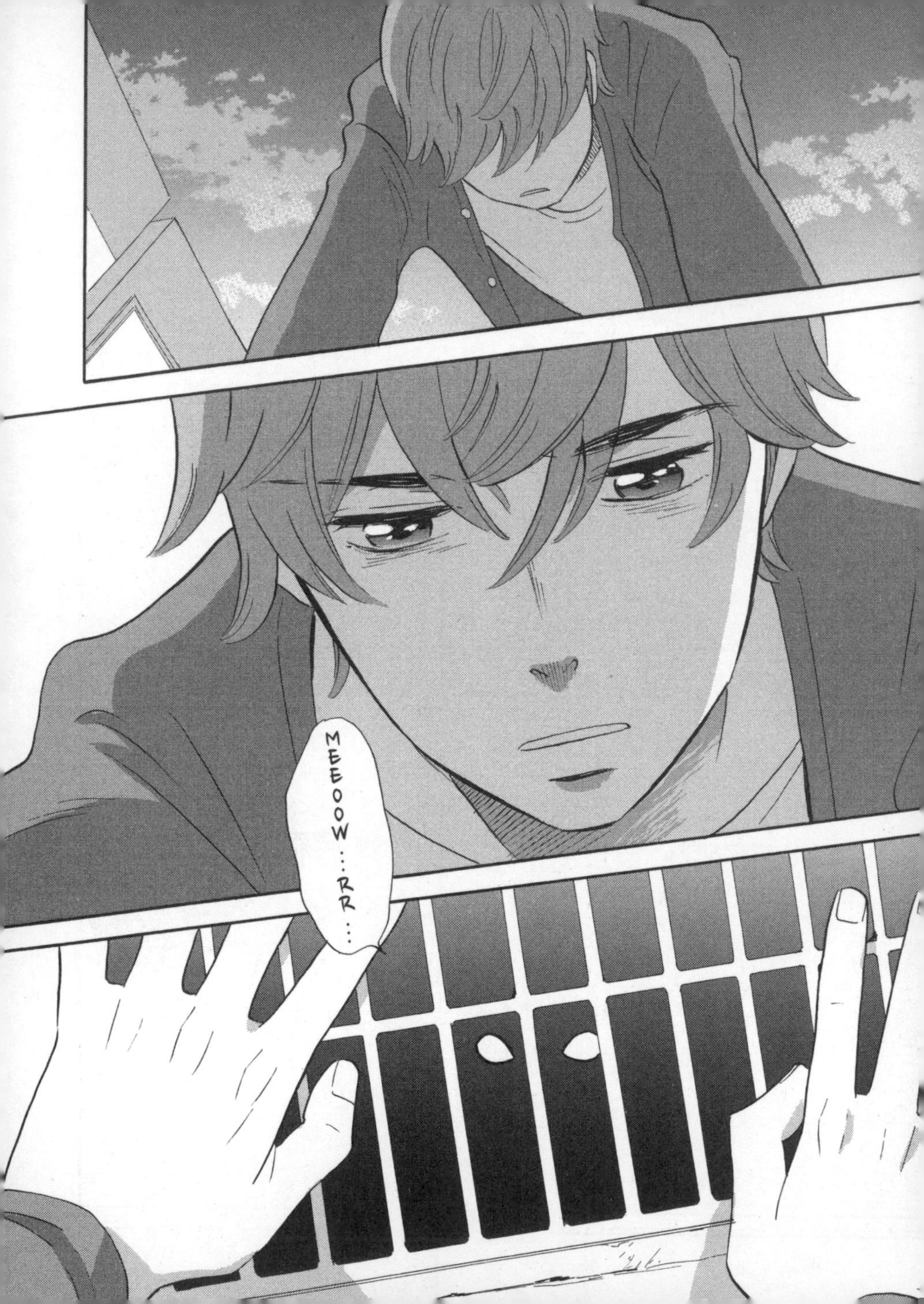
MEEOOW...RR...

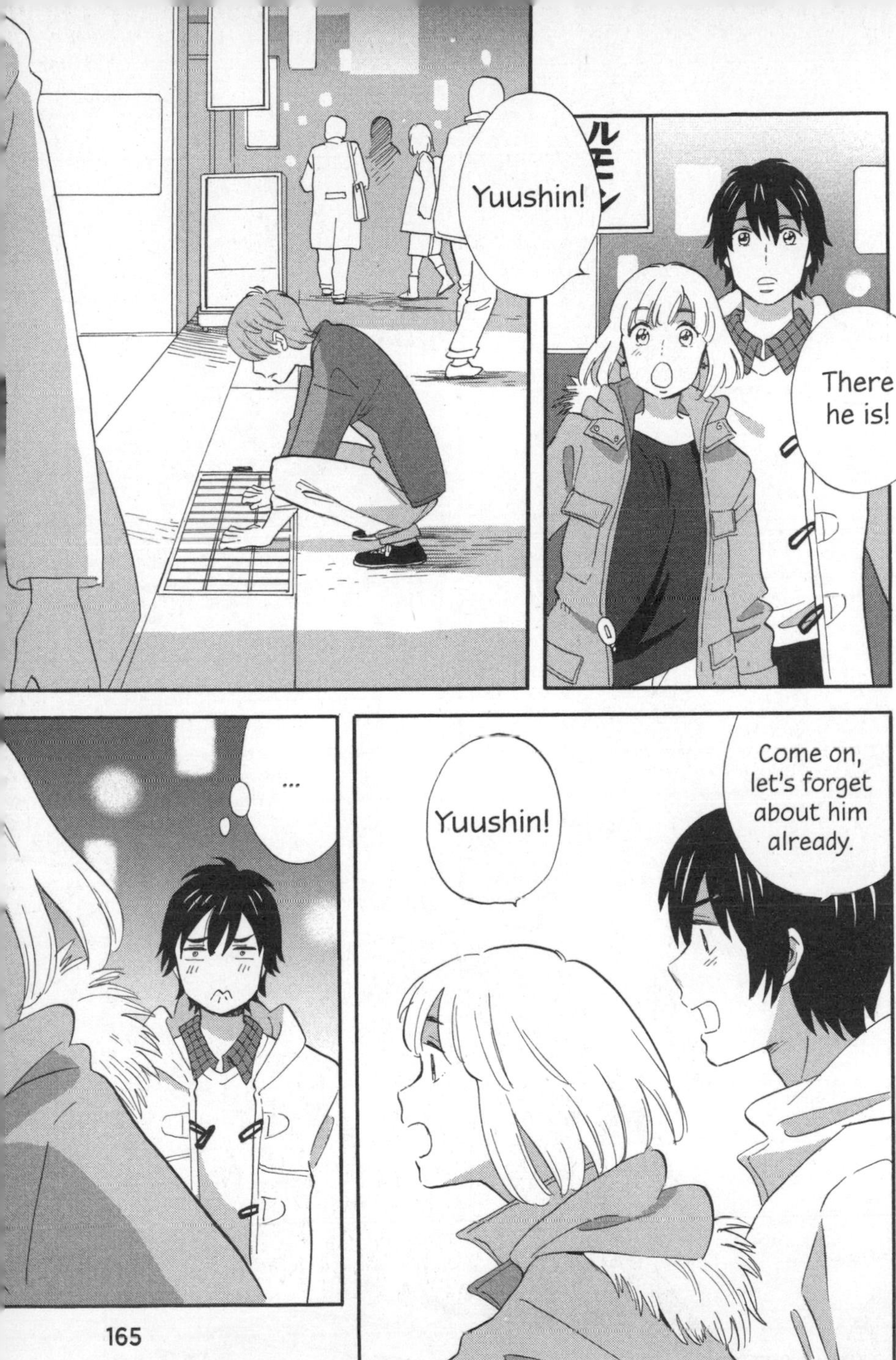
Yuushin!
There he is!
Come on, let's forget about him already.
Yuushin!
...

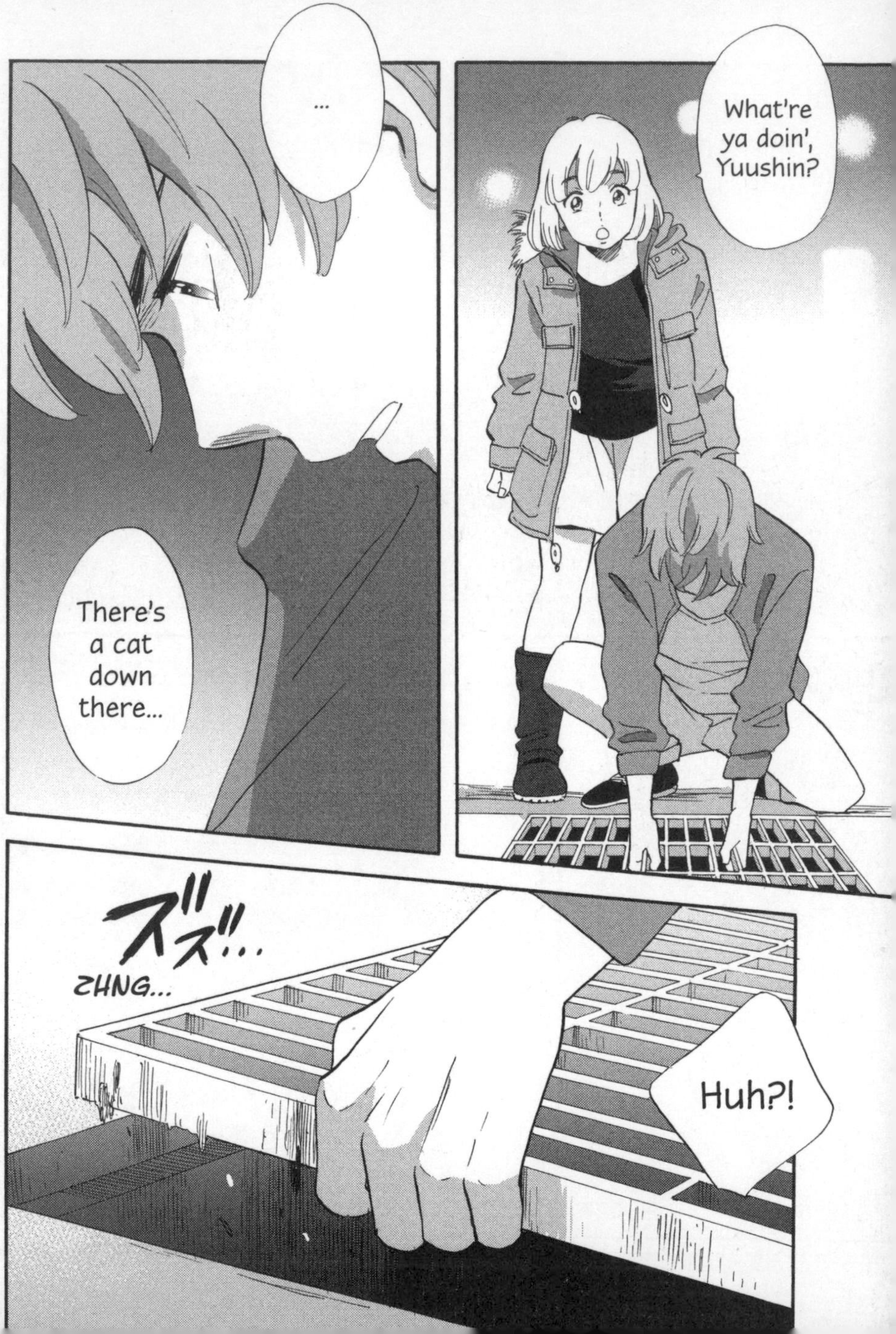
What're ya doin', Yuushin?
...
There's a cat down there...
ズズ...
ZHNG...
Huh?!

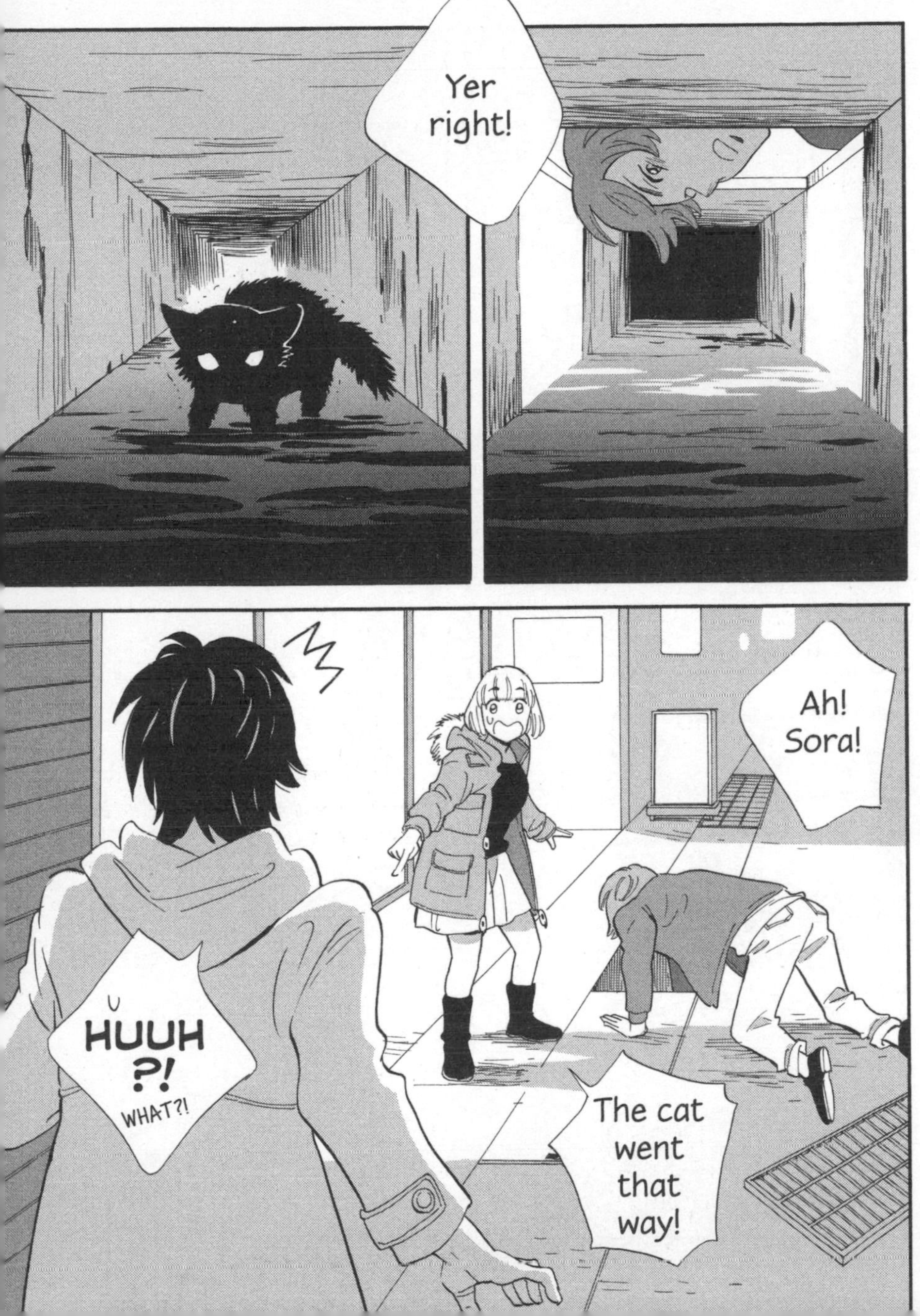
Yer right!
Ah! Sora!
The cat went that way!
HUUH?!
WHAT?!

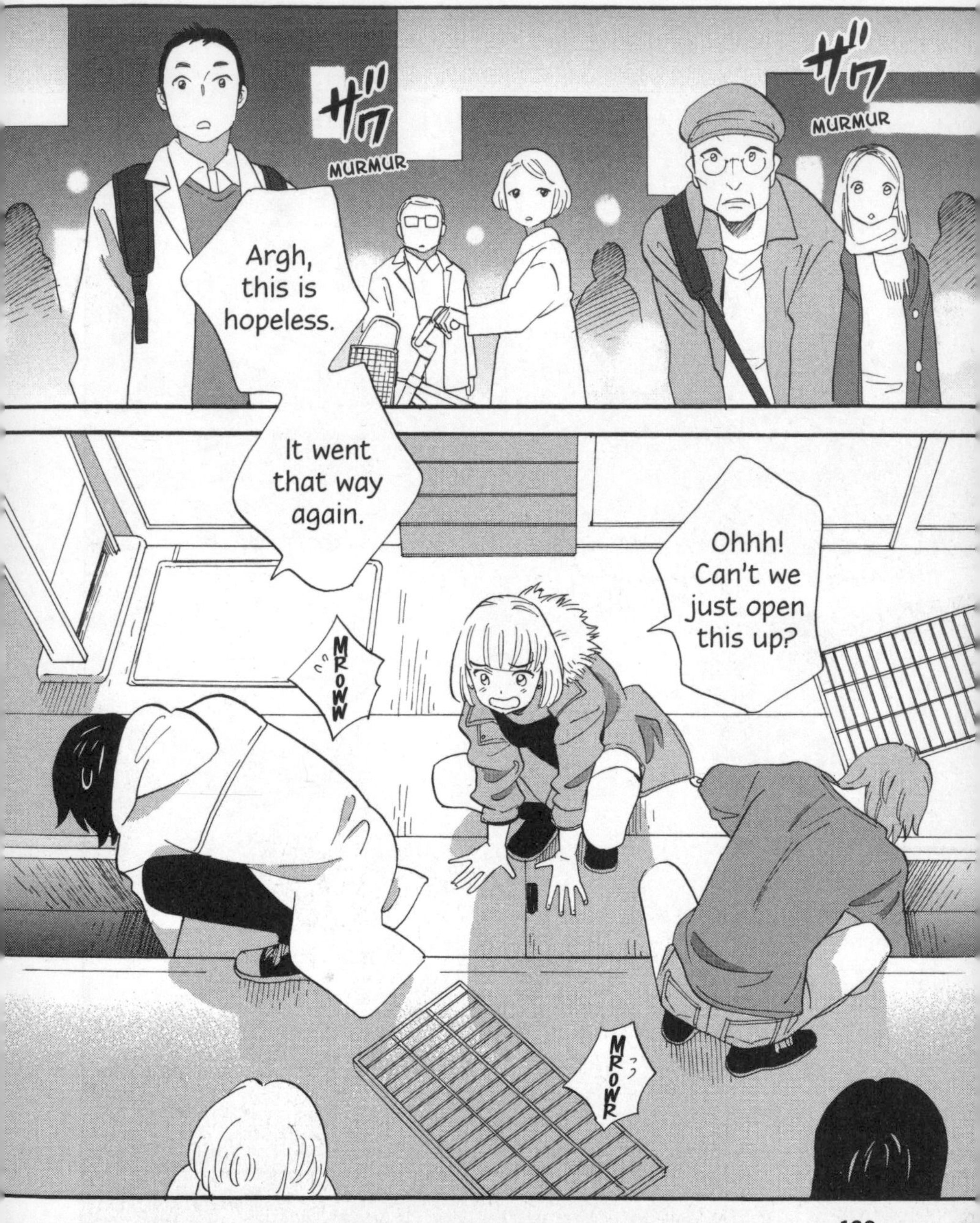
ザワ
MURMUR
ザワ
MURMUR
Argh, this is hopeless.
It went that way again.
Ohhh! Can't we just open this up?
MROWW
MROWR

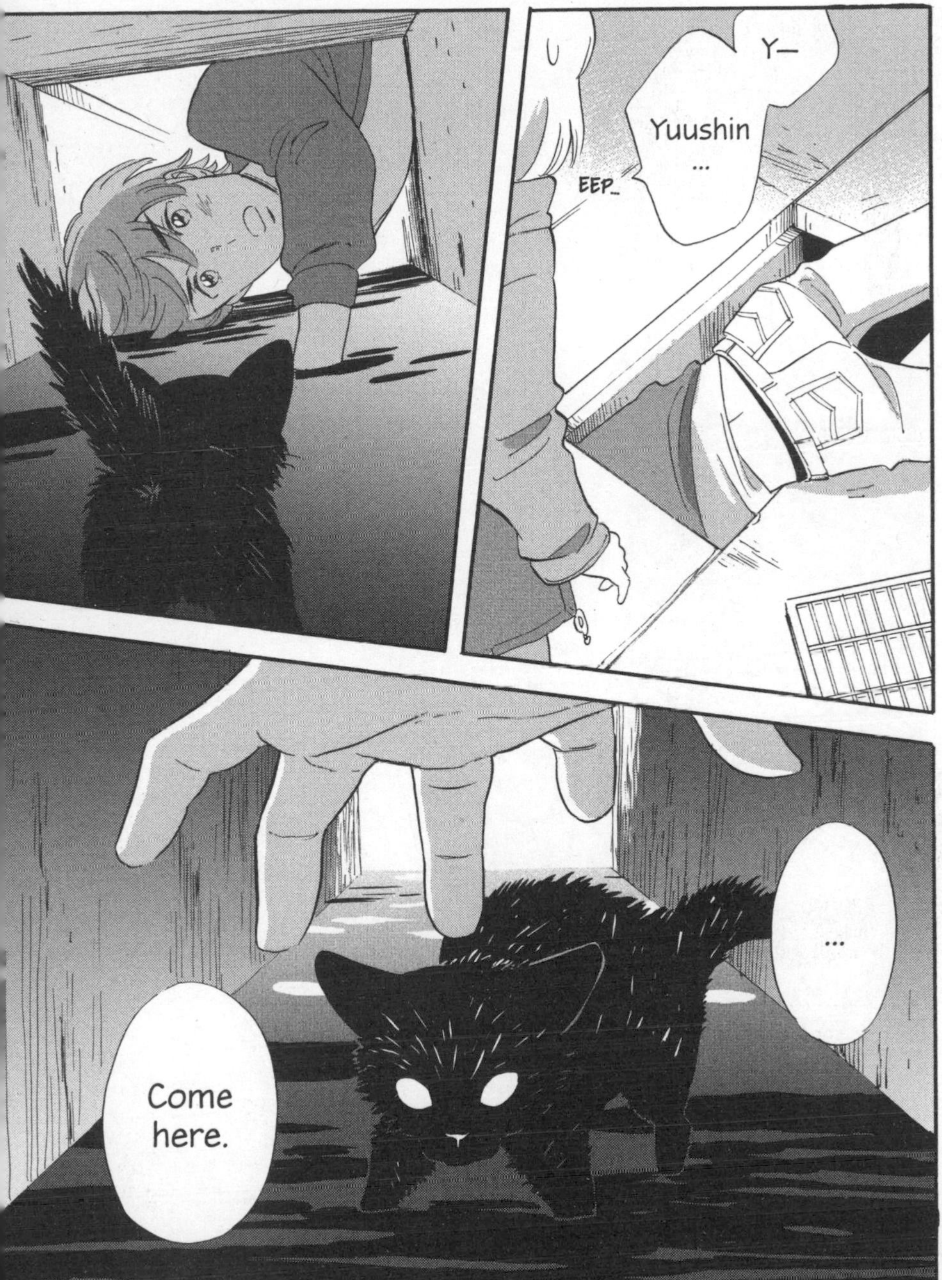
Y—
Yuushin ...
EEP_
...
Come here.

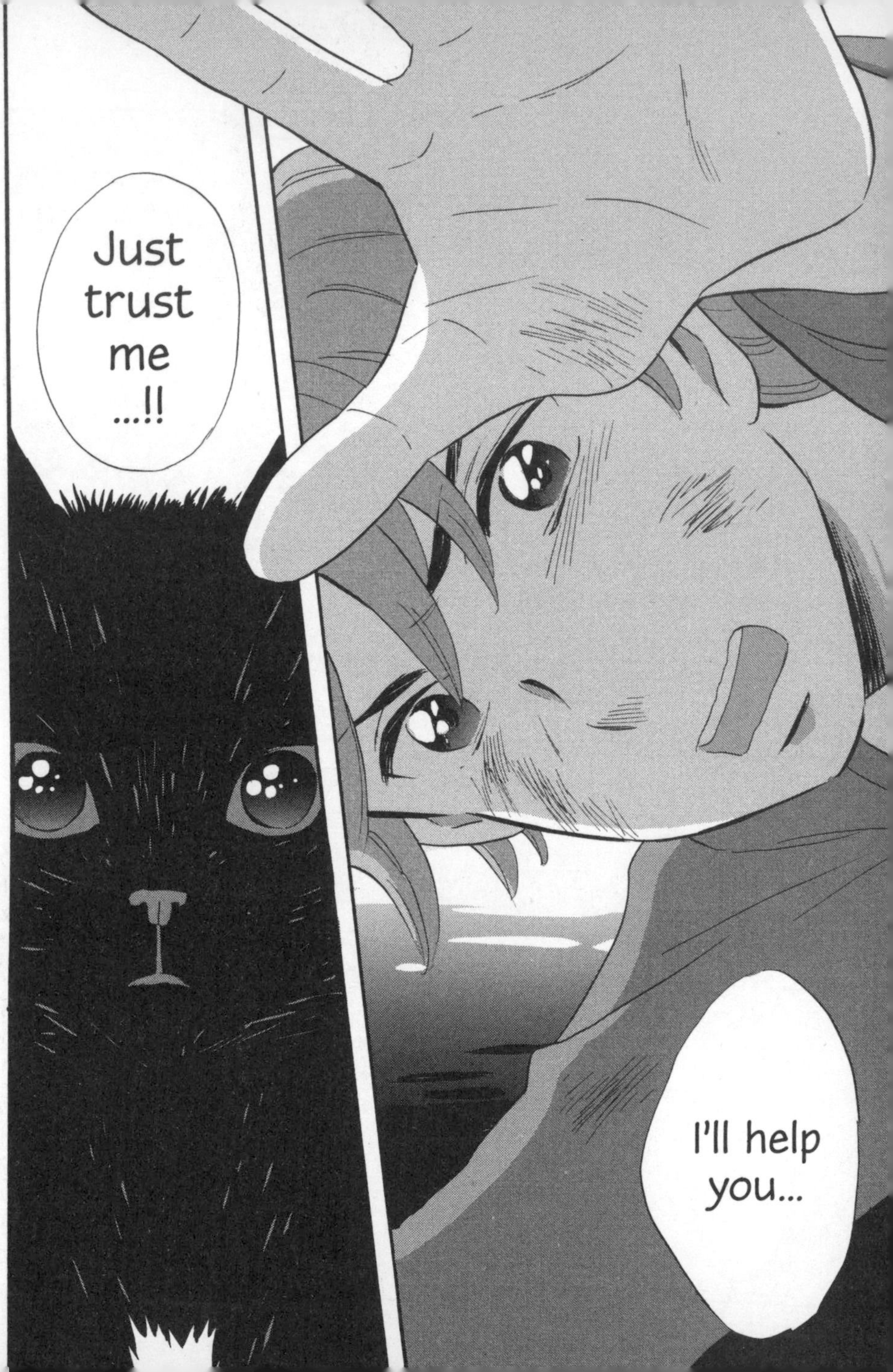
I'll help you...
Just trust me ...!!

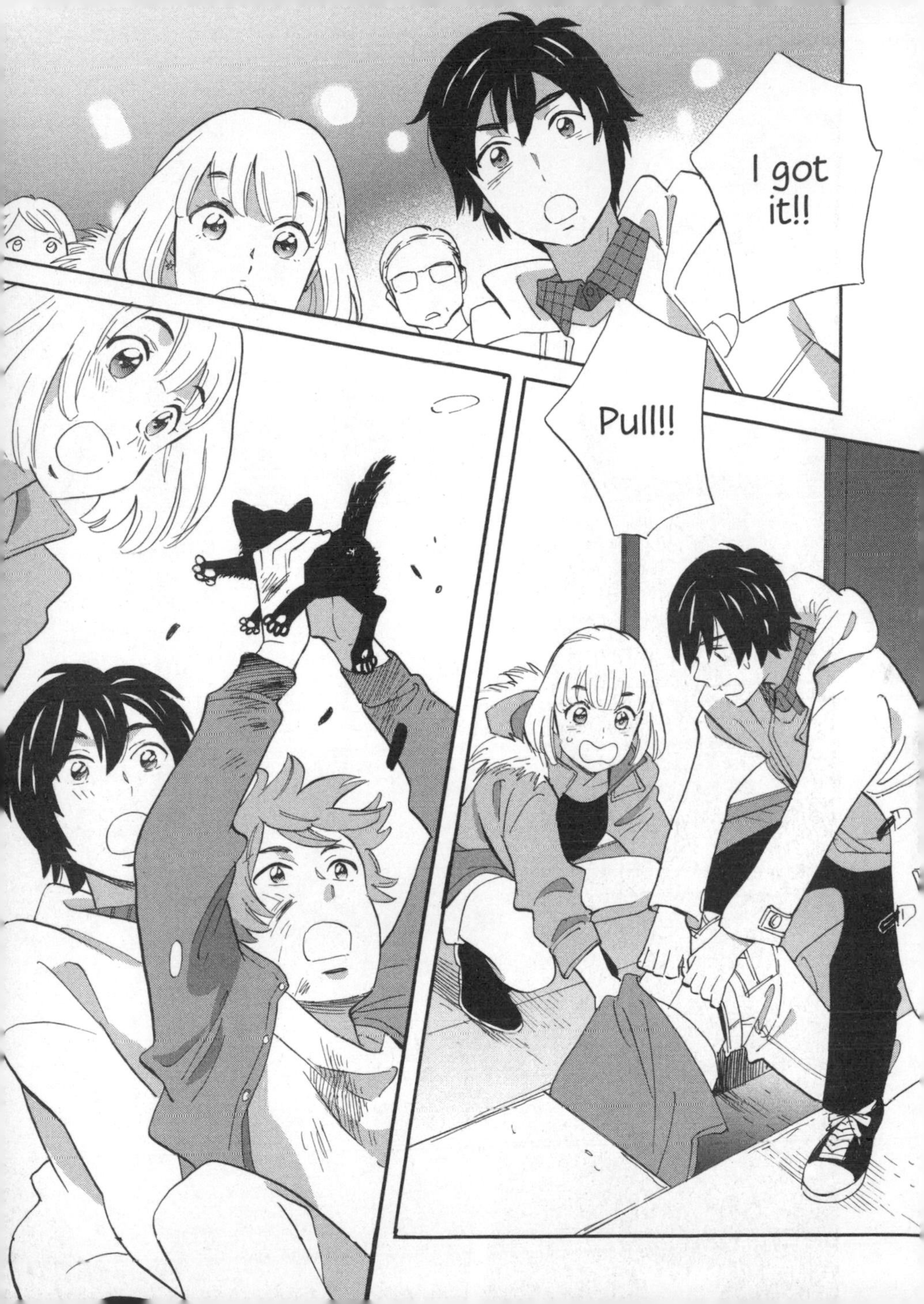
I got it!!
Pull!!

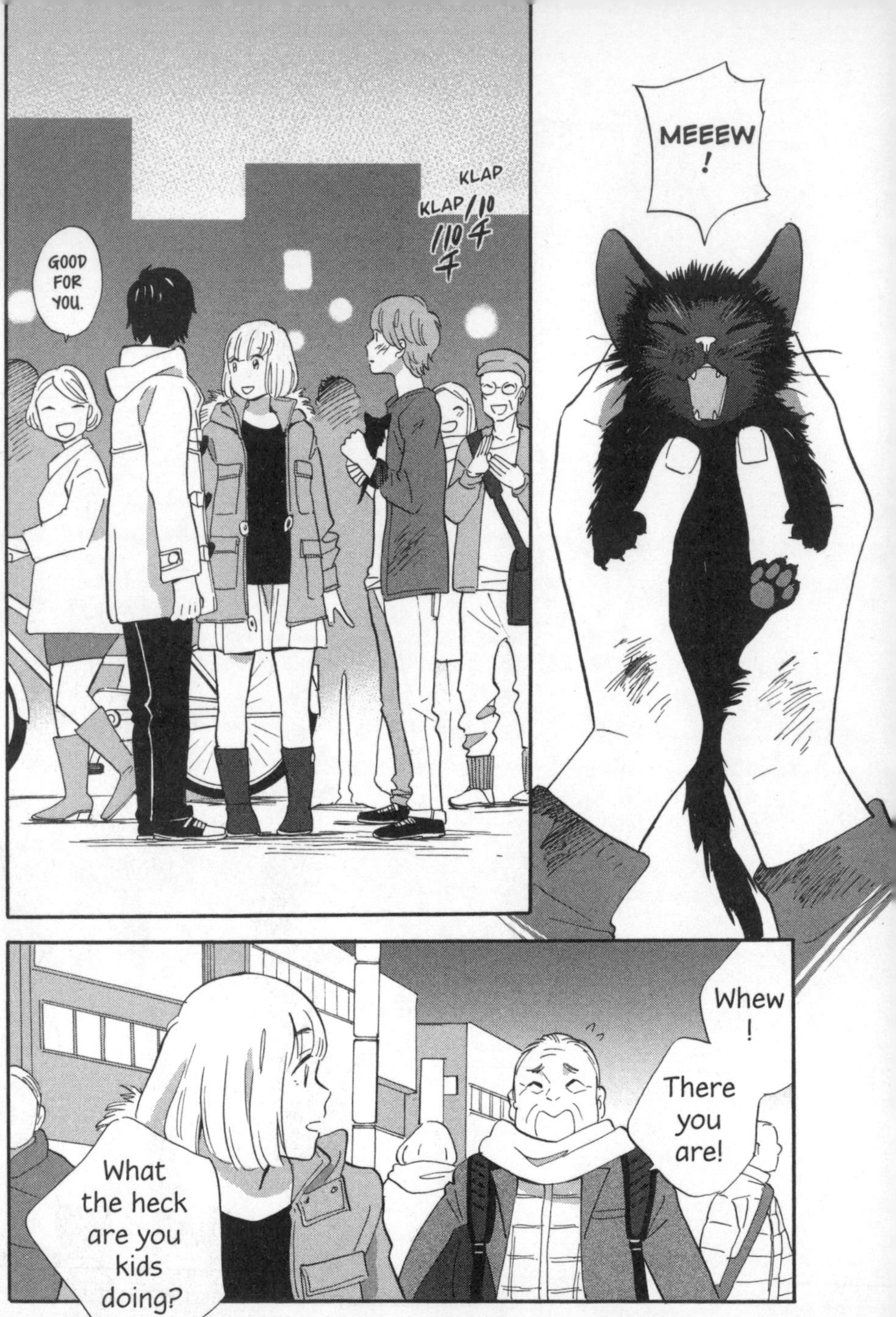
MEEEW!
KLAP
KLAP
GOOD FOR YOU.
Whew! There you are!
What the heck are you kids doing?

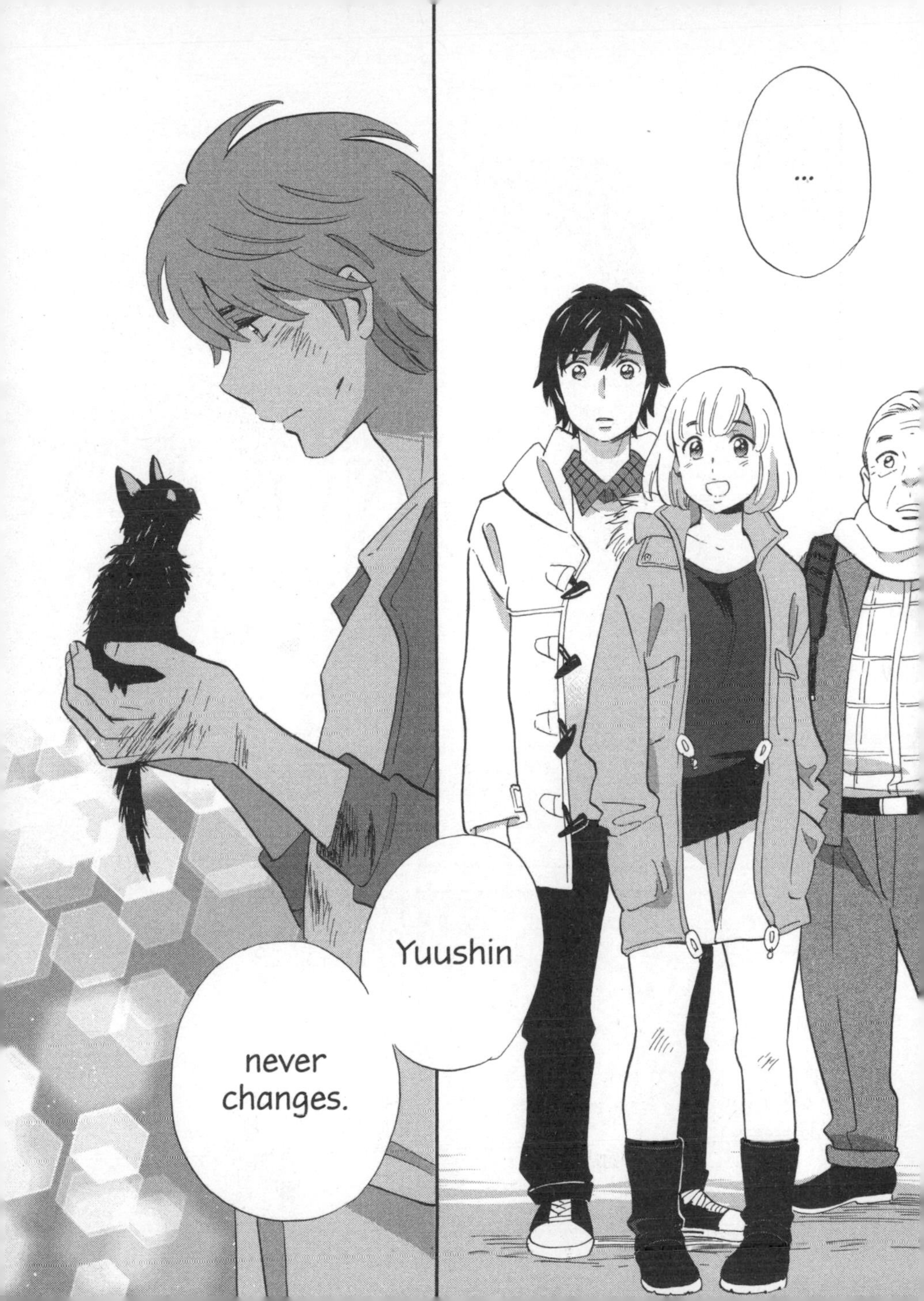
...
Yuushin
never changes.

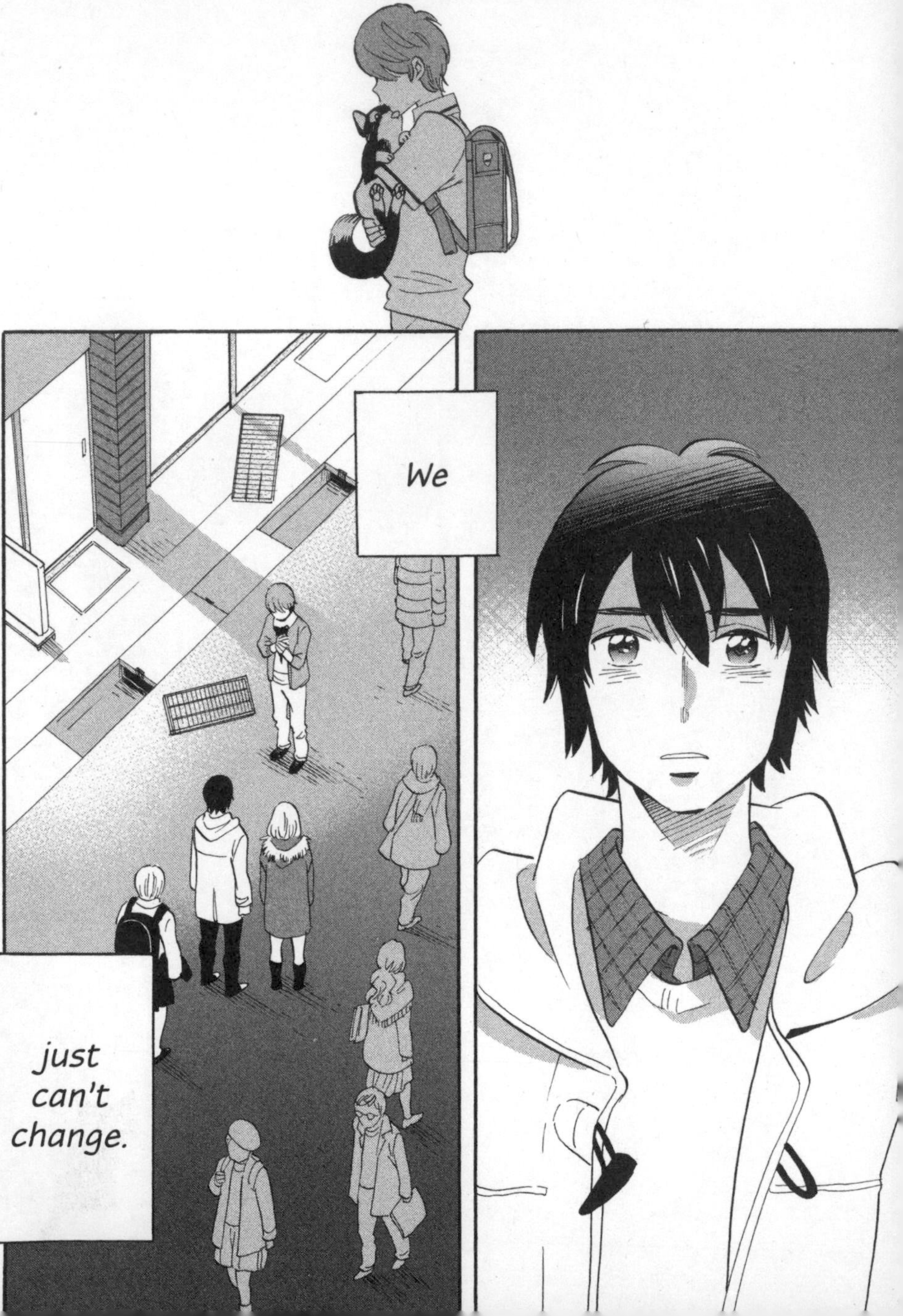
We
just can't change.

The Golden Sheep | continued in volume 3 |